American Poetics of History

American Poetics of History

FROM EMERSON TO THE MODERNS

Joseph G. Kronick

Louisiana State
University Press
Baton Rouge and London

810.9
K93a

Published with the assistance of a grant from the National Endowment for the Humanities.

LIBRARY OF CONGRESS CATALOGING IN PUBLICATION DATA
Kronick, Joseph G.
  American poetics of history.
  Bibliography: p.
  Includes index.
  1. American literature—History and criticism.
2. History in literature. 3. Metaphor. 4. Criticism. I. Title.
PS169.H5K7 1984   810'.9   83-24827
ISBN 0-8071-1152-X

85-8153

For my mother
and father

Among the various conflicting modes of writing history, there would seem to be two grand practical distinctions, under which all the rest must subordinately range. By the one mode, all contemporaneous circumstances, facts, and events must be set down contemporaneously; by the other, they are only to be set down as the general stream of the narrative shall dictate; for matters which are kindred in time, may be very irrelative in themselves. I elect neither of these; I am careless of either; both are well enough in their way; I write precisely as I please.

—Herman Melville, *Pierre*

Contents

Acknowledgments

I have incurred many debts in the writing of this book, not the least of which is owed to the late Eugenio Donato. He generously shared with me his considerable knowledge of nineteenth-century theories of history and science. His advice added immeasurably to the historical and theoretical background of my discussions of nineteenth-century writers. I thank Barbara Packer, with whom I first studied Emerson. It was in her seminar that I stopped thinking of Emerson as a second-rate Coleridge and learned to appreciate his greatness. Edgar A. Dryden read my manuscript and provided helpful comments. I have benefited from the many conversations I had with Kathryne Lindberg concerning several topics dealt with here. I am also grateful for the discussions I have had with Elton Fukumoto, Peter Hodgson, Roland Kipfstuhl, Harro Stammerjohann, and Stefana Sabin. Bainard Cowan has been gracious enough to offer close readings of my revisions during the final preparation of the manuscript. Adelaide Russo has been most helpful in assisting me in the translations from French. I also thank Beverly Jarrett, Catherine Barton, and the staff of the LSU Press, especially Barbara Phillips for her meticulous editing job. I am particularly pleased to acknowledge the support and encouragement offered by Lewis Simpson and Gale Carrithers. My greatest debt, however, is to Joseph Riddel, who has guided me through the writing of all the stages of this book. I, like so many others, have been the beneficiary of his inexhaustible generosity. He has rendered the kind of help and advice that can never be properly repaid. I only hope that I have learned from his example.

Williams, © 1969 by Florence H. Williams; *The Embodiment of Knowledge*, copyright © 1974 by Florence H. Williams; *Imaginations*, copyright © 1970 by Florence H. Williams; *In the American Grain*, copyright 1925 by James Laughlin, 1933 by William Carlos Williams; *I Wanted to Write a Poem*, Copyright © 1958 by William Carlos Williams; *Paterson*, copyright © 1946, 1948, 1949, 1951, 1958 by William Carlos Williams; *Pictures from Brueghel and Other Poems*, copyright © 1949, 1951, 1952, 1953, 1954, 1955, 1956, 1957, 1959, 1960, 1961, 1962 by William Carlos Williams; *Selected Letters*, copyright © 1957 by William Carlos Williams; *Selected Essays*, copyright 1954 by William Carlos Williams; *A Voyage to Pagany*, copyright © 1970 by New Directions Publishing Corporation; previously unpublished material by William Carlos Williams, copyright © 1983 by William Eric Williams and Paul H. Williams, used by permission of New Directions Publishing Corporation, agents; excerpt from "Rome" from *Iowa Review*, copyright © 1978 by the Estate of Florence H. Williams. All used by permission of New Directions Publishing Corporation.

Excerpts from the following works by Ezra Pound: *The Cantos of Ezra Pound*, copyright © 1934, 1937, 1940, 1948, 1950, 1956, 1959, 1962, 1963, 1965, 1966, 1968, 1970, 1971 by Ezra Pound, © 1969, 1972 by the Estate of Ezra Pound; *Gaudier-Brzeska*, copyright © 1970 by Ezra Pound, all rights reserved; *Guide to Kulchur*, copyright © 1970 by Ezra Pound, all rights reserved; *Literary Essays*, copyright 1918, 1920, 1935 by Ezra Pound; *Selected Letters of Ezra Pound, 1907–1941*, copyright © 1950 by Ezra Pound; *Selected Prose, 1909–1965*, copyright © 1973 by the Estate of Ezra Pound; *Spirit of Romance*, copyright © 1968 by Ezra Pound, all rights reserved. All used by permission of New Directions Publishing Corp. and Faber and Faber, Ltd.

Excerpts from manuscripts and notes for *Paterson*, Book IV, Part I, in the William Carlos Williams Collection, Collection of American Literature, by permission of the Beinecke Rare Book and Manuscript Library, Yale University.

Excerpts from letters of Wallace Stevens to Charles R. Barker, March 17, 1944, in WAS Box 72 (5), and to Emma Stevens Jobbins, December 27, 1944, in WAS Box 73 (15), by permission of The Huntington Library, San Marino, California.

Quotations from Brom Weber (ed.), *The Letters of Hart Crane, 1916–1932* (Berkeley, 1965), by permission of the University of California Press.

Excerpts from the following works by Wallace Stevens: *The Necessary Angel: Essays on Reality and the Imagination*, copyright 1942, 1944, 1947, 1948, 1949, 1951 by Wallace Stevens; *The Letters of Wallace Stevens: Selected and Edited by Holly Stevens*, copyright © 1966 by Holly Stevens; *Souvenirs and Prophecies: The Young Wallace Stevens*, copyright © 1966, 1976 by Holly Stevens; *Opus Posthumous*, edited and with an introduction by Samuel French Morse, copyright © 1957 by Elsie Stevens and Holly Stevens; *The Collected Poems of Wallace Stevens*, copyright 1923, 1931, 1935, 1936, 1937, 1942, 1943, 1944, 1945, 1946, 1947, 1948, 1949, 1950, 1951, 1952, 1954 by Wallace Stevens. All used by permission of Alfred A. Knopf, Inc.

A portion of Chapter One herein, which appeared, in somewhat different form, in "Emerson and the Question of Reading/Writing," *Genre*, XIV (Fall, 1981), 363–81, by permission of the editor.

Chapter Eight herein, which appeared, in somewhat different form, in "Of Parents, Children, and Rabbis: Wallace Stevens and the Question of the Book," *boundary 2*, X (Spring, 1982), 125–54, by permission of the editor.

Excerpts from *Collected Poems, 1909–1962*, *Four Quartets*, and *Selected Essays*, all by T. S. Eliot, by permission of Harcourt, Brace, Jovanovich Inc.; copyright 1936, 1950 by Harcourt, Brace, Jovanovich, Inc., copyright © 1943, 1963, 1964 by T. S. Eliot, renewed 1971, 1978 by Esme Valerie Eliot. Excerpts from *Selected Essays*, by T. S. Eliot, reprinted by permission of Faber and Faber, Ltd.

Lines by Hart Crane and prose excerpts are reprinted from *The Complete Poems and Selected Letters and Prose of Hart Crane*, edited by Brom Weber, by permission of Liveright Publishing Corporation. Copyright © 1933, 1958, 1966 by Liveright Publishing Corporation.

American Poetics of History

Introduction

It may very well be a cliché of literary history to call Emerson the father of American literature and his first book, *Nature*, the primal source not just for New England transcendentalism but for American modernism as well. Indeed, Richard Poirier has gone so far as to declare, "Emerson in many respects *is* American literature." A survey of commentary on *Nature* seems to confirm Poirier's claim. For every statement about the American writer's imperial self, denial of history, creation of self through style, emphasis on voice at the expense of content, and anxiety over the past, one can find similar remarks about *Nature*. If American literature, as Charles Feidelson, among others, has claimed, is primarily experimental and has yet to produce a masterpiece (which, in this parlance, means an aesthetically unified work), then Emerson's importance lies in his creating a poetic program that was only realized, if at all, in the works of Thoreau and Whitman. Richard P. Adams confesses that "in spite of its [*Nature*'s] many brilliant passages, [it is] a fundamentally unsatisfactory piece of work." Even Harold Bloom, Emerson's staunchest defender, reads *Nature* for its epiphanies, "abandoning the rest of it to time's revenges." If the Emersonian essay is to be salvaged, we must, according to these critics, recognize that it is a work in progress, a creative activity, not a finished product.[1]

Emerson's first book often serves as the starting point of attempts to define American literature. Thus, Poirier begins *A World Elsewhere* by stating his preference for American books that "are an image of the creation of America itself, of the effort, in the words of Emerson's Orphic poet, to 'Build therefore your own world.'" Like most critics, Poirier finds that

---

1. Poirier, *A World Elsewhere*, 69; Feidelson, *Symbolism and American Literature*, 4; R.P. Adams, "Emerson and the Organic Metaphor," 121; Bloom, *Agon*, 157. For discussions of the literary work as creative activity, see, in addition to Feidelson and Poirier, Pearce, *The Continuity of American Poetry*. Lawrence Buell begins his *Literary Transcendentalism* by admitting that "undoubtedly Emerson and his circle *are* more important for historical reasons than for the quality of their achievement in art, philosophy, and theology" (pp. 1–2).

Emerson's style is his saving grace; it rescues the work from a failed metaphysics or theology. For Poirier, questions of style are inseparable from questions of self. Roy Harvey Pearce, who shares with Poirier a dialectic that promises to negate history and preserve the self, has complained of Emerson's egocentrism; nevertheless, he finds in Emerson the paradigmatic example of an antinomian strain in American poetry that begins by saying no before transmuting the world into an image of self and humanity.[2]

A symbolic theory of language has held ground from F. O. Matthiessen's Coleridgean theory of organic language through Charles Feidelson's concept of symbolism to John Irwin's symbol of the hieroglyphic. This emphasis on style and the symbolic image has led critics to insist that the American writer has no interest in history. The Adamic myth served as the basis for R. W. B. Lewis' *The American Adam*, wherein he argued that the prescription for an American literature was to break away from Europe. Without any history behind him, a poet like Whitman *"projects* a world of order and meaning and identity into either a chaos or a sheer vacuum, he does not *discover it."* This belief in the American poet's metaphysical naïveté persists in Hugh Kenner's *A Homemade World*, where he states that "styles are *elected"* and that a writer such as Hemingway is "uncoerced by the dead writers his ancestor."[3] Through style, so these critics tell us, the writer resolves the conflicts between a desire to be original and the uncertain cultural, social, and political status of an emergent nation conscious of its foreign origin.

In an innovative essay, "Historicism Once More," which set the ground for *The Continuity of American Poetry*, Roy Harvey Pearce seemed to offer an alternative to the impasse that arose between formalist criticism and literary history. Rather than treat history as something extrinsic to the literary work, as a background for sources and influences, Pearce offered what he thought would be a formula for reconciling literature and history: "Through language history gets into literature." Pearce reverses the still-common perception of literature as a mere product of historical forces and

2. Poirier, *A World Elsewhere*, 3; Pearce, *The Continuity of American Poetry*, 153. No one has objected more to Emerson's so-called egocentrism than Quentin Anderson. See his *The Imperial Self*.

3. Irwin, *American Hieroglyphics*; R. W. B. Lewis, *The American Adam*, 5, 9, 51; Kenner, *A Homemade World*, 217.

suggests that language makes history. Reading, henceforth, will be the vehicle of historical continuity: "The art of reading a poem is an act of at once appropriating and being appropriated by its history." Pearce's dialectical scheme allows him to move from language as a relatively autonomous body to history as the lived experience of humanity. The literary work, therefore, is at once historically conditioned and the expression of man's unchanging and universal sense of selfhood that Pearce calls *humanitas*. As he says in another essay, "Literature—any literature—is at once in history and above it." Finally, as the past is available in language, it lives in the present through the continued life of literature. By means of his dialectic, Pearce introduces history into any assessment of literature while retaining the formalist's emphasis upon the work of art as an organic whole. Ultimately, history is superseded by the spirit, or humanitas, embodied within it. While literature may be "an expression *in* history," it has value because it alone is the realization of humanitas: "In literature, we could say, *humanitas* triumphs over history, even as it triumphs by means of history."[4] Pearce's inversion of that hierarchical relation wherein the literary work is subordinate to its historical background still proves to be as metaphysical and ahistorical as anything proposed by formalists or Adamists, for the values Pearce finds in literature are ultimately nonlinguistic and, thus, transcend history.

Although his dialectic is vitiated by a rather schematic and uncritical Hegelianism, Pearce does offer an alternative to formalism by pointing the way to bridge the artificial gap between history and literary studies. Most often, history, if it does enter into discussions of American literature, does so in the context of stylistics or thematic studies. Poirier, for instance, writes, "By being historical about American literature we have often missed the history which is particular in novels, poems, or essays, the history lurking in their stylistic and formal characteristics." For Poirier, history is the environment created within a text.[5] Style reflects the individual's desire to give shape to a personal identity, just as America's history tells of the struggle for a national identity.

More recently, in the essay "Writing Off the Self," Poirier follows the example of Harold Bloom and presents his theory as a radical alternative

4. Pearce, *Historicism Once More*, 8, 7, 26, 35, 31.
5. Poirier, *A World Elsewhere*, viii–ix, 4.

to the attack upon the concept of self in Continental criticism: "Writing is a struggle to impose voice or will on the intractable and fluid material of language, language which irresistibly refers to historical, social, and mythological implications that remain very much alive in it." Finding in America a rejection of the European writer's nostalgia for "humanistic and religious traditions," Poirier triumphantly announces, "American literature is, supremely, the literature that *knows* that distinction between voice and writing, and the problematic relation between voice and presence. It plays with these distinctions not for moral but for mortal stakes—the salvation of voice is nothing less than salvation of the will." Even though he begins by denying that America has ever shared the humanistic tradition wherein voice is the sign of self-presence, Poirier's theory of the dramatization of self through style rescues the metaphysics of self in a dialectic of negation. By denying that the self exists, the poet affirms the presence of self in and through style: "The performance of the poem is a signature of human will and power that affirms its presence in the very act of absenting itself."[6] Despite the appeal that Poirier's pathos-ridden language of crisis may have, his work does not represent a departure from the various Adamic myths wherein the poet creates a world in language, although Poirier is acutely aware that any writing is to some extent a fiction and, therefore, that the question of the self issues from a dialectic between reading and writing and cannot be resolved by a mimetic theory of language.

Poirier follows Bloom in characterizing American literature as a *gnosis*, a *knowing* that transcends everything natural, including history. According to Bloom, gnosis yields knowledge neither of eternity nor of this world but of oneself, or what he calls the *pneuma*. Gnosis, therefore, is beyond history. It is, writes Bloom, "a persuasive rhetoric, a language of desire and possession" and, hence, a voicing. The father of this gnosis, this "American religion," is, of course, Emerson, whose "gnosis rejects all history."[7] Because I turn to Bloom's concepts throughout my book, I will not enter into a critique of his theory here, except to point out that although his extravagant terminology has made his name anathema to traditional scholars and critics, he is the most ardent defender of the humanist tradition in American letters that these same critics wish to protect against the incur-

6. Poirier, "Writing Off the Self," 109, 132.
7. Bloom, *Agon*, 12, 170.

sions of Continental philosophy and criticism. Unlike his critics, Bloom recognizes the threat such thinkers as Paul de Man and Jacques Derrida represent for the humanist values to which he is so clearly committed. I therefore take him as the most significant proponent of this tradition in American literature today. His concept of gnosis represents the most vigorous attempt to revive a tired metaphysics grounded in the ahistorical self.

The hold of such notions as the ahistorical quality of American literature and its predominantly symbolic aesthetic confirms the mystifying power of metaphor. Even when a critic like Poirier asserts that history exists as style, he must eventually conclude that the world literature creates is sealed off from what might be called "objective" history and can only be entered momentarily as a fiction, or what Stevens would call the fiction of a belief beyond belief. Underlying this emphasis on voice and style in American literary criticism has been a symbolic aesthetic, which has close ties to an Adamic theory of language. The perception of a new world and a new nation would and should be, according to these critics, embodied in a new style. Consequently, the search for an "American" language has meant a denial of history. Emerson has suffered the most from this aesthetic. Unfortunately, critics can still read *Nature* and then write, "The turn to an American language so conceived was the ultimate and crucial turn away from history."[8] There has, however, been a shift away from an aesthetic of the literary symbol to a philosophical and rhetorical criticism that exposes the metaphysics of a humanistic heritage and, in doing so, uncovers the linguistic problematic underlying not just poetics and hermeneutics but also anthropology, philosophy, psychology, and history. I therefore follow the lead of those philosophers and critics who have challenged the traditional concepts of literary history and methodology. Rather than provide a list of names—names, I might add, that have achieved the status of buzz words in recent polemics—I will merely appeal to the writers whom I study, for they never felt any need to resist theory; in fact, Stevens may be taken as typical when he wrote of the pure good of theory.

In following the example, however eccentric, of the writers discussed herein, I focus on the question of metaphor in our understanding of tradition and history. Writers such as Whitman and Pound seek not to make it new but to make it old, that is, to write a poem containing history. But

8. Ziff, *Literary Democracy*, 34.

an "American" history is not founded upon a rejection of the past; the turn away from Europe is a re-turning—a troping—of the tropes that constitute history. History, I propose, is a rhetoric, for it consists of these tropological transformations. Hence, I find it characteristic of the American writer to treat history as a question of intertextuality, of reading and writing. A poetics of history shifts the ground of historical studies from epistemology to tropology, the rhetorical interplay that poses history as a problematic of reading wherein temporal relations are generated by a linguistic process of exchange.

A poetics of history will therefore be a poetics of reading, as well as writing, but reader and author exist neither as opponents in a dialectic nor as complementary halves in a mutual process of creation. Emerson provides the most searching, if diffuse, commentary on the place of the reader in history. It is as a reader that Emerson approached the world, for he, like Stevens, finds the world in a book. Thus New England transcendentalism represents a hybrid of Unitarianism, the physical and natural sciences, seventeenth-century British literature—especially Milton—British Romanticism, and German literature and philosophy. In a manner that was to be taken to an extreme by Henry Adams, Emerson turned to philosophy and the sciences in order to evolve his own theory of history. His desire to reconcile nature with spirit led him to speculate on language and history; in so doing, he uncovered the linguistic problematic hidden within any attempt at a systematic theory of nature and history. A more relentless process of disclosure can be found in *The Education of Henry Adams*. In this and other late works, Adams appropriates one scientific theory after another for his dynamic theory of history. Beginning with pre-Darwinian evolutionary theory and geological theories of catastrophic changes of the earth's surface, Adams eventually confronts thermodynamics and statistical mechanics, only to discover how the last reveals history to be merely a convenient fiction for explaining the distribution of energy that we call life.

Adams, who rarely figures in genealogies beginning with Emerson, had a profound influence on his fellow moderns, particularly Pound and Williams. Pound's ideas on translation and history often find expression in either scientific or economic metaphors. Williams was struck by Adams' writings on thermodynamics, as is revealed in *The Embodiment of Knowledge* and his passages on Madame Curie and radium in *Paterson*. Further-

more, the whore/virgin of *Paterson*, Book Five, a metaphor for the violation of history by trope, and the corrupt and fragmentary originals Pound
translates in the *Cantos* deny, as did Adams' radium, their God, that is, a
belief in origins and truth. The poet, like Adams' historian, follows the traces
of energy, which lead not to a pure origin but through the twists and turns,
the tropes, of writing. Rather than follow this en-tropic path through history, Crane, like Eliot, desires to recover the logos obscured by language
and history but finds his poems are overwhelmed by the quotations marking them as a repetition. On the other hand, Stevens joyfully affirms the
absence of the Word, for writing begins with the denial of God. Stevens
reveals, possibly with greater rigor than any other modern poet, the irreducible metaphoricity of any notion of origins or centers. All these writers,
from Emerson on, attempt to rethink history and thereby rewrite their genealogy, because the American writer can never forget his belatedness. Belatedness, however, is a condition of language—the poet piles up the fragments conveying history as an inscription, a foreign language that resists
translation. The problem of an "American" identity, therefore, is one of
reading, that is, of mapping the exchange of tropes between texts.

In the following chapters, I trace the interlineations of metaphors associated with architecture, farming, economics, geology, thermodynamics,
and genealogy—tropes, I might add, that do not come from foreign disciplines but are already inscribed in literature. Beginning with Emerson's
theory of quotation and originality, I discuss how the American writer's
anxiety over the question of a national literature surfaces in his obsession
with history. In his efforts to write a uniquely American history and, hence,
to assert his tradition, the poet reveals that nature and the past do not exist
outside of language: history is generated by metaphors of representation.
Whitman envisioned history as a self-reading, a semiotic wherein the text
interprets itself to a future audience. Adams reads history in terms of thermodynamics, Pound as a process of translation, Williams in metaphors of
physical contact, Crane according to the trope of the bridge, and Stevens
after the model of the family. Thus, America has always been inscribed in
the metaphors of a poetics of history.

CHAPTER ONE

Originality and Authority
in Emerson and Thoreau

Let me indulge the American habit of
quotation.
                —Pound to Williams

Homeliness is almost as great a merit
in a book as in a house, if the reader
would abide there.
                —Thoreau

For all symbols are fluxional; all
language is vehicular and transitive,
and is good, as ferries and horses are,
for conveyance, not as farms and
houses are, for homestead.
                —Emerson

In his brief essay "Emerson's Books (The Shadows of Them)," Whitman
says he will examine "the bare spots and darknesses" of Emerson's writings and ignore the "sunny expanses and sky-reaching heights." Whitman
defends his ungracious act by appealing to Emerson's philosophy: "But I
will begin by scarifying him—thus proving that I am not insensible to his
deepest lessons. I will consider his books from a democratic and western
point of view." Whitman invokes the familiar doctrine of self-reliance:
"Insist on yourself," Emerson admonishes his readers, "never imitate."[1]
All readers of Whitman know that he insisted on himself. But his self-pro-
motion did not prevent Emerson's influence from casting a shadow on his
claim for originality. Perhaps this created the need to scarify Emerson. The
OED defines *scarify* as follows: "To make a number of scratches or slight
incisions in (a portion of the body, a wound). Hence *gen.* to cover with
scratches." In modern use, it means "to subject to merciless criticism." Finally, it also means "to break up or loosen (ground) with a scarifier," an
instrument used in road making. To clear the ground for his own beginnings as a poet, Whitman will scratch out Emerson's text to make room for
his own. His criticism will break open a path in the surface of Emerson's

---

1. Whitman, *Prose Works 1892*, II, 515; E. W. Emerson (ed.), *The Complete Works of
Ralph Waldo Emerson*, II, 83, hereinafter cited as *W* with volume number and page reference.

texts, preparing the way for his independence. But might not Whitman fear that the traces of Emerson's writings will appear beneath his own? And doesn't the path to self-reliance lie within Emerson's tracks?

In a rather confused passage in the same essay, these questions turn Whitman's text against himself: "The best part of Emersonianism is, it breeds the giant that destroys itself. Who wants to be any man's mere follower? lurks behind every page. No teacher ever taught, that has so provided for his pupil's setting up independently—no truer evolutionist."[2] In the context of the essay, we might take this passage to mean that the giant bred by Emersonianism will destroy Emerson's texts, if not Emersonianism. In terms of the Freudian family romance, we can read this as the son slaying the father. *Itself*, however, grammatically refers to the giant, not to Emersonianism. Does the son kill himself? The answer is yes—in killing the father he kills himself. In Freud's account, the sons assuage their guilty consciences by turning the dead father into a god. In scarifying, or destroying, Emerson's texts, Whitman would raise them into a god called Emersonianism. And isn't this proper? Hasn't the son destroyed the father through the father's agency? Whitman would like to believe that originality and progress exist—a belief consistent with Emersonianism but not necessarily with Emerson. Yet Whitman recognizes that Emerson invites his readers to destroy his texts and to be their own begetters. It is particularly appropriate that Whitman sees this tradition of discontinuity, if I might be allowed this oxymoron, in terms of reading. For in this he recognizes what deprives him of originality. The reader always stands in debt to his predecessors, most particularly to a predecessor who makes possible the illusion of his independence.

Perhaps it requires a professed non-Emersonian to make the following statement: "The world is forever babbling of originality; but there never yet was an original man, in the sense intended by the world; the first man himself—who according to the Rabbins was also the first author—not being an original; the only original author being God. . . . [N]ever was there a child born solely from one parent." The author who believes he is original also believes he can be his own parent—illusions Melville dispels in *Pierre*. In a letter of March 3, 1849, Melville addresses the question of Emerson and originality quite explicitly:

2. Whitman, *Prose Works 1892*, II, 517–18.

Nay, I do not oscillate in Emerson's rainbow, but prefer rather to hang myself in mine own halter than swing in any other man's swing. Yet I think Emerson is more than a brilliant fellow. Be his stuff begged, borrowed, or stolen, or of his own domestic manufacture he is an uncommon man. Swear he is a humbug—then is he no common humbug. Lay it down that had not Sir Thomas Browne lived, Emerson would not have mystified—I will answer, that had not Old Zack's father begot him, Old Zack would never have been the hero of Palo Alto. The truth is that we are all sons, grandsons, or nephews or great-nephews of those who go before us. No one is his own sire.[3]

Origins, Melville says, are always at least double; furthermore, to be an author is to have many parents. As a reader, the author is the most indebted of men. And the son, as Whitman's text claims in spite of Whitman, affirms his belatedness every time he destroys his father; for in setting himself up as independent, he reifies the primacy of his predecessors. Like Melville, Emerson claims that nothing is original, that there is only quotation: "Every book is a quotation; and every house is a quotation out of all forests and mines and stone-quarries; and every man is a quotation from all his ancestors" (W. VIII. 176).

If all books are quotations, then originality disappears as a criterion for judging a book's value. In place of originality, use determines value. In Emerson's terms, the more a book is quoted, the better it is. Therefore, reading must share an equal place with writing in his theory of literature. In defining this aesthetic of use, Emerson frequently employs metaphors drawn from economics. For books are like paper money—having no intrinsic worth, they are valued as signs that stand in place of things. Unlike paper money, which ideally does not exceed the gold held in reserve, books are always excessive—they represent nothing, neither nature nor the self; both have been displaced by quotation.

Another son of Emerson, Thoreau, refuses to admit that originality is impossible—a refusal so opposed to Emerson's philosophy that it may be the most Emersonian act of all. But as I have suggested, the more the son excludes the father, the more he preserves him within himself. Emerson's and Thoreau's contrasting theories have a parallel in their metaphors. While Emerson's metaphors for reading and writing come from economics, Thoreau's metaphors come from building and farming. Emerson leaves his

3. Melville, *Pierre*, 259; Davis and Gilman (eds.), *The Letters of Herman Melville*, 78.

works to the vagaries of the literary marketplace, but Thoreau wishes to invest his work in a solid edifice. In opposition to Emerson's nonidealistic aesthetic of repetition, Thoreau's desire to break new ground and dwell in a home of his own construction reveals a deeply rooted nostalgia for originality. Of course, the hut Thoreau built by Walden Pond was far from original. In fact, it was a quotation—the boards came from another shanty.

The question of originality has plagued American writers since the European settlement of America, which was less an engendering of a new world than a disseminating of the old one. The question of an indigenous culture was a familiar one to both Emerson and Thoreau, and although they have had their ups and downs with readers, New England transcendentalism has been accepted, if not as the beginning of an American literature, then as the flowering of it. Transcendentalism was itself a search for an original relationship with God and nature. This conjunction of a religious movement with a literary one can hardly be considered fortuitous; for a new literature would require a new god, and a new language. But if we return to Melville's *Pierre*, we find that "silence is the only Voice of our God." As Melville suggests in this novel on writing, the first man was not original precisely because he was also the first author—language displaces man from a primary existence. And the writer, who is like a geologist, is the man most aware of this: "But, far as any geologist has yet gone down into the world, it is found to consist of nothing but surface stratified on surface. To its axis, the world being nothing but superinduced superficies. By vast pains we mine into the pyramid; by horrible gropings we come to the central room; with joy we espy the sarcophagus; but we lift the lid—and no body is there!—appallingly vacant as vast is the soul of a man!"[4] American poets have long been engaged in a search for a natural language—an American language. But the language of the earth, the geo-logos, is displaced by reading and writing. Nature, man, and books are as vacant as Melville's pyramid.

From transcendentalism to modernism, the question of originality has been bound up with the question of place. It's as though a new locality will of itself produce a new literature. This search for solid ground, or what Thoreau calls a *point d'appui*, is frequently coupled with an emphasis on writing at the expense of reading. Reading implies inferiority; therefore, we must scarify books. Whenever we "break ground" in search of direct con-

---

4. Melville, *Pierre*, 204, 285.

tact with nature, we encounter the remains of our ancestors instead. Hence, we must scratch out our ancestors' books beyond all recognition. Out of these mangled texts we will construct a new literature. Emerson stands as the major American theorist of the complicity between reading, writing, and death. His denial of origins, let alone originality, severs man from God and nature. Cut off from the metaphysical grounds of self and knowledge, the writer translates God, nature, and the self into a dead origin, the book. Quotation mimes a recovery of a source; the search for an origin leads the reader/writer back to mementos of origins, quotations. Rather than nostalgically search for a *point d'appui*, Emerson insists upon the violence of intertextuality whereby the solid ground is disfigured by the seeker.

As there is no original source to turn to, not even nature, the writer must borrow from other texts. Emerson excludes the following remark from the published version of "Quotation and Originality," his central document on reading: "All reading is a kind of quotation" (*W.* VIII. 399). This remark also appears with slight variations in a few journal passages.[5] Here is one of the more striking variants: "All our literature is a quotation, our life a custom or imitation, and our body is borrowed like a beggar's dinner from a hundred charities" (*JMN.* IX. 126). In "Quotation and Originality" this becomes: "Is all literature eavesdropping, and all art Chinese imitation? our life a custom, and our body borrowed, like a beggar's dinner, from a hundred charities? A more subtle and severe criticism might suggest that some dislocation has befallen the race; that men are off their centre; that multitudes of men do not live with Nature, but behold it as exiles" (*W.* VIII. 188). While these questions weaken the force of the journal entry, in the essay Emerson explicitly links quotation to man's inability to experience nature directly. God's book of nature can be known only through quotation, the original text having been lost. Consequently, reading becomes the primary form of writing. But it is writing with a vengeance; in quoting we distort and cover up the traces of our readings. In order for reading to assume the status of writing, we must forget that we are quoting.

Quotation, of course, belongs to the memory, but memory itself is a book: "There is no book like the memory, none with such a good index, and that of every kind, alphabetic, systematic, arranged by names of persons, by colors, tastes, smells, shapes, likeness, unlikeness, by all sorts of mysteri-

---

5. Gilman *et al.* (eds.), *The Journals and Miscellaneous Notebooks of Ralph Waldo Emerson*, IX, 112, X, 386, hereinafter cited as *JMN* with volume number and page reference.

ous hooks and eyes to catch and hold, and contrivances for giving a hint" (W.XII.93). As reading stores the memory with information, we must also note that Emerson describes the mind as a daguerreotype: "The memory collects and re-collects. We figure it as if the mind were a kind of looking-glass, which being carried through the street receives on its clear plate every image that passes; only with this difference, that our plate is iodized so that every image sinks into it, and is held there. But in addition to this property it has one more, this, namely, that of all the million images that are imprinted, the very one we want reappears in the centre of the plate in the moment when we want it" (W.XII.93). Like Freud on the mystic writing pad, Emerson here describes the mind as a machine; and, like Freud once again, he remarks on his metaphor's failure to explain how this stored information can be recalled at will. Having placed memory at the will's command, Emerson now sets memory in opposition to the self: "It sometimes occurs that Memory has a personality of its own, and volunteers or refuses its information at its will, not at mine" (W.XII.97). Deploring the shortness of memory, Emerson takes up Plato's attack on writing as "a barbarous invention which would weaken memory by disuse" (W.XII.99). Without contradicting himself, Emerson can go from deprecating defect of memory to praising forgetfulness as a characteristic of genius. Forgetfulness allows for invention—"indeed it is remarked that inventive men have bad memories" (W.XII.100). In Emerson's economy, we accumulate knowledge and new books by forgetting: "All the facts in this chest of memory are property at interest. And who shall set a boundary to this mounting value?" (W.XII.101). The "chest of memory" can accumulate interest forever because it is defective—that is, we forget what is already in it. If the coffer were filled, it would be a crypt. This threat, however, is dispelled by that "barbarous invention"—writing. Memory is entombed in the book, not the psyche. Emerson transforms Plato's attack on writing into a defense of it, and he does so by quoting Plato. We can imagine Emerson saying, "Yes, writing does weaken the memory, but where Plato finds fault, I find virtue." Far from being inimical to memory, writing, as Emerson says elsewhere, is the *telos* of memory: "Every faculty casts itself into an art, and memory into the art of writing, that is, the book" (W.XI.497). Since memory, as he says in "Self-Reliance," is a corpse, the art into which memory casts itself—the book—must be a kind of crypt.

Our excursion into Emerson's theories of memory and writing has led us into the crypt/book; we are now ready for his theories of forgetting and reading. This yoking is not merely fanciful; it defines Emerson's economy. If, as he says, "all things are double, one against another," then memory and writing exist only by virtue of forgetting and reading. It should be pointed out that Emerson's name for writing as the art of memory both follows and deviates from the line of metaphysical thought, exemplified by Plato's *Phaedrus*, in which writing is decried as unnatural to speech, the sign of presence. Yet the mind follows the book into the crypt. In "Self-Reliance," Emerson writes, "In every work of genius we recognize our own rejected thoughts; they come back to us with a certain alienated majesty" (*W.*II.45–46). But these thoughts were never our own. If, as Emerson says, everything is quotation, then the self is a collection of quotations. Following Derrida's analysis of Maria Torok and Nicolas Abraham on incorporation and introjection, we can say that what the mind reappropriates "is simultaneously rejected: which leads to the paradox of a foreign body preserved as foreign but by the same token excluded from a self which thenceforth deals not with the other but only with itself. The more the self keeps the foreign element as a foreigner inside itself, the more it excludes it."[6]

The preserving of a foreign body invokes the Hegelian *Aufhebung*—a simultaneous negation, preservation, and elevation. In the Hegelian dialectic of self and other, the other is preserved within the self *as the other*. Through this act of appropriation, the self is preserved for itself (*für sich*) by virtue of its existing for another. When this other is a conscious being, reciprocity leads to the preserving of the self as at once both individual and universal—that is, as an individual consciousness, I am recognized as a free individual by another person. And it is his recognition of me that preserves my individuality. And I, in turn, recognize him as an individual consciousness. Our reciprocal acknowledgment of each other's freedom binds us together in a community of individual consciousnesses that Hegel calls Universal Spirit.

The idealistic thrust behind the Hegelian *Aufhebung* is denied in Derrida's analysis, however, by the encroachment of incorporation on the realm of introjection. The Freudian pre-text for Derrida's analysis is "Mourning and Melancholia," which concerns the preservation of the dead in and for the living. In Freud's analysis, the loss of a beloved object frees the libido, which then withdraws into the ego. As all love is narcissistic, the ego identifies with the lost object and therefore fails to attach itself to another ob-

6. Derrida, "Fors," 72.

ject. "In this way," says Freud, "the loss of the object becomes transformed into a loss in the ego." According to Derrida's cryptography, the lost object is entombed within the self. In the Freudian text, says Derrida, introjection is a "gradual" and "mediated" process whereby the self is expanded by assimilating the object it desires. The work of introjection would be to assimilate the lost object within the self, thus freeing the libido to attach itself to an external object. Derrida shows how this attachment to an external object is irreconcilable with introjection. As the dead is kept "alive" within the self only to be refused as dead, the enlargement of the self, which defines introjection, is impossible. Introjection promises a synthesis of preservation and negation that it cannot fulfill; at this juncture, incorporation, a "fantasmic" and "unmediated" process, intervenes. But incorporation does not complete the process of introjection: "With the real loss of the object having been rejected and the desire having been maintained but at the same time excluded from introjection . . . incorporation is a kind of theft to reappropriate the pleasure-object." But this reappropriation is also rejected. If, as Freud says, the loss of the object means a loss in the ego, then the self deals only with itself in preserving and excluding a foreign body as foreign. "What the crypt commemorates," writes Derrida, "as the incorporated object's 'monument' or 'tomb,' is not the object itself, but its exclusion, the exclusion of a specific desire from the introjection process."[7]

Derrida's analysis of Freud suggests a similar reading of Emerson's comments on readers and writers. As in Freud, we find in Emerson a dialectic of self and other—living and dead. Reading parallels the gradual process of assimilation given the name introjection in the Freudian text. And as incorporation displaces introjection, so quotation displaces reading.

Reading presupposes that the thoughts of dead authors can be made living once more through their appropriation by the reader. This idealistic theory has been the foundation of the humanities—in fact, there would be no humanities without it. For this reappropriation (allow me to use the term *introjection*) means that the dead past can be brought alive in and for the present in such a manner that the past sustains and is yet subordinate to the present. Emerson undermines any tendency he may feel to embrace this idealism. The reader becomes a secondary man; he does not enjoy an "original relation to the universe"; instead, he lives through the eyes of "the fathers" (W.I.3). The past, then, is sealed off or entombed in a book

7. Freud, *General Psychological Theory*, 170; Derrida, "Fors," 72.

as the past—that is, as dead. And for that matter, the present itself is dead: it too is only a quotation. How then can the reader extend his self by taking in past literature? There remains the magic of quotation. Quotations give the illusion that we can read, or that we can make the past present. For Emerson, quotations are like the foreign bodies in the crypt of the book.

But quotations encompass everything from books to nature to selves. And what is the self but other selves the writer incorporates by quoting? The reader, like the book, seals off and marks as dead an other which is no one but his self. The other may be excluded by quoting it, but the more it is quoted, the more it remains inside "with a certain [always already] alienated majesty." Readers incorporate crypts/books. The internalizing of a crypt is similar to what Eugenio Donato has called "the representation of textual funerary monuments."[8] The past and nature can never be directly apprehended; they are only available to perception within a linguistic or pictorial system. In an analysis of nineteenth-century literature, Donato reveals the complicity between systems of representation and death, a complicity that finds its emblem in the pyramid. In Emerson, this complicity has its fullest expression in his concept of reading. The book, says Emerson, is a crypt. And crypts, like Melville's pyramid, contain nothing—death—they are hollow. Like the crypt, the book marks the absence of nature. Hence reading incorporates the incorporating system, the book/crypt. Like the book, the reader becomes a "funerary monument" marking the absence of natural presence.

Reading, or the struggle of reappropriation and exclusion (introjection), is facilitated by forgetfulness. Forgetting frees us to reappropriate what we have rejected. And forgetting is a preserving and negating par excellence. As Emerson's memory machine demonstrates, we never lose what has been imprinted in the mind; impressions remain hidden within the iodized plate. If our minds were iodized plates, they would soon be filled up by a few books. But as our reading is a quoting, we exclude the other by incorporating it— we forget it is the other and thus preserve it as the other.

To understand the relation between reading and forgetting, we must examine Emerson's attitude toward the past, an attitude Harold Bloom has reappropriated in his theory of influence. Bloom has revitalized Emerson's concept of reading under the title misprision. On the one hand, Bloom argues for the indeterminacy of texts; on the other hand, he implies that the

8. Donato, "The Ruins of Memory," 596.

poet's misreading of his precursors is determinable. Bloom attempts to recover meaning by mapping poetic language through a genealogy of misprisions commonly called Romanticism. In his theory meaning shifts from the text as book to the text as psyche.

Following Vico, Bloom says all language, "particularly poetic language, is always and necessarily a revision of previous language." In view of this belatedness, the poet's "art is necessarily an *aftering*, and so at best he strives for a selection, through repression, out of the language of poetry; that is, he represses some traces, and remembers others. This remembering is a misprision, or creative misreading, but no matter how strong a misprision, it cannot achieve an autonomy of meaning, or a meaning fully present, that is, free from all literary context."[9] Although Bloom adopts the concept of intertextuality, he breaks out of the infinite regress implicit in it by appealing to the poet's role within the system of poetic language. The strong poet distinguishes himself by successfully misreading his forefathers; he thereby clears a space for himself within the tradition by mistranscribing his precursors' poems within his own poems. The works Bloom gives most of his attention to, poems such as Browning's "Childe Roland" and Wordsworth's "Tintern Abbey," are themselves records of the poet's struggle with his precursors. (He would most likely say that this struggle is the only meaning in a poem.) Hence the linear progression in his genealogy of poets is recapitulated in the narrative line, which is typically genealogical, of the Romantic quest lyric. Bloom's concern for genealogy finds expression in his adoption of the Freudian family romance, the Viconian distinction between divine and human origins, and the Kabbalistic and Gnostic models of creation. Each one of these sources proposes a fiction in which origins are belatedly imagined. For Bloom, this means that the uncertainty of man's origins frees the poet to create an origin out of language.

Like the genealogical metaphor in Bloom's theory, Emerson's concept of reading both acknowledges and rejects the continued presence of the past. Forgetting merely defers the past, and Bloom will argue for the return of the past. But Emerson's theory of quotation refers to a past from which we are cut off. Quotation constitutes the present as that which it is not. The present is a lost presence; it is a time becoming space. In other words, the present is a quotation. The quotation signifies the interval within the present.

9. Bloom, *Poetry and Repression*, 4.

In order to create, Emerson must forget all that is anterior, which we can now say involves a forgetting of the self (self-forgetting). In "Circles" he asks, "Why should we import rags and relics into the new hour?" (W.II.319). In this and many other passages, Emerson is as vehement as Thoreau in asserting his originality. Yet Emerson will just as frequently confess that "our debt to tradition through reading and conversation is so massive, our protest or private addition so rare and insignificant,—and this commonly on the ground of other reading or hearing,—that, in a large sense, one would say there is no pure originality. All minds quote" (W.VIII.178). On the following page he asserts, "This extreme economy argues a very small capital of invention." In a listing of credits and debts, the present stands on the verge of bankruptcy. Emerson reveals his hostility to his literary ancestors by using the catachresis "protest" in place of "writing." The debt to the past grows even more oppressive when we find that "the originals are not original. There is imitation, model and suggestion, to the very archangels, if we knew their history. The first book tyrannizes over the second" (W.VIII.180). If we follow out Emerson's debunking of originality, we realize that "the first book" is only a fiction, albeit a tyrannical one. In a more conciliatory mood, he expresses a notion of writing wherein quotation is celebrated: "Great genial power, one would almost say, consists in not being original at all; in being altogether receptive; in letting the world do all, and suffering the spirit of the hour to pass unobstructed through the mind" (W.IV.191). Emerson here expresses a familiar Romantic trope, but his gesture toward passive receptivity is usually reserved for his comments on the greatness of past writers, as in the essay on Shakespeare; for his contemporaries, he remains the angry prophet decrying the lack of a true poet.

Emerson's hostility toward past literature does not extend to the Bible, which seems to have best claim to being "the first book." But what protects the Bible from his condemnation, surprisingly, is its lack, not possession, of sacredness. He looks upon the Bible as "the work of the whole communion of worshippers" and compares it to "an old Cremona; it has been played upon by the devotion of thousands of years until every word and particle is public and tunable" (W.VIII.182). Relying on Eichhorn's higher criticism of the Bible, with which his brother William, having studied at Göttingen, was personally acquainted, Emerson attributes the Bible's value to its collective authorship. He extends this principle to all great literature: "It is easy to see that what is best written or done by genius in the world, was no man's work, but came by wide social labor, when a thousand wrought like one, sharing the same impulse" (*W*.IV.199). Emerson sacrifices originality to his desire for the One. If he is struck by "the appearance that one person wrote all books" (*W*.II.232), it is because all literature repeats the same thing. Writing cannot account for diversity, let alone originality, but reading can. He writes of Vergil, "That author is a thousand books to a thousand persons. Take the book into your two hands and read your eyes out, you will never find what I find" (*W*.II.149). Being "public and tunable," the Bible, like all other books, is rewritten every time it is reread.

At this point, it appears that Emerson denies originality to the writer and grants it to the reader. But we need to recall that books, or quotations, were once our own, and they return to us as foreign bodies and are internalized the more they are rejected. Reading, being a kind of quotation, can be no more original than writing. Both take part in an economy of the incorporation of foreign quotations that paradoxically constitute the self. The traditional sign of the self, speech, serves as the main vehicle of reappropriation: "What he [the speaker] quotes, he fills with his own voice and humor, and the whole cyclopaedia of his table-talk is presently believed to be his own" (*W*.VIII.183). The voice reappropriates the written text and makes it the speaker's property. On the other hand, those who quote others rather than experience nature directly "live as foreigners in the world of truth, and quote thoughts, and thus disown them. Quotation confesses inferiority" (*W*.VIII.188). Quotation also makes impossible determination of proprietorship. It both acknowledges and obscures the debt. The only thing that counts in this economy is the rate of exchange: "This vast mental indebtedness has every variety that pecuniary debt has,—every variety of merit. The capitalist of either kind is as hungry to lend as the consumer to borrow; and the transaction no more indicates intellectual turpitude in the borrower than the simple fact of debt involves bankruptcy. On the contrary, in far the greater number of cases the transaction is honorable to both" (*W*.VIII.189). The number of transactions indicates the value of a literary work. It is only in the quoting that words take on significance. Even the "author" (the quotation marks should be sufficient warning of the status of this term in Emerson's works) must see "his" words quoted before he recognizes their worth: "Whatever we think and say is wonderfully better for our spirits and trust, in another mouth" (*W*.VIII.190). In this transaction the writer now stands in the quoter's debt; in fact, as the writer himself is a quoter, his debt extends both to his precursors and to his plagiarists. Yet he can eliminate his debt only by borrowing from other writers. The debt, then, between source and quoter is mutual. Emerson comes close to claiming their parity: "Next to the originator of a good sentence is the first quoter of it" (W.VIII.191). But as originality belongs only to God, the writer always remains secondary, a quoter. Emerson goes so far as to suggest that the borrower takes precedence over the author: "We read the quotation with his [the borrower's] eyes, and find a new and fervent sense"; and he says elsewhere, "Observe also that a writer appears to more advantage in the pages of another book than in his own. In his own he waits as a candidate for your approbation; in another's he is a lawgiver" (W.VIII.194, 195). Quotation declares the absence of the author, and in his absence, his words acquire authority.

In the early pages of "Quotation and Originality," Emerson sketches a theory of reading permeated by hostility toward the past. Intent upon denying the existence of originality, he grants a role to the reader that subverts the authority of the text, which is not only derivative but a veritable tomb without the reader. For literature to exist, it must operate within a system of exchange. Having no value in itself, the literary sign is like paper money; it only has value when it is spent—its value comes with use. The past provides the raw material in this economy: "We cannot overstate our debt to the Past, but the moment has the supreme claim. The Past is for us; but the sole terms on which it can become ours are its subordination to the Present" (W.VIII.204). At this stage in our analysis, we can say we subordinate by quoting. But this cannot be—quotation declares that what we write or speak does not belong to us. Quotation entombs the past in the self, thereby cutting the speaker off from both the past and the present. All is quotation; the past, let alone the present, is never present to itself. A quotation refers to what can only be another quotation.

The one exception to this rule is God: "The divine never quotes, but is, and creates. The profound apprehension of the Present is Genius, which makes the Past forgotten. Genius believes its faintest presentiment against the testimony of all history; for it knows that facts are not ultimates, but that a state of mind is the ancestor of everything. And what is Originality? It is being, being one's self, and reporting accurately what we see and are" (W.VIII.201). Having posited a theory of reading in which the book (and, for that matter, meaning itself) only comes into being through the absence of the author, Emerson retreats from this stance and affirms divine and human presence in an abrupt about-face. Yet his theory of reading undercuts his affirmation of the authority of the self and the immediacy of perception. Since everything is a quotation, the apprehension of the present must be a forgetting of the past. But forgetting the past cuts us off from the present. This self-destroying union of history and the present moment characterizes, in Paul de Man's analysis, literary modernity. In an Emersonian text such as Nietzsche's *Use and Abuse of History*, the desire to attain a true present free from the past requires the willful forgetting of the past, but modernity accepts the "present moment as an origin" only to discover "that, in severing itself from the past, it has at the same time severed itself from the future."[10] The present only exists by virtue of the memory giving continuity to isolated events. If we subordinate the past to the present by quoting, then we also reinstate the past under the name of the present. But as quotation declares the absence of the self, it marks the abyss between the quoter and the present. And the absence of the present means the loss of self-presence.

Nature is the preferred alternative to the past, but it too is condemned to be displaced by quotation. If we turn to Emerson's first book, *Nature*, we find that nature, which is structured like a language, must be read also; and, like language, it admits absence and difference into its being. At the opening of Chapter 4, "Language," he writes:

> Language is a third use which Nature subserves to man. Nature is the vehicle of thought, and in a simple, double, and threefold degree.
> 1. Words are signs of natural facts.
> 2. Particular natural facts are symbols of particular spiritual facts.
> 3. Nature is the symbol of spirit. (*W*.I.25)

Unlike Hegel, Emerson does not distinguish between sign and symbol, as his substitution of the latter for the former reveals. Although Hegel acknowledges that the "symbol is *prima facie a sign*," he distinguishes a symbol from a "mere sign": "In a mere sign the connection which meaning and its expression have with one another is only a purely arbitrary linkage. In that case this expression, this sensuous thing or picture, so far from presenting *itself*, brings before our minds a context foreign to it, one with which it does not need to stand in any proper affinity whatever."[11] As we shall see, Emerson's symbol resembles Hegel's "mere sign."

In Emerson's scheme, nature is the sign of spirit, and language is the sign

---

10. De Man, *Blindness and Insight*, 149.
11. Hegel, *Aesthetics*, I, 304.

of nature; language is thus a sign of a sign and is twice removed from spirit. Writing in the logocentric tradition of Western thought, Emerson asserts that a word's meaning is erased as it passes through many hands. Thus, the connection between nature and spirit is, as Hegel says, "a purely arbitrary linkage." In "White Mythology," Derrida refers to this process of erasure as the economy of metaphor,[12] a term particularly well suited for Emerson's own metaphors: "Every word which is used to express a moral or intellectual fact, if traced to its root, is found to be borrowed from some material appearance." As language decays, "old words are perverted to stand for things which are not; a paper currency is employed, when there is no bullion in the vaults" (W.I.25,30).

Emerson attributes a perverted language to the corruption of character: "When simplicity of character and the sovereignty of ideas is broken up by the prevalence of secondary desires,—the desire of riches, of pleasure, of power, and of praise,—and duplicity and falsehood take place of simplicity and truth, the power over nature as an interpreter of the will is in a degree lost" (W.I.30). Ideally, however, "man is an analogist, and studies relations in all objects." Man looks upon nature and finds signs of the universal soul: "The blue sky . . . is the type of Reason," and man embodies spirit "in his language as the FATHER" (W.I.27). Man, and here Emerson reflects Hegel, stands between spirit and nature; he is both and neither. When man's desires are directed toward spirit, he draws analogies from nature and thereby comes to know spirit. The purity of language depends upon man's spiritual distance from nature; the more physical his attachment to natural impulses, the more corrupt the relation between words and things. As man more actively pursues the spiritual life, the more truthful language becomes. Or so Emerson would have us believe. But we have seen how language itself is drawn from nature. Man's pursuit draws him away from the source of language. Spirit is knowable only in the concrete, the very thing that cuts man off from spirit. And nature itself is inaccessible: "The stars awaken a certain reverence, because though always present, they are inaccessible; but all natural objects make a kindred impression, when the mind is open to their influence" (W.I.7). It is from an inaccessible nature that man conceives what must be an inaccessible God.

Emerson would have a dialectic in which language would bring the world and God into relation. We conceive of spirit through analogies derived from

12. Derrida, *Margins of Philosophy*, 207–271.

nature. Nature, in turn, is conceived in language: "Parts of speech are metaphors, because the whole of nature is a metaphor of the human mind"
(W.I.32). Mind does not exist prior to language; it too is a product of metaphor. If "words are signs of natural facts," then they must be metaphors
of metaphors. There is no nature, only a surplus of dead metaphors—quotations so well worn that they have achieved the illusion of permanence.
What can nature be but a quotation from the mind of man, which is itself
a collection of quotations? Mind and nature can never get beyond tautology: mind is a metaphor of nature, and nature is a metaphor of mind. Metaphor always reveals the abyss between the object and its representation in
language. Finally, it cannot be said that language provides the grounds for
the concrete realization of spirit; instead, dialectic gives way to interminable quotations whereby death inhabits nature, self, and spirit in the form
of metaphors. In other words, the search for solid ground upon which Being
can manifest itself only uncovers the irreducible presence of metaphor.

As nature is language, it should be no surprise that it is meant to be read:
"There sits the Sphinx [a symbol of nature] at the road-side, and from age
to age, as each prophet comes by, he tries his fortune at reading her riddle"
(W.I.34). In the Sphinx, nature is a text, as Emerson indicates in the next
paragraph: "By degrees we come to know the primitive sense of the permanent object of nature, so that the world shall be to us an open book, and
every form significant of its hidden life and final cause" (W.I.35). The
gradual decipherment of nature promises the possibility of introjection, a
synthesis of man and nature. But the Sphinx is an excess of nature—a text,
an unnatural union of man and nature. We traditionally give the name culture to this union. This text, however, is lost to introjection. For introjection to be possible, language would have to mediate between self and other.
The Sphinx's decipherment came with the magical and immediate utterance of the word "man," whereupon she threw herself into the sea. Out-
stripped by nature, language must generate meaning by the fantasmic act
of naming. But the Sphinx's destruction reveals that reading destroys the
text the moment decipherment begins. A discontinuity between language
and nature prevents the reader from ever making contact with nature. To
experience nature, we must interpret it, which means we must violate it by
inscribing man and nature in the text of culture. The search for nature leads
into the pit of metaphor.

Emerson proves to be fully aware of the inadequacy of language. Consequently, he denigrates it in favor of God and identity: "The central Unity

is still more conspicuous in actions. Words are finite organs of the infinite mind. They cannot cover the dimensions of what is in the truth. They break, chop, and impoverish it. An action is the perfection and publication of thought" (W.I.44–45). If words that stand for abstract truth—words like "right" or "spirit"—represent a decay from a language of full presence in which words stand for things, then truth, which the mind apprehends, can never be properly put into words. Truth represented in language must be metaphorical, as Emerson must resort to metaphor himself; consequently, language takes us away from, rather than toward, truth.

In *Pierre*, Melville speaks of the search for truth as a digging into a crypt. Finding "nothing but surface stratified on surface," the geologist discovers absence at the center. In a journal passage strikingly similar to Melville's pyramid metaphor, Emerson also invokes the figure of the geologist who finds absence perpetually retreating behind the screen of representation: "Mediator mediation There is nothing else; there is no Immediate known to us. Cloud on cloud, degree on degree, remove one coat, one lamina, and another coat or lamina just like it is the result,—to be also removed. When the symbol is explained the new truth turns out to be only a symbol of ulterior truth. The Judgment Day is in reality the Past. We have been judged & we have judged all" (JMN.XI.424). As writing records the past, as well as nature, so books mark the permanent absence of truth, nature, and spirit.

In *Nature*, Emerson told his readers, " 'Build therefore your own world' " (W.I.76); Thoreau went to Walden Pond to build a house and write a book. The two tasks, building and writing, were one and the same for Thoreau. Like Whitman, he could never be content as "any man's mere follower"; he would build his own house, even if it was on Emerson's property.

A journal entry for January 1, 1852, reveals the close association books and homes had for Thoreau: "I wish to survey my composition for a moment from the least favorable point of view. I wish to be translated to the future, and look at my work as it were at a structure on the plain, to observe what portions have crumbled under the influence of the elements." Thoreau desires not only to be "translated to the future" but also to translate the book into a house and thereby leave a sturdy edifice. But he knows that some of it will erode with time, leaving only archives, fragments of a foundation. The building of a house is not unlike the writing of a book; they both require a firm foundation and solid financing: "When I consider how our homes are built and paid for, or not paid for, and their internal economy managed and sustained, I wonder that the floor does not give way under the visitor while he is admiring the gewgaws upon the mantelpiece, and let him through into the cellar, to some solid and honest though earthy foundation." The search for an earthy foundation is a search for a *point d'appui*, "a place," writes Walter Michaels, "we locate by asking questions. We know that we've found it when one of our questions is answered. The name we give to this place is Nature. The search for solid bottom is a search for . . . what is real, that is, natural, and not human."[13] Thoreau's objection to houses can be read as an objection to all human institutions, including language. Nietzsche called language a prison house; Thoreau thought all houses were prisons. Yet Thoreau does build his house; he even "took particular pleasure in this breaking of ground [digging the cellar]. . . . Under the most splendid house in the city is still to be found the cellar where they store their roots as of old, and long after the superstructure has disappeared posterity remark its dent in the earth" (*W*, p. 30).

In his eulogy for Thoreau, Emerson says Thoreau preferred New England to Europe because New England "is not based on any Roman ruins. We have not to lay the foundation of our houses on the ashes of a former civilization" (*W*.X.460). Thoreau will be his own architect, or technician of the *archē* (that is, the maker of origins), and lay the ruins for future generations. It is the foreign architect who arouses Thoreau's anger. The breaking of the ground is the inscription of an origin. Thoreau turns the fields and woods surrounding Walden Pond into a text. His sentences dig furrows in the ground marking the presence of the dweller. In a fascinating passage on Rousseau, Derrida comments on the *via rupta*, plowing and writing: "The furrow of agriculture, we remind ourselves, opens nature to culture (cultivation). And one also knows that writing is born with agriculture which happens only with sedentarization." Writing by furrows means that the linear movement remains unbroken as the line transverses from left to right and then right to left. Opening nature to culture involves a reordering of space that reveals the presence of man. In terms of writing, the space of the sentence marks the presence of the author; in other words, writing is consciousness becoming spatial. The objective of reading would be to erase the signifier (*i.e.*, writing) and recover the signified (*i.e.*, the au-

---

13. Stapleton (ed.), *H. D. Thoreau: A Writer's Journal*, 81, hereinafter cited as *WJ*; Thoreau, *"Walden" and "Civil Disobedience,"* 25, hereinafter cited as *W*; Michaels, *"Walden's False Bottoms,"* 137.

thor's consciousness). But this recovery of presence can only be thought of within writing, a system of representation owing as much to reading as it does to inscription. Writing does not follow the line of the plowman; reading by furrows is easier than writing by furrows. Writing is determined as much by the hand as by the eye. As Derrida puts it, "One does not only write, one reads a little blindly, guided by the order of the hand."[14] The successive movement of the written line breaks up the linear progression of agriculture. Writing doesn't exist in a genetic line running from consciousness to the sensible world. As writing is only intelligible by virtue of repetition—by occupying the space of reading—it represents a consciousness locked in a chain of signifiers.

In *Walden*, Thoreau refuses to acknowledge the doubleness of writing. Writing is always a reading and, therefore, can never be original. He would like to think of the writer as a maker, a man of action. The writer, for Thoreau, occupies that place which brings together nature and culture. But the writer, who should thus be a bringer of harmony, brings violence instead. The excess of writing transgresses the silent harmony of nature: "The volatile truth of our words should continually betray the inadequacy of the residual statement. Their truth is instantly *translated*; its literal monument alone remains" (*W*, p. 221). The ideal would be the erasure of the signifier, but ideals are hard to live up to. Let us turn to Thoreau on building, where we find only empty monuments, never truth.

Whenever Thoreau talks about building, he adopts the language of presence: "Architectural beauty . . . has gradually grown from within outward, out of the necessities and character of the indweller, who is the only builder" (*W*, p. 32). The language of this passage is remarkably Heideggerian. In "Building Dwelling Thinking," Heidegger writes, "*Only if we are capable of dwelling, only then can we build.*"[15] And like Heidegger, Thoreau also believes that the proper sense of dwelling has been suppressed by the excrescences of civilization—that is, by ornament and language. For Thoreau, architectural ornaments copied from European models mark the absence of spirit: "It [building without dwelling] is of a piece with constructing his own coffin,—the architecture of the grave, and 'carpenter,' is but another name for 'coffin-maker'" (*W*, p. 33). If we allow a foreign technician to construct our *archē*, we risk falling through the superstruc-

14. Derrida, *Of Grammatology*, 287.
15. Heidegger, *Poetry, Language, Thought*, 160.

ture and landing upon the relics of decayed civilizations. Instead, we must find unbroken ground upon which to build our home.

A *point d'appui* therefore requires a deliberate dwelling in nature—an incision that marks the origin of an American culture. To allow another architect to construct the house is to exchange the home for a coffin. The importation of European architecture has its parallel in the problem of translation. According to Thoreau, it is not enough to read the classics "in the character of our mother tongue"; these works "will always be in a language dead to degenerate times" (*W*, p. 69). But even knowledge of the original language may not suffice. "Books must be read as deliberately and reservedly as they were written. It is not enough even to be able to speak the language of that nation by which they are written, for there is a memorable interval between the spoken and the written language, the language heard and the language read" (*W*, p. 70). The interval between speech and writing measures the progress from savagery to culture. It is the difference between dwelling outdoors or in a house of one's own; it is the advent of agriculture. And as literature may be corrupted by the transcription from one country to another, so may architecture.

Let us pause to contrast Thoreau's rejection of translation with Emerson's praise for it. In a journal entry eventually used in "Books," Emerson writes:

> I thank the translators & it is never my practice to read any Latin, Greek, German, Italian, scarcely any French book, in the original which I can procure in an English translation. I like to be beholding to the great metropolitan English speech, the sea which receives tributaries from every region under heaven, the Rome of nations, and I should think it in me as much folly to read all my books in originals when I have them rendered for me in my mother's speech by men who have given years to the labor, as I should to swim across Charles River when ever I wished to go to Charlestown. (*JMN*.VIII.357)

Their contrasting attitudes toward translation may explain their equally different attitudes toward originality. If there is no original text as Emerson says, then to read a book in English is merely to choose one translation over another. English would even be preferable—its fragmented and indeterminable origin makes it a universal language. Containing elements from all other nations, English is a bastard language: although the mother may be identifiable, there are many candidates for the father. Thoreau, a believer in origins, makes much more of reading in the original language, as he values the father more than the mother.

As we might expect, the genealogical implications of the metaphor of a mother tongue are not lost upon Thoreau. He says speech is "a sound, a tongue, a dialect merely, almost brutish, and we learn it unconsciously, like the brutes, of our mothers." Writing, however, "is the maturity and experience of that [speech]; if that is our mother tongue, this is our father tongue, a reserved and select expression, too significant to be heard by the ear, which we must be born again in order to speak" (W, p. 70). The emergence of writing signifies a spiritual growth in society, as Thoreau's allusion to John 3:3 indicates. But writing has other associations. Derrida points out that "the birth of writing (in the colloquial sense) was nearly everywhere and most often linked to genealogical anxiety."[16] Those roots in Thoreau's cellar aren't just potatoes; they are the ancestors' (metaphorical?) remains. The incision of the line doesn't break new ground; instead, it reveals the path that has already been dug.

We need not be surprised that, however much Thoreau may insist on writing as the spiritual father, he favors speech. When he says writing "is the work of art nearest to life itself," he resorts to metaphors of self and presence: "It [the written word] may be translated into every language, and not only be read but actually breathed from all human lips;—not be represented on canvas or in marble only, but be carved out of the breath of life itself. *The symbol of an ancient man's thought becomes a modern man's speech*" (W, p. 71; my emphasis).

The written word is the transcription of a thought that awaits resurrection by the reader; in this, Thoreau's theory of reading resembles Emerson's. Thoreau, however, adheres more closely than does Emerson to the traditional metaphysics of presence—speech is the sign of presence, and writing is the substitute for speech. Writing represents, not presence, but the signs of presence. Speech guarantees the life of mind and culture. Thoreau also shares Emerson's belief that nature is a book: "The earth expresses itself outwardly in leaves, it so labors with the idea inwardly" (W, p. 209). (It's worth noting that this inside/outside metaphor operates within the same conceptual system as do thought/speech and writing/reading.) The pun on *leaf* appears again when he asks, "What Champollion will de-

16. Derrida, *Of Grammatology*, 124.

cipher this hieroglyphic for us, that we may turn over a new leaf at last?"
(*W*, p. 210).

The work of deciphering leads us back to the earth. Thoreau writes in a
journal entry for October 16, 1859: "Talk about learning our *letters* and
being *literate*! Why, the roots of *letters* are *things*. Natural objects and
phenomena are the original symbols or types which express our thoughts
and feelings, and yet American scholars, having little or no root in the soil,
commonly strive with all their might to confine themselves to the imported
symbols alone. All the true growth and experience, the living speech, they
would fain reject as 'Americanisms.' . . . A more intimate knowledge, a
deeper experience, will surely originate a word" (*WJ*, pp. 205–206). Just
as our architecture and literature are borrowed, so is our very vocabulary.
But Thoreau's alternative to foreign borrowings is a local borrowing. As
the newly dug cellar uncovered the roots of the ancestors, so will the roots
of words prove to lie in more words, not in things. The "deeper experience" sought by Thoreau leads to a search for a *point d'appui*, which is a
search for nature. By digging through the excrescences of civilization, he
hopes to uncover nature and, consequently, "the living speech." Writing
would thereby fall among the rubble of civilization as Thoreau seeks to break
the chains placed upon him by conventions and foreign sources. There must
be *extra vagance*, an opening of boundaries for the presence of the poet to
emerge on the horizon. Thoreau writes, "I fear chiefly lest my expression
may not be *extra-vagant* enough, may not wander far enough beyond the
narrow limits of my daily experience, so as to be adequate to the truth of
which I have been convinced. *Extra vagance*! it depends on how you are
yarded" (*W*, p. 221). (Thoreau's puns, like his living alone in the woods,
are a movement outside the boundaries, the decorum, of New England society.)

His desire for extra vagance resembles the Heideggerian sense of boundary as that "from which something *begins its presencing*." I would like to
return once more to Heidegger's essay "Building Dwelling Thinking" for
an analysis of the horizon. Heidegger says, "A boundary is not that at which
something stops but, as the Greeks recognized, the boundary is that from
which something *begins its presencing*. That is why the concept is that of
horismos, that is, the horizon, the boundary. Space is in essence that for
which room has been made, that which is let into its bounds." The digging
of the cellar and the erecting of the house at Walden Pond form the site
where Thoreau begins his presencing. Thoreau's yard does not pen him in;

rather, it allows for the location, as Heidegger explains it, "into which earth and heaven, divinities and mortals are admitted." But if the horizon is the site where presencing begins, it is also the site where presence remains almost, but never quite, present. Thoreau aims to recover full presence, the living speech; the poet's task, however, is one of inscription—digging and writing. Thoreau's wandering beyond boundaries leads him into the boundary's path. The effacement of boundaries that promises the emergence of the poet's presence comes to displace presence within the "structure of the trace." Yet this structure has no place; it is effaced by an inscription that "constitutes it as a trace."[17]

Emerson calls the tracing of traces "quotation," and its emblem is the horizon. In "Experience" he writes, "Men seem to have learned of the horizon the art of perpetual retreating and reference. . . . I quote another man's saying; unluckily that other withdraws himself in the same way, and quotes me" (W.III.46–47). As the sign of the approaching or retreating sun, the horizon serves as a sign for that which refers beyond itself to what it can never re-present. And, as we have seen, the writer, who is only a quoter, is never present. For, as Emerson suggests, to assert oneself is to withdraw one's self—the voice is the sign of the speaker's absence.

Thoreau, on the other hand, wishes to recover and assert presence. He speaks of presencing as taking place in both time and space. Time for transcendentalists, particularly Kantian ones, is recognized as a product of mind, and it can only be measured in terms of space. Thoreau employs metaphors of space when expressing his desire "to improve the nick of time, and notch it on my stick too; to stand on the meeting of two eternities, the past and future, which is precisely the present moment; to toe that line" (W, p. 10). What is this stick but a stylus, a pen? Thoreau's dwelling clears a space for the boundary within which he begins his presencing—declares his independence by writing his first book, A Week on the Concord and Merrimack Rivers. His objection to speech is that it is common—he must learn it from others. But by writing, he gains the mastery of the pen, which we might call a phallus, and in rewriting history, he inscribes his own origin. The master of the pen/phallus becomes his own father.

We must turn to Walden's conclusion and the fable of the artist of Kouroo to see how writing, genealogy, and history are linked in Thoreau's text.

---

17. Heidegger, Poetry, Language, Thought, 154, 155. For a discussion of the trace, see Derrida, Margins of Philosophy, 3–27.

Like Thoreau, the artist of Kouroo also carves a stick, but rather than notch the nick of time on it, he uses it to write the end of time in the sand: "Before he had given it the proper shape the dynasty of the Condahars was at an end, and with the point of the stick he wrote the name of the last of that race in the sand, and then resumed his work" (W, p. 223). The fable of the writer and his stick is Thoreau's inscribing of the boundary from which he will begin his presencing. But the possessor of the stylus does not master time; he can only translate it into the relic of the book. Thoreau wishes to master time through art. His book will set him free from history; but as the concluding fable shows, writing inscribes, even commemorates, the passage of time. Time is only thinkable within the path of the line, which the artist's stick traces. In spite of what his text tells him, Thoreau wishes to be the author—that is, the codifier of his own origin and the father of American literature. Ideally, the two origins would be connate. Let us turn to a journal entry for December 27, 1855, in which he lists the important dates in his life that a biographer would want to record: "Was graduated in 1837 (?). Began the big Red Journal, October, 1837. Found first arrowheads, fall of 1837. Wrote a lecture (my first) on Society, March 14th, 1838, and read it before the Lyceum" (WJ, p. 133). Thoreau's careers as writer, lecturer, autobiographer, and archaeologist begin with the recognition of his belatedness. He, too, must build on the ruins of another culture, one that has better claims to the home than does his own. His topic, society, is further proof of the distance from the origin of culture.

Although Thoreau saw fit to devote a chapter to reading in *Walden*, it is sounds, after all, that guarantee spirit and originality. If we only read books, Thoreau writes, "we are in danger of forgetting the language which all things and events speak without metaphor, which alone is copious and standard" (W, p. 77). Echoing the sentiment of Emerson's question, "Why should not we also enjoy an original relation to the universe?" (W.I.3), Thoreau asks, "Will you be a reader, a student merely, or a seer?" (W, p. 77). Thoreau looks upon nature as accessible to him who lives deliberately. The reader, then, is secondary; only the writer enjoys an original relation to the universe. But he can be original only by forgetting his belatedness; the writer must forget he is also a reader. Thoreau makes this clear when he says, "I did not read books the first summer; I hoed beans" (W, p. 77). In *Walden*, hoeing is synonymous with writing. He did not hoe beans so he could eat them, but "for the sake of tropes and expressions, to serve a parable-maker one day" (W, p. 112). But he breaks ground only to find remains of his precursors. Even he admits, "Decayed literature makes the richest of soils" (WJ, p. 85).

If Thoreau says culture is fertilizer, it's only because the world is a compost heap. The hieroglyphic of nature, Thoreau says, "is somewhat excrementitious in its character, and there is no end to the heaps of liver, lights, and bowels, as if the globe were turned wrong side outward; but this suggests at least that Nature has some bowels, and there again is mother of humanity" (W, p. 210). Growing out of this compost is language. Sitting by a railroad cut, Thoreau remarks: "You find thus in the very sands an anticipation of the vegetable leaf. . . . The overhanging leaf sees here its prototype. *Internally*, whether in the globe or animal body, it is a moist thick *lobe*, a word especially applicable to the liver and lungs and the *leaves* of fat, (λειβω, *labor, lapsus*, to flow or slip downward, a lapsing; λοβός, *globus*, lobe, globe; also lap, flap, and many other words,) *externally*, a dry thin *leaf*, even as the *f* and *v* are a pressed and dried *b*" (W, p. 209). In examining this passage and its debt to Walter Whiter's theory of a universal language, Michael West comments that "life and language are not only coordinates, but all life seems to aspire to linguistic expression."[18] To idealize this passage is to deny evidence of Thoreau's anxiety over his belatedness. Rather than give birth to living speech, the world will only permit the recomposition of a decomposed language. After all, *compost*, as the OED informs us, means both manure and literature.

Stanley Cavell takes a more humanistic view of Thoreau's metaphors. "In *Walden*," he writes, "reading is not merely the other side of writing, its eventual fate; it is another metaphor for writing itself. The writer cannot invent words as 'perpetual suggestions and provocations'; the written word is already 'the choicest of relics.'" Although Cavell sees writing and reading as analogous activities, the writer bears "a commitment to total and transparent meaning" that the reader is obliged to recover.[19] Cavell, like Thoreau, subordinates reading to writing. The writer escapes the secondariness of a reader by uncovering the sediment that has accumulated upon words and restoring their "transparent meaning." In effect, Cavell separates writing from reading. The recovery of lost time—that is, the assertion of originality—is to be accomplished by writing, which is spatial. But Thoreau's hoeing metaphors overturn Cavell's claim for a temporal recov-

---

18. West, "*Walden's* Dirty Language," 127.
19. Cavell, *The Senses of Walden*, 27, 30.

ery of presence. A deliberate dwelling, on the contrary, does not bring us into relation with nature. While hoeing, Thoreau does not recover the object; he uncovers "tropes and expressions"—metaphors—and metaphors are borrowed homes. Tropes are words which can be occupied by several meanings, none of which may dwell there permanently. And as agriculture affirms the presence of society and the loss of virgin nature, writing affirms that "meaning" is always already borrowed from the dung heap of literature upon which the foundation of *Walden* is built.

A final aside is in order here. We have heard from Melville and Emerson on the hopeless task of the geologist. It is only fitting that we allow Thoreau to contradict Emerson once more: "The earth is not a mere fragment of dead history, stratum upon stratum like the leaves of a book, to be studied by geologists and antiquaries chiefly, but living poetry like the leaves of a tree, which precede flowers and fruit,—not a fossil earth, but a living earth; compared with whose great central life all animal and vegetable life is merely parasitic. Its throes will heave our exuviae from their graves" (*W*, pp. 210–11). But Thoreau has just finished telling us that the living earth, which now appears to be in its death throes, is a heap of excrement. He wants to revivify nature by turning excrement into life, just as he wants to turn his geological metaphor into an organic metaphor. Thoreau stands self-condemned, since the site of his hut by the side of Walden Pond was a short distance beyond Emerson's home. In a discussion of host and parasite, J. Hillis Miller comes to the following conclusions on the definitions and etymologies of the Greek prefix *para*:

> "Para" is an "uncanny" double antithetical prefix signifying at once proximity and distance, similarity and difference, interiority and exteriority, something at once inside a domestic economy and outside it, something simultaneously this side of the boundary line, threshold, or margin, and at the same time beyond it, equivalent in status and at the same time secondary or subsidiary, submissive, as of guest to host, slave to master. A thing in "para" is, moreover, not only simultaneously on both sides of the boundary line between inside and outside. It is also the boundary itself, the screen which is at once a permeable membrane connecting inside and outside, confusing them with one another, allowing the outside in, making the inside out, dividing them but also forming an ambiguous transition between one and the other.[20]

20. J. H. Miller, "The Critic as Host," 441.

Thoreau's desire for extra vagance depends upon a distinct boundary within which he will be master—a place where contact with the particularities of nature will give rise to universal truth. But Thoreau is both master and slave. He boasts of living within his slight domestic economy, but he fails to say that he lives within his domicile by leaving his domestic economy to Emerson's charity—the house, after all, was built on Emerson's property.

We need to mention one more of Emerson's tenants, Whitman, who, like Thoreau, rejects the nihilism of the geological metaphor and turns to an organic metaphor in its place: "The science of language has large and close analogies in geological science, with its ceaseless evolution, its fossils, and its numberless submerged layers and hidden strata, the infinite go-before of the present. Or, perhaps Language is more like some vast living body, or perennial body of bodies. And slang not only brings the first feeders of it, but is afterward the start of fancy, imagination and humor, breathing into its nostrils the breath of life."[21] Apparently, both Whitman and Thoreau had in mind the following passage from Emerson's essay "The Poet" when they wrote of geology and language:

> The poets made all the words, and therefore language is the archives of history, and, if we must say it, a sort of tomb of the muses. For though the origin of most of our words is forgotten, each word was at first a stroke of genius, and obtained currency because for the moment it symbolized the world to the first speaker and to the hearer. The etymologist finds the deadest word to have been once a brilliant picture. Language is fossil poetry. As the limestone of the continent consists of infinite masses of the shells of animalcules, so language is made up of images or tropes, which now, in their secondary use, have long ceased to remind us of their poetic origin. (W.III.21–22)

Thoreau and Whitman want to affirm the poet's calling as the namer of things. They reject the skepticism that creeps into the following remark of Emerson's: "But the poet names the thing because he sees it, *or comes one step nearer to it than any other*" (W.III.22; my emphasis).

In "The Nature of Language," Heidegger writes of Stefan George, but he could just as well have been writing about American poets: "The decisive experience is that which the poet has undergone with the word—and with the word inasmuch as it alone can bestow a relation to a thing. Stated

21. Whitman, *Prose Works 1892*, II, 577.

more explicitly, the poet has experienced that only the word makes a thing appear as the thing is, and thus lets it be present. The word avows itself to the poet as that which holds and sustains a thing in its being. . . . The poet experiences his poetic calling as a call to the word as the source, the bourn of Being." What Thoreau fears is that the thing has been lost among the decomposed matter of language and nature. Just as he builds his hut with boards from a run-down shanty, so he composes his book out of the rotting remains of culture and nature. An inveterate punster, Thoreau hopes to regenerate a lost origin by exploiting the resources of language, particularly etymology. Thus, digging into the ground to build a firm foundation involves a recovery of the origin. This recovery is an uncanny (*unheimlich*) experience, as Freud finds out when tracing the etymology of *heimlich*: "What is *heimlich* thus comes to be *unheimlich*."[22] Thoreau experiences the uncanny as poetic naming—his puns obscure the thing as much as they sustain it. By punning, Thoreau attempts to restore the antithetical sense of words that have been worn down to a simple definition. But this uncovering of meaning is a fragmenting of origins—puns reveal the indetermincy of language. No wonder Thoreau complains that "in this part of the world it is considered a ground for complaint if a man's writings admit of more than one interpretation" (*W*, pp. 221–22).

Thoreau set out to build a house, but ended up with a compost heap. The history of American literature proves to be less a beginning than a continual destruction of the old. Emerson, who was capable of speaking of America as the new Eden, knew that literature thrives more on violence than it does on humanity: "The new continents are built out of the ruins of an old planet; the new races fed out of the decomposition of the foregoing. New arts destroy the old" (*W*.II.302). The American writer is always discovering that the road west leads east of Eden.

---

22. Heidegger, *On the Way to Language*, 66–67; Freud, *On Creativity and the Unconscious*, 129.

CHAPTER TWO

Emerson's Encyclopedia

I promise nothing complete; because any human thing supposed to be complete, must for that very reason infallibly be faulty.

—Melville

"The only exact knowledge there is," said Anatole France, "is the knowledge of the date of publication and the format of books." And indeed, if there is a counterpart to the confusion of a library, it is the order of its catalogue.

—Walter Benjamin

For the nineteenth century, the historian had the twofold task of translating textual artifacts and cataloguing them for inclusion in a universal encyclopedia. The desire to know the origin of the universe is as persistent as the desire to index and catalogue it. The tools of classification were borrowed from the emerging sciences of philology, geology, and zoology. A consistent pattern can be found in which biological metaphors were grafted onto the atemporal classifications of the natural sciences. Friedrich Schlegel, for example, not only adopts the metaphor of genealogy for geology and philology, he places these two sciences in a family relationship: "The geological branch of natural history may well be considered cognate to the inquiry [into the origin of languages] before us."[1] According to Schlegel, both geology and philology are concerned with studying antiquities and with classifying primary structures and their secondary offspring; thus the natural sciences and philology become affiliated in a process at once taxonomic and genealogical.

In Schlegel and many others, classification merges with genealogy to produce a system of historical discourse arranging man and nature in a spatial hierarchy. The obvious paradox—confusion may be more accurate—of accounting for a spatial hierarchy in genealogical terms derives from a transference of biological metaphors into the physical sciences and linguistics. Auguste Comte, for instance, argues for a hierarchical arrange-

1. Schlegel, *The Philosophy of Life,* 398.

ment of knowledge in what he calls "*dogmatic* order," as opposed to "*historical* order." He arrives at his hierarchical arrangement of the sciences by tracing the history of knowledge to its pinnacle in his own *Philosophie première*, using history to account for deviations from what is supposed to be the privileged and atemporal status of positivism. And by means of classification, the heterogeneity and discontinuities in nature and culture are read as only surface phenomena obscuring relationships waiting to be decoded and alphabetized by the historian.

The frequency with which the nineteenth century treated physical and cultural remains as textual materials to be arranged in a catalogue indicates the pervasive awareness that nature and man were caught within varying systems of representations. The historian's search for truth becomes a search for the metaphor that will recover truth by re-collecting lost resemblances. For instance, Michelet's *Introduction à l'histoire universelle* surveys history from the ancients to the moderns to prove that world history is the story of infinite progress. Nonetheless, Michelet's world view remains atemporal. France, to use his metaphor, links the past with the present and the East with the West in a hierarchical order determined by unchanging national characteristics. In both the encyclopedia and the universal history, the trope of resemblance becomes the *topos* of unity. The writing of the total book comes at the end of history—the order of the world appears in/ as a text to which the universal history or the encyclopedia stands as both preface and afterword. The perception of a unified natural world cannot be treated separately from the question of representation. The natural world disappears only to be reconstituted in a text as a lost presence or artifact.

In an essay on Poe's *Eureka* as a cosmogony, Paul Valéry remarks that "the world itself is not much older than the art of making the world." As soon as man appears, suggest Valéry, he sets to writing histories of the world. Borges' Pierre Menard, it seems, was not the first to think of history as the origin of reality rather than as a record of events.[2] Reality earns its name by being written in a book, for only when the event is documented can we recognize it as truth. Borges' tale reminds us that the historian neither creates an origin *ex nihilo* nor records an original event; instead, he can only retrace other texts to which his stands as an addendum. The historian never deals with an event free from its place within a system of rep-

2. Valéry, *Leonardo, Poe, Mallarmé*, 170; Borges, *Ficciones*, 45–55.

resentation. The Romantics reinterpreted the Fall as the substitution of mediation for perception and thereby opened up nature to the discontinuities of language and history. Consequently, Romantic literature continually retells the myth of the Fall as man's recognition that his ontological priority has been replaced by a temporal secondariness.

For Emerson, the Fall occurred when man discovered he exists: "It is very unhappy, but too late to be helped, the discovery we have made that we exist. This discovery is called the Fall of Man. Ever afterwards we suspect our instruments. We have learned that we do not see directly, but mediately, and that we have no means of correcting these colored and distorting lenses which we are, or of computing the amount of their errors" (W.III.75). At this point in "Experience," Emerson crystalizes in a few lines one of the great themes of Romanticism—self-consciousness. Yet the discovery that man has fallen is, as it must always be, a belated discovery. Emerson would modify Descartes' cogito to "I exist, therefore I am fallen." But only in saying "I exist" do I fall. By turning the question of Original Sin into a problem of mediation, the nineteenth century, as Kierkegaard demanded in *The Concept of Dread*, returned Adam to history.

In his analysis of Original Sin, Kierkegaard argues that myth inheres in the notion of firstness and not in sin. Sin is real, he says, and its reality comes from the fact that the individual contains in himself the whole race. To remove Adam from history one would have to suppose that the first sin of each individual could be defined by "its serial number (if we can think of such a thing) in the general sinking fund of the human race." In his inability to account for sin as that which "comes in as the sudden, i.e. with the leap," man turns Genesis into a myth about a perfect world into which sin comes little by little. What proves a "stumbling block to the understanding" is that "sin presupposes itself." Kierkegaard's objection to the myth of Eden is that it places Adam outside of history: "Owing to the fact that the race does not begin afresh with every individual the sinfulness of the race acquires a history. This however proceeds by quantitative determinants, while the individual by the qualitative leap participates in it. The race therefore does not begin afresh with every individual, for in that way the race would be no race, but every individual begins afresh with the race."[3]

3. Kierkegaard, *The Concept of Dread*, 28, 29, 30, 31.

The Myth of Eden is the myth of genealogy, a myth that there was a source free from indeterminate change and that descendants can once again attain the innocence that their father lost for them. Kierkegaard, however, erases the notion that Adam was different from his descendants merely because he precedes them: "Descent is only the expression for the continuity in the history of the race, which always moves by quantitative determinants and therefore is never capable of bringing forth an individual. . . . If the second man had not descended from Adam, he would not have been the second man but an empty repetition, and from this would have derived neither a race nor an individual." An individual, in Kierkegaard's pejorative use of the term, would be he who stands outside of time and change. In calling this second man an "empty repetition," Kierkegaard destroys the notion of firstness and originality. His use of "repetition," as opposed to "empty repetition," allows each man to enter history by losing, as did Adam, innocence through guilt. But this is not to say that innocence was a pristine state lost by sin. Instead, innocence "comes into existence by the very fact that it is annulled. . . . Immediacy is not annulled by mediacy, but when mediacy emerges it has that same instant annulled immediacy." In *The Concept of Dread*, published the same year as Emerson's *Essays, Second Series*, Kierkegaard reveals that the notion of origin, with its companion terms, "innocence" and "immediacy," exists only as a belated concept. In other words, mediacy and immediacy are coexistent, one is immanent within the other. Consequently, we cannot think of immediacy without mediacy, nor can we determine the demarcation that maintains the two. Kierkegaard's critique of generation and origin elaborates a notion of dialectic as an allegory of belatedness in which the usurpation of thesis by antithesis, in this instance immediacy by mediacy, is a fictive rendering of the immanence of the one within the other. This fiction can only be rendered as a temporal process or narrative of the Fall and consciousness of sin. Consciousness defers the Fall until consciousness differs from itself, that is, becomes self-consciousness. Kierkegaard warns that "innocence is not a perfection one ought to wish to recover; for as soon as one wishes for it, it is lost." Knowledge of innocence is made possible by guilt. The moment man reflects on innocence, he discovers he has lost it. For both Kierkegaard and Emerson, the knowledge we exist does not so much precipitate the Fall as it is the Fall. There never was a time when man was not in history and therefore not fallen. Wallace Stevens, another poet obsessed with origins, says much the same in "Notes Toward a Supreme Fiction": "The first idea was not our own. Adam/ In Eden was the father of Descartes."[4] To be human is to be self-conscious; that is, to be human is to be fallen. There is no first idea, no pure origin; the first idea had to be imagined as a belated explanation of the Fall of Man. We might even go so far as to say that belatedness is the Fall, for to know that we exist is to know that we have come too late.

The sense of belatedness proves to be particularly acute in American writers. Although Emerson announced in "The American Scholar" that America's dependence on European literature had come to an end, the optative mood did not stay with him. The pronouncements of the early lectures are frequently rhetorical stances aiming more to affect the audience than to present a consistent doctrine of Emerson's. Although he opens *Nature* by condemning the present age for being retrospective, dwelling more in tombs (the books) of the fathers than in nature, he could also call the earth a museum.[5] He does not refer to this term pejoratively in "The Uses of Natural History," but it indicates his recognition that representation cannot be confined to language and is not, as a reading of the chapter "Language" in *Nature* indicates, unproblematical. Entering into Emerson's unending meditation upon the relation between past and present, and innocence and mediacy, we enter into his metaphysics of reading and writing. A traditional concept of reading assumes that the past, in the form of a book, can be mastered by a writer who then produces a new text that is qualitatively different from previous texts. One masters the tradition and then adds to it. But this concept of tradition and originality presupposes that the past can be overcome through an unproblematic genealogical descent. Descent, however, only promises quantitative, not qualitative, difference. For a book to be qualitatively different from the tradition, it would have to be a first book. Hence, each book of the tradition would be a first book, and the tradition would be no tradition. Belatedness, as it appears in Emerson, does away with faith in originality, as I argued earlier. The poet neither carries on a tradition nor begins a new one; instead, he repeats the past by quoting a pre-text, thereby ripping the quotation from its context and posting it in a new one which he calls his own.

4. *Ibid.*, 31, 33, 34; Stevens, *Collected Poems*, 383.
5. Whicher, Spiller, and Williams (eds.), *The Early Lectures of Ralph Waldo Emerson*, I, 6, hereinafter cited as *EL* with volume number and page reference.

Yet the problem of belatedness, like that of representation, is not confined to literature. The fall into mediacy leaves man in the ruins of Babel.
The multiplication of languages, however, cannot be restricted to the literal
meaning of the word *language*, for systems of representation constitute
nature and the past as well as books. While the topos of God's book of nature has a long history, including, of course, the Puritan tradition of which
Emerson was an heir and of which he sought to divest himself, this theological metaphor was transformed during the eighteenth century with the
rise of archaeology and the natural sciences.[6] This transformation was as
much a transcendentalizing of the sciences as it was a secularizing of nature. The initial theories of geological formation, best exemplified and given
greatest currency by Baron Cuvier, attempted to reconcile the Bible with
natural history. As Michel Foucault has argued in *The Order of Things*,
deciphering nature was considered an archaeological task during the nineteenth century. But archaeology sought to decipher the past and to restore
it as well. In fact, decipherment and restoration are one and the same in this
system.

In the opening of *A Discourse on the Revolutions of the Surface of the
Globe*, Cuvier gives what can stand as a paradigmatic statement concerning
the task facing nineteenth-century theorists of nature and history: "An
antiquary of a new stamp [*espèce*], it was necessary at the same time to restore these monuments of past revolutions, and to detect their meaning: I
had to collect and arrange in their original order the component relics; to
remodel the creatures to whom the fragments belonged; to reproduce them
in their just proportions and with their proper characteristics; and then to
compare them with those beings now existing." Reconstructing history
means interpreting the relics of forgotten ages. Prehistoric ruins are the
writings of an age preceding man. Cuvier writes, "We admire that power
of the human mind, the exercise of which has enabled us to ascertain those

---

6. See Curtius, *European Literature and the Latin Middle Ages*, 319–26; Glacken, *Traces
on the Rhodian Shore*, 203–205. Curtius traces the metaphor of the book of nature back to
the Latin Middle Ages. Glacken finds the metaphor already well developed in the works of
John Chrysostom (345?–407).
    In the context of American Puritanism, Perry Miller contrasts Emerson's "mystic" and
"pantheistic" nature with the empty forms of Unitarianism. According to Miller's "From Ed-
wards to Emerson," transcendentalism was a reaction against the religion of reason that cul-
minated in Unitarianism. This essay, which first appeared in the *New England Quarterly*,
XIII (1940), 589–617, is in *Errand into the Wilderness*, 184–203. The onto-theological grounds
for metaphors linking language and nature are exposed in Derrida's *Of Grammatology*.

motions of the planets, which Nature seemed for ever to have held from us; genius and science have soared beyond the limits of space; some observations, developed by reason, have detected the mechanism of the world. Would it not be some renown for a man, in like manner, to penetrate beyond the limits of time, and to discover, by research and reflection, the history of the world, and of a succession of events which preceded the birth of the human race?" By reading geological strata, one discovers man's traces before his very existence. In consideration of the absence of human fossil remains in times of geological revolutions, Cuvier concludes that the establishment of human society must postdate the last revolution; consequently, "we clearly see that the last revolution and the establishment of present society, cannot be very ancient."[7] Although he does not say so explicitly, Cuvier places the origin of society after the Flood.

With the end of revolutionary eras, geologically speaking, geology "unites, in an unbroken chain, natural and civil history." Not only does civil history begin after an age of cataclysms, but it appears that natural history comes into existence with the creation of man. In Cuvier's theory, however, which was soon to be refuted by Charles Lyell, the geological events that shape the earth predate human history. Unlike the study of past political revolutions, which the historian can explain by looking at current intrigues motivated by human passions, the natural historian has no present before him by which he can account for the formation of the earth: "The thread of operations is broken; the march of nature is changed; and not one of her agents now at work would have sufficed to have affected her ancient works."[8] The appearance of man and civil history coincides not with the birth of natural history but with its end. Natural history proper entailed a series of epochs in which sudden catastrophic revolutions drastically altered the features of the earth. While there presently exist forces that continue to alter the earth's surface, they are merely residual powers and are far less significant in scope than what is properly the geologist's domain of study—the era preceding man. For Cuvier and, as I shall show, for Emerson, the beginning of human history means the end of nature.

Reconstructing events preceding written history was not thought of as a process standing outside a system of representation. In fact, natural his-

7. Cuvier, *A Discourse on the Revolutions of the Surface of the Globe*, 1, 2–3, 86.
8. *Ibid.*, 144, 28.

tory is synonymous with system: the methodical classification of objects of natural history "is what is usually termed a system of nature; or, a grand catalogue of nature's works, in which all things may have suitable names, may be recognized by distinctive characters, and be methodically distributed into divisions and subdivisions, from the appellations and characters of which the object classified under each may be immediately sought for and discovered." System, or philosophy, would be synonymous with classification. The aim of Romantic philosophy is to construct a system of representation that would name everything—philosophy would be a dictionary. Cuvier says precisely this about his method, but his dictionary would be the inverse of a normal one: "This scale of divisions, of which the superior contain the inferior, is what is called system or method. It is, in some respects, a sort of dictionary, wherein, from the properties of things, we proceed to discover their names, thus forming the inverse of ordinary dictionaries, wherein the names direct us to the properties." Natural history promises not only to reconstruct the history of the world but also to reverse the effects of the Fall and restore the unity of words and things: "Such a system will prove the surest means of generalizing the properties of such objects, of expressing them in the fewest, most comprehensive, and most significant terms, and of impressing them most successfully upon the memory."[9]

The measure of success for a taxonomic system will be the ease with which the terms will be remembered. As befits an Adamic myth of proper naming, the reader will presumably know the word is correct when he hears it. The art of Adamic naming can only be compatible with an approach to geology that equates this science with archaeology. If the world, as Emerson says and Cuvier implies, is a museum, then the geologist would be able to reconstruct its history by examining fragmentary ruins and refashioning them into a coherent whole. According to Eugenio Donato's succinct analysis of Cuvier's project, "The function of the geologist is to reconstruct a continuous temporal history out of the fragments handed down to him. His task, like that of the archeologist, is twofold: to reconstruct the entities to which the fragments belonged and then to arrange those same entities in a series so as to discover the history of the globe—a history which, inciden-

9. Cuvier, The Animal Kingdom, I, 7, 8, 9.

tally, is of necessity as anthropocentric as that proposed by archeology."[10] While the proper object of geological history is the earth before man ex‑ isted, the reconstruction of prehuman history proves possible only within an irreducibly human conception of existence. Cuvier's prehistoric earth is but the shadow prefiguring man; the shadow, however, is cast by man. If the names which the anatomist chooses for his subjects turn out to be "proper," it is only because they are the belated repetition of a history that first summoned the comparative anatomist and the geologist into the past.

The inherent paradox that underlies all nineteenth-century reconstruc‑ tions of history, human and prehuman, concerns a conception of history as that which is all-encompassing, or encyclopedic, and, at the same time, as that which deals with fragments from a distant age. In the Hegelian sys‑ tem, a study of all past history is subordinated to a present which contains within it all of the past. Hegel's introduction to *The Philosophy of History* concludes, "Thus, in dealing with the idea of Spirit only and in considering the whole of world history as nothing but its manifestation, we are dealing only with the *present*—however long the past may be which we survey." History would thus be an eternal repetition of the presence of Spirit in the world. Yet as Alexandre Kojève has shown in his analysis of the *Phenom‑ enology of Mind*, the story of the unfolding of Spirit can only be written from the point of view of someone who stands outside the story in which he is the main character. A universal history can only be written at the end of history. This helps explain the predominance of metaphors of burial and entombment whenever Hegel discusses the concept of *Erinnerung*.[11]

In *Henry von Ofterdingen*, Novalis also associates history with death and monuments. In this *Künstlerroman*, the poet meets a miner who tells how his desire to seek out the origin of nature led him into the depths of the earth. Desiring to know what gold and silver lay hidden in the mountains, "he had often contemplated these sparkling solids on the icons and relics of the near-by monastery church and had wished that they could talk to him and tell him about their mysterious origins." Nature, here repre‑ sented by the gold and silver ornamenting religious relics, is a monumental

10. Donato, "The Museum's Furnace," 228.
11. Hegel, *Reason in History: A General Introduction to the Philosophy of History*, 95; Kojève, *Introduction to the Reading of Hegel*. For an analysis of Hegel's theory of the sign and its relation to metaphors of entombment, see Derrida, *Margins of Philosophy*, 69–108.

sign of the end of civil and church history. The desire to seek out the secrets of nature has its origins in the relics of civilization. Origins and man prove to be inimical, as the miner/archaeologist can only write history after the death of man. Later in the same chapter, a hermit tells Henry and the miner, "The church is the dwelling place of history and the quiet court is its symbolic flower garden. Only aged and God-fearing people should write about history, people whose own history is ended and who have nothing more to hope for than being transplanted into the garden."[12] History, then, must be written from the grave, here represented by the garden, a reminder of Eden and the Fall of Man. And as the earlier passage suggests, the church is the monument marking the death of historical man.

In Hegel's *Phenomenology*, the death of Christ marks the end of history. His death means the death of the Abstract God. When the individual self-consciousness grasps the death of Christ, his individual existence is sublated (*aufgehoben*) and "this particular self-existence has become universal self-consciousness." Following Christ's death there is the unending repetition of the unfolding of individual self-existence and its sublation into universal self-consciousness. Toward the conclusion of the *Phenomenology*, Hegel writes that with the death of Christ, "death then ceases to signify what it means directly—the non-existence of *this* individual—and becomes transfigured into the universality of the spirit, which lives in its own communion, dies there daily, and daily rises again."[13] Spirit enters the world with the death of Christ, and with the entrance of Spirit, Absolute Being is attained and thus history ends. But as this end can only be recognized after reading Hegel's *Phenomenology*, the end of history may just as well be the writing of the *Phenomenology*.

Of course, the positing of an event that marks the end of history is problematical, if not hopeless. The "event" that ends history can be nothing but a reconstitution of an "event" within philosophical discourse. This "event," therefore, must be linguistic in nature; that is, it exists only as an event in language or as a moment in a text where the belatedness of the author is allegorized as an external occurrence in which a hierarchy is formed and then inverted. The antithetical relation between man and nature in Hegel's philosophy exists not, as he claims, because the presence of man raises natural history onto the plane of human and divine history, but be-

12. Novalis, *Henry von Ofterdingen*, 64, 84.
13. Hegel, *The Phenomenology of Mind*, 781, 780.

cause man and nature inhabit two systems of representation that lack a common language or, as we might say in light of Cuvier, a single dictionary. The encoding of nature within ontological categories, whereby a hierarchy ensures the privileged place of man in the natural world, merely confirms the privileged place of an anthropocentric system as opposed to, and this is the unthinkable, a natural system of representation.

We have seen in Cuvier how the reconstruction of fossil remains in turn becomes a history of man before man ever appeared. The medium for this hierarchical system of classification ("hierarchy" is precisely what Cuvier means by the word *method*) is memory. Memory, like fossil remains, is characterized by a system of self-identification—the resemblance of one idea to another allows the reconstruction of a system called mind or intelligence. As Cuvier's method of classification depended upon type, he could maintain the uniqueness of each species; at the same time, he could reconstruct extinct species on the basis of a fossil's resemblance to a living animal. Thus, he could have a synchronic hierarchical order that requires distinct demarcations between species, and simultaneously maintain a diachronic order on the basis of resemblance. Consequently, his system could account for the coexistence of identity and difference without allowing the resemblance between fossil remains and living species to disrupt the hierarchical order he thought was "natural."

There should be little wonder at Cuvier's having followed a Lockean theory of the association of ideas, for the common parentage which forms the basis of his definition of species also defines the association of ideas: "Ideas between which some similarity exists, or which have been acquired at the same period of time, have a tendency to recal [sic] each other to the mind. This tendency is termed the *association of ideas*, and in its order, extent, and quickness does the perfection of memory consist." Shared origin provides a filial link between ideas. The resemblance between ideas proves they are cognates. But what can this resemblance be but a union formed by a remembered origin? Acquisition and resemblance, however, are by no means proof of natural connection. Memory transforms simultaneity into a principle of contiguity. The more complete and systematic the arrangement of resemblances, the more advanced the intellect; hence, classification defines intelligence: "The understanding possesses the power of separating these accessory ideas from the objects of thought, and of uniting together, under a *general idea*, such qualities as are found to be alike in a diversity of objects. The power of framing this general idea, to which no corresponding type is to be found in actual existence, is usually dominated *abstraction.*" Cuvier's taxonomic system would be the perfect example of his model of intelligence. In addition, the analogy between mind and taxonomy extends to fossil remains and to writing. As taxonomy is a system constructed out of external evidence arranged into a "natural" order, the faculty of association of ideas transforms natural symbols and speech into an unnatural order—that is, the mediate and human order of writing: "Writing is a series of the latter sort of symbols [hieroglyphics], by which we represent the elementary sounds, and, by their combination, all those other symbols which relate to the sense of hearing, and of which speech [*parole*] is composed. Writing, therefore, is not a direct but a *mediate* representation of ideas."[14] Classification, whether it be of ideas or fossils, is a linguistic system best characterized by writing. Although in Cuvier's text the terms *langue* and *parole* do not have the meaning that they have attained since Saussure's work, the conjunction between his taxonomic system, theory of memory, and concept of language confirms the textual character of his, and any, archaeological project.

Classification, Emerson says repeatedly, is science and philosophy. Yet this avid reader of Cuvier, Laplace, Humboldt, even Sadi Carnot, denies, despite his affirmations to the contrary, that there could be an all-encompassing system of universal history. Emerson, into whose works so many of the great themes of English and Continental Romanticism find their way, may be considered the true encyclopedist of the nineteenth century. (In fact, he entitles one of his journals, which he used as a copybook, Encyclopedia.) Although he never read as much or as widely as Coleridge, Emerson could move from the Bhagavad-Gita to Cuvier and find all was a confirmation of his theory. Yet his theory could change from work to work, even from sentence to sentence. American transcendentalism can almost be considered a compendium of readings in philosophy, literature, and the natural sciences. The encyclopedia provides an appropriate image of Emerson's works—his essays consist of gleanings from his favorite, and not so favorite, readings. Quotation is his preferred mode of composition—he learned his Novalis, Schelling, Kant, and Hegel largely through the works

14. Cuvier, *The Animal Kingdom,* I, 53, 54.

of Carlyle, Coleridge, Henry Hedge, and J. C. Hare. Although he owned a set of Novalis' *Werke*, almost any quotation from Novalis found in his journals can be traced back to Carlyle's essays. If he is not quoting Carlyle quoting Novalis, or Coleridge quoting Schelling and Kant, he is quoting himself. When the reader turns to Emerson's works he finds them to be a patchwork of journal entries, lectures, and his previously published essays. When Emerson reemploys "every book is a quotation" as an epigraph to "Quotation and Originality," he is merely quoting himself from "Plato" in *Representative Men*. In "Experience" Emerson confesses, "I am a fragment, and this is a fragment of me. I can very confidently announce one or another law, which throws itself into relief and form, but I am too young yet by some ages to compile a code" (W.III.83). A linking together of fragments, a perpetual failure to achieve a final "code" or system—this is Emerson's corpus. Yet I do not say this in criticism of him, for he makes explicit what is ultimately the fate of any writer caught in the prison house of language.

For every statement in which Emerson calls upon his readers to "build therefore your own world," there can be found the skeptic's lament, "Once man was all; now he is an appendage, a nuisance" (W.I.76,127). Which is the real Emerson? The skeptic or the transcendentalist? But this question misconstrues the problem. The question should properly read, Is there a true Emerson? If we follow out Emerson's philosophy of reading, we can only conclude that Emerson is as real as the text he is quoting. Tradition threatens to turn his texts into an empty repetition. Descent, for Emerson, implies at once the failure of imitation and the promise of sublation. Yet neither promise nor failure comes into being, for quotation can never merely repeat the pre-text or move beyond it.

I refer, of course, to Harold Bloom's theory of influence. Yet the genealogical metaphor underlying his theory must be distinguished from the hereditary analogy adopted by literary historians who implicitly assume there is a natural connection between texts. In Bloom's family, the father, who is discontinuous with his offspring, breaks the familial bond that goes unquestioned by most literary historians. Opposed to the filiative bonds of genealogy is *affiliation*. Edward Said makes this significant distinction in his essay "On Repetition": "*Affiliation* is a joining together of people in a non-genealogical, non-procreative but *social* unity." In an analysis of Marx's *Eighteenth Brumaire of Louis Napoleon*, Said points out that the

affiliative method of linguistic analysis "portends a methodological revolution whereby, as in the natural and human sciences, the facts of nature
are dissolved then reassembled polemically, as during the nineteenth century in either the museum, the laboratory, the classroom, or the library,
facts are dissolved then assembled into units of didactic sense, perhaps more
to illustrate human power to transform than to confirm nature."[15] Said's
supplementing of filiation with affiliation repeats the methodological
blindness that we have found in Cuvier. The disruptive feature of affiliation makes it an appealing corrective to the theological term *filiation*, but
affiliation, as an atemporal order, serves the same function as the taxonomic system of genus and types instituted by Cuvier. Although Said is a
critic preeminently aware of the self-justifying, and self-deluding, practice
of masking human actions as nature and truth, his analysis rests too
comfortably on the possibility that a system, whether it be natural or social, can escape the disruptive and discontinuous properties inherent in all
discourse.

If we return once again to Emerson, we can see how his concept of quotation disrupts the genealogical descent of tradition and reinscribes it as a
textual product existing only within a nonlinear, nonhierarchical process
of writing. Descent is commonly thought of as a nonproblematic system of
identity and difference. The confusion begins with the biological analogy
of generation, or as Kierkegaard warns: "What often deludes people and
helps to start all sorts of fantastic notions going is the fact of generation, as
if the subsequent man were essentially different from the first because he
is a descendant."[16] If Emerson's collection of quotations were merely a descendant of previous texts, his works would be, in Kierkegaard's term, "an
empty repetition," just as they would be if they stood outside of history.
Historians, as Said reminds us, must avoid biological and genealogical
analogies. However, until the advent of thermodynamics, the nineteenth
century's search for a universal theory was predicated upon certain theological concepts transplanted into the language of the natural sciences. (It
should be pointed out that the second law of thermodynamics lends itself
to a reinstatement of quantitative descent. I will return to this topic in my
discussion of Henry Adams.)

15. Said, "On Repetition," 146, 158.
16. Kierkegaard, *The Concept of Dread*, 31.

The onto-theological grounds of science were not missed by Emerson: "The progress of physics & metaphysics is parellel[;] at first it is lowest instinctive life loathsome to the succeeding tribes like the generation of sour paste. . . . As the races advance & rise order & rank appear, & the aurora of reason & of love" (*JMN*.IX.124). If physics and metaphysics are parallel, it is because they both demand a belief in progress. Yet the infinite progression of man is hardly the sole pattern of metaphysics; infinite decomposition is equally metaphysical or, better still, theological. The Fall, after all, holds a preeminent place in Western thought. A belief that a linear movement through time means a qualitative change in descendants can only be held if the concept of a simple origin remains undisturbed. Although Emerson never explicitly called into question the metaphysics of origin, he had few illusions about the metaphysical character of history, as this journal entry indicates:

> There are always two histories of man in literature contending for our faith. One is the scientific or skeptical, & derives his origin from the gradual composition, subsidence, & refining, from the negro, from the ape, progressive from the animalcule savages of the waterdrop, from volvox globator, up to the wise man of the nineteenth century. The other is the believer's, the poet's, the faithful history, always testified by the mystic & the devout, the history of the Fall, of a descent from a superior & pure race, attested in actual history by the grand remains of elder ages, of a science in the east unintelligible to the existing population. (*JMN*.IX.241–42)

As Emerson says in "Circles," the New World is built upon the decomposition of the Old. In the passage above, the scientist who looks to man as the supersession of inferior races bases his conclusions on comparative anatomy and fossil remains. The devout, on the other hand, look at grand ruins to confirm that man has fallen. History, physical and metaphysical, is a branch of archaeology.

In one of his earliest journals, "Wide World," Emerson discusses the ancient materials of history. He concludes that the only permanent remainders are graves. Graves, therefore, are not just the repositories of human remains; they are the first records of civilization: "A nation which exists when the means are few of transmitting their memory, is remembered, not by any partial or local institutions, which their neighbors can neither copy nor understand; but derive their best chance for immortality from their modes of embodying the principles which all feel—from their obedience to the common necessities of human nature. Thus, the burial of the dead is a custom so natural and necessary, that we have easily traced its forms in every different nation" (JMN.I.67). Civil institutions are unique to particular cultures and, thus, untranslatable; therefore, they are inadequate transmitters of a nation's memory. Graves, on the other hand, which provide evidence of a belief in immortality, pass on the memory of a nation's existence, even though the individual is forgotten. As historical artifacts, graves are reminders of universal principles and individual mortality. The idea of immortality suggests that "the only bond of connection which can transverse the long duration which separates the ends of the world and unite the first people to the knowledge and sympathy of the last people, is religion" (JMN.I.62). But the medium, the writing, that ensures the continuity between the first man and the last is the tomb. Curiously enough, Emerson's tombs do not hold a promise for the immortality of the deceased; instead, they are monuments that ensure the preservation of the nameless dead. Like Hegel's signs, these tombs have only universal, never particular, meaning.

If it should be thought that calling tombs writing is a catachresis, then it is a familiar one to the nineteenth century. All remains serve as written texts in history; however, the tomb is particularly appropriate. As Carlyle remarks, "History has been written with quipo-threads, with feather-pictures, with wampum-belts; still oftener with earth-mounds and monumental stone-heaps, whether as pyramid or cairn."[17] The preservation of corpses is connate with culture, religion, and writing. That which marks the beginning and end produces religion and history. The connection is hardly unusual, for the association between writing and death appears repeatedly in Romantic literature and philosophy, so that which codifies death also inscribes within a single conceptual framework the two systems that exist for the purpose of overcoming death—religion and history. Tombs are evidence of a belief in immortality; they are also the first signs of civilization and thus one of the primary texts for the historian.

In the first of his essays on epitaphs, Wordsworth argues that a sense of immortality is implanted in man at birth. All children, says Wordsworth, wonder about "whence" and "whither." He therefore concludes, "Origins and tendency are notions inseparably co-relative." The epitaph is the sign

17. Carlyle, "On History," 60.

of the coeval birth of this inherent concern for beginnings and endings among all people. The first writing, says Wordsworth, was epitaphs: "As soon as Nations had learned the use of letters, Epitaphs were inscribed upon these monuments." Writing first functioned to preserve the memory of the dead. As Wordsworth insists that language should be "the incarnation of thought," we should expect the epitaph to promise the incarnation of the dead, yet he explicitly requires an epitaph to be a record *"in close connection with the bodily remains of the deceased."* The strange emphasis upon bodily remains draws together writing and death in a rather bizarre physical union. In commenting on another passage in this series of essays, Frances Ferguson remarks, "To insist upon language as incarnation in essays devoted to epitaphs is a strange track, because the incarnation of language comes into direct opposition with the factual deaths, the de-incarnation of the actual human beings who are memorialized in the epitaphs."[18] Writing in Wordsworth's works is indissolubly linked with death; if language reincarnates thought, then writing buries it.

A similar pattern of associations emerges in Emerson's journal of 1822, written when he was only nineteen. Unlike Wordsworth, Emerson directly associates writing with religious institutions, and his ambivalence toward writing is far more pronounced than Wordsworth's. In a passage referring to his discussion of tombs and religion, Emerson associates writing with political oppression in a manner that looks back to Rousseau and forward to Levi-Strauss:[19]

> We have said that the first nations were remembered religion;—and in tracing down their history a little farther until the time of written languages we find that the first efforts which the human genius made to commit its ideas to permanent signs were exercised upon the great topic which stood uppermost in an unperverted mind. Poetry attempted to fashion a probable picture of the Creation, to explore the character of Providence, to impress upon mankind the enlightened views of a moral government in the world which had been disclosed to her own eye. History alarmed the mind by reciting the vengeance which waited and fell on impiety; and the dark imaginations which conceived the destruction of the Giants, the fire and vulture of Prometheus, the abode of the Furies and of the dead, suffi-

---

18. Wordsworth, "Essay on Epitaphs," in Zall (ed.), *Literary Criticism of William Wordsworth*, 93, 92, 125, 96; Ferguson, *Wordsworth*, 31.

19. I refer to Derrida's analysis of Levi-Strauss's and Rousseau's defenses against the threat of writing. See *Of Grammatology*, 101–140.

ciently attest the nature of the principles which excited their hearts and
founded their traditions. Philosophy set out from rude speculations upon
the Being of God and borrowed from another age or gathered from its own
observation the notion of Destiny. But the date of *writing* marks the second age in the history of Religion and we have parted from the second
more attractive memory of the first. (*JMN*.I.71–72)

Inaugurating what Emerson calls "the second dispensation," writing, in the
colloquial sense, replaces tombs and graves as the record of the remains of
earlier ages. And like tombs, writing deals strictly with the past: Poetry
sought to create a cosmogony; history recorded tales of punishment dealt
out to earlier inhabitants of the earth; and philosophy either borrowed an
ontology from earlier times or fashioned destiny out of present observations. The first writing is not at all original, as it is inscribed upon the traces
of tradition.

Tombs—the traces of death, civilization, and religion—preempt writing's claims as the first encoder of culture. The "first" writing, Emerson
indicates, is always secondary, always belated. It repeats the myths of earlier ages. When Emerson says that writing marks a second age of religion,
he also suggests it marks a second (or is it a third?) Fall. Writing does not
merely separate man from a pure or natural religion; it separates him from
the "more attractive memory of the first." The first religion was always a
memory—we are not cut off from an unfallen religion; we are cut off from
the memory of such a thing.

Writing itself becomes for Emerson the sign of man's belated entry into
this world, and the American writer comes into the world when nothing
remains to be written. Perhaps the American poet can be defined as he who
is belated. The problem, as I have said, is certainly one of tradition and
originality, but it cannot be confined to a dialectic of past and present in
which old forms are revitalized and renewed.

Composition and decomposition are as much a feature of geology and
history as they are of writing. Emerson's interest in the natural sciences
and history extended from his first lectures to his last. In fact, one of the
first lectures he ever read was called "The Uses of Natural History," and
one of his last lecture series was titled *The Natural History of Intellect*. As
the titles indicate, Emerson held that the mind was part of nature and, at
the same time, above it. Just as the geologists and astronomers have revealed the natural history of the earth and the stars, so Emerson recounts

the "natural history"—or progress—of the intellect. Nevertheless, he offers to write not an essay on human evolution, but rather a history of mind, which can be read in the history of nature: "No matter how far or how high science explores, it adopts the method of the universe as fast as it appears; and this discloses that the mind as it opens, the mind as it shall be, comprehends and works thus; that is to say, the Intellect builds the universe and is the key to all it contains" (W.XII.4–5). To study nature is to unfold the processes of intellect, for "every object in Nature is a word to signify some fact in the mind" (W.XII.5). The objects of nature have their origin in the mind of man, or so Emerson will claim at various times. Later in the same essay he says, "This slight discontinuity which perception effects between the mind and the object paralyzes the will" (W.XII.44). Emerson's use of the word *perception* here is indistinguishable from the concept of mediation. What concerns Emerson is the *medium* of perception; we can never see the thing-in-itself because the medium of the senses intervenes between self and object. Perception forever divides mind from nature. It is the effect of the Fall, the recognition that man exists. Emerson compares the effects of this discontinuity to cutting a block in two and trying to join it back together: "You can indeed bring the particles very near, but never so near again that they shall attract each other so that you can take up the block as one. That indescribably small interval is as good as a thousand miles, and has forever severed the practical unity. Such is the immense deduction from power by discontinuity" (W.XII.44).

Man is forever divided from nature. Perception, the means by which man comes to understand nature, severs him from the world: "The intellect that sees the interval partakes of it, and the fact of intellectual perception severs once for all the man from the things with which he converses. Affection blends, intellect disjoins subject and object" (W.XII.44). Man dwells in the in-between; he belongs neither to the self nor to nature. We cannot hope that the affections can heal the wounds of the intellect, for they come too late—the discovery that we exist precludes any redemption by mere affection. The Fall has thrown man into the division between subject and object. This is Emerson writing a history of the Fall; what remains is a history of science or progress.

Living in between as he does, Emerson will write a history of progress that will bend back the linear history of the Fall and return man to Eden: "All inquiry into antiquity[,] all curiosities respecting the pyramids, the

excavated cities, Stone-Henge, Rome, Babylon, is simply & at last the desire to do away this wild, savage, preposterous *Then*, & introduce in its place
the *Now*: it is to banish the *Not Me* & supply the *Me*; it is to abolish *difference* & restore *Unity*" (*JMN*.VII.111). Emerson hopes to humanize nature by finding evidence of man's presence in all of history. The restoration
of man will be through archaeological excavation—man will dig down into
the earth in order to uncover the past. This metaphor appears in the continuation of the above passage:

> Belzoni digs & scratches & climbs & gropes, until he can see to the end of
> the difference between the monstrous work, & himself. When he has satis-
> fied himself in general & in detail that it was made by such a person as
> himself . . . the problem is then solved; his *Me* lives along the whole lines
> of the temples, sphinxes, & catacombs; passes through them like a creature
> soul with satisfaction, & they live again to the mind, or are *Now*. And this
> is also the aim in all science, in the unprofitable abysses of entomology, in
> the gigantic masses of geology, & spaces of astronomy,—simply to trans-
> port our consciousness of cause & effect into those remote by us uninhab-
> ited members, & see that they all proceed from "causes now in operation"
> from one mind, and that Ours. (*JMN*.VII.111)

History is made possible by *différance*. The present is always other than
itself—it is made intelligible by the lag between cause and effect; thus,
the present is constituted by its difference and distance from the cause that
produces it. Therefore, one cannot think of the Now as a past made present; it is, as Hegel's analysis of the *Hic* and the *Nunc* in the *Phenomenology* reveals, a product of language. Hegel asks, "What is the Now?" and
answers that "the Now is night-time." He continues, "To test the truth of
this certainty of sense, a simple experiment is all we need: write that truth
down. A truth cannot lose anything by being written down, and just as little by our preserving and keeping it. If we look again at the truth we have
written down, look at it *now, at this noon-time*, we shall have to say it has
turned stale and become out of date." Writing treats the Now as something
that *is*, but the Now maintained in writing "proves to be rather a something which is *not*." The Now maintains itself as the not-night, as day, and,
at the same time, it is also the not-day, "altogether something negative."
Hegel comments, "This self-maintaining Now is therefore not something
immediate but something mediated; for, *qua* something that remains and
preserves itself, it is determined through and *by means* of the fact that
something else, namely day and night, is *not*." The self-maintaining Now

exists only in language. The Now only maintains itself by the existence of its negation; therefore, the Now can never be a particular Now, but must be universal, for a universal alone is neither this nor that and is either this or that. And whenever we say "This," it is always the universal "This." Hegel makes it clear that language is the vehicle of mediation: the Here and the Now are never before our mind, "but we *utter* what is universal; in other words, we do not actually and absolutely say what in this sense-certainty we really *mean*. Language . . . is the more truthful; in it we ourselves refute directly and at once our own 'meaning'; and since universality is the real truth of sense-certainty, and language merely expresses *this* truth, it is not possible at all for us even to express in words any sensuous existence which we 'mean.' "[20] Sense-certainty promises contact with nature, but instead we are left with words, which are universal and never concrete. In Hegel's dialectic we are threatened with a universal regress in which sign refers to sign *ad infinitum*. At the moment that we appear to be lost in the continual falsity of the Here and the Now, we find that language, in the sense of *langue*, as opposed to *parole*, tells the truth every moment we are speaking lies. Language expresses the impossibility of sense-certainty. The *Aufhebung* has come to the rescue and has lifted man from the realm of the particular to that of the universal.

Emerson's meditation on history suggests an inversion of Hegel. Whereas writing in Hegel maintains self-certainty as its negation and leads to the recognition that sense-certainty deals only with the universal, writing in Emerson appears as an unproblematic record of past events. The ruins discovered by the archaeologist maintain their particularity while they also indicate the presence of the universal. Oddly enough, archaeology is not so much a recovery of lost time as it is a thrusting of man back to the remote ages he has uncovered. This historical/archaeological task shares its methodological principles with philology and the natural sciences. In the journal entry quoted above (*JMN.* VII.111), Emerson alludes to the subtitle of

---

20. *Différance* is a neologism introduced by Derrida that combines the two meanings of the verb *différer*, to defer and to differ. The word indicates that the process of signification presupposes that the sign represents the absent thing for which it stands—the sign differs from the thing and defers or postpones the moment we can come into contact with the thing itself. The thing, or present element, is never present to itself (which would require that it be free from language); it is always related to something other than itself and is constituted by its relation to this other. See Derrida, *Margins of Philosophy*, 3–27. Hegel, *The Phenomenology of Mind*, 151–52.

Lyell's *Principles of Geology: Being an Inquiry How Far the Former Changes of the Earth's Surface are Referable to Causes Now in Operation* (first published in 1830 in England, it appeared in America in 1837).

Lyell, who shared with Cuvier an anthropocentric view of science, begins his book with an extended analogy between geology and history. Lyell admits that geology will not "obtain a full and connected account of any series of events beyond the reach of history, but the testimony of geological monuments, if frequently imperfect, possesses at least the advantage of being free from all suspicion of misinterpretation. We may be deceived in the inferences we draw . . . but our liability to err is confined to the interpretation, and, if this be correct, our information is certain." Lyell's great work refuted Cuvier's theory of geological cataclysms and anticipated Darwin's theory of evolution. For our purposes, it is important to note how Emerson appropriated the methodology and extended it to cultural studies, a borrowing sanctioned by Lyell's opening analogy. Emerson adopts the principle that past monuments, cultural and natural, have the same causes as do present events and artifacts. Although this contradicts Cuvier's thesis, Lyell himself finds in Cuvier's adoption of the same generic name for both fossils and living species a preparation for his own method: "It was an acknowledgment [by Cuvier], as it were, that part at least of the ancient memorials of nature were written in a living language."[21] Nature is, for Lyell, as it was for Emerson, a textual artifact waiting to be deciphered. Cuvier's theory, to use Emerson's words, situates the past in a "wild, savage, preposterous *Then*"; Lyell transformed it into "the *Now*." The earth, we might say, maintains itself as the Here and the Now in writing—that is, in the monuments and "living language of Nature."

If nature is ever present, that is because it has been preserved in a museum: "The earth is a museum, and the five senses a philosophical apparatus of such perfection, that the pleasure we obtain from the aids with which we arm them, is trifling, compared with their natural information" (*EL*.I.6). It is likely that Emerson's visit to the Jardin des Plantes suggested this metaphor. The manuscripts for the lectures are dated November 4, 1833, and Edward Waldo Emerson conjectures that they were begun while Emerson was waiting for a boat in Liverpool at the end of his first visit to Europe.

21. Lyell, *Principles of Geology*, I, 19, 79.

Rusk has called Emerson's visit to the Jardin des Plantes "one of the memorable experiences of his life. His mind seemed to leap forward with a new vision."[22] In his journals, Emerson described his walk through the cabinet of natural history as a revelation: "The Universe is a more amazing puzzle than ever as you glance along this bewildering series of animated forms . . . & the upheaving principle of life everywhere incipient in the very rock aping organized forms. Not a form so grotesque, so savage, nor so beautiful but is an expression of some property inherent in man the observer,—an occult relation between the very scorpions and man. I feel the centipede in me—cayman, carp, eagle, & fox. I am moved by strange sympathies, I say continually 'I will be a naturalist'" (*JMN*.IV.199–200).

The journal passage, which reappears in "The Uses of Natural History," hints at the highly contrived design of the cabinet. When Emerson writes of the "occult relation" between man and nature, he reveals the persistence of the old concept of the chain of being, wherein a single plan controls all organisms. Here he reflects the thought of Geoffroy Saint-Hilaire rather than that of Cuvier, who broke the chain of being by introducing four divisions (Vertebrata, Articulata, Mollusca, Radiata) into the classification of species, thereby dividing the natural world into "little isolated islands supported by impassable channels."[23]

A walk through the Jardin, however, allowed the visitor to see the chain of evolution stretched out before him. The artifice of this natural display is unmistakable in Emerson's description of it for his audience: "There is the richest collection in the natural curiosities arranged for the most imposing effect." The overwhelming rhetorical force of this arrangement has been ensured by ransacking nature "to furnish whatever was rich and rare" (*EL*.I.7). The museum's emphasis on the unusual makes the garden sound more like a collection of exotica than a natural display of animal and plant life. If the arrangement accords more with rhetoric than with science, it may be because the garden, in Emerson's description of it, is a grammar and a dictionary: "Moving along these pleasant walks, you come to the botanical cabinet, *an inclosed grammar plot, where grows a grammar of botany*— where the plants rise, each in its class, its order, and its genus. . . . If you have read Decandolle [Augustin Pyrame de Candolle], with engravings, or

22. Rusk, *The Life of Ralph Waldo Emerson*, 187.
23. Jacob, *The Logic of Life*, 108–109. See also Orr, *Jules Michelet*, 20n.

with a *hortus siccus,* conceive how much more exciting and intelligible is *this natural alphabet, this green and yellow and crimson dictionary,* on which the sun shines, and the winds blow" (*EL.*I.8; my emphasis).

The Jardin des Plantes is a primer—a handbook introducing the reader to the syntax and lexicon of nature. This same image figures prominently in Flaubert's *Bouvard and Pécuchet.* In a reading of Flaubert's last work, Eugenio Donato points out the significance of the museum and its linguistic arrangement: "The Museum of Natural History was, strictly speaking, the first French museum. Its function was to give an ordered representation, a spectacle of Nature. By displaying plants, metonymically selected and metonymically ordered, it meant to produce a *tableau* of Nature."[24] *Bouvard and Pécuchet,* in Donato's analysis, traces the displacement of the teleological metaphors of nature as museum by the nihilistic metaphors of thermodynamics. In his chronicle of two copyists' efforts to master nature, Flaubert exposes the gulf between the system of language and the system of nature.

Although I have quoted Emerson to similar purposes, he could never quite reconcile his skepticism with his faith in universal law. "And this," says Emerson, "because the whole of nature is a metaphor or image of the human mind": "The very existence of thought and speech supposes and is a new nature totally distinct from the material world; yet we find it impossible to speak of it and its laws in any other language than that borrowed from our experience in the material world" (*EL.*I.24). Beginning with F. O. Matthiessen's *American Renaissance* (1941), passages such as this have traditionally been read as evidence supporting Emerson's Coleridgean theory of the symbolic character of language and his faith that nature is commensurate with mind. More recently, R. A. Yoder has argued that "at the summit of Emerson's natural history is man joining poetry and science, for poetry re-creates nature in a conscious act of mind." Joel Porte has gone so far as to claim that Emerson was among the first to understand that "all our symbols are *natural,* and all nature is symbolic, because the very act of making verb and noun, by means of which we take possession of the

24. Donato, "The Museum's Furnace, " 229–30. This article presents an important critique of Foucault's taxonomic archaeology of knowledge. For a rhetorical, rather than taxonomic, analysis of the museum, see, in addition to this article, Donato, " 'A Mere Labyrinth of Letters,' " 885–910. See also Schwab, *La Renaissance oriental,* 410ff.

world, is constitutive of reality for us."[25] According to this symbolic theory, language constitutes nature, thereby bridging subject and object. But the discontinuity between mind and nature is absolute. Like Heidegger before an abyss, Emerson throws a bridge across the gulf separating man and nature. Nature, claims Emerson, is a metaphor of the mind; at the same time, he says we can only speak of the mind in a language "borrowed from our experience in the material world." Even the language that we speak partakes of this discontinuity; in fact, language is discontinuity. The discovery that mind precedes nature is a belated recognition that language situates itself between a mute nature, which is ontologically prior to mind, and intellect, which is an a posteriori epistemological construct. Language does not link mind and nature, for nature has its own visual grammar, and intellect must borrow a language. No wonder Emerson says that after the Fall we suspect our instruments of mediation. In a symbolic scheme of language, metaphor should bridge the gap between subject and object, but in Emerson's theory, language creates the abyss wherever it appears. The hieroglyphics of nature have not found their Champollion. The decipherment of nature proceeds by seeking in the past evidence of man's continual presence. The uncovering of man's remains, oddly enough, assures the historian, the archaeologist, and the geologist that nature is subordinate to man. However, this unearthing of cultural artifacts becomes a reminder, for the historian of the Fall at least, that nature has been lost to man. The "existence of thought and speech" suggests that man lives apart from nature, although metaphor supposes that the distinction can be both overcome and maintained, but as the passage on mediation from "Experience" reveals, thought contains its negation—that which supposes the perfectibility of human spirit also supposes the Fall.

In light of Emerson's coupling of thought with speech and the Fall with mediation, we can conclude that Fall and Redemption exist within language. Mediation, or language, makes possible the thinking of difference between man and nature, present and past, Eden and the Fall.

The preeminent role of language helps explain the consistent equation of philology with archaeology and geology in nineteenth-century dis-

25. Yoder, *Emerson and the Orphic Poet in America*, 56; Porte, *Representative Man*, xiv–xv.

course. The Jardin des Plantes, for example, represents a collection of natural exotica that seems to belie the museum's expressed purpose of providing a grammar and lexicon of nature. In a journal entry of 1824, Emerson suggests that the American landscape is a text wherein one can read the history of humanity by traveling from east to west: "History it seems is not, an account of the order of society in any time or land, but an account of the *exceptions* to such order. But travelling is a practical history which answers both these ends, & Talleyrand said that in a new country as N America to travel 1 or 2000 miles is as good as to go, in *time*, one or 2000 years; for, in so doing, you pass from the highest pitch of Civilization, to the verge or the midst of savage life (*JMN*.II.232). The traveler in North America recovers the past as he moves farther and farther west. In this respect, he repeats the archaeologist's discovery of contemporary man among ancient ruins. The primitive state of western America not only provides a living record of early man, it also holds out the promise for America's future. The uncivilized West offers hope that America will escape English influence. In "The Naturalist," Emerson laments, "All American manners, language, and writing are derivative. We do not write from facts, but we wish to state facts after the English manner. . . . It is the tax we pay for the splendid inheritance of the English literature. We are exonerated by the sea and the revolution from the national debt but we pay this which is rather the worst part" (*EL*.I.75). Emerson offers the study of nature as a curative for imitation of English culture. Implicit in this argument is the belief that America failed to make a fresh start and must try to do so once again. Belatedness, however, is not so easily overcome. Just as the archaeologist brings his own expectations concerning man when he digs into the past and makes the Then a Now, the traveler heading west brings the East with him.

Belatedness, as Harold Bloom has argued, is not a peculiarly American phenomenon, though in America it takes a unique form; the poet's belief that he has come too late into the world was shared by most nineteenth-century writers. In the foregoing discussion, I have tried to show how the sense of belatedness is less a psychological condition and more a condition of language. Speech, Emerson suggests, reminds man that a void exists between humanity and nature. A symbolic theory of language would suppose that this abyss can be bridged, but language names the void and does not bridge it. Although the concept of belatedness has most often been treated in terms of poetic influence, it should not be restricted to its appearance in literature. The archaeological metaphors that abound in nineteenth-century science and historiography indicate the pervasiveness of this theme. *Archaeology* functions as a generic term for any effort to strip away layers of mediation, whether they be geological or etymological, in order to unveil a hidden source or a pristine origin. The separation of philosophy, geology, and archaeology into unique disciplines denies their common metaphors linking all sciences in a universal anthropology. Even geology, as is suggested in Cuvier and made explicit in Emerson, is a study of man. Here is Emerson, in "The Relation of Man to the Globe": "By the study of the globe in very recent times we have become acquainted with a fact the most surprising—I may say the most sublime, to wit, that Man who stands in the globe so proud and powerful is no upstart in the creation, but has been prophesied in nature for a thousand ages before he appeared" (*EL*.I.29).

Man is a Narcissus who, in Wallace Stevens' words, "did not expect, when he looked in the stream, to find in his hair a serpent coiled to strike, nor, when he looked in his own eyes there, to be met by a look of hate, nor, in general, to discover himself at the center of an inexplicable ugliness from which he would be bound to avert himself. On the contrary, he sought out his image everywhere because it was the principle of his nature to do so."[26] Nature, Emerson says, is a metaphor of the mind of man; I suggest this be emended to say that nature is a tautological re-presentation of man. Man goes out into the world seeking to recover the lost unity of mind and nature, but he stops by the first stream or pool of water he comes to, satisfied that he has found an image of himself.

The metaphor of the reflecting pools plays an important role in two key passages in Coleridge's prose. For an elucidation of belatedness as it appears in ontological terms, I would like to turn to Coleridge's famous definitions of symbol and allegory in *The Statesman's Manual*:

> Now an Allegory is but a translation of abstract notions into a picture-language which is itself nothing but an abstraction from objects of the senses; the principal being more worthless even than its phantom proxy, both alike unsubstantial, and the former shapeless to boot. On the other hand a Symbol (which is always tautegorical) is characterized by a translucence of the Special in the Individual or of the General in the Especial or of the Universal in the General. Above all by the translucence of the Eternal through

26. Stevens, *The Necessary Angel*, 79.

and in the Temporal. It always partakes of the Reality which it renders intelligible; and while it enunciates the whole, abides itself as a living part in that Unity, of which it is the representative.[27]

In his influential article, "The Rhetoric of Temporality," Paul de Man has already remarked on the common transcendental origin of both symbol and allegory.[28] Allegory, in de Man's analysis, renounces the symbol's nostalgia for the irrecoverable union of sign and referent, and acknowledges that the signifier always comes too late to properly name the signified. I also wish to point out how closely Coleridge's definition of allegory resembles Emerson's comment on the relation between language and nature. Were Emerson simply to maintain that nature is a representation of the mind, then nature would resemble the Coleridgean symbol—it would partake of that which it represents. This uncomplicated movement between the idea and its representation is confounded when Emerson claims that man conceives the intellect in a language derived from nature. With this reversal and displacement of the hierarchy idea/form, language represents neither mind nor nature; instead, it reassembles the bric-a-brac of time and nature in provisional identities. Hence, language must be empty allegories—translations into a picture language of abstractions drawn from nature, which is itself a "phantom proxy" of the mind.

The allegorical sign—which, as de Man suggests, is the only sign there is—exists as a reminder of the natural world's absence. If we turn to the sentence immediately following Coleridge's distinction between symbol and allegory, we find an allegory about allegory: "The other [allegories] are but empty echoes which the fancy arbitrarily associates with apparitions of matter, less beautiful but not less shadowy than the sloping orchard or hillside pasture-field seen in the transparent lake below."[29] Coleridge condemns allegories for giving pale copies of nature, but he does so in an allegory. Although he does not find, as Narcissus did, an image of man reflected in the waters, we might say that the allegorization of allegory is precisely the reflecting in language of the distance between thought and its objectification.

Two years later in his Essays on the Principles of Method, originally intended as an introduction to an encyclopedia, Coleridge repeats this image

27. Coleridge, Lay Sermons, 30.
28. De Man, "The Rhetoric of Temporality," 173–209.
29. Coleridge, Lay Sermons, 30–31.

of the reflecting pool in an allegory describing, of all things, the symbolizing powers of the mind. In the last of eight essays, Coleridge speaks of the man of spirit who seeks

> some ground common to the world and to man, therein to find the one principle of permanence and identity, the rock of strength and refuge, to which the soul may cling amid the fleeting surge-like objects of the senses. Disturbed as by the obscure quickening of an inward birth; made restless by swarming thoughts, that, like bees when they first miss the queen and mother of the hive, with vain discursion seek each in the other what is the common need of all; man sallies forth into nature—in nature, as in the shadows and reflections of a clear river, to discover the originals of the forms presented to him in his own intellect. Over these shadows, as if they were the substantial powers and presiding spirits of the stream, Narcissus-like, he hangs delighted: till finding nowhere a representative of that free agency which yet is a *fact* of immediate consciousness sanctioned and made fearfully significant by his prophetic *conscience*, he learns at last that what he *seeks* he has *left behind*, and but lengthens the distance as he prolongs the search. [30]

The intuition that man will find objectified in nature what he has represented to himself leads him to discover only the pale reflections of an irrecoverable origin. Thought takes man on a journey away from the immediate and away from nature, for the latter too is only found in "shadows and reflections." The absence disclosed by the allegorical search for unity is recovered by the narrative: by allegorizing the signifier's failure to coincide with the signified, the narrative suggests that the path leading man away from unity can be retraced and, hence, identity between nature and language can be restored. The narrative promises an end to the tyranny of linguistic indeterminability, but the allegory undoes itself as the promise points toward the past, not the future. Unity—like Eden, we are told—has been left behind, but his former unity is not confirmed until the moment man discovers it has been lost. The idea of Eden and the Fall is made possible by the temporal condition of language as that which reminds man of his lost innocence and at once bars him from returning to this mythical state—a state that exists only within language. As that which mediates and separates—for mediation and separation are, as the Romantics tell us, synonyms—language postulates the Fall at the very moment it promises Redemption. This returns us to Kierkegaard's comment that mediacy inheres

30. Coleridge, *The Friend*, Pt. 1, pp. 508–509.

within immediacy. We cannot think innocence without thinking the Fall. Sin and redemption are the postulates of language. When turned into polar opposites, they serve orthodoxy, which masquerades under the name of coherence.

In a journal entry for 1834, Emerson speaks of the bipolar nature of man in terms of translation. Translation changes polarity into a principle of unity and atemporality: "Every man is bipolar; never a circle; somewhere therefore in each one of never so many million you shall find the contrariety[,] inconsistency of his nature. And as language translates language, verb verb, & noun noun so could their surfaces be adjusted to each other[,] might we find one age corresponding to another age in every minute peculiarity and every one man to every other man" (*JMN*.IV.331). Translation would presumably overcome multiplicity as any one word can be translated into another language. Emerson assumes, of course, that languages are perfectly correlated to each other, even if men are not. The principle of multiplicity allows him to argue that an individual contains the race. This is one way of protecting man from temporality. But by taking man out of history, he subjects him to empty repetition.

Implicit within Emerson's atemporal scheme is a concept of history as perpetual allegories. If we return to Coleridge's definitions of allegory and symbol, we find that the former is temporal and the latter transcendental. If the first man is a symbol, then the second man is an allegory—a pale copy of the first. Adam, Coleridge says in *Aids to Reflection*, is a symbol: "Must not of necessity the first man be a symbol of mankind in the fullest force of the word symbol, rightly defined;—a sign included in the idea which it represents—that is, an actual part chosen to represent the whole, as a lip with a chin prominent is a symbol of man." In Coleridge's philosophy, in contrast to Kierkegaard's, Adam stands outside of nature because there can be no origin in nature: "Nature is a line in constant and continuous evolution. Its beginning is lost in the supernatural: and for our understanding therefore it must appear as a continuous line without beginning or end. But where there is no discontinuity there can be no origination, and every appearance of origination in nature is but a shadow of our own casting."[31] Nature shares with metaphor and allegory a purely temporal mode of existence which excludes the eternal from its being. If nature partakes of time,

31. Coleridge, *Aids to Reflection*, 270n, 272n.

then it is allegorical—it is a pale copy of what can only be a pale copy. In Coleridge's allegories from *The Statesman's Manual* and *Essays on the Principles of Method*, nature reflects a unity lost to man in the temporal dimensions of representation. In the above passage from *Aids to Reflection*, however, the appearance of an origin in nature remains just that—an appearance—for unity, a cognate of origin, exists only as a reflection that disrupts the continuity of nature without pointing toward a transcendental source. The continuum on which nature exists is the temporal line of narrative. The origin is visible as a shadow or distorted reflection produced by the presence of man, whose temporal existence intrudes upon nature's separate narrative. Nature and man constitute two notions of history, the former as narrative and the latter as repetition. Both man and nature imply the possibility of an original creation, but when we pursue our search for origin in nature, we either lose ourselves in an endless line of evolution or we seek to rise above nature by thinking of an origin outside of it. The idea of perfection suggested by the search in nature reveals the discontinuity between man and the material world. When we turn to man and seek the origin in him, we conceive of the source in a language derived from the imperfections of nature. The difficulties Coleridge encounters whenever he tries to disclose the transcendental realm hidden from man center around the problem of language. At crucial points in various texts where he takes up the question of origins, he soon finds that he must speak instead of the difficulties of representation in language or, to be more specific, of allegory and symbol. The search for an origin free from the impurities of time is but a displaced search for a pure language to express the source it invariably obscures.

In a discussion of Poe that touches on problems similar to those I have been examining in Emerson and Coleridge, Joseph N. Riddel writes, "In Poe there is no natural language, and no nature. Nature is not an origin but a run-down trope. This is a fable Poe obsessively retells, the wearying struggle to purify language through language, the poetic repetition of some idea of 'absolute perfection' or some idea of purity that in the same gesture reveals the mark of its own discontinuity with any original form, idea, truth, reality. The Poesque realm of dream, which is the realm of language, is always a realm of the 'unfulfilled.' "[32] The "Poesque realm of dream" and

32. Riddel, "The 'Crypt' of Edgar Poe," 122.

the Coleridgean realm of allegory repeat the stories of their failures to represent an original truth or reality. Emerson undertakes the same doomed search for truth in history, which joins dream and allegory in the realm of textuality. In an isolated journal entry, Emerson writes under the heading "Symbol": "Yes, History is a vanishing allegory, and repeats itself to tediousness a thousand & a million times" (JMN.XI.435). This passage underscores what remains only a hint in Coleridge—nature and man are empty repetitions. Cut off from Adam, and therefore history, man and the natural world exist as mismatched interlinear texts, neither of which can translate the other's allegory.

The paradox is that Emerson and Coleridge have an ahistorical view of man, but they must tell their accounts of the Fall in an allegorical, and therefore temporal, language. Man, insofar as he partakes of time, is a part of nature, but insofar as he is a creature of the Will, he is free from time. That which "has its principle in itself," writes Coleridge, "so far as to originate its actions, can not be contemplated in any of the forms of space and time; it must, therefore, be considered as spirit or spiritual . . . and by spiritual I do not pretend to determine that the will is, but what it is not— namely, that it is not nature." Coleridge's orthodoxy is evident—man is both a part of nature and a part of spirit. He emphasizes the Will as that which lifts man above nature because his definition of Original Sin depends on man's freedom from time: "It is evident that the phrase, Original Sin, is a pleonasm, the epithet not adding to the thought, but only enforcing it. For if it be sin, it must be original; and a state or act, that has not its origin in the will, may be calamity, deformity, disease, or mischief; but a sin it can not be."[33] The Will, that which lifts man above nature, also casts him into it. Coleridge warns his readers that the Will cannot be considered as pure and inviolate, for sin is immanent within the Will (perhaps his uneasiness over Kant's ethics stems from the recognition that insofar as man has a will, he must sin). Temporality would then be the punishment for man's transgressions. If to think of an origin is to move beyond nature, then origin also has bound up within it the sin that keeps man within nature. In other words, to be original is to sin. Coleridge's symbolic theory of language would be the sublation of history and nature, but his commitment to religious orthodoxy, in this case Original Sin, allows him only to write

33. Coleridge, *Aids to Reflection*, 154, 274.

allegories of a lost innocence that can never be recovered. The aim of the symbol would be to recuperate an original innocence; but if "Original Sin" is a pleonasm, then "original innocence" must be an oxymoron.

Coleridge's orthodoxy forces him to divide history into two distinct epochs each with its own language: there is innocence and symbolic language, and then there is the fallen age and allegorical language.[34] Emerson has no such claims to orthodoxy, although his theory of history has much in common with Coleridge's theories of language. We have seen how Coleridge denies temporality by insisting on the supernatural agency of the human will. He must do so in order to preserve both an orthodox concept of sin and to protect man from a temporality that removes him farther and farther from his origin. The scene of this struggle, however, is the distinction between allegory and symbol. Whenever Coleridge wishes to confirm either man's will or the permanence of biblical truth, he has recourse to definitions of allegorical and symbolic languages. Although he affirms that language can give adequate embodiment to the truth, he relies on allegorical accounts that admit to the temporal slippage of a language that always undoes his desire for permanence.

Emerson, on the other hand, finds that any attempt to embody revelation is doomed to transgress that which it is supposed to express. The foremost affronter of divine truth is the church: "But the Revelation and the Church both labor under one perpetual disadvantage. They need always the presence of the same spirit that created them to make them thoroughly valid. . . . The truest state of thought rested in, becomes false. Thought is like manna, that fell out of heaven, which cannot be stored. It will be sour if kept; and tomorrow must be gathered anew. Perpetually must we *east* ourselves or we get into irrecoverable error starting from the plainest truths, and keeping, as we think the straightest road of logic" (*EL*. II. 92–93). We can see why Emerson refused to administer the Holy Communion on the grounds it displeased him. Like the belated poet, the seeker of truth must trace his own path if he is to be original, originality being coeval with truth. In Emerson's metaphor, however, we must retrace the path of the

34. The division of history into two moments and two languages is common to Romantic poetry. Donato comments on Schiller's "The Gods of Greece": "The past lost forever dooms the modern poet to a belatedness that divides history into two distinct moments: one of Gods and 'golden years of nature' and one of elegaic poets and presumably art" ("Divine Agonies," 92).

sun's ecliptic—we must go east, we must travel to the point of origin. Beginning anew would be a process of perpetual repetition.

In "Goethe; or, the Writer," Emerson returns to a similar problem when considering the man of action:

> Men's actions are too strong for them. Show me a man who has acted and who has not been the victim and slave of his action. What they have done commits and enforces them to do the same again. *The first act, which was to be an experiment, becomes a sacrament.* The fiery reformer embodies his aspiration in some rite or covenant, and he and his friends cleave to the form and lose the aspiration. The Quaker has established Quakerism, the Shaker has established his monastery and his dance; *and although each prates of spirit, there is no spirit, but repetition, which is anti-spiritual.* (W.IV.267; my emphasis)

A sacrament is a sin. We might even say that Emerson looked upon it as the embodiment of sin, for it was his refusal to administer the sacrament that led to his decision to leave the church. In the Lord's Supper we find the grounds for Emerson's rejection of empty repetition and symbolic language. Any attempt to give definite form to spiritual or natural truths is doomed to failure. Emerson rejects fixed form for the same reason he rejects empty repetition: both deny the temporal condition of man. To say the entire Bible is divinely inspired and therefore capable of yielding only one reading would, to cite Coleridge on this topic, turn it into "a colossal Memnon's head, a hollow passage for a voice, a voice that mocks the voices of many men, and speaks in their names, and yet is but one voice and the same."[35]

One reason why Emerson ultimately prefers writing to speech is that the former admits as many interpretations as there are readers. The attack on Swedenborg rests precisely on the question of symbolic language. He accuses Swedenborg of fastening "each natural object to a theologic notion. . . . The slippery Proteus is not so easily caught. In nature, every individual symbol plays innumerable parts, as each particle of matter circulates in turn through every system. The central identity enables any one symbol to express successively all the qualities and shades of real being" (W.IV.121). It seems unlikely that the central identity can be recognized amid its constantly shifting representations, yet it is precisely this indeterminability that frees the poet to re-create in perpetually new forms the central identity.

35. Coleridge, *Confessions of an Inquiring Spirit*, 52.

Emerson's theory of history is irreconcilable with a doctrine of identity and permanence. The illusion of permanence is a matter of perspective. Emerson would like to have a fixed hierarchy that affirms man's privileged place in the world, but if man finds that all nature serves him, it is because he finds himself wherever he looks: "Nature proceeds from a mind congenial with ours. Nature is overflowed and saturated with humanity" (EL.II.33). We have already examined Emerson's statement that nature is a product of the mind; here he suggests the underlying unity of man and God. But the unity of nature is hardly apparent; it must first be read in order to be understood. Emerson enlists science for his *explication de texte:* "Science is the arrangement of the phenomena of the world after their essential relations. It is the reconstruction of nature in the mind. This is at once its ideal and its historical aspect" (EL.II.27). Science shores up the ruins of a fragmentary world by classifying the diverse forms of nature according to an anthropocentric scheme. The ideality of nature is a belated product of a historical reconstruction. Reading nature is no different from reading human history. For this reason it is significant that the first chapter, following an introduction, in his lecture series *The Philosophy of History* is called "Humanity of Science."

The similarity between science and history extends beyond their anthropological biases; they are both textual. "The study of one natural object," says Emerson, "is like the study of a book in a foreign language. When he has mastered one book, the learner finds with joy that he can read with equal facility in ten thousand books" (EL.II.26). Nature, like man, is metonymically arranged—the reduction of nature's multiplicity to the proper name, a taxonomic label, permits the reader to move from effect to cause, or from history to spirit. Or so Emerson believes until he reaches his next paragraph: "But whilst the laws of the world coexist in each particle, they cannot be learned by the exclusive study of one creature. . . . All her secrets are locked in one plant; but she does not unlock them in any one. . . . She writes every obscure and minute facet in colossal characters somewhere" (EL.II.26). The failure to read nature's secrets comes from the lack of a proper vantage point. Man cannot see the present and proximate. He must have nature reconstructed in a metonymical order, as in the Jardin des Plantes, for it to become visible to him. When nature wishes to conceal something, writes Emerson, "she hides facts by putting them next to us" (EL.II.31). To perceive a law we must stand at a distance. This is as true of history as it is of nature: "History is the group of the types of representative men of any age at only the distance of convenient vision. We can see the arrangement of masses, & distinguish the forms of the leaders. Mythology is the same group at another remove, now at a pictorial distance; the perspective of history. The forms & faces can no longer be read, but only the direction of the march, & the result. . . . Distance is essential. Therefore we cannot say what is *our* mythology" (*JMN.*X.289–90). The inability to see the proximate is paralleled by man's incapacity to see the present. Geology is both science and history for Emerson, as it makes the present past and the near-at-hand far away.

In a journal entry that was later modified and used in the essay "Nature," Emerson writes, "The use of geology has been to wont the mind to a new chronology. The little dame school measures by which we had gauged everything we have learned to disuse, & break up our European & Mosaic & Ptolemaic schemes for the grand style of nature & fact. We knew nothing rightly for want of perspective" (*JMN.*IX.123–24). Emerson recognizes that geology mixes the temporal with the spatial and thus makes the past visible to the observer. He tells us that he always found it best to study geology the morning after an earthquake. The chasms opened up by the quake allow him to look into the ground and the past at the same time. The geological layers are "leaves of the *Stone Book.*" This metaphor from Robert Chambers' *Vestiges of the Natural History of Creation* (p. 58) is hardly original; it is merely explicit. Emerson works the metaphor to greater advantage when he describes Cuvier standing before a broken mountainside: "In the rough ledges, the different shades and superposition of the strata, his eye is reading as in a book the history of the globe . . . he is hearkening to infallible testimony of events whereof is no chronicle but in the memory of God" (*EL.*I.18). Contrary to the final claim, geological strata contain the traces recording each event. The layers themselves form a chronicle that can be read like the rings in a cross section of a tree. There is no need for God; nature contains within itself the memory of the events which Cuvier decodes.

Geology, as Emerson describes it, is the perfect science for a belated man. The history of the earth can only be studied after it has ended. As a reader of Cuvier, Emerson looked upon geology as a science that held before him the completed history of his subject. Although he knew from Lyell that present changes could account for the surface features of the globe, he still considered the history of the earth as complete. If current processes could explain present geological formations, the study of previous changes in the earth foreshadowed an ultimate death. In a passage written too early for Emerson to have been aware of the second law of thermodynamics and heat death, he finds in history the threat of universal death: "Every science is the record or account of the dissolution of the objects it considers. All history is an epitaph. All life is a progress toward death. The world is but a large Urn. The sun in his bright path thro' Ecliptic but a funeral triumph. for [*sic*] it lights men & animals & plants to their graves[.] There is a duration to which a century is but the turning of an hour glass. There is but one principle that is eternal. In the decays of time we flee to the gospel. We are driven to Truth by the decays of the Universe" (*JMN*.III.220).

This entry precedes any mention by Emerson of anything to do with the second law of thermodynamics (he did read Sadi Carnot late in life); however, he could just as well have formulated this view from his readings in geology. He says repeatedly that the soil that proves so fecund for plant and animal life is the decomposition of earlier ages. Composition, says Emerson, is made possible by decomposition. (The question of the eternal return suggested by this remark lies outside the scope of this chapter.) There emerges in Emerson's comments a series of metaphors relating to reading, writing, history, and science. A process of decay, repetition, and belatedness can be found throughout his reflections on man and nature. Science takes a subordinate position behind man, but not because it is of less value than history; science, in this case geology, is but one branch of the human sciences. The study of man is properly an encyclopedia of knowledge.

When Emerson set out to write a philosophy of history, he was guided by the nineteenth-century topos of the encyclopedia. A history of man requires a universal history: "Man is explicable by nothing less than all his history" (*EL*.II.13). And as the individual must be explained by the universal, so the universal appears in the individual: "Where you behold a man there you see the origin of the whole encyclopedia of facts" (*EL*.II.14). The lectures entitled *The Philosophy of History*—with their various chapters on art, politics, religion, society, ethics, and manners—are an attempt to write a comprehensive history. Emerson's failure to complete such an enterprise hardly needs to be remarked upon, although a cursory glance at the titles collected in *Essays* reveals he had not abandoned this vision of a universal history. There were other attempts and other failures in the nineteenth century, the most significant perhaps being Hegel's *Encyclopedia of the Philosophical Sciences* and Comte's *Philosophie première: Cours de philosophie positive*. If we include cosmogonies and universal histories, we may add to the inventory Michelet's *Introduction à l'histoire universelle*, Novalis' *Fragments*, Poe's *Eureka*, Coleridge's projected and incomplete magnum opus, and Emerson's *Nature*.

I would like to turn briefly to Auguste Comte, who offers an extreme example of how the belief in the universal progress ushered in by modern science could be combined with an ostensibly secular philosophy of history. Michel Serres has been one of our most perceptive commentators on the onto-theological grounds of science and history, which find their most grandiose expression in Comte's *Cours*. In his introduction to that work, Serres comments on the ideological force underlying Comte's attempt to bring the disciplines of history, mathematics, and science under the rubric of philosophy. "Taking into account," writes Serres, "that the history is that of reason, it tells of the formation of the encyclopedic, the progressive construction of a scale of hierarchies." In what Emerson calls history according to science, nineteenth-century man is seen as the goal of a temporal order that is at once chronological and hierarchical. The hierarchical element in positivism is what separates Emerson's theory from Comte's. As Serres points out, the philosophical dictionary is arranged according to the order of books in a library, and the plan of the *Cours* follows that of the encyclopedia: "The entire *Cours*, globally speaking, is the encyclopedia of a history, or the dictionary of a text."[36]

Comte, we might say, reduces history to an encyclopedia: "The principal goal that one must have in sight is to arrange natural sciences in the order of their natural sequence, according to their mutual dependence; in such a way that one may be able to set them forth successively without ever being drawn into the slightest vicious circle." To escape the vicious circle of the book, Comte proposes to replace "the *historic* order" with "the *dogmatic* order." The linear, or chronological, mode of arranging a work becomes more and more impractical as knowledge advances, and one can no longer go through the intermediary stages of studying science in a historical order. "By means of the second [dogmatic order]," writes Comte, "one puts forth the system of ideas such as it would be conceived today by a sin-

36. Serres, Introduction to Comte, *Philosophie première*, 1, 2.

gle mind, which, placed at a fitting standpoint and provided with sufficient knowledge, would apply itself to remaking science in its entirety."[37] Comte, who rejects theology and metaphysics in the name of science, reinstates the privileged observer, the scientist as god and king, to arrange society into a hierarchical encyclopedia mirroring the "natural" order of the world. While Emerson shared with Comte a desire to arrange the circle of knowledge in a book, he never satisfied his desire, in the manner of Comte, to close the circle of history by turning a metaphor into a metaphysics. Emerson remains acutely aware of the tropological power of language and, therefore, resists the tendency to grant autonomy to any one trope, including that of Absolute Spirit or God.

As the atemporal record of the "natural" order of science, the encyclopedia completes the philosophy contained within its covers. In other words, it writes a history which is fulfilled by its very existence, thereby transforming the encyclopedia, or circle of knowledge, into a self-engendering circle. Positivism announces itself as the historical goal of science's progress toward a system that maintains itself as atemporal and speculative. The encyclopedia is aligned with science in a system that stands outside the vicissitudes of time. The obvious analogue is Hegel's Absolute Spirit. In both Hegel and Comte, the book records the gradual unfolding of what proves to be the end of history.

Before turning to Emerson's treatment of the metaphor of the encyclopedia, I would like to examine the trope of the self-engendering circle of universal knowledge in Michelet's *Introduction à l'histoire universelle*. Presenting his work as what was originally intended to be a history of France, Michelet explains that he found he could not write a history of France without writing a history of the world. With the loss of the unified world of antiquity, the modern world has become so complex that one must study the mutual engagement of the world's nations "in their intimate harmony." Comte offers a similar argument for the atemporal study of the sciences. Michelet, however, criticizes Hegel and his followers for petrifying history: "The social world has become a god in their hands, but an immovable, insensitive god, completely suited to comfort and prolong the national lethargy." Hayden White has characterized Michelet's rejection of a mechanistic philosophy of history as an escape from irony, along with

---

37. Comte, *Philosophie première*, 50.

the tactics of metonymy and synecdoche: "Michelet denied all worth to Mechanistic (causal) reductions and to Formalist (typological) integrations of the historical field. The Metaphorical apprehension of the essential sameness of things overrides every other consideration in his writings." Thus, Michelet offers, in opposition to the petrified god of mechanistic philosophy, a view of history as identity and difference, wherein the opposition between man and nature is effaced by the translation of history into geography.[38]

History, according to this early work of Michelet's, is the articulation of geography:

> If in natural history, animals of a higher order, man, the quadruped, are better *articulated*, so as to be most capable of the various movements which their activity imparts; if among languages those succeed which respond, by the variety of their inflections, the richness of their feats, the suppleness of their forms, to the infinite needs of intelligence, shall we not also judge that in geography certain countries have been designed according to a more favored plan, carved more carefully into gulfs and ports, bounded in a better way by seas and mountains, with valleys and rivers which pass through them in a more favorable fashion, that is, if I dare say it, better *articulated*, that is to say, more capable to accomplish everything which liberty would want to extract from them. (pp. 410–11)

Like Hegel in his preference for phonetic writing, Michelet associates the flexibility of spoken language with the easy intercourse between nations. In a refutation of Leibniz's defense of hieroglyphics, Hegel writes, "Leibniz's practical mind misled him to exaggerate the advantages which a complete written language, formed on the hieroglyphic method . . . would have as a universal language for the intercourse of nations and especially scholars. But we may be sure that it was rather the intercourse of nations . . . which occasioned the need of alphabetical writing and led to its formation."[39] Michelet's analogy, on the other hand, proposes that the earth's topography, not speech, leads to intercourse between nations. In his analogy, speech is secondary to writing since the mountains, gulfs, ports, and so on, are visual signs articulating an otherwise mute earth. Michelet does

---

38. Michelet, *Introduction à l'histoire universelle*, 425, 432; White, *Metahistory*, 150; Orr, *Jules Michelet*, 12. As my discussion of Michelet is limited to an early text, see Orr's work for a thorough analysis of the relation between Michelet's historical writings and his works on natural history. See also Kippur, *Jules Michelet*, 71–83.

39. Hegel, *Philosophy of Mind* [and] *Zusätze*, 215.

not have to dig into the ground to read the earth; he sticks entirely to the surface.

In this articulate geography, France holds a special place: "Paris was at that time for Europe the capital of dialectics" (p. 449). In its central position on the Continent, France is the meeting place of East and West, North and South, and, as we shall see, past and future. Hegel's dialectic, which begins with the *Hic* and the *Nunc*, originates within language; Michelet's dialectic is also linguistic—in fact, it is governed by the logos: "France will explain the Word [*Verbe*] of the social world which we see beginning" (p. 467). The Word translates the articulate map of the world into a historical order of infinite progress. In opposition to the immobile god of German philosophy, the god Michelet envisions will be the logos, the Word made flesh. There will be, it seems, a new dispensation—the dead letter of Hegelianism will be revivified by France.

Michelet writes in his conclusion that France, like Janus, faces both the past and the future. As language, France mediates between the ancient world of the Greeks, the modern world of Europe, and the future of America. Yet to maintain the history of infinite progress, Michelet must turn away from language and rely on spirit: "That which is youngest and most fertile in the world is by no means America, that serious child who will imitate for a long time; it is aged France, renewed by the spirit" (p. 469). The articulate geography that speaks the universal progress of the world hints of a movement from east to west with France linking Europe and Asia to the New World. As the logos, France alone exists in the present tense—it remains both mature and ever new as it unites the characteristics of the classical and Eastern civilizations with the fertility of the New World. To prevent France from lapsing into the dead letter of mechanistic philosophy, Michelet must appeal to the ahistorical spirit to enter into his temporal system and maintain France's privileged position against the threat posed by his own commitment to progress and egalitarianism. He fashions his universal history on the organic model of interacting bodies which pass from periods of growth to those of decay. He maintains his "natural" system by the mechanism of translation which repeats the text of God throughout the world body.

While the nineteenth century hardly can be considered unique for producing cosmogonies and universal histories, its coupling of history and science led to a confusion of metaphors of biology and geology with those of history. The earth becomes the fossil record of its continual growth and decay. Geological science joins biology as one of the organic sciences. The metaphors of the natural sciences slip into historical and philosophical discourse, producing various organic philosophies. With a conceptual base formed by metaphors of growth and transition, a conflict arises between the mechanical sciences and the organic sciences. In Michelet, for instance, we find that the metaphors and theories of geography merge with those of history. The physical migrations of people quite literally become the articulation of the earth. Michelet adopts the biological metaphor of evolution and writes history as the story of infinite progress. But the same metaphor that supplies his dynamic theory of history serves as the guiding principle of a static philosophy. Michelet describes man as alternating between periods of composition and decomposition: "Humanity proceeds, we have said, eternally from decomposition to composition, from analysis to synthesis. In analysis, all the relationships disappear, all the ties are broken, the social and divine unity becomes imperceptible. But little by little the relationships reappear in science and in society, unity returns in science and in society, unity returns in the city and in nature" (p. 465).

The world, writes Michelet, will one day return to "the image of the divine order." Whereas Comte is blind to the theological implications of a scientific theory of eternal return, Michelet appears blind to the scientific grounds of his explicitly theological reading of the eternal return. We live in a period of analysis; science concerns itself with the minutest details. Unity, Michelet predicts, will return because of science and the same analytic method that is a cause of the present dispersal: "Unity and this time free unity, reappearing in the social world; science having, through the observation of details, acquired a legitimate foundation to erect its majestic and harmonic edifice, humanity will recognize the accord of the double world—natural and civil—in the benevolent intelligence which made the bond" (p. 466). Science will be an encyclopedic organization of knowledge, and the edifice it builds is a book classifying the articulate geography of nations. Finally, the encyclopedia will encode Genesis in a scientific system.

Comte's *Cours* represents a similar effort to bring under the aegis of science the theological concepts of stasis and unity. I return once more to Michel Serres on the nineteenth century's effort to close history. Serres remarks how each of the major figures in Comte's pantheon of positivists created systems designed to reduce nature to laws that would elimate "a chance of history."[40] Laplace's *Exposition du système du monde* represents one such effort. Another example would be Cuvier's anatomical theory. Cuvier bases his taxonomy not on visible features, but on the internal organs of animals. In addition, he placed great emphasis on the interaction between these organs. By looking at the body as a closed system, Cuvier reduces it to a set of functions, or forces, and rejects history in the form of evolution. Denying the external evidence of fossil bones and living animals that species develop and alter, he bases his rigid classification on nonvisible internal forces. The equivalent to this would be Michelet's stress on the universal interaction between people as the only way to write history in a chaotic age. The world becomes a system measured by interaction, yet maintains a fixed distinction between nations. Unity exists in the interstices between nations which are internally fragmented. In light of Michelet's metaphor of an articulate geography, we might conclude that although each language is distinct, translation is possible because of the incompleteness that requires the supplementation of one language/nation with another.

Science puts the world in order. Emerson may have had Cuvier in mind when he wrote that "history is Zoology & 'not a chapter of accidents.'" (*JMN*.XIII.92). Cosmogony, as Serres says, becomes a science—Poe's *Eureka* would be the perfect example, although for Poe, as well as Emerson, science is poetry. The system of the world will contain all sciences and all philosophies. The system will, as all systems must, account not just for order but the variation from order. Michelet, as we have seen, achieves this by reading science as the source of disorder and of order as well, just as Poe's cosmogony in *Eureka* begins with dispersal of atoms at the Creation and predicts their eventual return to their original state. The world has been catalogued and arranged into a library where each volume tells the same story—the system and the world are one. What Serres says of Comte applies to Cuvier and Michelet and, with some reservations, to Emerson: "The house of man is in order and the inventory is finished. Fitted out, henceforward for nautical technology present or future. There are no longer any voyages other than circular ones, on the globe, in space or in the metaphor

40. Serres, *Hermes III*, 162.

of ideas. Philosophical systems mimic the system of the world or embellish an already organized niche."[41] With the termination of the inventory, the circle will be closed, and the traveler will move throughout the globe/metaphors—the encyclopedia will be the book of the total science.

In a preface on Hegel's prefaces, Jacques Derrida finds in the metaphor of the book the problematic of beginnings and endings of systems. This is known to be true of Hegel's preface to the *Phenomenology*, which was written after the completion of the book. Derrida asks, Does the preface stand outside or inside philosophy? Does it produce philosophy or does philosophy produce it? This problem is particularly acute in a philosophy that is supposed to be an encyclopedia of all knowledge. The ideal form of an encyclopedic philosophy is, as Derrida says, the book: "The ideal form of this [the ideal opus] would be a book of total science, a book of absolute knowledge that digested, recited, and subsequently ordered all books, going through the whole cycle of knowledge." The conception of the cycle presents, as we have seen in Comte, unusual problems. The preface that introduces the work is at once the end of the work. The cycle of knowledge begins where it ends—in a self-engendering circle: "If the preliminary explanation is absolutely prior to the encyclopedic circle, then it stays outside it and explains nothing. It is not philosophical and in the extreme remains impossible. If on the other hand it is engaged within the philosophic circle, it is no longer a *pre*-liminary operation: it belongs to the actual movement of the method and to the structure of objectivity. Engenderer and consumer of itself, the concept relieves [*relève*] its preface and plunges into itself. The Encyclopedia gives *itself* birth. The conception of the concept is an autoinsemination."[42]

The encyclopedia that speaks the language of nature only speaks the language of its own writing. Yet the question of engenderment is not so easily resolved. The concept of self-insemination includes the dissemination of a meaning that returns in the figure of the logos. The self-created totality of the book is contingent upon a concept that is anterior to the circle of the encyclopedia. In his *Fragments*, which is also known as the *Encyclopedia*, Novalis raises the question of the form of the book in terms of writing. In

41. *Ibid.*, 163–64.
42. Derrida, *Dissemination*, 46, 48.

Derrida's analysis of Novalis' projected and fragmentary work: "Novalis, in his *Encyclopedia* . . . explicitly poses the question of the *form* of the total book as a *written* book: an exhaustive taxonomical writing, a hologram that would order and classify knowledge, *giving place* to literary writing."[43]

In Emerson's Encyclopedia, indexed under "Nature," is a quotation from Novalis that he found in Carlyle: " ' What is Nature? An encyclopedical systematic Index or Plan of our spirit. Why will we content us with the mere Catalogue of our Treasures? Let us contemplate them ourselves & in all ways elaborate & use them' " (*JMN*.VI.219). As Derrida points out, the problem of the indexing of nature is not only one of dissemination, it is also one of supplementation: "A fulfilling productivity that comes not to repeat but to complete nature through writing, would mean that nature is somewhere incomplete, that it lacks something needed for it to be what it is, that it has to be supplemented."[44] As the book of nature needs indexing, its writing is not complete. Yet the cataloguing will be in excess of nature, for, as Novalis claims, nature can only be completed by the human spirit. This catalogue, as it indexes both nature and spirit, would supplement nature with the spirit of man. Man, too, is not complete. If he is the supplement of nature, it is only because nature is the supplement of him. I have already quoted Emerson on the incompleteness of man—he is an arc and never a circle. We find the same image repeated in a journal entry acknowledging the failure of his Encyclopedia to close its circle:

> *Systems*[.] I need hardly say to any one acquainted with my thoughts that I have no System. When I was quite young I fancied that by keeping a Manuscript Journal by me, over whose pages I wrote a list of the great topics of human study, as, *Religion, Poetry, Politics, Love,* &c in the course of a few years I should be able to complete a sort of Encyclopedia containing the net value of all the definitions at which the world had yet arrived. But at the end of a couple of years my Cabinet Cyclopedia though much enlarged was no nearer to a completeness than on its first day. Nay somehow the whole plan of it needed alteration nor did the following months promise any speedier term to it than the foregoing. At last I discovered that my curve was a parabola whose arcs would never meet, and came to acquiesce in the perception that although no diligence can rebuild the Universe in a model by the best accumulation or disposition of details, yet does the

43. *Ibid.*, 50.
44. *Ibid.*, 53.

World reproduce itself in miniature in every event that transpires, so that all the laws of nature may be read in the smallest fact. (*JMN*.VII.302–303)

Emerson begins this passage by dismissing empirical and taxonomical efforts to define, and thereby control, the world. But the turn toward the microcosm resurrects his belief in man's ability to construct a universal history. The shift from the catalogue to the miniature represents a distinction between two methods of reading. As a reader who desired to overturn other texts, Emerson's project for the Encyclopedia was destined to be rejected because it would relegate him to a mere copyist of other people's definitions. By accumulating the gross sum of knowledge, Emerson would simply have reproduced a preconstructed history. This linear model of history rests on a biological analogy of descent and growth in which all systems of knowledge stand in an unproblematic relationship to one another. Each science would develop in filial fashion—present-day science would be the offspring of its forebears—Laplace, therefore, would be the son and heir of Newton. Each field of science, in turn, would be linked by familial bonds to other sciences, the sum total presumably descending from a common origin in philosophy. Generation, however, does not proceed by quantitative accumulation but by disruption and dislocation instead. The former model would reproduce empty repetitions or imitations masquerading as originals. Yet reading nature, which is no different from reading books, requires a distortion and a reappropriation of the pre-texts as an other or a foreign body. In the previous chapter, I describe these two methods of reading as an unproblematic versus a problematic reading that I call, after Emerson, quotation. The disruptive tendency of quotation is reflected in Emerson's comments on the "progress" of science: "*Generalization*. The studies of Cuvier showed that the classification of animals must be based on organs. But Bichat showed that the organs depended on tissues, & so undermined Cuvier's system. But/ newer inquiries/ Schwan/ showed that tissues depended on cellular structure, & so undermined Bichat. And, when the microscope is improved, we shall have the cells analysed, & all will be electricity, or somewhat else" (*JMN*.XIV.174).

Emerson's skeptical tone indicates a certain dissatisfaction with the pretensions of science. Because of the repeated displacement of ever more refined instruments, the Encyclopedia would have to be revised daily. In the journal passage Emerson places nature against science, but he does not do so out of any belief in the permanence of the natural world as opposed to the ephemerality of science. Nature resists reduction to a numerical index system; the Proteus will not be so easily named—for science would be an affixing of proper names to nature. The passage on systems was rewritten and used in "Intellect," which appeared in *Essays*. In the paragraphs leading up to his disavowal of systems, Emerson introduces the image of the horizon, a metaphor of limitation and supersession: "Every thought is a prison also. I cannot see what you see, because I am caught up by a strong wind and blown so far in one direction that I am out of the hoop of your horizon" (*W*.II.339). The horizon is an arc circumscribing, or imprisoning, the thinker, yet it is also the foremost point of vision and, as such, represents the forever-unarrived-at future.

As Emerson says along with Serres and Derrida, the metaphor of the system/encyclopedia is the circle. The failure to close the circle signifies an inability to seal man off from time. The metaphor of circles appears most memorably in the essay bearing the word for its title. Yet in "Circles" Emerson does not treat the circle as an image of completion; like the horizon, the circle is a metaphor of transformation: "The eye is the first circle; the horizon which it forms is the second; and throughout nature this primary figure is repeated without end. It is the highest emblem in the cipher of the world" (*W*.II.301). To read nature aright, we must learn how to decipher this emblem, but this figure will not admit of definition. In this respect, it too is protean. In itself, the circle never changes; what changes are its readers. Nature seems to be one text that does not remind the poet of his belatedness. Nature resists quotation. The moment we are settled within a circle, we find another has been drawn around it: "Our life is an apprenticeship to the truth that around every circle another can be drawn; that there is no end in nature, but every end is a beginning; that there is always another dawn risen on mid-noon, and under every deep a lower deep opens" (*W*.II.301).

The discovery of a new circle does not so much presuppose a progress in the growth of the intellect as it signifies a new reading of the book of nature. Once man becomes a reader, he finds all is unsettled, as each apparent fixture in nature is in truth medial. For the writer who declares himself "an endless seeker with no Past at my back" (*W*.II.318), the circle promises a life of perpetual beginnings without end—it is the myth of America. But in the allusion to Milton's *Paradise Lost*, Emerson transforms the hope of a fresh beginning into a complex interlacing of texts whereby the reader is caught between epiphany and despair.

Emerson's first allusion is to Book V, lines 310–11, when Adam calls to Eve when he sees Raphael approaching like the sun:

> Haste hither *Eve*, and worth thy sight behold
> Eastward among those Trees, what glorious shape
> Comes this way moving; seems another Morn
> Ris'n on mid-noon; some great behest from Heav'n
> To us perhaps he brings, and will voutsafe
> This day to be our Guest.[45]   (V, 308–313).

When Adam sees this emblem of the sun and God, he reads it as an omen of God's good will. A second morning prefigures the second Adam, Christ, and the redemption he brings to man. Though Raphael does not exactly bring redemption, he does forewarn Adam of the Fall. While consideration of the complexity of Milton's attitudes toward God is well outside the scope of this chapter, it is important to note how the image that Adam reads as beneficent carries with it a warning of impending doom. Before his fall, Adam can only read what may be called unfallen texts—he finds himself wherever he looks.

Satan is also visited by a representative of God, and he too finds himself:

> O thou that with surpassing Glory crown'd,
> Look'st from thy sole Dominion like the God
> Of this new World; at whose sight all the Stars
> Hide their diminisht heads; to thee I call,
> But with no friendly voice, and add thy name
> O Sun, to tell thee how I hate thy beams
> That bring to my remembrance from what state
> I fell.   (IV, 32–39)

One may note in Satan's reading of the sun a doubleness similar to that found in Adam's reading of the approaching archangel. Satan recognizes the sun as a symbol of hope, but this very recognition plunges him deeper into despair and brings us to Emerson's allusion:

> Me miserable! which way shall I fly
> Infinite wrath, and infinite despair?
> Which way I fly is Hell; myself am Hell;

45. Milton, *Complete Poems and Major Prose*, ed. Hughes. All citations from *Paradise Lost* are from this edition.

> And in the lowest deep a lower deep
> Still threat'ning to devour me opens wide,
> To which the Hell I suffer seems a Heav'n.   (IV, 73–78)

Like Adam, Satan looks into the sun and finds a mirror of himself. His long speech on doctrine and his fall is a process of self-definition. A circle in nature is a text which any reader may pick up and it will be a thousand books to a thousand readers. Nature is medial, for it serves, as does language, as a conveyance between points. But a point in Emerson's cosmogony appears only as another circle and never a fixed *point d'appui*.

Literature may provide an exception to this rule, for it "is a point outside of our hodiernal circle through which a new one may be described. The use of literature is to afford us a platform whence we may command a view of our present life, a purchase by which we may move it" (W.II.311–12). As befits a system, the controlling force must stand outside or else it will be subject to the same perturbations as that which it controls.[46] From the perspective of society, literature is likewise circles upon circles. Only as an observer of the other does a man discover firm footing; once he looks upon himself, he falls. Either man is caught between the discontinuity of perception, wherein he is forever divided from what he perceives, or what he perceives is characterized by instability and dislocation. Stability can only be a momentary illusion—a false perspective. Emerson admits as much when he announces, "I unsettle all things. No facts are to me sacred; none are profane; I simply experiment" (W.II.318). Whenever Emerson reaches a point of absolute relativism or skepticism, he does not quite retreat, but instead leaps over the abyss he has opened and affirms a central identity: "This incessant movement and progression which all things partake could never become sensible to us but by contrast to some principle of fixture or stability in the soul" (W.II.318). Yet the affirmation is soon obscured as Emerson continues to extol indeterminacy: "The one thing which we seek with insatiable desire is to forget ourselves, to be surprised out of our propriety, to lose our sempiternal memory and to do something without knowing how or why; in short to draw a new circle" (W.II.321). Insofar as a man is fixed, there is no hope for him. Emerson's doctrine of circles is a philosophy suited to the American condition. To draw a new circle we

46. For an examination of the paradoxical relation between center and structure, see Derrida, *Writing and Difference*, 279.

must forget the past—that is, forget that the circle we draw only traces the outlines of other circles. Emerson's circular transcendentalism is a model of a system: it permits maximum spontaneity and variability only by affirming the fixity of a central being. To create man anew each and every day there must be a fixed point at the center of the system. This fixed point not only stabilizes the system, it also prevents it from undergoing any change. The constantly shifting forms of nature and society are reduced to mere epiphenomena that repeat a similar story from different points of view. The apparently random process of historical change is mere seeming which masks the permanence of Being.

It appears that we have closed Emerson's circle, but this too is mere seeming—a seeming that has nothing to do with Being. If we turn to Emerson's *Nature,* we find the image of the circle repeated in the famous "transparent eyeball" passage: "Standing on the bare ground,—my head bathed by the blithe air and uplifted into infinite space,—all mean egotism vanishes. I become a transparent eyeball; I am nothing; I see all; the currents of the Universal Being circulate through me; I am part or particle of God" (W.I.10). In "The Instructed Eye: Emerson's Cosmogony in 'Prospects,'" Barbara Packer has pointed out that "the Transparent Eye-ball is a circle whose center is everywhere and its circumference nowhere." In an extended analysis of this passage and "the axis of vision" passage in "Prospects," Packer uncovers Emerson's desire to evade temporality. The spatial images of the circle and the eye are Emerson's replacement of the temporal myth of the Fall with a spatial one of states of Being.[47] To create a new myth Emerson must draw a new circle. It is the circular system of *Nature* that I would like briefly to examine.

I have discussed in the previous chapter Emerson's tripartite theory of language. Here I merely wish to point out the circular structure of it. As "words are signs of natural facts," and the latter are "symbols of particular spiritual facts," "Nature is the symbol of spirit" (W.I.25). Nature represents spirit, and words represent nature. At this point, the connection between words and spirit appears to be only through the agency of nature. The connection becomes even more baffling when Emerson says, "Parts of speech are metaphors, because the whole of nature is a metaphor of the human mind" (W.I.32). We appear to have found our self-enclosed circle:

47. Packer, "The Instructed Eye," 220; Packer, *Emerson's Fall,* 63–84.

words are metaphors because nature is a metaphor, and words represent nature. But the third element, which inseminates the circle, is mind. So our circle now reads: words are metaphors of the metaphor of mind. We might ask, How does the mind learn that it creates nature? The answer is through language: we know of the mind through a metaphorical language borrowed from a metaphorical nature. Therefore, our discovery that nature resembles the mind takes place within language. In Emerson's version of the *speculum*, the mirror is language. Nature is a metaphor of the mind, and mind, recognizable only within language, is a metaphor of a metaphor. Emerson transforms the necessarily belated discovery of mind in nature into an atemporal relationship.

History will henceforth be read and written "in the light of these two facts, namely, that the mind is One, and that nature is its correlative" (W.II.38). Emerson presents *Nature* as a new cosmogony affirming the correspondence between the One and the many, past and present, God and man. But wherever we turn in Emerson, and *Nature* is no exception, we find that history, God, and nature never exist outside of language. The atemporal metaphor of correspondence covers over the time-bound and fragmentary process of translation. The circle of language, nature, and God is a series of overlapping, but ill-fitting, arcs. As late as the lecture series *The Natural History of Intellect*, Emerson would still affirm the correspondence of mind and nature, but he abandons the system that would complete the arc; in other words, he abandons cosmogony for history:

> My contribution will be simply historical. I write anecdotes of the intellect; a sort of Farmer's Almanac of mental moods. . . . I cannot myself use that systematic form which is reckoned essential in treating the science of the mind. But if one can say so without arrogance, I might suggest that he who contents himself with dotting a fragmentary curve, recording only what facts he has observed, without attempting to arrange them within one outline, follows a system also,—a system as grand as any other, though he does not interfere with its vast curves by prematurely forcing them into a circle or ellipse, but only draws that arc which he clearly sees, or perhaps at a later observation a remote curve as the same orbit, and waits for a new opportunity, well assured that these observed arcs will consist with each other. (W.XII.11–12)

Emerson's rejection of systems that proclaim completeness reflects his distrust of language's claims that it can cover the grand dimensions of truth and nature. His faith tells him the One exists; perception, which includes all forms of mediation, including language, tells him that all is fragmentary and discontinuous.

Emerson remains caught between the chaos of the library and the questionable order of its catalogue. The impulse to affirm the universal presence of God threatens to turn the world into a petrified symbol. The circle of knowledge would be transformed into a circle of sin—a reified view of nature and man that reduces history to empty repetition. The Comtean encyclopedia would make America an appendage to an already completed history. Michelet even denies that America is the New World. The American writer turns away from the dream of the total book and produces fragments and drafts.

It is Melville, not Emerson, who offers the most lucid, if mad, vision of the patchwork that characterizes the American encyclopedia. In the chapter "Cetology" of *Moby-Dick*, Melville/Ishmael offers to present to the reader a library catalogue of whales/books. Melville claims his is "no easy task. The classification of the constituents of a chaos, nothing less is here essayed." This chaos, however, is not the whales in the sea, but is instead the sources Melville has plagiarized in the writing of his book. He confesses he is a letter sorter, for this "ponderous task" requires not a writer, but an extraordinary postal clerk: "No ordinary letter sorter in the Post-office is equal to it." And Melville continues his jokes on his plagiarisms: "I have swam through libraries and sailed through oceans; I have had to do with whales with these visible hands; I am in earnest; and I will try."[48] Whales, of course, are books classified according to their size—folio, octavo, and duodecimo.

The book must of necessity remain incomplete: "My object here is simply to project the draught of a systematization of cetology. I am the architect, not the builder."[49] Melville shares with Emerson a distrust of completed texts. The similarity also extends to their mutual claims to be only the proposers of future works rather than the authors of completed books. (In his announcements concerning the coming of an American bard, Emerson plays John the Baptist to Whitman's Christ.) As a compiler, Melville will merely refashion his sources into a preliminary catalogue. In this library/world everything must remain incomplete, for completion means

48. Melville, *Moby-Dick*, 116–17, 118.
49. *Ibid.*, 118.

death. Melville's nihilism may answer Nietzsche's complaint that we have not gotten rid of God because we still believe in grammar. The grammar, which reminded the "late consumptive usher" of his mortality, has the same status of the finished book—it is a tomb for dead authors.

Melville's fascination with the incomplete book, whether it be Pierre's genealogy or Bartleby's history, cannot be separated from his denial that either a writer or a nation can be original. History remains a series of mutilated texts which the author assembles willy-nilly into a narrative that draws attention to its own textuality. Emerson's essays are repeated attempts to graft together his quotations from Carlyle, Coleridge, and Swedenborg, among hundreds of others, into an encyclopedic account of the main concerns of man. The remarkable extent of Emerson's repetitions ultimately points to the inconclusiveness of his textual bric-a-brac.

Melville's famous disavowal that his stolen books have been perfected into a system rejects the nineteenth century's belief in the total book comprehending God, culture, science, and history:

> It was stated at the outset, that this system would not be here, and at once, perfected. You cannot but plainly see that I have kept my word. But I now leave my cetological System standing thus unfinished, even as the great Cathedral of Cologne was left, with the crane still standing upon the top of the uncompleted tower. For small erections may be finished by their first architects; grand ones, true ones, ever leave the copestone to posterity. God keep me from completing anything. This whole book is a draught— nay, but a draught of a draught. Oh, Time, Strength, Cash, and Patience![50]

50. *Ibid.*, 127–28.

CHAPTER THREE

Whitman and Time

"We will not anticipate the past . . .
our retrospection will now be all to the
future."
                           —Mrs. Malaprop

The nearly cotemporaneous emergence of evolutionary theory with the geological and philological sciences seemed to open the earth and language to history. The ever-increasing perfection of the biological order seemed to promise man a similar drive toward perfection in his social existence. In preserving a teleological understanding of the ends of man, evolutionary theory transformed the book of nature into a variable system of signs that could only be deciphered if read in historical terms, whereas God's Creation was eternal and, insofar as the world is the logos, embodied a fixed and unitary meaning. Historical sense, therefore, was not needed to understand what was the shadowy type of a transcendent world. Although history according to evolutionary theory is the story of progress, philology suggested a decline from an original plenitude when words more closely adhered to what they denominated and when they had not yet succumbed to the decay that comes with use. Unlike a myth of Adamic naming, this history of language has close analogies with the debasement of coins— having passed through so many hands, words, like coins, begin to lose their distinctive marks along with their value.

Whitman's corrective to this debasement was a return to slang, or the idioms peculiar to each language. Slang, however, is not to be confused with either natural language or speech, that is, a form of language existing outside the fixed grammar and lexicon of a derivative written language. English, says Whitman, is a composite language as old as any other:

> View'd freely, the English language is the accretion and growth of every
> dialect, race, and range of time, and is both the free and compacted compo-
> sition of all. From this point of view, it stands for Language in the largest
> sense, and is really the greatest of studies. . . . The scope of its etymolo-

gies is the scope not only of man and civilization, but the history of Nature in all departments, and of the organic Universe, brought up to date; for all are comprehended in words, and their backgrounds. This is when words become vitaliz'd, and stand for things, as they unerringly and soon come to do, in the mind that enters on their study with fitting spirit, grasp, and appreciation.[1]

The composite nature of English makes it the universal language; all other languages flow into it; leaving behind the sediment that contains the history of the universe. Thus, Whitman compares philology with geology at his essay's conclusion: "The science of language has large and close analogies in geological science, with its ceaseless evolution, its fossils, and its numberless submerged layers and hidden strata, the infinite go-before of the present" (PW.II.577). By equating philology with geology, Whitman transforms history into language—words do not tell the story of man; they *are* the story of man. Moreover, as English is the composite of all languages, it alone is history. As it is the last of languages, English is the first: having reduced the past to the fragmentary particles that constitute English, Whitman asserts that only the present is a whole because it brings the universe "up to date."

Origins, therefore, are without any value: "*Language cannot be Traced to First Origins.*—Of the first origins of language it is vain to treat, any more than of the origin of men and women, or of matter, or of spirit. . . . Language makes chronology petty; it ante-dates all, and brings the farthest history close to the tips of our ears. No art, no power, no grammar, no combination or process can originate a language; it grows purely of itself, and incarnates everything" (NYD, p. 56). Language is at once the most ancient of things—it exists before man—and the newest. As that which incarnates everything, language carries history in and as itself; hence, the remote past is made present to man. The past exists for man as interpretable signs; furthermore, as the compound product of linguistic signs, history is a semiotic wherein sign interprets sign. Man merely need listen to

---

1. Whitman, *Prose Works 1892*, II, 572, hereinafter cited as *PW* with volume number and page reference. The following abbreviations will be used for Whitman's texts: *CW*—Bucke, Harned, and Traubel (eds.), *The Complete Writings of Walt Whitman*; *LG*—*Leaves of Grass*, ed. Bradley and Blodgett; *LG 1855*—*Leaves of Grass: The First (1855) Edition*, ed. Cowley; *LG 1860*—*Leaves of Grass: Facsimile Edition of 1860 Text*, ed. Pearce, *NYD*—*New York Dissected*, ed. Holloway and Adimari. All ellipses in quotations from Whitman's texts are in the original except where placed in brackets.

the history carried in language; the signs will interpret themselves. Therefore, words "stand for things," as Whitman writes, insofar as they contain
within their scope all history, that is, all languages. The things represented
by words are themselves signs. Finally, we may conclude that slang is not
an original speech but what we might call an ur-rhetoric, a "primary" metaphoricity that permits the continuous production of signs.

Slang is that element in Whitman's speculations that moves him from
philology, or an evolutionary theory of language, to a rhetoric wherein both
the linear temporality implied by the geological metaphor and suprahistorical organic metaphors fail to suffice: "Slang, profoundly consider'd, is
the lawless germinal element, below all words and sentences, and behind
all poetry, and proves a certain perennial rankness and protestantism in
speech. . . . Such is Slang, or indirection, an attempt of common humanity
to escape from bald literalism, and express itself illimitably, which in highest walks produces poets and poems, and doubtless in pre-historic times gave
the start to, and perfected, the whole immense tangle of the old mytholo-
gies" (PW.II.572–73). As the "germinal element" underlying words, slang
is an ever-present origin allowing for the simultaneous investigation into
the past and present of words. This investigation, however, does not follow
a linear path, for it must be indirect, that is, rhetorical. In defining slang as
"indirection," the desire "to escape from bald literalism," Whitman turns
slang away from a primal speech toward a belated attempt to return language to metaphor.

Later in the essay, Whitman offers a curious foundation of slang as a belated origin: "Daring as it is to say so, in the growth of Language it is certain that the retrospect of slang from the start would be the recalling from
their nebulous conditions of all that is poetical in the stores of human utterance" (PW.II.574). To recall the poetical hidden within language, one
must begin by looking back. Slang, we may conclude, is an "original" recapitulation of the poetical and, as such, is a "first" metaphor, a reminder
of the figurative status of beginnings.

Whitman's conception of Leaves of Grass varied over the years. In "A
Backward Glance," he speaks of it as the record of one man's thoughts and
observations. In a note his executor, Bucke, dates June, 1857, Whitman refers to his third edition as "The Great Construction of the New Bible"
(CW.IX.6). At other times he describes it as a work of history or even as a

type of encyclopedia. But the one thing he continually denied to *Leaves of Grass* was any claim to originality—in the vulgar sense. In "Song of Myself," he embraces the past: "These are the thoughts of all men in all ages and lands, they are not original with me" (*LG 1855*, p. 41). The past, however, is not present to the poet; it must be discovered: "No result exists now without being from its long antecedent result, and that from its antecedent, and so backward without the farthest mentionable spot coming a bit nearer the beginning than any other spot" (*LG 1855*, pp. 20–21). Whitman dispels any belief in a simple origin, a generative point from which all history descends, for his endless chain of antecedents does not return history to a fixed origin, however remote it may be. Moreover, he rejects linear temporality altogether. No one point in time comes any nearer to a beginning than does any other point. The use of "beginning" rather than "origin" casts doubt upon the very notion of cause and effect, for the beginning is but the "antecedent result" and, thereby, both beginning and end. Henceforth, says Whitman,

> You shall no longer take things at second or third
> hand . . . . nor look through the eyes of the
> dead . . . . nor feed on the spectres in books,
> You shall not look through my eyes either, nor take
> things from me,
> You shall listen to all sides and filter them from
> yourself. (*LG 1855*, p. 26)

Because the antecedent no longer is privileged by a notion of temporal priority, the concept of the self is also without priority. If the reader "shall possess the origin of all poems," he will not do so through the agency of the poet. Having removed from the present a fecundating origin, Whitman also removes from behind the poem a creative consciousness. There is no antecedent for the Me Myself. Consequently, Whitman does "not talk of the beginning or the end. There was never any more inception that there is now" (*LG 1855*, p. 26). Inception lies all around us waiting to be discovered in the present moment.

The poet's pathway to the present, however, must be through language, and this pathway, says Whitman, proceeds originally by indirection, or diacritically, but not dialectically, regardless of his identification of his theory with "Hegelian formulas." In the 1855 preface he writes, "The expression of the American poet is to be transcendent and new. It is to be indirect and not direct or descriptive or epic. Its quality goes through these to much more" (*LG 1855*, p. 8). Although Whitman also writes that the poet "shall go directly to the creation," the path leading there has already been laid. The poet's aim is not to find, in the manner of Thoreau, new ground to break, for the scarifier has left no place unturned, and the compositions of the past have already fertilized the ground. To go directly to the creation, he must proceed indirectly along the byways of language, for it is in the byways that the "new" is discovered. "Laws for Creations," Whitman writes, are headed by "the divine law of indirections": "There shall be no subject but it shall be treated with reference to the ensemble of the world, and the compact truth of the world—And no coward or copyist shall be allowed;/ There shall be no subject too pronounced—All works shall illustrate the divine law of indirections" (*LG 1860*, p. 185). The copyist is he who respects "bald literalism," the facts, but indirection has no place for facts: "The facts are useful and real . . . . they are not my dwelling . . . . I enter by them to an area of the dwelling" (*LG 1855*, p. 47). To find a suitable dwelling, the poet must give himself over to the indirect, that is, to writing and history.

Whitman's escape from "bald literalism" is an escape from both linear and cyclical conceptions of time, for history, along with the new, lies in language. Thus, Whitman closes his essay on slang by comparing philology to geology. The recovery of the past will be through means of a linguistic retrospection—an original remembering of the past. There can be no direct knowledge of the past, for that would mean a lapse into the dualism he rejects: "The indirect is always as great and real as the direct. The spirit receives from the body just as much as it gives to the body" (*LG 1855*, p. 19). Like language, the body too is defined as "indirection," which conforms to Whitman's equation of writing with the poet's body. To speak, therefore, of "a retrospect from the start" as an original re-membering means that the reader re-gathers the limbs of Osiris, or the poet; hence, his claim that "The reader will always have his or her part to do, just as much as I have had mine" (*LG*, p. 570).

The poet's part, writes Whitman, is to bring "the spirit of any or all events and passions and scenes and persons some more and some less to bear on your individual character as you hear or read. To do this well is to compete with the laws that pursue and follow time" (*LG 1855*, p. 12). While he never quite spells out what the laws that follow time are, Whitman does indicate that the poet rejects the possibility that time is bound by laws; thus, he refers to laws that follow time and not laws of time. His attack focuses on a linear concept of time that says the grandeur of man lies in the past, and the poet must "trot back generation after generation to the eastern records! As if the beauty and sacredness of the demonstrable must fall behind that of the mythical" (*LG 1855*, p. 6). Once time is conceived upon a linear model, "beauty and sacredness" are consigned to an irrecoverable past. Whitman never denies the past in some belief that an absolute present could thereby be reached. He began his career by announcing, "America does not repel the past" (*LG 1855*, p. 5). And toward the end of his life, he wrote in "A Backward Glance," "The New World receives with joy the poems of the antique" (*LG*, p. 567).

When R. W. B. Lewis writes that Whitman "moved forward because it was the only direction (he makes us think) in which he could move; because there was nothing behind him," he does not take into account Whitman's declarations that America does not reject the past.[2] Rather than turn his back on the past, Whitman goes as far as to claim the poet is not at all original. To resurrect the dead is to place the past before him, whereas accepting the past as dead cuts oneself off from the present. Philology, according to Whitman, would be the articulation of the present into a past and a future that, as we shall see, prevent the present from coming into existence. We know the present only in retrospect. To compete with the laws that pursue time, therefore, is to reject precisely that belief in history that says the past is lost and the future is yet to be.

In place of this demeaning concept of time, Whitman announces: "Past and present and future are not disjoined but joined. The greatest poet forms the consistence of what is to be from what has been and is. He drags the dead out of their coffins and stands them again on their feet . . . he says to the past, Rise and walk before me that I may realize you. He learns the lesson . . . he places himself where the future becomes present" (*LG 1855*, p. 12). In a splendid analysis of Whitman's Preface, Paul Bové points out how this passage reveals Whitman's acute sense of time: "Because the past, present, and future do not exist independently, the American poet who hopes to build a tradition out of the present for the future must begin by rediscovering what the now 'defunct' tradition of Europe offers. The 'les-

2. R. W. B. Lewis, *The American Adam*, 44.

son' the poet learns is of the failure of the past, why it is no longer adequate, what America must do differently to succeed."[3] Whitman's repeated use of the metonymy equating the body with the text allows us to
conclude that this resurrection of the tradition is textual—he calls, as one
from the midst of the crowd, to the texts of the past to stand before him so
he may realize them, that is, repeat them. His poem will be a retrospect
from the start, a looking behind that will bring forth a "new" poem. The
poet is he who begins by looking backward.

Whitman's declaration is a translation of Emerson's admonishment, "Our
age is retrospective. It builds the sepulchres of the fathers" (W.I.3). To ap-
prehend the past is to give it shape, albeit a cadaverous one. Whitman,
however, implies that the past responds to his call before he can realize it.
Thinking, therefore, is belated, a realizing of what is always already at hand.
Consequently, the poet does not place himself in the present, because
Whitman's denial of the immediacy of either perception or conception displaces the present in the undecidable difference between reading and writing. The present, therefore, is realized only in and through language. The
question remains, however, whether a rhetorical model of history can be
resolved by a hermeneutics, for this would, as Bové claims for Whitman,
locate temporality in the individual.

The poet, writes Bové, opens up the future, thereby demonstrating,
"man's being as potentiality": "The poet lives on the verge, on the boundary between what is and has been within life and tradition and what is not
yet; he creates in the gap between the actuality defined by the past and
present and the potentialities which the future, growing out of the past and
present with which it is conjoined, presents."[4] Bové goes on to point out
the inappropriateness of the term *presents* when discussing Whitman's
sense of history, because the poet's vision into the "realms of death and
Being" is a vision into the "ineffable" or "un-presentable." Bové here
transforms indirection into a failed means of representation, an approxi-
mating in language the visionary insight of the poet.

The place "where the future becomes present" is not the present; it is
the place where reading occurs. I use the term *reading* to distinguish a rhetorical analysis of Whitman from Bové's Heideggerian hermeneutics. In

3. Bové, *Destructive Poetics*, 145.
4. *Ibid.*, 147.

order to establish Whitman as the poet of unending process, Bové must resort to a fairly traditional scheme of literary history. Whitman's break with
a merely aesthetic concept of tradition, one that lacks "true" historical sense,
depends upon a misreading of Emerson. To maintain the divisions between
Romanticism, modernism, and post-modernism, Bové must read Emerson
as tradition has taught us to read him—as an idealist. Whitman, therefore,
fails to be truly radical because he retains Emerson's "mystified" rhetoric
of the " 'Soul' " and "of the correspondence between this world and another spiritual realm."[5] Despite his failure to free himself from tradition,
Whitman represents a new beginning for American poetry that Stevens and
Charles Olson were to extend along two distinct lines descending from
Leaves of Grass.

Bové's Emerson is a fiction, as every reading of Emerson must be, designed to provide a "tradition" against which Whitman can rebel. He could
have turned to Emerson himself, who warns in "Brahma": "They reckon
ill who leave me out;/ When me they fly, I am the wings" (W.IX.195).
Emerson makes possible the flight from influence that he urges upon all
poets and thereby assures all will fail to escape him. (Emerson's monstrous
joke upon America was to set himself up as the patron saint of self-reliance
and then deny independence to posterity. Perhaps the only effective way
to escape Emerson is to be his slavish imitator.) Bové also has Whitman's
essay, "Emerson's Books, (The Shadows of Them)," to sanction this misappropriation. But rather than turn there for Whitman's praise of Emerson's acute awareness of the writer's need to destroy his precursors, I will
examine but one of several instances where Whitman appropriates Emerson's lesson. Near the end of "Song of Myself" he writes,

> I am the teacher of athletes,
> He that by me spreads a wider breast than my own
>   proves the width of my own,
> He most honors my style who learns under it
>   to destroy the teacher. (*LG 1855*, p. 81)

Whitman will almost quote this last line verbatim twenty-five years later
at the conclusion of his essay on Emerson. He also expresses the same sentiment in the 1860 poem, "So Long!," where he writes, "I invite defiance,
and to make myself superseded" (*LG 1860*, p. 452). Whitman displaces

5. *Ibid.*, 151.

Emerson as the giant and calls upon his ephebes, as Stevens calls the young poets, to destroy him, thereby proving Emerson's continued dominance, for Whitman can only repeat a gesture that he learned from Emerson and, hence, ensures that his teacher will be resurrected, even if it means the present will remain interred.

Bové's reading of Whitman is another such belated response to Emerson. This emerges when he complains of Whitman's failure to realize that his "belief in the centrality of a transcendent realm [a belief Bové attributes to Emerson's influence] is in direct opposition to his discussion of ongoing dis-covery as 'ceaseless rings,' which he suggests are to dis-orient and unsettle the habitual." The metaphor of "ceaseless rings" is certainly Emersonian and could very well be drawn directly from "Circles," where Emerson writes of life as "a self-evolving circle" of ever-enlarging rings and declares his aim is to "dis-orient": "Do not set the least value on what I do, or the least discredit on what I do not, as if I pretended to settle anything as true or false. I unsettle all things. No facts are to me sacred; none are profane; I simply experiment, an endless seeker with no Past at my back" (W.II.318). Although Bové might call the final remark an example of Emerson's denial of history, "Past" is here used as a synonym for tradition. In order to turn Whitman into the source of a decentered poetics wherein openness to history is maintained, Bové must read Emerson as a mystified spokesman for an Adamic literature, thereby providing the semblance or illusion from which Whitman's truth can emerge. In other words, the residual language of self, origins, and the new that remains in Whitman's text is the historical sediment of an Emersonianism that Whitman inherits and must use in the very process of destroying it. Whitman's language, therefore, is authentic; Emerson's remains mystified. Hence, Bové can maintain the priority of a literary language as opposed to the language of the "they," to use his Heideggerian term for the public language that levels down all possibilities of Being to mere averageness.[6]

Emersonianism, therefore, is the other from which Whitman must wrest an authentic self. Bové restores to Emerson's texts the language of traditional humanism that Whitman will subsequently destroy. Without this Emerson, there will be no veil that a hermeneutics will destroy in order that truth may emerge. If, as I have been suggesting, no such Emerson exists for Whitman, then his poetry only appears to lend itself to a Heideg-

6. Ibid., Heidegger, Being and Time, 164–65.

gerian hermeneutics that confirms the presence of Dasein in the world. In place of this hermeneutics, I propose that we substitute a rhetorical mode of reading suggested by Emerson's "Quotation and Originality," wherein the endlessness of interpretation is not attributed to a dialectical relation between error and truth but is the inevitable product of language itself. Whitman's texts are not a destruction of Emerson's but a troping of them— a doubling of an "original" metaphoricity that denies the possibility of reading as that which permits the discovery of truth. Emerson's theory of quotation disrupts the temporal relation between reader and text, or writer and language, that allows one to speak of conceptualizing truth or recovering from a sedimented language the ontological grounds for truth.

This problematic of discovery locates itself in the horizon, the place where each of the three *ecstases* of temporality—"the future, the character of having been, and the Present"—discloses itself. The future is always mentioned first, says Heidegger, because "primordial and authentic temporality temporalizes itself in terms of the authentic future and in such a way that in having been futurally, it first of all awakens the Present. *The primary phenomenon of primordial and authentic temporality is the future.*"[7] The common understanding of time is that of an unending succession of nows.

Emerson seems to retain this "inauthentic" understanding of time when he writes, "Life is a series of surprises, and would not be worth taking or keeping if it were not. God delights to isolate us every day, and hide from us the past and the future. . . . 'You will not remember,' he seems to say, 'and you will not expect'" (W.III.67–68). The inability to recall the past or anticipate the future frees man to live in the present. For Emerson, however, this failure of memory—the future cannot be anticipated without a past from which one projects one's expectations—is part of a refusal to maintain the principle of self-identity upon which the metaphysics of originality rests. Therefore, rather than insist upon the purity of the present moment, Emerson allegorizes our understanding of temporality as an opposition between either reader and text or the Me and Not Me, which Whitman translates into the Me Myself and the "other I am."

In the introduction to *Nature*, Emerson writes, "Undoubtedly we have no questions to ask which are unanswerable. We must trust the perfection of the creation so far as to believe that whatever curiosity the order of things

7. Heidegger, *Being and Time*, 377–78.

has awakened in our minds, the order of things can satisfy. Every man's condition is a solution in hieroglyphic to those inquiries he would put. He acts it as life, before he apprehends it as truth" (W.I.3–4). To ask a question we must already possess the answer, and our answers are found in the structure of the world—in order to think, there must be an object at which thought must be directed. So far, Emerson seems to be arguing for the compatibility between world and mind, but when he declares that "man's condition is a solution in hieroglyphic," he translates the phenomenological relation between mind and nature into tropology, a doubling of what is already a metaphorical and, therefore, multiple sign. Even when he says man acts the answer "before he apprehends it as truth," he not only reveals the belatedness of what we call "truth" but also defines truth as tautology. "Language" presents the fullest statement on this concept of truth, but "The Poet" offers a succinct formulation of this principle: "Words and deeds are quite indifferent modes of the divine energy. Words are also actions, and actions are a kind of words" (W.III.8). Thus, if words are acts and acts are words, we cannot speak, on the one hand, of life in terms of immediacy and, on the other, truth as a reflective mirroring of life. The relation of truth to life resembles that of the figurative to the literal, except that in Emerson's scheme the literal is itself a figure—the figure of the Sphinx, to be precise, which is itself a catachresis.

When Emerson asks, "Why should not we also enjoy an original relation to the universe?" (W.I.3), he is not asking for unmediated access to truth. Although "original relation" means a nonderivative relation, *original* may also mean "derived from something" and, therefore, "derivative" (OED). But even if we dismiss this uncanny negation of the word's "primary" meaning, the phrase "original relation" is itself an oxymoron. Although *relation* is defined as "connection" or "association," it also means "the act of relating in words" or "narration." Emerson's question contains its own answer—an "original relation" is a fiction derived from the inquiries man puts to nature, which are themselves the belated interpretations of actions and, consequently, not without their presuppositions. The position one has relative to the universe is determined by language. To ask a question is to discover the "solution in hieroglyphic"; that is, in the interpretation that renders past action as "truth," we discover our past as that which lies before us.

What Emerson calls the "solution in hieroglyphic," Heidegger calls the "fore-conception" we have in advance of any interpretation: "An inter-

pretation is never a presuppositionless apprehending of something presented to us. If, when one is engaged in a particular concrete kind of interpretation, in the sense of exact textual Interpretation, one likes to appeal
[*beruft*] to what 'stands there,' then one finds what 'stands there' in the
first instance is nothing other than the obvious undiscovered assumption
[*Vormeinung*] of the person who does the interpreting." The meaning that
is discovered there in the text "has been presented in our fore-having, our
fore-sight, and our fore-conception."[8] What distinguishes Emerson's concept of the past from Heidegger's is the essential role played by the interpreter in the latter's hermeneutics. No interpreter is needed in Emerson's
theory of signs; this is precisely the point where Whitman converges with
Emerson. And although Bové amply demonstrates the great value a Heideggerian hermeneutics has for the reading of American poetry, Josiah
Royce's reading of C. S. Peirce offers an "American" strategy for understanding the relation of language to history.

Royce may have been the first to recognize the possibility of a semiotics
of history. Although in *The Problem of Christianity* he confuses Peirce's
"interpretant" with "interpreter" and ultimately appropriates semiotics for
onto-theological ends, he points the way to a semiotic, rather than her-
meneutical, process of relating past, present, and future. He applied Peirce's
triadic system of interpretant, representamen, and object to a theory of
interpretation modeled after translation: "One of the three terms is the interpretant; a second term is the object—the person or the meaning or the
text—which is interpreted; the third is the person to whom the interpretation is addressed." Here is the passage from Peirce that Royce adapts:

> A sign stands *for* something *to* the idea which it produces, or modifies. Or,
> it is a vehicle conveying into the mind something from without. That for
> which it stands is called its *object*, that which it conveys, its *meaning*; and
> the idea to which it gives rise, its *interpretant*. The object of representation
> can be nothing but a representation of which the first representation is the
> interpretant. But an endless series of representations, each representing
> the one behind it, may be conceived to have an absolute object at its limit.
> The meaning of a representation can be nothing but a representation. . . .
> So there is an infinite regression here. Finally, the interpretant is nothing
> but another representation to which the torch of truth is handed along;
> and as a representation, it has its interpretant again. Lo, another infinite
> series.

8. *Ibid.*, 191–92.

It is essential to note the unending chain of signification that Peirce calls "semiosis." As Paul de Man has said, "The interpretation of the sign is not, for Peirce, a meaning but another sign; it is a reading, not a decodage, and this reading has, in its turn, to be interpreted into another sign, and so on *ad infinitum*."[9] Thought, therefore, is an unlimited chain of representations that can never lead to a pure or innocent referent—to an object "outside" of language or to a univocal meaning *within* it—or to a thinking subject.

Royce, however, still maintains the subject, but as Umberto Eco has demonstrated, "The *interpretant is not the interpreter.* . . . The interpretant is that which guarantees the validity of the sign, even in the absence of the interpreter." As Peirce says in the passage quoted above, the interpretant is another representation. I have no wish to belabor the fact that Royce misinterprets Peirce. What is important, however, is his application of the triad to the terms *past, present,* and *future.* The continuity of history depends upon the infinite process of interpretation that renders the past for the future. The present is defined as "the interpretation of the past to the future." What makes Royce's adaptation interesting is his reduction of experience to "a realm of signs." We regard the signs of past time as real "because we view our memories as signs which need and possess their interpretations," and "we regard our expectations as signs of a future."[10] The present, therefore, does not exist; it is the interpretation of the past for the future. Thus, Royce offers in semiotic terms Heidegger's existential concept that the past lies in our future. What distinguishes a semiotic from a hermeneutic formulation of this scheme is that the former denies the possibility that the past, present, and future can be unified or that there can be any going beyond the chain of signs. Royce, however, does not share Peirce's logical rigor and, thus, turns the semiotic process into a teleological one. It is Whitman who provides a semiotic model of time.

I would like to return to Whitman's curious formulation of the poet's place in history: "he places himself where the future becomes present." This place

9. Royce, *The Problem of Christianity*, II, 142; Hartsthorne and Weiss (eds.), *Collected Papers of Charles Sanders Peirce*, I, 171; de Man, *Allegories of Reading*, 9. I am grateful to Charles Bigger for introducing me to Royce's *The Problem of Christianity* and explaining its importance for hermeneutics and the philosophy of history.
10. Eco, *A Theory of Semiotics*, 68; Royce, *The Problem of Christianity*, II, 147, 289–90.

is most emphatically not a pure present. He does not stand with Thoreau "on the meeting of two eternities, the past and future, which is precisely the present moment" (*W.* p. 10). The place "where the future becomes present" is the past, the place where retrospection begins. The risen corpse of the past walks in the future but is realized by the poet in what is never quite the present. We have already seen how Royce defines the present as that which interprets the past for the future; consequently, there is no present available for consciousness. To Royce's triad of past, interpreter, future, which is based on Peirce's representamen, object, interpretant, we may add Whitman's triad of poet, reader, text. But Whitman is closer to Peirce than to Royce in that his semiotic is without a subject; thus, he denies that his text is original, let alone complete.

I admit, to deny there is a subject in Whitman's poems, including "Song of Myself," may seem heretical, even foolish. After all, no single topic in Whitman criticism has received so much attention and given cause for so little anxiety as the Whitmanesque trope of the self. The following remark by Roy Harvey Pearce is typical of this untroubled acceptance of Whitman's Me Myself: "Whitman is the supremely realized Emersonian poet— the simple, separate person sufficiently free of theoretical concerns to let his ego roam . . . and endow the world with its utterly human perfection." Affirmations of the integrity of the poetic self in Whitman can easily be multiplied. Even recent challenges to our common understanding of Whitman have not strayed too far from an unproblematic view of the Whitmanesque self. John Irwin, for instance, writes that in Whitman's trope of song, "the poet's self [fuses] with the song, and the song with the world." Irwin takes as metaphor what is, in fact, a metonymy and, thus, idealizes Whitman's text. Even Harold Bloom, a critic who thrives on so-called heresies, finds in "Song of Myself" several Whitmans, variously referred to as "my self, my soul and the real Me or Me myself," which he easily assimilates to a notion of persona, thereby transforming the potentially disintegrative force of these multiple selves into outer expressions of an "inmost self."[11] Bloom's Whitman begins to sound suspiciously like T. S. Eliot.

The number of selves in Whitman's poetry, however, is hardly exhausted by Bloom's catalogue. Nevertheless, enumerating these Whit-

---

11. Pearce, *The Continuity of American Poetry*, 164; Irwin, *American Hieroglyphics*, 39; Bloom, *Agon*, 26–28.

AMERICAN POETICS OF HISTORY / 104

mans will bring us no closer to what is at issue, for Whitman's insistence upon the physicality of both the soul and his book provides the totalizing metaphor that apparently reconciles multiplicity with the One: the book is at once the poet and the focal point into which all things flow; hence, the poet is the least personal of men. This metonymy—the song is its creator—has all the force of a metaphor. Furthermore, it represents an attempt to undo Emerson's denial of the union of voice, book, and self. The Not Me, after all, includes writing.

In order to sustain the totalizing force of his metaphor, Whitman must suppress its status as metonymy. As metaphor, the poet/book is a spatial representation of a narrative process, the passage of the self toward the integration in the Real Me. The contingency of a metonymy is denied in favor of the necessary link of metaphor to what it represents.[12] In order to present his text as metaphor, however, he must turn from figure to statement. In other words, the spatialized narrative threatens to break down into a fragmented series of contiguous events. He therefore asserts the unity by declaring himself "the poet of the body,/ And [. . .] the poet of the soul" (*LG 1855*, p. 44), thus transforming the Not Me into the Me and maintaining the two in a closed system where the narrative is a self-reading.

The Peircean triad as translated by Royce, wherein the present interprets the past to the future, becomes the poet interpreting his text to himself. Yet the interpretation always remains belated; it can never be a direct representation of consciousness. Instead, it is the interpretation of a sign (the text or the past) for the reader (a receiver who waits in the future) by a poet who is himself a sign constituted by this chain of signification. To transform the diachronic process of reading into a stable moment, Whitman will present his narrative as a self-reading, but as we shall see, the self can only be read if it is absent.

The task of disclosing the past, however, does not rest entirely with the poet, nor does the new demand stylistic innovation. If this were the case, Whitman would merely be repeating platitudes about originality, rather than presenting the radical revision of history that he does. In his Preface, his argument for the impersonality of the poet is closer to Emerson's theory than to Eliot's: "The greatest poet has less a marked style and is more

12. De Man, *Allegories of Reading*, 63.

the channel of thoughts and things without increase and diminution, and is the free channel of himself. He swears to his art, I will not be meddlesome, I will not have in my writing any elegance or effect or originality to hang in the way between me and the rest like curtains. [. . .] What I experience or portray shall go from my composition without a shred of my composition. You shall stand by my side and look in the mirror with me" (*LG 1855*, p. 13). What begins as a fairly familiar argument for the poet as spokesman for his age turns into a rejection of language as either mediation or the embodiment of unmediated vision. The poet and the reader will stand together before the mirror, his book. Nor is this a recuperation of a mimetic theory of language and, thus, a return to mediation. Whitman's shocking proposition is that his book *is* nature and nature is his book.

When the child asks, "What is the grass?" we are compelled to think that one answer is the poem itself. And this is more than a mere pun on Whitman's part. Yet he never directly gives this answer; instead, he suggests "it is a uniform hieroglyphic"

> Or I guess it is the handkerchief of the Lord,
> A scented gift and remembrancer designedly dropped,
> Bearing the owner's name someway in the corners, that
> we may see and remark, and say Whose? (*LG 1855*, p. 29)

The grass, then, is the reminder of God's absence: it is a metaphor, His uncertain signature, that forces man to think that there must be a designer who has left this sign. The textualizing of the grass continues when Whitman says,

> And now it seems to me the beautiful uncut hair
> of graves. [. . .]
> This grass is very dark to be from the white
> heads of old mothers,
> Darker than the colorless beards of old men,
> Dark to come from under the faint red roofs of mouths.
>
> O I perceive after all so many uttering tongues!
> And I perceive they do not come from the roofs of
> mouths for nothing.
>
> I wish I could translate the hints about the dead
> young men and women,
> And the hints about old men and mothers, and the
> offspring taken soon out of their laps. (*LG 1855*, p. 30)

I will return to Whitman's insistence that he is a translator when I examine "Out of the Cradle Endlessly Rocking." Here, I wish to point out the conflation of the metaphor of the grass with God, hieroglyphics, signatures, death, the body, and tongues. In various ways, these are all images for *Leaves of Grass*, which Irwin has shown to have been conceived "as a kind of hieroglyphic Bible."[13] Whitman's association of the poem with a hieroglyphic does not, as Irwin proves, turn his book into a picture book mirroring the natural and spiritual worlds, for the book does not lead beyond its signs to spirit or nature but is no different from either one. Whitman's world is an ensemble, to use his word, where everything is equal, that is, without distinction of surface and depth, inside and outside, or body and spirit. Speech, therefore, does not represent the self, for Whitman uses "tongues" not as a metonymy for speech but as a synecdoche for the body and, ultimately, as a metaphor for writing.

Not only is the text a sign, but so are the poet and reader. They are locked in the chain which produces meaning. What Whitman calls the ensemble is a semantic field of signs leading to signs *ad infinitum*. This is why history is not to be conceived of as a tracing back of antecedents to a pure origin—no one sign is greater than another sign. "The great poet," writes Whitman, "is the equable man" (*LG 1855*, p. 8).

"Crossing Brooklyn Ferry" presents most succinctly Whitman's rhetoric of history. (Peirce's characterization of semiotics as "pure rhetoric" allows for this substitution of *rhetoric* for *semiotics*.[14] I choose the former because it conveys a notion of reading, and, as we shall see, Whitman's semiosis is generated by tropes.) The poem is staged as the poet's apostrophe to his future readers while he crosses from Manhattan to Brooklyn. Thus, the present moment is pictured as a literal and figural crossing. The figural crossing of time takes place when Whitman turns from the scene before him and addresses his future readers: "And you that shall cross from shore to shore years hence, are more to me, and more in my meditations, than you might suppose" (*LG 1860*, p. 379). The poet's address is a projection, to use one of Whitman's favorite terms, of a nonexistent audience, his future readers. In other words, his poem contains its readers, who are, along

13. Irwin, *American Hieroglyphics*, 31.
14. See "Division of Signs," in Hartshorne and Weiss (eds.), *Collected Papers of Charles Sanders Peirce*, II, 135–36.

with the poet, "disintegrated, yet part of the scheme,/ The similitudes of
the past, and those of the future." Historical time, "the scheme" that joins
past, present, and future, is a trope, an allegory of poets and readers.

The poet's address to his future readers is predicated on the infinite repetition of the scene of crossing—his future readers will see the same sun-
set, flood and ebb tide. Yet this is not simply an anticipation of what is to
come—only the later Whitman will confuse apostrophe with prophecy—
it is a retrospection from the start, a remembering of what the future will
bring:

> It avails not, neither time or place—distance
>   avails not,
> I am with you, you men and women of a generation,
>   or ever so many generations hence,
> I project myself—also I return—I am with you, and
>   know how it is.   (LG 1860, p. 380)

As in "Out of the Cradle Endlessly Rocking," the poet projects into the future what is, in fact, a past experience. The aim of poetry is to make the
future present, and in order to so, he must return to the past. Hence, the
poet no longer speaks of an audience to be, but writes of a poet who once
looked upon the river and sky and was "one of a crowd," "Just as any of
you is one of a living crowd." Apostrophe has brought him "face to face"
with the future and, in so doing, has given face (prosopopoeia) to the past.
Paul de Man has written, "Prosopopoeia, the trope of apostrophe . . . means
to give a face and therefore implies that the original can be missing or nonexistent." [15] We might say of Whitman's poetry that reading gives a face
to the poet and time.

The reversal of present and future, or metalepsis, is the product of the
exchange of prosopopoeia for apostrophe. The direct discourse of apostrophe gives the illusion of addressing an audience; it is, to borrow de Man's
phrase, the "rhetorization of grammar," a transformation of the second-
person pronoun into a trope. It is not, however, a representation of an
imaginary audience, for it does not bring the poet before the audience, but
points to the distance between him and the reader. The reader, Whitman
implies, is an imaginary sign that exists as a function of grammar—it is
the "you" of direct discourse. Whitman's hyperbolic extension of the tem-

15. De Man, "Hypogram and Inscription," 30. I am also indebted to de Man's discussion
of disfiguration in "Shelley Disfigured," 39–73, esp. 68–69.

poral distance separating poet and reader places the book in the past. His apostrophe, therefore, projects into the future what is fixed in the writer's past, thereby breaking the illusion of the permanent presence of writing. Finally, apostrophe gives way to prosopopoeia as the projection into the future gives face, not to the audience, but to an absent poet, one who calls from the past. In other words, he addresses his audience in the present tense, but speaks of himself in the past. He can, therefore, say, "I too many a time crossed the river" (*LG 1860*, p. 381). The single crossing with which the poem began has multiplied, but only as the poet has transformed the voice of self-presence into a call from the grave.

A similar moment of projection and return occurs in Section 25 of "Song of Myself" when the poet announces:

> My voice goes after what my eyes cannot reach,
> With the twirl of my tongue I encompass worlds
> and volumes of worlds.
>
> Speech is the twin of my vision . . . . it is
> unequal to measure itself.
>
> It provokes me forever,
> It says sarcastically, Walt, you understand enough
> . . . . why don't you let it out then?   (*LG 1855*, pp. 50–51)

The voice is the forerunner of the eternal world, but Whitman does not invest the voice with the weight of self-presence. Just as both body and soul never quite seem to be the I Am, but are the "other I am," an other without a dialectical opposite, so the voice is something other than the poet or his poem. To be "unequal to measure" means not only that the voice is beyond calculation but also that it exceeds tradition, that is, the measure of the English iambic pentameter line. Rather than serve as a sign of self-presence, speech is apostrophe, a self-address that leads him into an unrealized future. Yet he resists the voice that provokes: "Come now I will not be tantalized . . . . you conceive too much of articulation" (*LG 1855*, p. 51). The body of writing, the book, fails to encompass the poet:

> Writing and talk do not prove me,
> I carry the plenum of proof and every thing else
> in my face,
> With the hush of my lips I confound the topmost
> skeptic.   (*LG 1855*, p. 51)

Whitman rejects writing as the embodiment of speech or the externaliza-
tion of an interior self. Consequently, the face that carries "the plenum of
proof" denies the dualism inherent in a conventional notion of speech and
reinscribes the self as a memory trace, thereby transforming the inside/
outside metaphor of mind/body or self/writing into a temporal relation
wherein the self is known only as an inscription or, better, as prosopopoeia,
the personification of the past.

This rejection of dualism is part of Whitman's disruption of linear temporality and the metaphysics of self-presence that guarantees the conformity of past and future with the present. When Whitman tells his readers
of a "hundred years hence," "I project myself to tell you—also I return,"
he divorces language from voice (*LG 1860*, p. 382; this line was eliminated
in 1881). The address depends strictly upon the phenomenality of inscription and, thus, on the necessary absence of the self. For the moment exists
where the future become present, that is, in the past, where we find the
poet looking forward to the reader:

> The men and women I saw were all near to me,
> Others the same—others who look back on me,
>   because I looked forward to them,
> (The time will come, though I stop here to-day
>   and to-night.)   (*LG 1860*, p. 382)

By looking forward, the poet retrieves the future and makes it the past,
which is precisely the "present" moment—the present is a similitude, an
allegorical crossing between past and future. In other words, the present is,
to borrow de Man's term, an allegory of reading, a narrative of the act of
reading that tells of the the impossibility of reading.[16]

Whitman's trope for reading is the chiasmus, or the crossing wherein
the past becomes the future, and the future becomes the past. In this crossing, the present moment exists, it seems, as the act of reading, which repeats the temporal crossing allegorized as the poet's crossing on the Brooklyn ferry. There is never an unmediated moment wherein the consciousness
of a reader recovers the consciousness of the poet. Whitman stages the
reading as a look backward into the past that repeats the poet's gesture of
looking forward into the future. The common link between these two mo-

16. De Man, *Allegories of Reading*, 77.

ments is the iterability of the crossing itself. Thus, the poem offers itself as a metaphor—the crossing is a figure for the act of reading.

Yet the relation between the figural (the crossing) and the literal (the reading) depends upon metonymy, the crossing that brings literal and figural into a contingent relationship. This contingency is insisted upon as the reader's glance backward is made possible by the poet who "looked forward to them." Whitman's use of the past tense at this point displaces the reading from a present—the relation between past and future is recognized belatedly as a conjoining of two moments in the body of the poem: "I too had received identity by my body,/That I was, I knew was of my body—and what I should be, I knew I should be of my body" (*LG 1860*, p. 383). These lines reflect Whitman's rejection of the Cartesian cogito; that he *was* and what he should be, he knew by his body. Again, the present seems to appear only as a statement, as a direct address to the reader. The tense of the assertion, however, is the past. What the poet *is*, we might say, is the lines of his poem. But if this moment is to be realized, it must be in the consciousness of a reader who actualizes the consciousness of the poet:

> Closer yet I approach you,
> What thought you have of me, I had as much as you
>   —I laid in my stores in advance,
> I considered long and seriously of you before you
>   were born.
>
> Who was to know what should come home to me?
> Who knows but I am enjoying this?
> Who knows but I am as good as looking at you now,
>   for all you cannot see me?   (*LG 1860*, pp. 384–85)

Whitman's trope for the poem as the poet's body argues for a coincidence of the text and its producer. According to this interpretation, the Now exists in the act of reading. The poem's narrative is the metaphor of a specular reflection of anticipation and memory. We might claim for Whitman's narrative what de Man says of Proust: "The 'moment' and the 'narrative' would be complementary and symmetrical, specular reflections of each other that could be substituted without distortion. By an act of memory or of anticipation, the narrative can retrieve the full experience of the moment. . . . Narrative is the metaphor of the moment, as reading is the metaphor of writing." The anticipation of his future readers, which draws him to them, is mirrored by the retrospective reflections on his crossing of the river. Thus, the act of writing the narrative, as de Man argues for Proust, "would then be coextensive with the act of self-reading by means of which the narrator and the writer, now united in one, fully understand their present situation . . . by means of the retrospective recapitulation of its genesis."[17] The apostrophe to his anticipated readers brings him closer to the future, thus recapitulating the crossing of the river. In other words, the crossing of the river is synonymous with the crossing of time.

The coherence of Whitman's poem depends upon substituting the reader for the poet—in crossing the river, we cross time to see the same sights as did the poet. To achieve this substitution, however, there must be a crossing of future with past, the temporal with the spatial, and the figural with the literal. As metaphor, the narrative totalizes the processes of reading and writing in the chiastic figure of the crossing; but the proper meaning of the metaphor, the coincidence of present and future in the past, is disrupted by the temporalization of the figure. The crossing that promises to reduce the figural and literal to a specular moment ends up pointing to an irreducible temporality wherein signification is attained by an endless series of displacements. To prevent this, the poet switches from figural speech to statement:

> It is not you alone, nor I alone,
> Not a few races, nor a few generations, nor a few
>   centuries,
> It is that each came, or comes, or shall come, from
>   its due emission, without fail, either now, or
>   then, or henceforth.   (LG 1860, p. 385)

These lines, eliminated in later editions, operate according to a familiar Whitmanesque scheme—the totalization of mankind and history in the present moment, which is both the moment of writing and the address to the reader, is a metonymic, rather than metaphorical, process. There is no substitution of writer for reader here; instead, there is a denial of the necessity of either in favor of the knowledge that the succession of generations guarantees the totality that "envelops the Soul for a proper time." This succession, however, is not strictly a genetic one.

We have already noted Whitman's transformation of metaphor into narrative—the substitution of reading for writing is presented as a meta-

17. Ibid., 68, 67.

phor of crossings; a trope of logic masquerades as a trope of representation. The moment of crossing turns, by an act of anticipation, into a narrative joining past, present, and future. But this conjoining of temporal units in a successive process is a function of grammar—the conjugation of *come* and the reduction of the present moment to a syntagmatic relation ("either now, or then, or henceforth"). A present moment of writing is transformed into an infinite duration. The process whereby Whitman projects himself into the future and then turns upon the present moment of writing translates the scene of writing, the crossing, into a scene of self-reading, which, to borrow once more de Man's characterization of a similar situation in Proust, unites writer and reader in the present "by means of the retrospective recapitulation of its genesis."

The call that projects the writer into the future also draws him from out of the past. Thus, he writes, "But I was a Manhattanese, free, friendly, and proud!/ I was called by my nighest name by clear and loud voices of young men as they saw me approaching or passing" (*LG 1860*, p. 384). This acknowledgment and celebration of the physicality of existence serves as a pseudobiography accounting for the genesis of the poet and his poem. This retrospection is, we might say, a spatializing of a diachronic moment. Reading is allegorized as calling the poet's name and touching his body. By addressing a future audience on the readability of his poem, he places the understanding between poet and reader in the past. Once he locates the reading of the poem in the past, he comes into contact with the future:

> Curious what Gods can exceed these that clasp me
>   by the hand, and with voices I love call me
>   promptly and loudly by my nighest name as I
>   approach.
> Curious what is more subtle than this which ties me
>   to the woman or man that looks in my face,
> Which fuses me into you now, and pours my meaning
>   into you.   (*LG 1860*, p. 385)

On one level, the acts of touching, calling, and looking are metaphors for reading. But the totalization, or fusion, promised by contact in a spatialized moment is undone by the temporal structure of the poem, which transforms these spatialized metaphors into metonyms—contact between reader and poet is determined by contiguous relations described by the narrative.

The pouring forth of his meaning takes us back to the metaphor of crossing. The continuous flow of history that will carry him into the future is spatialized by the metaphor of sight, whose proper meaning is reading. Operating alongside these metaphors of crossing, looking, calling, and touching is the strictly spatial metonymy of the book as the poet. To hold the book is to hold the poet. Whitman's literalizing of this metonymy gives it the force of a metaphor—we are guaranteed the totalizing process whereby reading becomes a convergence of two consciousnesses, the poet's and the reader's, and of meaning and understanding:

> We understand, then, do we not?
> What I promised without mentioning it, have you not
>   accepted?
> What the study could not teach—what the preaching
>   could not accomplish is accomplished, is it not?
> What the push of reading could not start is started
>   by me personally, is it not?   (*LG 1860*, p. 386)

Whitman eventually canceled this last line, which denies the mutual participation between reader and poet in the act of understanding. Yet the line only makes obvious the shifting polarity of temporality/reading and spatiality/writing. Reading would be the metaphor that achieves the reconciliation of motion and stasis, for it is through reading that meaning and understanding come together.

Whitman, however, never states a meaning—understanding is achieved prior to any statement. What the final version implies, the canceled line makes explicit: writing is guaranteed by a narrative that makes writing a self-reading. The future reading, according to this scheme, repeats the act of writing. To peruse the book is to stare into a mirror: "Consider, you who peruse me, whether I may not in unknown ways be looking upon you" (*LG 1860*, p. 387). The look transposes the past act of anticipation into a present moment. Every time the book is read, the anticipation is realized in a present moment. Anticipation, we may conclude, constitutes one mode of reading, wherein the understanding of the text is repeatedly realized in the future.

Memory, or retrospection, constitutes the second mode of reading as the recapitulation of the genesis of the poem. These two modes appear to be symmetrical, as the retrospection is made possible by an "original" anticipation, and the act of anticipation elicits a retrospection of the moment of writing. The power of this totalizing scheme has led critics to interpret "Crossing Brooklyn Ferry" as a hymn to "the joy of the sensuous body," the aesthetic expression of the unity of soul and body culminating "in an ecstacy of understanding," "a vision of the eternal destination of the soul," or the articulation of "a theory of imagination in which self and reality are viewed as merging in a form that transcends mortality and links mind to mind in a timeless communal bond." All these readings affirm a reconciliation of body and soul, time and the eternal, and life and death. The river serves as the undercurrent of Being that unites the individual with the eternal. Reading, therefore, is an unproblematic passage from text to the soul. Diane Middlebrook offers a succinct formulation of this interpretation: "But of course the reader is not face to face with Whitman; if the enterprise has been successful he is face to face with the poem. 'I' is the poem."[18] Like the majority of Whitman's commentators, Middlebrook moves unwaveringly from the poem as thing to the creating self that is said to lie behind it.

The poem itself becomes a metaphor, a "natural" substitution, for the poet. "Whitman"—the poem produced by him—is, as I have said, a metonymy that has all the force of a metaphor. The question, however, is whether the poet can succeed in making the writing coextensive with a self-reading and, thus, transform the present moment into an infinite duration. The poem begins with a "face to face" meeting that anticipates the meeting of poet and reader:

> Flood-tide below me! I watch you, face to face;
> Clouds of the west! sun there half an hour high!
> I see you also face to face.   (*LG 1860*, p. 379)

The poem's opening trope is a metonymy; the convergence of river, poet, and sun is, dare we say, literally a case of contingent proximity and not the causal necessity required for metaphor. From this metonymy, the poem generates all successive tropes. On the one hand, there are various tropes for reading and, on the other, there are tropes of crossing. The latter is a generalizing of the former, turning reading and the substitution of the poem for the "I" into an allegory of temporal crossings.

When, in a passage deleted from later editions, the poet declares the realization of the soul, the trope is no longer that of analogy but of synecdoche:

> We descend upon you and all things—we arrest you
> all,

18. E. H. Miller, *Walt Whitman's Poetry*, 199; Coffman, " 'Crossing Brooklyn Ferry,' " 70; Allen, "Mutations in Whitman's Art," 42; Middlebrook, *Walt Whitman and Wallace Stevens*, 106, 108–109.

> We realize the Soul only by you, you faithful
>   solids and fluids,
> Through you color, form, location, sublimity,
>   ideality,
> Through you every proof, comparison, and all the
>   suggestions and determinations of ourselves.   (*LG 1860*, pp. 387–88)

The "We"—body, soul, and the poet—realizes the soul by means of material objects. What at first seems to be a fairly standard metaphor ordered on the model of material representation of the idea and of interior being proves to be an allegory—the crossing tells of the unbridgeable gap separating the poet crossing the river from the one who apostrophizes the future audience. The illusion of convergence of the biographical figure and the speaker is given by the trope of book as body. But this trope is radically incompatible with the metaphysics of presence upon which metaphor depends, for Whitman so closely associates the body with death that the voice of the poet calling out of the book is a prosopopoeia, a speech given to an absent person. In projecting himself toward his imagined audience of the future, he displaces the narrator into the past. The future, in the crossing, lies in the past. Thus, he runs ahead of his audience and in the final apostrophe addresses his audience from a "present"—that is, a past that lies in the future:

> You have waited, you always wait, you dumb,
>   beautiful ministers! you novices!
> We receive you with free sense at last, and are
>   insatiate henceforward,
> Not you any more shall be able to foil us, or
>   withhold yourselves from us,
> We use you, and do not cast you aside—we plant
>   you permanently within us,
> We fathom you not—we love you—there is
>   perfection in you also,
> You furnish your parts toward eternity,
> Great or small, you furnish your parts toward the Soul.   (*LG 1860*, p. 388)

In these final lines, Whitman recuperates metaphysics, as the reader's part changes from completing the poem to completing "eternity" and the "Soul." Yet completion is not in sight because the reader, like the poet, is but one sign in an unlimited semiosis. Futhermore, as a sign, the reader exists as a grammatical function, and as such, language speaks through him—he is, writes Whitman, "dumb," a mute through whom language projects its "voice." The reader, finally, gives face to the poet; he memorializes the writer as an inscription. Reading is made possible by virtue of memory—the future is an a posteriori reconstruction of the past. The future, in other words, lies in the past in/as writing.

What distinguishes Whitman's concept of time from a hermeneutic one is that, for him, time is structured like a rhetoric; it is a system of tropes. At the risk of oversimplification, we might characterize a hermeneutics of temporality as a process wherein reading becomes the realizing of the past in the future; that is, the past attains meaning only through a process of interpretation that transforms the future into an actualization of our understanding of the past. Thus, we might say that Royce's misinterpretation of Peirce translates the latter's semiotics into a hermeneutics. Whitman, on the other hand, is closer to semiotics, if we understand semiotics as "pure rhetoric," to use Peirce's term once more. Pure rhetoric, as opposed to "pure grammar," is concerned with how one sign-thought gives rise to another, not with the representation or the embodiment of meaning in a sign.[19] What in a hermeneutics operates as an epistemology functions as a system of tropes in a pure rhetoric.

In "Crossing Brooklyn Ferry," he turns from the present to apostrophize an absent reader and, thereby, gives bodily existence to an imaginary speaker, one who speaks from the past, not the present. In the final Calamus poem, which immediately precedes "Crossing Brooklyn Ferry" in the 1860 edition, he writes,

> When you read these, I, that was visible, am become
>   invisible;
> Now it is you, compact, visible, realizing my poems,
>   seeking me,
> Fancying how happy you were, if I could be with
>   you, and become your lover;
> Be it as if I were you. Be not too certain but
>   I am now with you.   (LG 1860, p. 378)

Rather than read *Leaves of Grass* as autobiography, we should follow what is suggested in these lines and throughout the text: *Leaves of Grass* is an example of *auto-écriture*; it is a text that reproduces itself in its readers and, in so doing, tells the life of its writing. Regardless of any biographical spec-

19. Hartshorne and Weiss (eds.), *Collected Papers of Charles Sanders Peirce*, II, 135–36.

ulations, we can say that Whitman's audience comes into existence upon the poet's death. The invisible poet becomes visible in his readers. It would not be at all inaccurate to say that reading personifies, which is one definition of prosopopoeia, the poet; that is, reading gives a face to the dead. But the relation between apostrophe and prosopopoeia is not homologous; these two tropes do not lead to the totalization that says the reading makes the poem forever present. To bridge the gap separating the poet and the reader—past and future—Whitman must turn from metaphors of voice and, hence, self-presence to the metonymy of the book as self and, therefore, as sepulcher. To realize the past, to make the corpse rise from the grave, the poet must give a face (prosopopoeia) to death.

When Whitman changed the title of "A Word Out of the Sea," which was first published as "A Child's Reminiscence," to "Out of the Cradle Endlessly Rocking," he substituted a trope of eternity for one of death. This substitution is also reflected in the change from the past participle to the present in the first line, which read "Out of the rocked cradle" in 1859. In his introduction to the reprint of the third edition, Roy Harvey Pearce argues that the change is from the sea as "a fact of life" to sea as "symbol." According to Pearce, the later version blurs the original's clear distinction between the literal experience of the boy and the metaphorical experience of the poet.[20] Yet the role of memory in this poem, even in the earlier version, makes it difficult to maintain such a neat distinction between the literal and the figural. Experience becomes literal by virtue of notation, writing as memory trace, not by the facticity of direct experience.

The song is triggered by, among other things, "the memories of the bird that chanted to me." The bird's song, moreover, is a trope for the past. It is the phenomenalization of a childhood memory:

> From the myriad thence-aroused words,
> From the word stronger and more delicious than any,
> From such, as now they start, the scene revisiting.   (LG 1860, p. 270)

The long series of prepositional phrases culminates with the word "death," the word "more delicious than any." Yet all elements of the series, from the rocked cradle to death, are textual markers, signs out of which his poem issues:

20. Pearce, "Introduction," Leaves of Grass, xlvii.

> I, chanter of pains and joys, uniter of here and
>   hereafter,
> Taking all hints to use them—but swiftly leaping
>   beyond them,
> A reminiscence sing. (LG 1860, p. 270)

To unite the "here and hereafter," the present and the future, the poet returns to the past. This return is prompted by the signs, particularly that of death, beyond which he must leap to bring forth his memorial song. What in "Crossing Brooklyn Ferry" was characterized as a gap separating author and reader is here set forth as a division between the author and his future. And in both poems, the future is located in the past. We must distinguish Whitman's reminiscence, however, from a nostalgia for lost innocence, because the future exists in and as a memory, the notation or inscription without which there can be no temporality.

Although the adult claims to transcend language, or the hints that first stir his memory, the child refuses anything of the sort. The scene to which the adult returns is presented to us as a scene of writing, a linguistic encoding of an experience by the child who absorbs and translates the bird's song. What allows the consciousness of the past to be awakened is that this consciousness exists as a memory trace, a notation. Nor is this memory one of an unmediated childhood experience: the child is a vehicle for translation.

The first song the child hears concludes, *"Singing all time, minding no time,/ If we two but keep together"* (LG 1860, p. 271). This lie against death, as Bloom would put it, presupposes the presence of the unnamed third, the boy as translator. This poem, more than any other by Whitman, conforms to Bloom's map of poetic crossings. Taking Bloom as our Baedeker, we find the movement from the introduction to the reminiscence is the Crossing of Election, when the poet "faces the death of the creative gift." The second, the Crossing of Solipsism, occurs after the end of the love aria and recounts his "struggles with the death of love." The third and final crossing, the Crossing of Identification, which comes after the repetition of the word "death," is "the psychic act of so identifying oneself with something or someone outside the self that time seems to stand still or to roll back or forward."[21] This is the confrontation with death.

---

21. Bloom, *Wallace Stevens*, 13–14, 403.

What is at stake in Bloom's reading is the psyche of the poet, which he fears, and correctly so, I might add, is being threatened by the critical projects of de Man and Derrida. Thus, in "Out of the Cradle," the reminiscence is not strictly "a commonplace or a memory place [but] more nearly *the place of a voice*, the place from which the voice of the dead break through. Hence, a *topos* is an image of voice or of speech, or the place where such an image is stored. The movement from *topos* to *topos*, the crossing, is always a crisis." The crossing that concerns Bloom is that between speech and writing, or topos and trope. In one of his characteristic sleight-of-hand tricks, Bloom defines the rhetoric of tropes as *ethos*, "the Greek word for 'custom,' 'image,' 'trait,' [which] goes back to a root meaning 'self.'" Rhetoric of persuasion he defines as *pathos*, "the Greek for 'passion,' [which] goes back to a root meaning to 'suffer.'" The *aporia* that falls between them is *logos*.[22]

Bloom not only returns to rhetoric the fully humanistic concepts of self and passion but in a polemical spirit, attributes this formulation to de Man. Finally, he characterizes the crossing in the Romantic crisis-poem as

> what intervenes as the crisis-point in each of the three pairs, that is, at the point where a figuration of *ethos* or Limitation yields to a figuration of *pathos* or Representation. I think that there are only two fundamental tropes, tropes of action and tropes of desire. Tropes of *ethos* are the language of what Emerson and Stevens call "poverty," of imaginative need, of powerlessness and necessity, but also of action, incident, and character. Tropes of *pathos* are the language of desire, possession, and power. In poetry, a trope of action is always an irony, until it is further reduced to metonymy and metaphor; whereas a trope of imaginative desire always begins as a synecdoche, until it is further expanded to hyperbole and metalepsis, the trope that reverses temporality.[23]

I quote this lengthy passage because it reveals how his dialectic moves toward a union that denies not temporality, and a linear temporality at that, but irony, that which threatens representation, the psyche, and the linear temporality upon which Bloom's genealogy of poets depends. The dialectic between ethos and pathos takes place at each of the three crossings, but he significantly drops any mention of an aporia and substitutes identification,

22. *Ibid.*, 399, 382.
23. *Ibid.*, 401–402.

which has its beginning in synecdoche. In other words, he opposes Coleridgean symbolism to de Manian allegory. Whatever Bloom may say about misreadings, his theory always asserts that reading is possible; that is, language allows the mediation between consciousnesses and between mind and world. The crisis, for Bloom, is the *self*-created abyss that opens up between the psyche and the object of desire. The abyss, furthermore, is necessary for the continuity of Bloom's genealogy because it is the place where the poet transumes his precursors and thereby transforms the abyss, or aporia, into a logos, or an image of voice.

Bloom's theory of crossings may well have been derived from Whitman's "Out of the Cradle," just as his concept of the anxiety of influence appears to be directly indebted to Emerson, particularly the Emerson of "Self-Reliance" and "The American Scholar," but *not* the Emerson of "Quotation and Originality." Let us, therefore, return to the child, whom we left listening to the bird's song. The trope here is, once again, prosopopoeia, which appears to confirm the song as an image of voice. Furthermore, there can be no question of the boy's identification with the bird. What, therefore, is the nature of this identification? For Bloom, the relation must be a dialectical one between the singers and the poet. The song, however, denies the presence of a listener, for the denial of time depends strictly upon the birds' mutual fulfillment of desire for one another. The poet, consequently, is an intruder, a third element that does not dialectically subsume the two; he disrupts their harmony. As the translator, he gives voice not to the birds but, as the introduction makes clear, to his memory of them, making the song a memory of place and not a place of voice. And since the song is a reminiscence, a function of memory, we can conclude that it owes its appearance to its pastness, not to a fictive present. It has existence only as a memory of words, as notation.

The continuity of the song does not depend on the fulfillment of desire; it depends on the absent object of desire, an absence already "present" before the disappearance of the she-bird. Thus, the boy's role does not change; he continues as translator: "Listened, to keep, to sing—now translating the notes,/ Following you, my brother" (*LG 1860*, p. 272).

The boy, however, is not the only translator in the poem; there is also the mockingbird. In "A Word Out of the Sea," "imitation" means not representation but repetition. Throughout the course of his lament, the he-bird warns its mate not to confuse the voice of the sea with his own or asks the "husky-voiced sea" to cease so his own voice can be heard. The opposition between the voices, the bird's and the sea's, equates the absence out of which poetry emerges with the word out of the sea, which is "death." Thus, the sea at once drowns out the voice of the bird, echoes it, and answers it. All three modes of response are a translation of the bird's song; both sea and bird speak the word "death," the word out of which language begins. The bird sings to the sea, "*Murmur! Murmur on! / O murmurs— you yourselves make me continue to sing, I know not why*" (LG 1860, p. 274). Whitman later canceled these lines, possibly because he wished to obscure the semiosis that makes the bird's, the sea's, and the boy's songs all intertranslations and replace it with a more schematic opposition between the sea and the bird. Yet he kept these lines (except for the final two words):

> The colloquy there—the trio—each uttering,
> The undertone—the savage old mother, incessantly
>   crying,
> To the boy's Soul's questions sullenly timing—
>   some drowned secret hissing,
> To the outsetting bard of love.   (LG 1860, p. 275)

The trio of bird, sea, and boy all echo the "undertone," the "secret hissing" of the word "death." Perhaps Whitman's decision to call himself simply a "bard" instead of the "bard of love" was a repressing of the union between love and death. Nevertheless, it is the echoing of the songs in the boy's soul that calls him forth as the bard.

This awakening to his calling, however, is another of Whitman's retrospective recapitulations of his genesis. But into this triad he inserts a fourth, the adult who is also a translator:

> Bird! (then said the boy's Soul,)
> Is it indeed toward your mate you sing? or is it
>   mostly to me?
> For I that was a child, my tongue's use sleeping,
> Now that I have heard you,
> Now in a moment I know what I am for—I awake
> And already a thousand singers—a thousand songs,
>   clearer, louder, more sorrowful than yours,
> A thousand warbling echoes have started to live
>   within me,
> Never to die.   (LG 1860, pp. 275–76)

It becomes increasingly uncertain at this point who speaks: is it the boy, his soul, or the adult? The moment of hearing appears to be the moment of writing, for it is only in the recapitulation that he hears the bird. Experience is an a posteriori reconstruction that does not make the past present to consciousness but projects it into the future: "O you demon, singing by yourself—projecting me, O solitary me, listening—never more shall I cease imitating, perpetuating you" (LG 1860, p. 276). Whereas in "Crossing Brooklyn Ferry," the poet projects himself into the future, here language, in the form of the bird's song, projects him. Projection, furthermore, is the trope of metalepsis, for it allows the a posteriori reconstruction of the past to appear as the past and, hence, creates the fiction of genealogy, for what the song awakens in him is yet to be fulfilled. The adult will go on "imitating" (Whitman later canceled this word) and thereby, "perpetuating" the bird's song.

The bird's projection of him and his perpetuating of the bird appear at first to be homologous. The bird's song awakens him to his calling, which he realizes in the future, and he reaches back into the past and perpetuates the bird's song, thus guaranteeing it an afterlife. The process, however, is that of translation, which exchanges not writer's poetry for bird's lament but present for past. The present exists in the mind as a memory without an object. For the song, he writes, will

> Never again leave me to be the peaceful child I was
>   before what there, in the night,
> By the sea, under the yellow and sagging moon,
> The dusky demon aroused—the fire, the sweet hell
>   within,
> The unknown want, the destiny of me.   (LG 1860, p. 276).

According to Bloom, this moment of crisis where the poet questions his identity as poet has its fulfillment in the answer, the word whispered by the sea—"death." But death can never be what Bloom calls a topos, an image of voice, for it resists representation. "The word final, superior to all" is a trope—prosopopoeia, to be more precise. When he asks of the sea, "Are you whispering it, and have been all the time, you sea-waves?" he gives not an image to the voice but a face, a figure, instead. Whereas image requires some relationship between the figural and the literal—it is, in other words, a representation—prosopopoeia is a trope operating in a system of translation.

In the final stanza, the song of death enters into this system:

> Which I do not forget,
> But fuse the song of two together,

> That was sung to me in the moonlight on Paumanok's
>   gray beach,
> With the thousand responsive songs, at random,
> My own songs, awakened from that hour,
> And with them the key, the word up from the waves,
> The word of the sweetest song, and all songs,
> That strong and delicious word which, creeping
>   to my feet,
> The sea whispered me.   (*LG 1860*, p. 277).

Memory functions as translation, a fusing together of all songs into one, that of death. This poem of poetic calling does not end in the denial of time that Bloom's theory requires. The place where the voice breaks through is always already the past. We might even say that because the present exists as a memory, the voice is only heard as an echo, a repetition that is belatedly characterized as having already been experienced. Finally, the orderly process of translation breaks down as the songs "awakened from that hour" are coexistent with "the word up from the waves," the word "The sea whispered me." The Me Myself is a trope for death. Whitman's tropes of song, sea, and death are, in view of his master trope, metonymy, all images of writing. What Whitman promised in "Song of Myself" to reveal as "the origin of all poems" proves to be memory, the perpetuating of song as a translation without boundaries.

CHAPTER FOUR

Henry Adams and
the Philosophy of History

Physics Stark Mad in Metaphysics.   A. A violent order is disorder; and
           —Henry Adams   B. A great disorder is an order. These
                                        Two things are one. (Pages of
                                        illustrations.)
                                               —Wallace Stevens

Emerson's few and relatively inconsequential appearances in *The Education of Henry Adams* confirm that tradition is at best an ambiguous concept. As I have pointed out, Emerson's philosophy unsettles the classical notion of tradition as a continuous linear descent that, despite its temporal form, tends to be conserved as an atemporal hierarchy. Adams typically invokes Emerson as the "duenna" of New England transcendentalism, a philosophy for which the "eighteenth century child," as Adams called himself, felt little affinity. It was only during his student years at Harvard, when he sensed his inheritance of the Adamses' eighteenth-century principles slipping away, that he turned to Concord. But, as Adams says, "He never reached Concord."[1] The pun on *concord* suggests both the loss of his literary and philosophical parents and the failure of his education. Yet the pun itself, which bespeaks his inability "to be transcendental," is, as it were, the very issue of that which it denies; Adams stole it from Thoreau's *A Week on the Concord and Merrimack Rivers*.

In that text Henry and John take their boat as far as Concord, New

---

1. Henry Adams, *The Education of Henry Adams*, 63, hereinafter cited as EHA. The following abbreviations will be used for citations from Adams' works: *DDD—The Degradation of the Democratic Dogma*; Cater—Cater (ed.), *Henry Adams and His Friends*; *History—History of the United States of America During the Administrations of Jefferson and Madison*; Letters I—Ford (ed.), *Letters of Henry Adams (1858–1891)*; Letters II—Ford (ed.), *Letters of Henry Adams (1892–1918)*; *LN—Letters to a Niece and Prayer to the Virgin of Chartres*; *MSMC—Mont-Saint-Michel and Chartres*.

Hampshire: "We were hospitably entertained in Concord in New Hampshire, which we persisted in calling *New* Concord, as we had been wont, to distinguish it from our native town, from which we had been told that it was named and in part originally settled. This would have been the proper place to conclude our voyage, uniting Concord with Concord by these meandering rivers, but our boat was moored some miles below its port."[2] Having been forced to leave the boat moored below the town, Thoreau is literally unable to reach concord. If the repetition of the name was supposed to translate people from Concord and keep them in concord, then Thoreau's pun underscores the diacritical space between proper name and idealist concept. Adams' theft of the pun similarly marks that cleft in transcendentalism which can only be handed down or handed on to a later generation as a radically displaced and even degenerate metaphysics. In denying his literary ancestry, Adams surreptitiously indicates that any tradition must be a theft—that is, a translation—of a previous theft, just as New England transcendentalism was an appropriation (and misprision) of German transcendental philosophy.

In perpetuating these series of thefts, Adams transforms autobiography into the history of ideas. The subject of the *Education*, called Henry Adams, is but a manikin dressed out in the latest philosophical and/or scientific theory. The phase of transcendentalism gives way to Darwinism, which, in turn, is displaced by the dynamic theory of history conceived as a layman's scientific understanding of thermodynamics. With the emergence of thermodynamics, what remains of faith in the orderly progression of time disappears. Linear descent, which is based on a theory of temporal succession, proves impossible in Adams' education. His genealogy left no place for the nineteenth century—he was "a child of the seventeenth and eighteenth centuries . . . required to play the game of the twentieth" (*EHA*, p. 4). In Adams' genealogy the line descends from grandfather to grandson; the father, the sign of both authority and mediation, is absent. Under the guise of a strict year-by-year account of Adams' life, the *Education* unsettles the classical notion of time by contrasting the orderly chronology signified by the chapter titles (the original private edition had only dates, no chapter headings) with the author's search for a philosophy of history fit for the twentieth century. Without the father to ensure stability in his-

2. Thoreau, *A Week on the Concord and Merrimack Rivers*, 303.

torical time, the sons turns from the genealogical line of descent to the lines of force represented by the Virgin and the dynamo. And it is only in the dynamic theory of history that we find his autobiography.

Adams spent his life outside the main sequence of force. Displaced by his eighteenth-century inheritance, he tried to recover a lost origin by educating himself for the twentieth century. If he did not inherit a nineteenth-century life, he then could write his own in the monumental *History of the United States*. History, or properly, a theory of history, can restore to time the sequence of cause and effect and, perhaps, account for the absence of the nineteenth century.

Adams, of course, never described his task like this, although the pose of having inherited from his ancestors an inability to adapt to the nineteenth century served to explain his peculiar position: "For him, alone, the old universe was thrown into the ash-heap and a new one created" (*EHA*, p. 5). The *Education*, then, is Adams' account of his confrontation with the "problem of running order through chaos, direction through space, discipline through freedom, unity through multiplicity" (*EHA*, p. 12). But it should not be read as autobiography—the ironic self-deprecation and the (willful?) errors of fact are two reasons why. As Adams says, the facts have "no interest for education"; memory is all that matters. Thus, when he writes of his first visit to Washington, he suggests that it is impossible to reconstruct a past event: "This was the journey he remembered. The actual journey may have been quite different, but the actual journey has no interest for education. The memory was all that mattered" (*EHA*, p. 43).

For a historian, this is a curious admission, but one we should expect from a writer sophisticated enough to question the metaphysics underlying any claim that history can be written. At one time Adams could declare his "historical indifference to everything but facts" (*Letters*.I.372), only later to dismiss facts as details whose value is merely convenience. In "The Dynamo and the Virgin," he describes the metaphysical assumptions underlying historicism: "Historians undertake to arrange sequences—called stories, or histories—assuming in silence a relation of cause and effect. These assumptions, hidden in depths of dusty libraries, have been astounding, but commonly unconscious and childlike" (*EHA*, p. 382).

Like Melville's poor sub-sublibrarian, who collects a hodgepodge of quotations while trusting that the weight of written records will metamorphosize fragments into "gospel cetology," historians uncover documents in order to transform the order of a library into the order of time. The book produced by this method is a patchwork of texts—as Adams ironically said of his "Letter to American Teachers of History": "I am incapable of comprehending the simplest, as the most complex reasoning. Therefore I don't reason; I try only to plaster other people's standard text books together, so as to see where we are" (*Letters*.II.541). In this manner, or accidental method, he recuperates a teleological notion of history—he recuperates, in fact, the concept of the book, wherein eclectic theories and random facts are arranged in what is thought to be a "natural" order. History is therefore reduced to the copying of texts: "Long before history began, his education was complete, for the record could not have been started until he had been taught to record. The universe that had formed him took shape in his mind as a reflection of his own unity, containing all forces except himself" (*EHA*, p. 475). In Adams', curriculum, history does not begin until there is writing; in fact, writing produces the sequence of thought called history. The universe itself is but the a posteriori reflection of his mind, yet this reflection, to the degree it is a copy of a copy, excludes the generating source. The subject, that which grounds unity in a source, is absent.

For lack of a unifying subject, Adams, like the tailor in the preface, dresses Thought in the garments of history. In both cases, "the object of study is the garment, not the figure" (*EHA*, p. xxx). Following Melville's example in *Pierre*, Adams borrows from Carlyle the clothes metaphor to serve as a reminder of the patchwork that goes into any composition, whether it be man or book. Adams' professed reluctance to publish emerges in his transforming the author into a tailor who "adapts the manikin as well as the clothes to his patron's wants." But in this case, Adams has selected his patrons: "The tailor's object, in this volume, is to fit young men, in universities or elsewhere, to be men of the world, equipped for any emergency; and the garment offered to them is meant to show the faults of the patchwork fitted on their fathers" (*EHA*, p. xxx). Set up as a geometrical model to be "used for the study of relation," the manikin, along with its ill-fitting patchwork, reconstitutes education as a field of forces stitched together by the needle/pen. Although the autobiography records in a strict sequential form Adams' lifelong search for an education, the life which the book retells is, as the preface indicates, a product of memory, not a record of facts and certainly not a chronology. As the garment worn by the tailor's dummy is patched together from who knows how many tattered remains, so the book, as well as the life recounted therein, is a ragbag: it consists of the worn-out scraps of hand-me-downs that mock the author's desire to recover truth or a pure origin. This metaphor, borrowed from Carlyle and Melville, to mention only the most obvious of its previous "owners," is, as Joseph Riddel writes of its use in *Pierre*, "surely a reminder that writing has always been implicated in a series of conventions and complications which preclude an access to its origins in the 'poetic nature.' "[3]

Adams offers his book as a patchwork of memories, but he also implies that his education ends before the *Education* begins. The failure of the education explains his inability to complete the book. Without the tools to prepare for the twentieth century, Adams is unable to find the point of origin that would reconcile history with evolution. For an autobiography (and it should be remembered that the subtitle, *Autobiography*, was, as Ernest Samuels notes in his edition, added by the editors of the posthumous 1918 edition), one's birth seems a suitable place to begin, but as Adams' awareness of his inheritance makes clear, the birth is, in a figurative if not literal sense, an arbitrary point. The lines of force have been at work well before his actual birth. In the "Editor's Preface," Adams, under the nom de plume Henry Cabot Lodge, cites "The Abyss of Ignorance" for an explanation of the companion volumes *Mont-Saint-Michel and Chartres* and the *Education*: " 'Any schoolboy could see that man as a force must be measured by motion from a fixed point. Psychology helped here by suggesting a unit—the point of history when man held the highest idea of himself as a unit in a unified universe' " (*EHA*, p . xxvii).

Although Adams' insistence that his life was determined before his birth has only a metaphorical sense, he shared with his brothers a feeling that his generation marked a significant decline from the highpoint of the Adams family's fortune. For his brother Brooks, the greatest figure was John Quincy Adams, whom Brooks regarded as "the most remarkable mind ever produced in America."[4] In "The Heritage of Henry Adams," his introduction to *The Degradation of the Democratic Dogma*, Brooks places Henry in direct descent from John Quincy: "Regarded philosophically, Henry's life is, in effect, a continuation of his grandfather's" (*DDD*, p. 103). Brooks merely refers to Henry and John Quincy's mutual devotion to science, but

3. Riddel, "Decentering the Image," 329.
4. Brooks Adams to Henry Adams, March 6, 1909, in Beringause, *Brooks Adams*, 312.

it is more than a biographical curiosity that the younger Adamses' highly regarded father, Charles Francis, is absent from this genealogy. The long introduction to this volume of essays appears to be a resurrection of Brooks's unfinished biography of John Quincy, a figure to whom he was far more devoted than was Henry. Nevertheless, the rupture in genealogy was not another of Brooks's eccentricities, for this idea also emerges in a more general form in the *Education*.

In a discussion of the energetics of Wilhelm Ostwald and Ernst Mach,[5] Adams concludes, "A student of history had no need to understand these scientific ideas of very great men; he sought only the relation with the ideas of their grandfathers and their common direction towards the ideas of their grandsons" (*EHA*, p. 453). This could be read as a theory of history in which past facts are gathered and interpreted in order to predict the future—and Adams felt drawn to making predictions. However, the student who, like Adams, stands outside historical time hopes that by gathering the scraps of history he can build a bridge which not only spans past and future but also creates linear time in a sequence of cause and effect.

We must still map out the various points in Adams' work where education and genealogy converge in a textual entanglement. If the student's task is to find a fixed point from which motion can be measured, then both the *Education* and *Mont-Saint-Michel* are descriptions of Adams' writings—they tell the genealogy of autobiography.[6] The *Education* recalls the life of its author in what, after Derrida, we have come to call a supplementary manner. The *autos*, or self, is recalled as "an object of study," that is, as a manikin. In recalling the manikin, Adams recalls, even renames, him-

5. Energetics was first developed in the 1890s by Ostwald, who substituted the notion of invisible forces of energy for the discrete particles of atoms. Energy was held to be the general substrate of all appearance. Although Mach said his 1872 work, *Conservation of Energy*, was compatible with the fundamentals of energetics, he came to oppose it for the same reasons he opposed atomism: as an ontological phenomenalist he "denied the reality of everything that could not be a sensation, and held that *all* theories whether 'atomism,' 'energetical,' or whatever were merely historical stages, of at best provisional value, which science might pass through on its way to the end goal of scientific simplicity in the form of mathematical functions." See Blackmore, *Ernst Mach*, 118.

In a letter dated January 29, 1908, Adams thanks Margaret Chanler for getting him a copy of Keyser's *Mathematics* and remarks, "In brief intervals of rolling on the ground and tearing out my grey locks of hair, I discover that I am a pupil of Ernst Mach, and an enemy of [Henri] Poincaré; that I am mathematical in method, since I do not assume immutable order" (*Letters*.II.488).

6. My discussion of autobiography is indebted to Derrida, "Coming into One's Own," 114–48.

self. The use of the third-person pronoun is more than just a device behind which he can maintain his ironic pose; the rightful name cannot belong to the "I" who writes until the completion of the work. Only with the acquisition of the tools that will prepare him for twentieth-century life can the student recover the genealogy guaranteeing the proper name.

Its education ending in failure, the *autos* never comes into being. Although we should never take Adams at his word, the work, according to the "Editor's Preface," remains unfinished because the historical theory "became unnameable as he approached the end" (*EHA*, p. xxviii). Translation can never adequately link the *autos* with biography. The movement from biography to philosophy has its obvious precedent in St. Augustine's *Confessions*. And for Adams, as most assuredly for Augustine, the contemplation of history is the fulfillment of the work. In the *Education*, however, the inscription of the philosophy becomes the reason for being. As this inscription must remain incomplete, so too must the self. "Avowedly incomplete" as the work may be, its unfinished character does not merely rest on the supposed difficulties with the philosophical chapters. The dynamic theory of history is the legacy Adams bequeaths to his readers, a legacy which, if true, will not find many more readers. Adams' incessant urge to speculate about the future opens up the scene in which the manikin can act his part. Having no children, Adams had no alliance with the future, and with the death of his wife, his ties to the past were also broken. To restore the continuity of the genealogical line, he had to follow the bypaths of nieces and nephews.

Adams' predicament, as the preface to *Mont-Saint-Michel* makes clear, is that of any author: if the genealogical descent is threatened, so is the relationship between reader and writer. He opens his preface by quoting these Elizabethan lines: "Who reads me when I am ashes,/ Is my son in wishes." He comments: "The relationship, between reader and writer, of son and father, may have existed in Queen Elizabeth's time but is much too close to be true for ours" (*MSMC*, p. xiii). As direct descent is no longer possible, the best a writer can hope for is that the book will allow an imaginative genealogy, not of father and son, but of uncle and niece. The myth of descent is that history progresses in an unequivocal line of cause and effect; Adams rejects this for the indeterminacy of lines of force which upset the temporal order upon which the earlier *History* was based:

The utmost that any writer could hope of his readers now is that they should consent to regard themselves as nephews, and even then he would expect only a more or less civil refusal from most of them. Indeed, if he had reached a certain age, he would have observed that nephews, as a social class, no longer read at all. . . . Finally, the metre does not permit it. One may not say: "Who reads me, when I am ashes, is my nephew in wishes." The same objections do not apply to the word "niece." The change restores the verse, and, to a very great degree, the fact. Nieces have been known to read in early youth, and in some cases may have read their uncles. The relationship, too, is convenient and easy, capable of being anything or nothing, at the will of either party, like a Mohammedan or Polynesian or American marriage. No valid objection can be offered to this change in the verse. Niece let it be! (*MSMC*, p. xiii)

While the language of direct communication may have existed in past ages, though Adams casts doubt even on this, it is lost to the modern writer. Barred from the parental position that turns the writer into an author(ity), Adams chooses the secondary path of uncle. Although his joke on "nephew" and meter should not be pushed too far—it is well known that he preferred the company of his nieces—the suggestion that restrictions of language force him to undertake the role of an uncle should not be discounted. The uncertain status of the relationship between writer, text, and reader destroys the grounds upon which the author could be considered the engendering father, transmitting culture and linguistic significance to the reader/son. The medieval world must be staged in a language denying that the so-called unity of twelfth-century France can be transmitted to twentieth-century descendants.

The inability to restore unity to nature dictated Adams' early ambivalence toward evolutionary theory. When in London with his father during the Civil War, Adams met Sir Charles Lyell and at Sir Charles' request wrote a review of *Principles of Geology*. In the chapter called "Darwinism" in the *Education*, Adams remarks on the theory of evolution's appeal: "Natural Selection led back to Natural Evolution, and at last to Natural Uniformity. This was a vast stride. Unbroken Evolution under uniform conditions pleased everyone—except curates and bishops; it was the very best substitute for religion, a safe, conservative, practical, thoroughly Common-Law deity" (*EHA*, p. 225). He treats Darwinism as a conservative force impos-

AMERICAN POETICS OF HISTORY / 132

ing unity on a universe that continually flies in the face of theory and facts. Unlike the church, which assumes unity at the start, science, like Augustine, worked from multiplicity to unity: "Unity and Uniformity were the whole motive of philosophy, and if Darwin, like a true Englishman, preferred to back into it—to reach God *a posteriori*—rather than start from it, like Spinoza, the difference of method taught only the moral that the best way of reaching unity was to unite. Any road was good that arrived" (*EHA*, p. 226). Instead of arguing from primal cause to secondary effect, the evolutionary theorist argued from multitudinous effects to simple cause. Little wonder that Adams found in it "the charms of art." The persistence of this failure in methodology can be found in the recent works of sociobiologists.

Adams' own attempt to start from the end and work to the beginning fails before it begins. Told by Sir Charles that the first vertebrate was the fish *Pteraspis*, whose fossil remains could be found at Wenlock Abbey, Adams discovers in this prehistoric ancestor a symbol of the illusion of progress—the *Pteraspis* remains exempt from time. How fitting that its home should be Wenlock Abbey: "The peculiar flavor of the scenery had something to do with absence of evolution; it was better marked in Egypt: it was felt wherever time-sequences became interchangeable. One's instinct abhors time" (*EHA*, p. 228). Here Adams seeks a legitimate parentage for man, but his ancient father could just as well be plucked from the Severn: "In the scale of evolution, one vertebrate was as good as another." And, it may be added, one father is as good as another: "To an American in search of a father, it mattered nothing whether the father breathed through lungs, or walked on fins, or on feet" (*EHA*, p. 229). Adams seeks the certainty of a father, but all he discovers are limitless cousins. Determining ancestry is cognate with writing history, that is, determining a line of cause and effect. Cousinship leaves him with collateral issue and no central line. Descent from parents would guarantee history as a story of progress, but seek as he may for evolution, "all he could prove was change. . . . [B]ehind the lesson of the day, he was conscious that, in geology as in theology, he could prove only Evolution that did not evolve; Uniformity that was not uniform; and Selection that did not select" (*EHA*, pp. 230–31).

Although critics are quick to point out the liberties Adams takes both with his autobiographical account and with the scientific theories he examines, they tend to treat autobiography and science as separate topics or to relegate science to a subsidiary position in the *Education*, which is itself a violation of the genre. It is of more than passing interest that Viktor Shklovsky characterized the violation of genre as an eccentric inheritance: "In the liquidation of one literary school by another, the inheritance is passed down, not from father to son, but from uncle to nephew."[7] We might say that the *Education* records the displacement of autobiography by the history of ideas, but in doing so, Adams' book undercuts the common ground of these two modes of writing—that is, a linear theory of time. Adams' theory, if not an absolute embarrassment to his readers, is at least something to be explained away as an imaginative, though misguided, attempt to recapture the unity absent from the modern world. In one sense, he resembles Emerson in his astonishing ability to run through such diverse topics as geology, physics, evolution, history, art, economics, and theology and make them all confirm his beliefs. If the young man is, as the preface states, to manage the economy of his forces, then the theories Adams encounters in his education are there to be consumed and discarded when their value is used up. He recognizes, as did Emerson, that writing itself is the least economical of acts.

Even if it were mere coincidence, Adams did not treat the turn from Darwinism to economics as such. What could be more consistent with the logic of cause and effect than to move from *The Origin of Species* to the payment of specie? Capitalists, like geologists, believe in natural origins. Having, in his words, "confus[ed] his ideas about geology to the apparent satisfaction of Sir Charles . . . Adams turned resolutely to business, and attacked the burning question of species payments. His principles assured him that the honest way to resume payments was to restrict currency" (*EHA*, p. 233). The geologist has turned capitalist, but whereas his caution and confusion kept him safely within the acceptable boundaries of theory, his moral resolution leads him straight into error. Restriction of currency proved disastrous to England, yet Adams' investment in the article demands that he publish. Upon receiving a letter of acceptance from the *North American Review*, "Adams looked at it as though he were a debtor who had begged

---

7. Quoted in Jameson, *The Prison-House of Language*, 53. For a brief summation of the critical reevaluation of Adams' works, see Colacurcio, "The Dynamo and the Angelic Doctor," 696–712.

for an extension. He read it with as much relief as the debtor, if it had brought him the loan. The letter gave the new writer literary rank" (*EHA*, p. 234).

"Darwinism" recounts not only Adams' encounter with uniformitarian geology and natural selection but also his passage from private secretary to writer—or from copyist to author. But the student's mastery of his tools is questionable. The loan he has taken, which gives him access to the press, at the same time places him at the mercy of a market where only the cheapest survive.[8]

Adams' insistence upon the displacement of the modern writer from the hierarchical order of the family line is inextricably bound up with his readings in geology and physics. We find these diverse interests expressed in a letter apparently intended as a preface to "The Rule of Phase Applied to History." After thanking the anonymous recipient for having read the *Education*, he stresses the privacy of the book while acknowledging his inability to ensure that his wishes are obeyed: "Every ward politician teaches us the first lesson of politics, that only direct, personal contact exerts influence; and since the distances which separate us make personal contact impossible, we can only fall back on the archaic resource of letter-writing; like Cadmus, whose date I have tried in vain to fix, but who, somewhat like myself, probably stole the idea" (Cater, p. 781). Although Adams' fear that the written word lacks authorial control was real, he repeats an idea as old as writing. To assert his authority over the reader, he appeals to Cadmus not as the inventor of writing but as the first to steal the idea. To write is to steal, for this letter introduces Adams' misappropriation of Willard Gibb's phase theory.

At the same time, the letter serves as a link between the *Education* and "The Rule of Phase," which is a continuation of the unfinished earlier work. This purloined letter, then, asserts the genealogical link between the *Education*, which Adams refers to as a personal letter, and the purloined es-

---

8. In a letter of 1899 to Brooks, Henry merges Marx with Herbert Spencer: "I can now, with fair confidence, formulate Marx's theory of history, as 'the survival of the cheapest until it becomes too cheap to survive' " (*Letters*.II.248). After the financial crisis of 1893, both Henry and Brooks became convinced that laws of economics determine the direction of history. Brooks developed his theory in *The Law of Civilization and Decay*. But by the early 1900s Henry was telling Brooks to replace *Money* with *Energy*.

say. The manikin has fathered a book every bit as piecemeal as itself. To-gether, these works are to produce "a universal formula for reconstructing and rearranging the whole scheme of University instruction so that it shall occupy a field of definite limits, distinct from the technical" (Cater, p. 784).

Adams envisions the *Education* and, in particular, the late essays col-lected by Brooks as the basis for a reconstruction of the university estab-lishing historical methodology as the centerpiece of the curriculum, thereby returning history and genealogy to the world of thought. The instructor, says Adams, "will conceive of the University as a system of education grouped about History; a main current of thought branching out, like a tree, into endless forms of activity, in regular development, according to the laws of physics; and to be studied as a single stream, not as now by a multi-versal, but by a universal law; not as a scientific but as a historical unity; not as a practise of technical handling, but as a process of mental evolution in history, controlled, like the evolution of any series of chemical or electric equilibria, by one general formula" (Cater, p. 784). Adams models his ed-ucational system after the genealogical tree with the parent, history, serv-ing as the trunk, and the secondary disciplines forming the collateral branches. Upon the science of genetics, which will guarantee the hierar-chical order of the sciences, Adams grafts the laws of physics, which will regulate the translation of the parental discipline into its stations on the genealogical tree.[9] Although historical and metaphorical, not scientific, unity will prevail in this system, the family tree's regular development is en-trusted to the laws of physics. Adams translates physics and history into a gene-alogy, a logic grounded upon the hidden order of genotypes, in con-trast to the visible disorder of phenotypes. Threatened by the increasing entropy described by thermodynamic processes, Adams turns into an in-tellectual horticulturist, translating Gibbs's phase rule into a genealogical order and thereby stabilizing the shifting currents of evolution.

In Gibbs's phase rule, Adams found the metaphor that would replace evolutionary theory. The cyclic processes in Laplace's adaptation of New-tonian mechanics, which exercised a profound influence on many thinkers of the first half of the nineteenth century, were challenged and ultimately replaced by the new physics of thermodynamics. Although Newton ob-

9. For my discussion of the entanglement of physics and genealogy, I have relied on Serres, *Hermes III*, esp. 15–41.

served the irreversible flow of heat from a hot body to a cold one, he conceived of atoms as inelastic hard bodies, unchanging in size or shape, which would not rebound upon contact. Consequently, all atomic motion would come to a standstill, and there would be no kind of conservation law for motion. Without a first law of thermodynamics, there cannot be a second law, although, in fact, the second law appeared before the first. Newtonian mechanics, however, defines irreversibility as a decrease in motion, not as entropy.[10] Furthermore, the model for molecular mechanics was taken from astronomy. Falling earthly and celestial bodies are governed by the law of gravitation. As all change is the result of external force acting upon an inert mass, the laws governing atomic matter are the same as those governing macroscopic phenomena. Finally, as matter is unchanging and all motion is the result of external force, Newtonian mechanics is essentially time reversible. A conflict arose, therefore, between irreversible heat flow on the macroscopic level and the reversible processes of Newtonian mechanics on the microscopic level. If the movement of atoms was not time directional, how then could the heat flow be explained since all observable motion is supposed to be reducible to atomic laws?

One of the first steps in answering this question developed out of Sadi Carnot's work with steam engines. Carnot observed that the loss of heat meant the loss of energy. His essential discovery was that the motive power of a steam engine depended solely on the temperatures of warm and cold bodies: *"wherever there exists a difference of temperature, motive power can be produced."* Although Carnot accepted caloric theory, which defines heat as a substance and attributes all phenomena of heat to the forces of repulsion and attraction, he thought that "heat is conserved in the steam-engine cycle . . . [and not] converted into mechanical work." From this revision of caloric theory and the denial of the possibility of perpetual motion, Carnot arrived at the principle of what came to be known as the second law of thermodynamics. Rudolf Clausius is credited with equating heat with work and thus with formulating the law of entropy; however, Carnot himself arrived at this same equation in the posthumously published notes to his famous essay on the motive power.[11]

10. Brush, *Kind of Motion*, 546. I have relied heavily on this work for my discussion of the history of thermodynamics.
11. Carnot, *Reflections on the Motive Power of Fire*, 9; Brush, *Kind of Motion*, 569.

In a paper presented to the Royal Society of Edinburgh on April 19, 1852, William Thomson, later Lord Kelvin, offers these propositions, which Adams quoted in "A Letter to American Teachers of History," in response to Carnot's principle of the dissipation of what by then was called mechanical energy:

1. There is at present in the material world a universal tendency to the dissipation of mechanical energy.
2. Any *restoration* of mechanical energy, without more than an equivalent of dissipation, is impossible in inanimate material processes, and is probably never effected by means of organized matter, either endowed with vegetable life or subjected to the will of an animated creature.
3. Within a finite period of time past the earth must have been, and within a finite period of time to come the earth must again be, unfit for the habitation of man as at present constituted, unless operations have been or are to be performed, which are impossible under the laws to which the known operations going on at present in the material world are subject.[12]

Though Clausius and Kelvin had worked out these principles in papers published in 1851, I turn to the paper of 1852 for the clarity of its presentation. Kelvin's first proposition states the second law of thermodynamics; his second, which denies perpetual motion is possible, states that mechanical energy can only be restored by an outside force which, in its turn, will undergo a dissipation of energy. The third proposition concerns heat death: the eventual cooling of the earth will result in an end to life in a few thousand years. These calculations by such physicists as Kelvin, P. G. Tait, and James Clerk Maxwell in England, and Clausius and Hermann von Helmholtz in Germany served as the major scientific argument against the uniformitarian geology of Lyell and its theoretical companion, Darwinian evolution. For our purposes it suffices to point out that calculations for the loss of energy due to friction, eventual cooling of the earth's interior (experiments were conducted in mine shafts), and calculations for the rate of the sun's dissipation of heat all led Kelvin to deny the length of time required by Lyell's and Darwin's theories and to restrict the limit of past time to approximately one hundred million years.[13]

12. Thomson, "On a Universal Tendency in Nature to the Dissipation of Mechanical Energy," 306.
13. See Kelvin, *Popular Lectures and Addresses*, II, 10–64.

But it was not until the 1865 paper of Clausius that the term *entropy* was introduced for the first time. The paper concludes with these famous theorems of the mechanical theory of heat: "The energy of the universe is constant. . . . The entropy of the universe tends to a maximum." In a lecture delivered in 1867, Clausius stated the consequence of his second theorem: "The more the universe approaches this limiting condition in which entropy is a maximum, the more do the occasions of further changes diminish; and supposing this condition to be at last obtained, no further change could evermore take place, and the universe would be in a state of unchanging death."[14]

At this stage in the development of thermodynamics, entropy was thought to be a physical fact that described the loss of mechanical energy in the form of heat. This in part could explain the *fin de siècle* fascination with the approaching end of the universe. Both Henry and Brooks Adams were absorbed in calculating the date of ultimate collapse—Brooks doing so in despair, Henry with ironic glee. To Elizabeth Cameron, Henry wrote, "My figures coincide in fixing 1950 as the year when the world must go to smash. This gives a comfortable margin for us to get out" (*Letters*.II.393). At other times, he expresses his satisfaction that the world, to use his own phrase, was rotting faster than he was.

As long as entropy is considered to be a qualitative and not a mathematical description, Adams' simpler remarks on the degradation of man can be explained; however, when we come to his statements about anarchy, force, and will, only a statistical account for entropy will suffice.[15] In an important letter written in 1905 to the medievalist Henry Osborn Taylor, a former student of Adams' at Harvard, Adams remarks that he is "trying to work out the formula of anarchism; the law of expansion from unity, simplicity, morality, to multiplicity, contradiction, police" (Cater, p. 558). Two years earlier, he wrote to Brooks: "The only question of serious interest to the world is the atom. What is the atom? Is there an atom? I hold, as a working hypothesis, that an atom is a man" (Cater, p. 545). The disorder that Adams speaks of is compatible with a theory of entropy that is statistical and not absolute; otherwise, the reconciliation of equilibrium with

14. Brush, *Kind of Motion*, 577, 578.
15. I disagree with Jordy's assertion that "Adams does not seem to have known of Gibbs' suggestion that the universality of the second law is doubtful after all if thermodynamics be considered in a statistical sense" (*Henry Adams*, 166–67).

disorder would be impossible. The molecular disorder of an entropic system is perceived as a state in equilibrium. Extreme molecular order, however, provides great available energy and is therefore perceived as anarchy. Thus, Adams may read entropy as a linear and irreversible process, and at the same time maintain that the perceived disorder of the world is an order, or a state in equilibrium, such as a democracy. More important than any concern for a simple source for Adams' use of the theory of entropy—and these sources are a problem—is the epistemological grounds for a statistical account for the dissipation of energy. To explain this we must turn to Maxwell's demon and the work of Ludwig Boltzmann.

The refutation of the second law's mechanical character took the unusual form of the famous Maxwell's demon. In response to his contemporaries' claim for the absolute validity of the second law (see, for instance, Kelvin's propositions above), Maxwell proposed that an exceedingly agile creature possessing superb vision could sort out slow-moving molecules from fast-moving ones and thus produce a perpetual motion machine, thereby violating the second law of thermodynamics.[16] The "hotter" body would therefore take "heat" from the "colder" body. I use quotation marks to draw attention to how Maxwell's theory defines temperature as a product of the kinetic energy of gas. Heat, then, is a product of the movement of molecules and the countless number of times they strike one another within a second.

According to Newton's mechanical theory, the direction in which an atom moves is not time directional. Forward and backward have no meaning in molecular physics. Reversibility then seems to hold true on the molecular level, even though entropy seems to be irreversible. Maxwell's demon, and the work of Boltzmann, established that the second law has only statistical validity. With the millions of molecules constituting the smallest particle of matter, it would be very unlikely that the molecules would spontaneously sort themselves out according to the individual molecule's speed. It would be as likely as the evaporated molecules of a bottle of alcohol returning to the bottle—theoretically it is possible, but statistically it is most improbable. Finally, it must be pointed out that Maxwell's demon is as important for introducing the notion that *entropy is a mixing of different*

16. For a concise explanation of Maxwell's demon, see Kelvin, *Popular Lectures and Addresses*, II, 144–48.

molecules as it is for introducing the more famous concept of the possible violation of the second law of thermodynamics. It remained for Boltzmann to equate entropy with disorder.[17]

Using Newtonian mechanics to analyze molecular collisions, Boltzmann attempted to prove that collisions of molecules will increase the entropy of a gas. This is known as Boltzmann's H theorem, which states that H (negative entropy) is generally above its minimum value, or H (min.), for the greater part of the time. In answer to the objection that the function H must decrease, Boltzmann replied in a paper of 1895, "On Certain Questions of the Theory of Gases," that equations of motion alone will not prove "that the minimum function H must always decrease. It can only be deduced from the laws of probability that if the initial state is not specially arranged for a certain purpose [see Kelvin's second proposition, which concerns the reversibility of entropic movement], but haphazard governs freely, the probability that H decreases is always greater than that it increases."[18] By turning to statistical analysis, Boltzmann was able to show that as the universal tendency is toward increasing states of disorder, the likelihood of a decrease in entropy is exceedingly rare, especially as the occurrence of H above its minimum value is itself highly improbable, though mathematically certain. Thus, if we were to call H above its minimum value H_1 and plot it on a curve, taking time as the axis of abscissas, we would find that the ordinates on either side of it would be on a downward slope indicating an increase in entropy. Consequently, as movement in either direction will mean a decline in the value of H_1, we can conclude that *entropy will increase whether we move forward or backward in time.*

As the H-curve is not time directional, thermal equilibrium lies in our "past" as well as our "future." Boltzmannian time must be distinguished from Newtonian time, for Newtonian mechanics is deterministic and does not deal with dissipation. Boltzmann, on the other hand, introduces both chance and dissipation into interpretations of the world. If we were to place the earth on an imaginary H-curve, we would discover that entropy increases in either direction on the time axis. Hence, Clausius' second proposition, "entropy increases with time," is a tautology. Therefore, time, ac-

17. For a more detailed discussion of reversibility, see Layzer, "The Arrow of Time," 56–69. For a nonmathematical presentation of Boltzmann's theory, see his *Theoretical Physics and Philosophical Problems*, 13–32.
18. Boltzmann, *Theoretical Physics and Philosophical Problems*, 205.

cording to Stephen Brush's analysis of Boltzmann's theory, is statistical, perhaps even subjective.[19]

We must further distinguish Boltzmann's subjective—*statistical* would be the better word—notion of time from idealist philosophy. Ernst Mach, a philosophical opponent of Boltzmann and a professed phenomenalist, first said Clausius' second proposition is a tautology. In fact, he went so far as to speculate that the second law of thermodynamics defined, not measured, time.[20] Mach argued that time and space exist as sensations and not as objective realities in the phenomenal world. Boltzmann's statistical definition of time, however, does not reduce space and time to sensations but rather insists on the presence of the observer who interprets physical phenomena—physical processes go on regardless of man's presence; man interprets physical phenomena and assigns temporal value to the dissipation of mechanical energy.

The significance of Boltzmann's concept of entropy for Adams involves the latter's equation of increasing molecular disorder, or the eventual heat death, with historical time. For Adams, time is degradation. But in Boltzmann's statistical theory, molecular processes are independent of time—time, in fact, has no meaning on the microscopic level. It is a function of language; that is, it describes changes in molecular configurations. Adams seizes upon physics as a metaphorical language not only because it is best suited to mirror the indeterminacy of history but also because it tries to maintain within itself the knowledge that language, mathematical or conventional, is inherently inadequate to fulfill its express purpose. This can be illustrated by examining the diffusion of gases.

In his preface to *Elementary Principles in Statistical Mechanics*, J. Willard Gibbs describes the relation between probability and thermodynamics: "The laws of thermodynamics, as empirically determined, express the approximate and probable behavior of systems of a great number of particles, or, more precisely, they express the laws of mechanics for such systems as they appear to beings who have not the fineness of perception to enable them to appreciate quantities of the order of magnitude of those which relate to single particles, and who cannot repeat their experiments often enough to obtain any but most probable results. The laws of statis-

19. Brush, *Kind of Motion*, 240.
20. Blackmore, *Ernst Mach*, 88.

tical mechanics apply to conservative systems of any number of degrees of freedom, and are exact."[21] In Gibbs's explanation, the laws of thermodynamics are formulated by beings who wish to explain macroscopic behavior through microscopic mechanics. We can imagine the possibility of a much different set of laws if there existed a being, such as Maxwell's demon, with perception acute enough to see atomic particles. Probability is therefore inseparable from the observer's physical limitations. Gibbs's theories of probability and subjective limitation offered little comfort to those who feared the approaching heat death.

Gibbs's theory of equilibrium made it possible for thermodynamics to include the study of nonhomogeneous bodies. The law of entropy failed when applied to those systems in which neither the number of gases nor the degree of their complexity—that is, mixture—is known. This is called Gibbs's paradox. If two identical gases are mixed, there would not be any change in total entropy before or after mixing. If, however, the mixture were of two identical gases which differ in respect to the attractions between their atoms and those of other substances, and thus differ in their tendency to combine with other substances, then their mixing would involve an increase in entropy, but it would be impossible to distinguish this situation experimentally from the mixing of two gases that were absolutely identical. Maxwell takes this a step farther and points out that we can mix two gases which we think are identical and later discover that they are separable by a reversible process. We would then discover that the entropy in the system has a positive value. Consequently, in Stephen Brush's words, "entropy is not an observable part of the system itself but depends upon our knowledge of the system."[22]

The absence of information is just as responsible for physics as it is for metaphysics. When Boltzmann considers the question of origins, he relies upon statistical mechanics and the concept of the random motion of individual molecules. Consequently, any definition of origin based upon random motion cannot be an origin at all: "That the mixture [of molecules] was not complete from the start, but rather that the world began from a very unlikely initial state, this much can be counted amongst the fundamental hypotheses of the whole theory and we can say that the reason for

21. Quoted in Wheeler, *Josiah Willard Gibbs*, 151.
22. Brush, *Kind of Motion*, 604, 593.

it is as little known as that for why the world is as it is and not other-wise."[23] Thermodynamics appears to close the door to consideration of the origin of the universe. Origin simply means a decrease in entropy. Although it is possible to consider a state of molecular regularity, there would be no reason to distinguish this state according to a past or future.

This hardly means that world history is a single unit free from change and measurable according to some absolute standard. On the contrary, Boltzmann's theory takes the radical step of dissolving the link between time and memory. In what we might call the classical notion of time, memory is what binds time between the points of origin and end. It is on these grounds that Nietzsche, in *The Will to Power*, attacks the concept of infinite progress:

> Lately one has sought several times to find a contradiction in the concept "temporal infinity of the world in the past" (*regressus in infinitum*): one has even found it, although at the cost of confusing the head with the tail. Nothing can prevent me from reckoning backward from this moment and saying "I shall never reach the end"; just as I can reckon forward from the same moment into the infinite. Only if I made the mistake—I shall guard against it—of equating this correct concept of a *regressus in infinitum* with an utterly unrealizable concept of a finite *progressus* up to this present, only if I suppose that the direction (forward or backward) is logically a matter of indifference, would I take the head—this moment—for the tail.[24]

Nietzsche's stress upon the moment as that which distinguishes past and future is not a recuperation of linear temporality. He rejects progress for imposing on the world an end which, according to him, does not exist. But he warns that "the old habit . . . of associating a goal with every event and a guiding, creative God with the world, is so powerful that it requires an effort for a thinker not to fall into thinking the very aimlessness of the world as intended." Metaphysics is so deeply ingrained in man's thought that apparent randomness is transformed into the belief that the world is

> supposed to be capable of the divine power of creation. . . . [I]t is supposed to possess not only the intention but the *means* of avoiding any repetition; to that end, it is supposed to control every one of its movements at every moment so as to escape goals, final states, repetitions—and whatever else

23. Boltzmann, *Theoretical Physics and Philosophical Problems*, 172.
24. Nietzsche, *The Will to Power*, 548.

> may follow from such an unforgiveably insane way of thinking and desir-
> ing. It is still the old religious way of thinking and desiring, a kind of long-
> ing to believe that *in some way* the world is after all like the old beloved,
> infinite, boundlessly creative God. . . . [T]he world, as force, may not be
> thought of as unlimited, for it *cannot* be so thought of; we forbid ourselves
> the concept of an infinite force as incompatible with the concept "force."[25]

Nietzsche unveils the connections between teleological thinking and infinite creativity. If there is a beginning and an end, then there is infinite novelty. Every point in the eternal unfolding of the world would in itself be
both a beginning and an end; the world would therefore achieve being, or
stasis, and maintain itself as infinitely new. That which reconciles eternal
novelty with being is memory or, what is much the same, God. To break
the hold of religious thinking on man, Nietzsche measures history by the
value of the moment.

Although Adams does not write of eternal recurrence, he, too, in his attack on teleological thinking stresses the moment. His choice of the twelfth
century as a moment of unity is arbitrary—it provides a point from which
he can calculate the dissipation of energy. Yet, as the following remark to
Henry Taylor suggests, the past can only be measured by the present: "You
need to be thorough in your study and accurate in your statements. Your
middle-ages exist for their own sake, not for ours. To me, who stand in
gaping wonder before this preposterous spectacle of thought, and who can
see nothing in all nature so iconoclastic, miraculous and anarchistic as
Shakespeare, the middle-ages present a picture that has somehow to be
brought into relation with ourselves. To you, there is no difficulty in trans-
ferring ourselves into the middle-ages" (Cater, pp. 559–60). With its faith
in facts and documents unchallenged, conventional historicism can reach
back into the past and restore its presence for contemporary man. To one
who lacks this faith in facts, the past has no independent existence—it can
only be judged according to the present. If the medieval period differed significantly from the twentieth century, it is a difference produced by a failure of memory. And to recover the past is to distort it.

Boltzmann's concept of recurrence, however, is quite different from
Nietzsche's: according to the physicist, the repetition of a similar molecular configuration is possible, though improbable, and it is distinguished

25. *Ibid.*, 546, 546–47.

by a restoration of energy after equilibrium has been reached. The problem becomes more complex if it becomes a question whether equilibrium can ever be reached. Nietzsche explicitly denies that it can, and he relies upon statistical theory to refute William Thomson's materialism: "If the world could in any way become rigid, dry, dead, *nothing*, or if it could reach a state of equilibrium, or if it had any kind of goal that involved duration, immutability, the once-and-for-all (in short, speaking metaphysically: if becoming *could* resolve itself into being or nothingness), then this state must have been reached. But it has not been reached: from which it follows . . . the mechanistic theory stands refuted."[26] We have seen how Boltzmann has denied the absolute validity of the second law—and it is against the absolute validity of entropy that Nietzsche is arguing.

Immediately following his considerations of the physical origins of the universe, Boltzmann offers another possibility suggested by statistical mechanics:

> States of great disentanglement, that is great temperature differences, are not absolutely impossible according to the theory, but merely highly improbable, although in an almost inconceivable degree. If only, therefore we imagine the world as large enough, then according to the calculus of probability there will supervene now here now there regions of the dimensions of the system of the fixed stars that have quite an improbable distribution of states. Both during their formation and during their dissolution the temporal course will be uni-directional; if there are intelligent beings in such a location they must gain the same impression of time as we do, although the temporal course of the universe as a whole is not uni-directional.[27]

Boltzmann's universe denies the existence of historical time as anything other than discrete irregularities which have no significance beyond the individual moment of appearance, thus aligning him with Nietzsche and Adams on the importance of the present moment. Conditions governing an original creation have no meaning—we can only speak of the condition for life as an irregular configuration of molecules that allows for the excess of mechanical energy above H (min.). Michel Serres has indicated the philosophical implications of Boltzmann's work: "The final equilibrium à la Fourier or Boltzmann implies an ignorance of initial conditions and of du-

26. *Ibid.*, 549.
27. Boltzmann, *Theoretical Physics and Philosophical Problems*, 172.

ration. Whatever the origin of history may be, its end is unequivocal, determined, everywhere identical and necessary, no matter what the length of the process is. Universal equilibrium, monotonous distribution, maximum entropy. . . . Inevitable, the boltzmannian world is without individualizing memory, it wipes out progressively both memory banks and differences. It has its discrete events, without causal preconditions; it is subject to this single linear law which gives a distribution over an orderless space as the end-point of history." Denied an origin, reduced to undifferentiated energy, history loses all that which gives it meaning—that is, origin, memory, and difference. In "The Museum's Furnace," Eugenio Donato quotes this same passage from Serres and concludes, "What thermodynamics makes impossible is a history conceived as archeology."[28] The search for history will be a search for difference—an irregular distribution of energy. As the summits of energy appear without precondition out of a uniform distribution of molecules, temporal order and, hence, memory have no role. Moments of difference are without precondition and without significance—all will return to a state of undifferentiated equilibrium. To write history is to codify discrete events and link them in a causal, or genetic, chain.

Adams was hardly alone in his fascination with, and dread of, the coming degeneration of available heat (energy, according to the first law of thermodynamics, cannot disappear; according to the second law, it will be degraded into an unusable form). Baudelaire, Flaubert, Zola, and Nietzsche are just a few of the more prominent names associated with nineteenth-century nihilism.

Critics have tended to treat Adams as a late-nineteenth-century nihilist who looked nostalgically back upon twelfth-century unity. According to Robert Mane, *Mont-Saint-Michel* extols the efficacy of faith. But it is wrong to speak of Adams as taking refuge in a dead religion or in abstract ideas. "Imagination was Adams' real 'refuge,'" writes Mane; "therein is to be found the 'unity' of *Mont-Saint-Michel and Chartres* without which there would be no 'meaning.' Instead of a sentimental nihilism, what we shall see is the triumphant affirmation of Art." Although not all readers of Adams are so generous, they typically oppose a unified past and a fragmented

28. Serres, *Hermes III*, 62; Donato, "The Museum's Furnace," 236. The translation of this passage in Serres is Donato's.

present in a dialectic resolved by the artistic imagination. Yvor Winters finds in Adams' writings this opposition, but he argues that this theory reflects Adams' personal life, not twentieth-century history: "Henry Adams saw modern history as a progress from unified understanding, or the illusion of such, in the century following the year 1150, toward the dispersion of understanding and force in the twentieth century. In regard to himself he was correct; and as for modern history, his view of it . . . [is] scarcely defensible."[29] Winters sees Adams as a misguided Puritan and morally condemns him as a nihilist and a hedonist.

The quotations from critics asserting Adams' metaphysical nostalgia can easily be multiplied. Although critics are quick to point out his misinterpretations of American history, medieval theology, art, and architecture, as well as twentieth-century science, they are just as quick to defend these as imaginative constructs affirming the unifying power of art. An exception is John Rowe's reading of *Mont-Saint-Michel and Chartres* as "a quest for an historical and ontological origin in the thirteenth century." Rowe writes: "The uncle takes his niece on a journey into the medieval consciousness in order that they may find some relation to that imagined age of unity. But, if only on the evidence of the niece's Kodak, the journey is an affirmation of twentieth-century multiplicity and the disappearance of the Virgin's harmony."[30] Rowe acknowledges that the search for a lost harmony merely emphasizes present disorder, but his phenomenological approach places the onus of failure on Adams' modern sensibility and thus avoids a more radical questioning of the metaphysics of history and science. Multiplicity and unity, or the dynamo and the Virgin, are not dialectical opposites in Adams' work. They are different names for force.

Unlike other so-called nihilists, Adams is distinguished by the depth and extent of his study and application of current research in thermodynamics. Although there are no references to Boltzmann in Adams' published works and letters (however, both visited the St. Louis exposition in 1904), he was familiar with Clausius, Maxwell, Lord Kelvin, Henri Poincaré, and Gibbs. The last named is of great significance to Adams' late theoretical writings.

As mentioned above, Gibbs's phase rule, originally presented in his 1876–1878 papers "On the Equilibrium of Heterogeneous Substances," is the

29. Mane, *Henry Adams on the Road to Chartres*, 225; Winters, *In Defense of Reason*, 374.

30. Rowe, *Henry Adams and Henry James*, 45.

source for Adams' essay "The Rule of Phase Applied to History." It is unlikely that Adams was able to rely solely on Gibbs's extremely sophisticated papers; Adams' source, perhaps his only one, was Alexander Findlay's *The Phase Rule and Its Applications*, containing an introduction by Sir William Ramsey. (Adams owned a copy of the second edition, published in 1906.) Unlike Boltzmann, who began his work in kinetic theory and then turned to statistical theory, Gibbs was first concerned with statistical mechanics and systems of thermodynamic equilibrium. The phase rule was devised for consideration of physical and chemical equilibriums.

We have already discussed Gibbs's theory of equilibrium. It was the problem concerning the mixture of identical gases that led to his reducing the second law of thermodynamics to statistical probability. This in turn led to the enunciation of his phase rule, which defines the conditions of equilibrium as a relationship between what are known as the phases and the components of a system. Gibbs proceeded from the common knowledge that "at any given temperature within certain limits . . . water and vapour can exist permanently in contact with each other—or, as it is said, be in equilibrium with each other—only when the pressure has a certain definite value." [31] The questions that Gibbs set out to answer were: Is it true of all liquids? Is it valid for solutions? A pure liquid in equilibrium, like water, can exist in three forms, or phases—ice, water, and vapor—only at one definite temperature and pressure. If a salt solution is added to the water, the solution may maintain its equilibrium at different temperatures and pressures. A solution which is uniform throughout—that is, possesses identical physical properties and chemical composition—is *homogeneous*. But if the solution contains different physical properties which can be separated from each other by boundary surfaces, it is said to be *heterogeneous*. When water is in a state of equilibrium, it is said to be in heterogeneous equilibrium. The homogeneous and distinct portions of water in heterogeneous equilibrium are called *phases*. The number of phases that can exist in contact with each other depends on the system. It will presumably increase with the number of substances in the system, but equilibrium is independent of the number of phases present.

A *component* is not synonymous with a constituent of the system; components refer only to "those constituents the concentration of which can

---

31. Findlay, *The Phase Rule and Its Applications*, 1.

undergo *independent* variation in the different phases." Finally, we must add "that the Phase Rule is concerned merely with those constituents which take part in the state of real equilibrium; for *it is only to be the final state, not to the processes by which that state is reached, that the Phase Rule applies*" (my emphasis). Clifford Truesdale has criticized Gibbs for having accepted the restrictions Clausius added to his theory in his retreat from irreversible processes and having "eliminated processes altogether and recognized the subject [thermodynamics] in its starved and shrunken form as being no longer the theory of motion and heat interacting, no longer thermo*dynamics,* but only thermo*statics.* . . . Gibbs proceeded to construct a strictly static theory, *in which change in time played no part at all.*"[32]

I emphasize Gibbs's restriction of his theory to a static system in equilibrium precisely because Adams does not get through the second page of his essay before he begins to apply Gibbs's phase theory to motion: "The common idea of phase is that of the solution itself, as when salt is dissolved in water. It is the whole equilibrium or state of apparent rest. It means, perhaps, when used of movement, a variance of direction, but it seems not to have been so much employed to indicate a mere change in speed" (*DDD,* p. 268). A simple misunderstanding is not the question here; Adams knew well enough that thermodynamics introduced an epistemological revolution unsettling any faith the historian may have had in sequential history. Time may be reduced to changes in phase or of equilibrium—the sensation of temporal movement, according to Mach, if not Boltzmann, too, derives from an increase in entropy. Whatever the rate of change in phase, says Adams, "the interest of the equilibrium lies in its relations, and the object of study is the behavior of each group under new relations" (*DDD,* p. 269).

For the eighteenth- and early-nineteenth-century taxonomists and geologists, such as Lamarck, Cuvier, even Lyell, the study of natural history was a study of relations. As I have argued earlier, for the first half of the nineteenth century, history was conceived as an archive whose catalogue needed to be decoded. Yet Lyell's uniformitarian theory implied, despite its name, that the geological descent of nature was a process of decomposition leaving fragmentary remains to be reconstructed belatedly in a genealogical hierarchy. This process, as the following quotation from Darwin suggests, is one of translation:

32. *Ibid.,* 7; Clifford Truesdale, *The Tragicomedy of Classical Thermodynamics,* 83.

> For my part, following out Lyell's metaphor, I look at the natural geological record, as a history of the world imperfectly kept, and written in a changing dialect; of this history we possess the last volume alone, relating only to two or three countries. Of this volume, only here and there a short chapter has been preserved; and of each page, only here and there a few lines. Each word of the slowly-changing language, in which the history is supposed to be written, being more or less different in the interrupted succession of chapters, may represent the apparently abruptly changed forms of life, entombed in our consecutive, but widely separated formations.

Defending his theory of evolution against the charge that the geological records he relies upon are incomplete, Darwin appeals to the metaphor of the world as a book whose lacunae can be filled by conjectures based upon comparative textual analysis. Uncertain in its dialect, marred by errors and missing pages, the book represents a unity that we can only know by its absence. The appeal to the book is an appeal to origin and end, for if the world has a beginning and an end, its middle must be complete. This can be contrasted with the metaphor of a dialect, which has no boundaries or definable origin—as Darwin himself says earlier in *The Origin of Species*: "A breed, like a dialect of a language, can hardly be said to have had a definite origin."[33] Discontinuity and decay undercut the archaeological enterprise of nineteenth-century historians and natural scientists. Evolutionary theory eventually clashed head on with the second law of thermodynamics.

In Adams' account of the battle between Lyell and Kelvin, Lyell won by asserting his uniformitarian theory over Kelvin's objections that the world could not have existed long enough to allow the changes that Lyell's theory rested upon. Adams recognized the philosophical victory embedded in the scientific one: "Lyell's conservative system of evolution, resting on several broad assumptions of fact, became not merely a physiological, but even more a philosophical dogma, and in a literary point of view the Victorian epoch rested largely,—perhaps chiefly,—on the faith that society had but to follow where science led; to—'Move upward, working out the beast,/ And let the ape and tiger die'; in order to attain perfection" (*DDD*, p. 159). Religious dogma gives way to scientific dogma, the latter being as metaphysical as the former. Evolutionary theory's inherent metaphysical bias lies in its

33. Darwin, *The Origin of Species*, 316, 97.

appeal to linear time. Adams' meditation on Rome and history in the *Education* reaffirms his inability to accept history as a sequence of cause and effect:

> Rome was actual; it was England; it was going to be America. Rome could not be fitted into an orderly, middle-class, Bostonian, systematic scheme of evolution. No law of progress applied to it. Not even time-sequence—the last refuge of helpless historians—had value for it. The Forum no more led to the Vatican than the Vatican to the Forum. Rienzi, Garibaldi, Tiberius Gracchus, Aurelian might be mixed up in any relation of time, along with a thousand more, and never lead to a sequence. The great word Evolution had not yet, in 1860, made a new religion of history. (*EHA*, p. 91)

Adams' rejection of Darwinian evolution is a rejection of metaphysics, or an attempt at such; for Adams, physics is metaphysics.

Like Nietzsche, Adams criticizes a notion of history that measures the present moment in terms of a linear progression that has infinity as its starting point and culmination. In its place, they propose a historicism that measures time by the present moment, without regard to a sequence that can explain the present. In "The Rule of Phase Applied to History," Adams claims the mechanical theory of the universe lends itself to a mathematical treatment of history. As the starting point in this history is a state of equilibrium, origin has no meaning—it can only be an arbitrary point chosen for the purposes of computation. A system in equilibrium will undergo a change in phase if temperature or pressure is changed. Adams' explicit concern is the direction that any change must take: "The matter of Direction was more vital to science than all kinematics together. The question how order could have got into the universe at all was the chief object of human thought since thought existed; and order . . . was but Direction regarded as stationary, like a frozen waterfall. The sum of motion without direction is zero, as in the motion of a kinetic gas where only Clerk Maxwell's demon of Thought could create a value" (*DDD*, p. 279). Motion without direction is Adams' description of maximum entropy, which, on the molecular level, means that the atoms are thoroughly mixed—that is, in a state of disorder. Direction, which means a decrease in entropy, can only be explained by laws of probability—direction, and therefore life, is an accident. The concept of origin loses all meaning since it neither explains duration nor affects history, which is only the product of lines of force. Adams writes: "History, so far as it recounts progress, deals only with such induction or direction, and therefore in history only the attractive or inductive mass, as Thought, helps to construct. . . . The processes of History being irreversible, the action of Pressure can be exerted only in one direction, and therefore the variable called Pressure in physics has its equivalent in the Attraction, which, in the historical rule of phase, gives to human society its forward movement" (*DDD*, p. 280). If history is an irreversible process, then it tends toward a state of equilibrium or, in Adams' words, motion without direction.

Adams misapplies the phase rule to historical periods, which are said to exist in a period of equilibrium until the powers of attraction or acceleration usher in a new phase. We can find the same theory at work in his *History of the United States*: "Should history ever become a true science, it must expect to establish its laws, not from the complicated story of rival European nationalities, but from the economical evolution of a great democracy" (*History*, p. 404). Social evolution has ceased in America. Free from the disruptions experienced by Europe and Asia, America, like an inert mass undisturbed by external forces, has reached the end of history: "In a democratic ocean science could see something ultimate. Man could go no further. The atom might move, but the general equilibrium could not change" (*History*, p. 406). This early application of atomic theory is more compatible with Newtonian mechanics than with thermodynamics. Comte, whom Adams had at one time admired, followed the mechanical view and ended history with the emergence of positivism. As critics have pointed out, Adams' phase rule is reminiscent of Comte's *états*; but whereas Comte thought the final *état positif* had been reached, Adams was intent upon mapping the coming phases that would end with complete annihilation of life. This urge to prophesy appears as early as the *History*, where, in the final paragraph, Adams questions the finality he has just projected: "With the establishment of these conclusions, a new episode in American history began in 1815. New subjects demanded new treatment, no longer dramatic but steadily tending to become scientific. The traits of American character were fixed; the rate of physical and economical growth was established; and history . . . became thenceforward chiefly concerned to know what kind of people these millions were to be" (*History*, p. 417). Adams' *History* marks the end of narrative and the rise of scientific methodology. History becomes a study of force in phase theory. The problem, as Adams comes to see it, is "fixing the limits of the Phase that preceded 1600" (*DDD*, p. 293). Adams' rule of phase modifies the *Education*'s law of acceleration and ultimately bears little resemblance to Gibbs's phase rule.

Adams' essay reaches its height of eccentricity when he plots his graph of social acceleration according to the law of inverse squares. According to Adams, "the average motion of one phase is the square of that which precedes it" (DDD, p. 305). Jordy identifies this as the "law of electrical squares."[34] Adams defends his appeal to physical law with an admission of his distortion of nature: "Nature is rarely so simple as to act rigorously on the square, but History, like Mathematics, is obliged to assume that eccentricities more or less balance each other, so that something remains constant at last, and *it is compelled to approach its problems by means of some fiction*,—some infinitesimal calculus,—which may be left as general and undetermined as the formulas of our greatest master, Willard Gibbs, but which gives a hypothetical movement for an ideal substance that can be used for relation" (DDD, pp. 291–93; my emphasis). Gibbs's phase rule provides Adams with the convenient fiction upon which he can base philosophical speculations. The generality of these formulas permits him to take great liberties in his study of historical relations. Of particular significance is the arbitrariness of a starting point chosen for the purpose of calculations. The idea of a convenient fiction is not merely a substitute for a lost faith. As thermodynamics strips away all the metaphysical props that give meaning to isolated events, the historian must himself arrange events into a significant order—an *ensemble*, to use the word Adams adopted from thermodynamics.

In the previously mentioned letter to Henry Osborn Taylor, Adams writes of his *Mont-Saint-Michel and Chartres*: "I care very little whether my details are exact, if only my *ensemble* is in scale" (Cater, p. 559). Although Adams may not have read about Gibbs's ensemble theory by 1905—his confusion of Willard with Wolcott Gibbs in the *Education* makes this appear likely—he could have appropriated the term from other physicists. Maxwell and Boltzmann introduced the term *ensemble* in papers written during the 1870s and 1880s. Boltzmann had introduced the term in his discussion of ergodic systems—an ensemble of systems with a certain distribution in phase where the atoms in a system will pass through all possible positions and velocities compatible with the given energy of a system.[35]

Gibbs refined the ensemble method as developed by Boltzmann and adapted it for calculating equilibrium properties. This transfer from kinetic

34. Jordy, *Henry Adams*, 144.
35. See Brush, *Kind of Motion*, 363–72.

to combinatorial methods permitted "one to give the complicated details of collision processes, so that one simply needs to enumerate the possible configurations and compute their energies." By the term *phase* of a mechanical system, Gibbs meant the condition of the system as specified by its configurations and velocity together. A great number of such systems identical in nature but differing in phase is termed an ensemble. The ensemble provides a basis for statistical reasoning when dealing with a great number of independent systems identical in nature with the first but differing in phase: "We imagine the first system to be repeated many times, each time with a different arrangement and with different momenta of its constituents. External bodies are located with respect to every system of the ensemble as they are with respect to the first. It is to be understood that the construction of such an ensemble is a purely creative act of reason and that there is nothing in nature which corresponds to it."[36] In a universe where all macroscopic phenomena are overdetermined by an incalculable wealth of discrete molecular configurations, ensemble theory offers a method to wrest an interpretation from facts. Adams' lack of concern for facts is hardly a sign of scholarly slovenliness; rather, it reveals a sophisticated awareness that the old faith in history as a sequence of cause and effect can no longer hold in a world where sequence is meaningless and equilibrium leads to death.

The obvious paradox I have been hinting at concerns Boltzmann's definition of entropy as maximum disorder. Once thermodynamics developed beyond its initial stages as an outgrowth of factory work with steam engines, the definition of entropy as loss of heat gave way to a definition of it as a mixing of molecules. Disorder of a system in maximum entropy means stasis or death. Adams insisted on moving directly from the disorder of the invisible to the disorder of the visible. His fears of the promised dissolution of the world derived from his awareness of the significance of thermodynamics and a discomfort with the rapid development of technology. Adams is a modern—he conceives of history as being without appeal to any notion of truth, or, what is much the same, memory, which would transform incongruous lines of force into a genealogical narrative explaining the present condition of man. Along with linearity, Adams rejects di-

36. *Ibid.*, 419; Wheeler, *Josiah Willard Gibbs*, 153; Lindsay and Margenau, *Foundations of Physics*, 220.

alectics; all hope of an ultimate synthesis is discarded in recognition of the molecular anarchy threatening to overwhelm the world.

In his letter to Taylor of January 17, 1905, Adams half-jestingly suggests he would translate thermodynamics into history: "According to my score of ratios and curves, that, at the accelerated rate of progression shown since 1600, it [science] will not need another century or half century to tip thought upside down. Law, in that case, would disappear as theory or *a priori* principle, and give place to force. Morality would become police. Explosives would reach cosmic violence. Disintegration would overcome integration" (Cater, pp. 558–59). The key question raised by Adams concerns the point from which measurement begins. He describes his procedure for measurement as a formulation for "the ratio of development in energy, as in explosives or chemical energies. . . . Radium thus far is the term for these mechanical ratios. The ratio for thought is not so easy to fix" (Cater, p. 558). In his search for a basis for a scientific history, Adams finds that the new forces cannot be controlled, and radium's spontaneous transformation proved this most dramatically: "Radium denied its God—or, what was to Langley the same thing, denied the truths of his Science. The force was wholly new" (*EHA*, p. 381). Nevertheless, Adams insists upon "necessary sequence" as the basis of science: "Any science assumes a necessary sequence of cause and effect, a force resulting in motion which cannot be other than it is" (*DDD*, p. 129). Radium, however, is without sequence—it changes without cause—and in denying cause and effect, it denies definition and, consequently, God.

St. Augustine, having placed unity outside of himself and in God, could work from the multiplicity of the self in the world to the unity of the self maintained in God. In a letter to William James, Adams makes clear that the question of unity in history is as much a matter of writing as it is of faith: "Did you ever read the Confessions of St. Augustine, or of Cardinal de Retz, or of Rousseau, or of Benvenuto Cellini, or even of my dear Gibbon? Of them all, I think St. Augustine alone has an idea of literary form,— a notion of writing a story with an end and object, not for the sake of the object, but for the form, like a romance" (*Letters*.II.490). Being a lesser artist, Adams writes for the sake of the object—an education—and hopes thereby to achieve form. The lines of force gathered together in man are redirected in an external construct called history. Conceived as a product of a universe that shapes and yet excludes him, modern man asserts himself over a history that threatens dissolution by transforming the nondirectional equilibrium of the universe into a process of cause and effect. This transformation takes place through writing. Writing produces history as an image refracted from a disjointed self. But writing is not the medium through which lines of force pass; rather, it is the boundary which produces forces as isolated events without cause or effect.

History is without beginning, end, and duration: "History is a tangled skein that one may take up at any point, and break when one has unravelled enough; but complexity preceded evolution. The *Pteraspis* grins horribly from the closed entrance. One may not begin at the beginning, and one has but the loosest relative truths to follow up" (*EHA*, p. 302). Adams' dissatisfaction with evolutionary theory was not only confined to its inherent concept of progressive improvement; he rejects the theory for its adherence to linear descent. The tangled skein of history preempts evolution as multiplicity replaces simple origins—the many precedes the One. As origin does not serve as a point on a line, but breaks open an involuted web, thereby producing many lines running in many directions. Truth gives way to truths which are but stray threads to be gathered up. The *Pteraspis*, a ganoid fish that never evolved, is the reminder that history is without memory.

If "complexity precedes evolution," then history is closed to us whichever way we turn. Notions of progress and stasis are replaced by concepts of diffusion and disorder. To plot history requires only that one anticipate increasing disorder. Returning once more to Adams' letter to Henry Taylor, we find him breaking the skein at the twelfth century: "This [anticipated disintegration] was the point that leads me back to the twelfth century as the fixed element of the equation. From the relative unity of twelfth-century conceptions of the Prime Motor, I can work down pretty safely to Karl Pearsen's [*sic*] Grammar of Science, or Wallace's Man's Place in Nature [*sic*], or to Mack [Ernst Mach] and Ostwald and the other Germans of today. By intercalating Descartes, Newton, Dalton and a few others, I can even make almost a time ratio. This is where my middle-ages will work out" (Cater, p. 559). Calculations for his dynamic theory of history require a fixed point from which he can work out his ratios. The point itself is arbitrary—at best, it represents a moment of intense energy, but not unity. If we read this as a construction of an ensemble, then the first phase is the twelfth century and every other period of time is another system identical in nature but differing in phase. Sounding more like Foucault than like Comte, Adams states, "The history of the new phase has no direct relation with that which preceded it. . . . The connection of thought lay in the human reflection of itself in the universe" (DDD, p. 290). We have seen how the same metaphor in the *Education* is turned into a reminder of multiplicity. The mind's capacity to create figures of unity does not point toward an underlying unity in the universe, but implies the unchanging nature of thought, which continually forgets initial conditions and thereby frees itself to reproduce a system under ever-changing guises. At the end of "The Rule of Phase," Adams declares, "Always and everywhere the mind creates its own universe, and pursues its own phantoms; but the force behind the image is always a reality" (DDD, p. 310). In spite of this apparent endorsement of an idealist concept of mental creation, Adams makes it clear that the product, the universe, excludes the mind. Force exists in nature and operates through various media—electrical current, magnetism, chemical energy, and even mind—all cast as images giving expression to the ubiquitous force.

According to the second law of thermodynamics, force, or energy, must continually be degraded into an unusable form. In his "Letter to American Teachers of History," written two years after the first version of "The Rule of Phase," Adams employs the law of entropy in a refutation of evolution; man, too, is subject to the law of degradation. In a fusion of Will with energy and entropy with genealogy, Adams demands that the ontologist "regard the will-power of every stem as the source of variation in the branches, and to admit, as a physical necessity, that the branch which has lost the power of variation should be regarded as an example of enfeebled energy falling under the second law of thermodynamics" (DDD, p. 194). Fixity of species must be treated as a sign of decay. This may explain Adams' frequently noted disdain of reason. Reason is but enfeebled Will. As the Will develops from a parental source, it undergoes progressive degradation. Poe's Usher family, which has undergone direct descent without collateral issue, encapsulates this metaphor for Adams—man's Fall is a genealogical and entropic descent.[37]

Descent, like ascent, is a thoroughly metaphysical concept. Although Adams defines the historian's task as the tracing of the decay of vital energy, or instinct, he condemns all evolution, whether it be upward or

37. For a discussion of the entanglement of genealogy and representation in Poe, see Riddel, "The 'Crypt' of Edgar Poe," 117–44.

downward: "The figure of Rise and Fall has done infinite harm for the beginning of thought. That of Expansion and Contraction is far more scientific, even in history" (*DDD*, p. 210). In discussing the conflict between unmediated instinct and mediated, and therefore degraded, intellect, Adams
previously acknowledged that if Will is not self-motivating, but is only
"mechanical attraction," then the historian is forced to choose between
teaching history as mechanical dissolution or retreating into affirmation of
a supernatural Will as the highest product of nature. Hence, in searching
for a compromise with the physicist, Adams seeks to escape the metaphysical constraints of a historicism conceived on the model of either the
biblical Fall or Darwinian evolution. Were the historian to turn from evolution to phase theory, "history would then become a record of successive
phases of contraction, divided by periods of explosion, tending always towards an ultimate equilibrium in the form of a volume of human molecules
of equal intensity, without coördination" (*DDD*, p. 213). Although the evolutionist would be forced to reject this theory, it accounts for the differences between species, as opposed to evolutionary developments, and the
ultimate degradation of energy. Contrary to the evolutionist who wishes
to save man by granting him sole exception to the second law of thermodynamics, the physicist claims that man does most to dissipate energy; he
is the least economic of creatures. Transformation replaces evolution in
a nondirectional theory of history; an epoch, or phase, neither determines
what follows it nor is determined by what precedes it. In fact, *precede* and
follow are only terms of convenience in this history without memory.

Earlier, in "The Abyss of Ignorance," Adams tells how his substitution
of force for Will was itself without explanation: "Adams never knew why,
knowing nothing of Faraday, he began to mimic Faraday's trick of seeing
lines of force all about him, where he had always seen lines of will. . . . By
this path, the mind stepped into the mechanical theory of the universe before knowing it, and entered a distinct new phase of education. This was
the work of the dynamo and the Virgin of Chartres" (*EHA*, pp. 426–27).
Adams repeatedly compares the forces unleashed by the new science and
represented by the dynamo with the twelfth-century power of faith in the
Virgin.

The church claims to have found the prime mover. Science, on the other
hand, merely tries to escape chaos: "Nihilism had no bottom. For thousands of years every philosopher had stood on the shore of this sunless sea,

diving for pearls and never finding them. All had seen that, since they could not find bottom, they must assume it" (*EHA*, p. 430). Caught between an inability to lose himself in faith and an unwillingness to accept science's threat of nihilism, Adams settles for the convenient. Unity, like the fixed point in a historical equation, is a necessary convenience, and it was over similar questions that battle lines were drawn between the energetics of Mach and Ostwald and the atomic theory of Boltzmann. Mach and his followers argued against atomic theory on phenomenological principles because the existence of atoms was not confirmed by the senses. Adams acknowledges this debate: "The scientific synthesis commonly called Unity was the scientific analysis commonly called Multiplicity. The two things were the same, all forms being shifting phases of motion" (*EHA*, p. 431).

Adams' likely source for this analysis is John Bernhard Stallo's *The Concepts and Theories of Modern Physics*, which he read in a French translation. Stallo attacks the mechanical theory of Clausius, Maxwell, and Boltzmann as being "founded upon propositions destructive of the very basis upon which alone a consistent superstructure of atomic mechanics can be reared." What is most interesting for the reader of Adams is Stallo's accusation that mechanical theory treats the concepts matter and motion as "distinct and real" entities: "The mechanical theory, in common with all metaphysical theories, hypostasizes partial, ideal, and, it may be, purely conventional groups of attributes, or single attributes, and treats them as varieties of objective reality. Its basis, therefore, is essentially metaphysical. The mechanical theory is, in fact, a survival of medieval realism." (We will see how Adams will interpret St. Thomas Aquinas as a forebear of William Thomson.) Stallo further defines two forms of the metaphysical system: the synthetic and the analytic. According to the former, "the varieties of objective reality are held to be due to a synthesis of substance and accidents." The analytic view is "presented in evolutionary or pantheistic systems in which the lower conceptual or real forms are supposed to be contained or implied in the higher forms and to be derived from them by processes of evolution or development."[38] In both the analytic and synthetic views, according to Stallo, reality lies in the unseen force that either forms the substance, of which visible objects are accidents, or energizes molecular particles producing the evolutionary changes in visible matter.

38. Stallo, *The Concepts and Theories of Modern Physics*, 38, 150, 152.

Adams regards both scientific synthesis and analysis as failures in the attempt to define unity. The appeal to ultimate energy is a lapse into pantheism—the heresy, says Adams in *Mont-Saint-Michel*, the church most dreaded. Just as the church swerved from doctrines that rendered its existence superfluous, so science sought to avoid the chaos of colliding atoms: "Science itself had been crowded so close to the edge of the abyss that its attempts to escape were as metaphysical as the leap" (*EHA*, p. 431). In *Esther*, Adams examines an individual's inability to make the leap of faith by an act of will, but he clearly distinguishes between faith in God and faith in science. His spokesman for science, George Strong, declares, "Mystery for mystery science beats religion hollow" (*Esther*, p. 191). When asked by Esther if science is true, Strong says no, yet he qualifies his answer: "There is no science which does not begin by requiring you to believe the incredible" (*Esther*, p. 199). Strong's faith, however, rests not upon a belief in transcendent truth but upon a need for convenience. Adams makes this far more explicit in the *Education*, where convenience is the last bastion against contradiction: "Always and everywhere the Complex had been true and the Contradiction had been certain. Thought started by it" (*EHA*, p. 455).

Complexity, supported by contradiction, set the force called thought in motion, but once in motion, thought seeks to fabricate an origin that would place it on firm ground. The historian confronted with the implications of this is forced to admit that the "mathematical paradise of endless displacement" must replace sequence as the grounds for his inquiry (*EHA*, p. 455). The mathematician's paradise is the historian's hell. Rejecting the failed experiment of his *History of the United States*, Adams attempts to borrow from science a method for writing history—a method that can make do without truth: "The historian must not try to know what is truth, if he values his honesty; for if he cares for his truths, he is certain to falsify his facts. The laws of history only repeat the lines of force or thought" (*EHA*, p. 457). The historian can no longer accept as truth the idea that society educates itself or works toward a goal; the lines of thought are without determinacy or continuity. They are natural forces antagonistic to man: "As Nature developed her hidden energies, they tended to become destructive. Thought itself became tortured, suffering reluctantly, impatiently, painfully, the coercion of new method" (*EHA*, p. 486). Adams' tortured and tortuous explanations of his dynamic theory of history match nature's destructive power for their refusal to be arranged in a logical and sequential order.

Toward the close of the nineteenth century, Adams had begun his calculations for the phases of history, but, as I have indicated, a change of phase is not a product of time. This is of particular importance in *Mont-Saint-Michel*. Both Michael Colacurcio and John P. McIntyre, S.J., have argued that *Mont-Saint-Michel* accents the temporal erosion of twelfth-century unity. Father McIntyre has commented that *Mont-Saint-Michel* moves from summit to grave, that is, from the striking opening, "The Archangel loved heights," to the buried pathos of the final page.[39] The final lines invite this ascription of formal unity to the book. Speaking of the Gothic church, Adams writes: "The delight of its aspirations is flung up to the sky. The pathos of its self-distrust and anguish of doubt is buried in the earth as its last secret. You can read out of it whatever else pleases your youth and confidence; to me, this is all" (*MSMC*, p. 377). But this conclusion ties in just as well, if not better, with the preface, for the latter also raises the question of reading, and it does so by pointing not to the internal unity of the text but to the external disorder represented by a preface that controls access to the work.[40] Yet the uncle's claim upon the niece is not binding like that of either father and son or author and reader. The relationship of uncle and niece is "capable of being anything or nothing." Just as history has been transformed from a chronology of unquestioned facts to a study of interpretative relations, reader and writer have lost the implicit genealogical tie that gave a determined meaning to a text—or a Gothic church, for it too can be "anything or nothing." The reader seeking relations or meanings must bring them to the text. The Gothic church, like the "Study in Twentieth-Century Multiplicity," tells of a desire for unity, not of a unity achieved, for the aspiration which captivates the viewer has its foundation in the emptiness and doubt "buried in the earth." If the outburst of great art from 1150 to 1250 received its substance from the Virgin, then it issued forth from the tomb. But this is not a dialectic of plenitude and absence; as the final description of the church suggests, absence inhabits plenitude and makes possible the difference that leads to the production of art and thought.

39. Colacurcio, "The Dynamo and the Angelic Doctor," 699; McIntyre, "Henry Adams and the Unity of Chartres," 161.
40. I refer to Derrida, *Dissemination*, 1–59.

The play of presence and absence has been as fecund for twentieth-century science as it was for thirteenth-century theology. In Chapter 14 of *Mont-Saint-Michel*, Adams presents the dilemma as a debate between Abelard, the nominalist, and William of Champeaux, the realist. Together these two medieval metaphysicians represent for Adams the two trends in nineteenth-century physics decried by Stallo. William holds that universals are substances; Abelard claims that substances have no reality, the only reality being concepts. In Adams' imaginary debate, William's account of their difference over the existence of a triangle sums up their opposition: " 'My triangle exists as a reality, or what science will call an energy, outside my mind, in God, and is impressed on my mind as it is on a mirror, like the triangle on the crystal, its energy giving form. Your triangle you say is also an energy, but an essence of my mind itself; you thrust it into the mind as an integral part of the mirror; identically the same concept, energy, or necessary truth which is inherent in God' " (*MSMC*, p. 298). Abelard is the medieval Boltzmann claiming that concepts, in place of the latter's atoms, be treated as the basis of reality. William is the medieval Mach, claiming that objective reality is the basis for every concept and that the most general concept is the highest reality. For the church, the problem seemed interminable: realism leads to materialism, and nominalism leads to pantheism. In both cases, energy is the underlying principle. This debate, says Adams, is just as heated in the twentieth century: "Science has become too complex to affirm the existence of universal truths, but it strives for nothing else, and disputes the problem, within its own limits, almost as earnestly as in the twelfth century" (*MSMC*, p. 289). The question is "whether unity or diversity is ultimate law" (*MSMC*, p. 288).

In the final chapter Adams turns to St. Thomas Aquinas, albeit a fictional Thomas, as having made the last great effort to construct a system reconciling unity with multiplicity. Adams' advice to his niece on reading St. Thomas holds for his own work as well: "Saint Thomas's architecture, like any other work of art, is best studied by itself as though he created it outright; otherwise a tourist would never get beyond its threshold" (*MSMC*, p. 345). The unity ascribed to Thomas' work is wholly imaginary—like all Gothic churches, it is unfinished. A new arch can be thrown or a new buttress added, to permit a never-ending modification of the building. (It should be remembered that Adams thought of his *Education* as a fragment.) By means of a mistranslation,[41] Adams transforms Thomas into a physicist: " 'I see motion,' said Thomas: 'I infer a motor!' This reasoning, which may be fifty thousand years old, is as strong as ever it was; stronger than some more modern inferences of science; but the average mechanic stated it differently. 'I see motion,' he admitted: 'I infer energy. I see motion everywhere; I infer energy everywhere' " (*MSMC*, p. 347).

Thomas, however, infers a fixed, intelligent motor. The mechanic can work with this theory as well as another, but it can only remain a theory—it is not proof. Adams' mechanic replies to Adams' Thomas: " 'To your old ideas of form we have added what we call force, and we are rather further than ever from reducing the complex to unity. In fact, if you are aiming to convince me, I will tell you flatly that I know only the multiple, and have no use for unity at all' " (*MSMC*, p. 348). Answering for all twentieth-century men, the mechanic also shows that hidden in the elaborate design of the *Summa* is a twentieth-century scientist. Modern science, like St. Augustine, starts from multiplicity; the lesser artists, St. Thomas and Henry Adams, start from unity. Temporal periods are reversed, and all efforts to derive the unified vision are reduced to arbitrary starting points—either the unity of God or the multiplicity of experience.

Neither one has priority, for even if multiplicity were prior, that would mean it had a substantial reality that would promise an ultimate reconciliation. Instead, both multiplicity and unity are lost in complexity, or the unresolvable, as they are for Thomas and the physicist:

> Avowedly science has aimed at nothing but the reduction of multiplicity to unity, and has excommunicated, as though it were itself a Church, any one who doubted or disputed its object, its method, or its results. The effort is as evident and quite as laborious in modern science, starting as it does from multiplicity, as in Thomas Aquinas, who started from unity; and it is necessarily less successful, for its true aims, as far as it is science and not disguised religion, were equally attained by reaching infinite complexity; but the assertion or assumption of ultimate unity has characterized the Law of Energy as emphatically as it has characterized the definition of God in theology. If it is a reproach to Saint Thomas, it is equally a reproach to Clerk-Maxwell. In truth, it is what men most admire in both—the power of broad and lofty generalization. (*MSMC*, p. 371).

41. Michael Colacurcio points out that Adams mistranslates Thomas' *movens* as motor. Mover is the common translation. See "The Dynamo and the Angelic Doctor," 701.

Science, like theology, is ultimately metaphysical, although the former tries to hide it. In a letter to Brooks, written at the same time Henry was working on Thomas Aquinas, Henry confirms his "having always had a weakness for science mixed with metaphysics. I am a dilution of Lord Kelvin and St. Thomas Aquinas" (*Letters*.II.392). Adams himself embodies the play of presence and absence represented by the Virgin and the dynamo. And although Adams restrains himself from reading for the higher synthesis, he recognizes that the moment one speaks, one enters into metaphysics. The marvelous wit of the principles of Conservative Christian Anarchy reveals his delight in trying to evade a dialectic that can never contain the diversity of energy. Like a good Hegelian, he says that "the great principle of contradiction . . . was itself agreement, a restriction of personal liberty inconsistent with freedom; but the 'larger synthesis' admitted a limited agreement provided it was strictly confined to the end of a larger contradiction. . . . [T]he process was arduous, and while Adams, as the older member, assumed to declare the principle, [Bay] Lodge necessarily denied both the assumption and the principle in order to assure its truth" (*EHA*, p. 406). With his final contradiction, Lodge assures the final synthesis that swings everything back to the unity which Conservative Christian Anarchists deny. Unity is chaos.

In his "Prayer to the Virgin," Adams expresses a similar concept, but in a manner which condenses *Mont-Saint-Michel*, the *Education*, and the final theoretical essays into an ambivalent acknowledgment that unity is most distant when it is attained. Like Christ who went about his Father's business, Adams seeks unity in the Father:

> I did not find the Father, but I lost
>   What now I value more, the Mother,—
>   You!
>
> I thought the fault was yours that foiled my search;
>   I turned and broke your image on its throne,
> Cast down my idol, and resumed my march
>   To claim the father's empire for my own.
>
> Crossing the hostile sea, our greedy band
>   Saw rising hills and forests in the blue;
> Our father's kingdom in the promised land!
>   —We seized it, and dethroned the father too.
>
> And now we are the Father, with our brood,
>   Ruling the Infinite, not Three but One;

> We made our world and saw that it was good;
>> Ourselves we worship, and we have no Son.   (*LN*, pp. 126–27)

The seeker attempts to restore direct descent of father to son, but to do so he usurps the father's place and now is both son and father. Wishing to be his own begetter, he only discovers the hollowness of unity. Having raised man to take God's empty throne, the supplicant finds that the One is but another name for the infinite complexity of energy. To this he prays in the poem within the poem, the "Prayer to the Dynamo." But on the dynamo "prayer is thrown away," for it is "only force and light" (*LN*, p. 129).

The dynamo is pure energy without meaning; its destructive force racks nature and destroys man:

> Seize, then, the Atom! rack his joints!
>> Tear out of him his secret spring!
> Grind him to nothing!—though he points
> To us, and his life-blood anoints
>> Me—the dead Atom-King!   (*LN*, p. 130)

It is from this ultimate degradation of energy that Adams flees in the remainder of the poem. His theological dynamo forces him into recognition that his nihilism is but a return to metaphysics. The God of energy and man as the Atom-King are but the lifeless versions of a once fecund belief in the presence of God. The object of that belief, the Virgin, receives Adams' devotion in his retreat from nihilism:

> Help me to bear! not my own baby load,
>> But yours; who bore the failure of the light,
> The strength, the knowledge and the thought of God,—
>> The futile folly of the Infinite!   (*LN*, p. 134)

But Adams cannot bear this faith either, for the infinite plenitude is but another name for the nihilistic power of the dynamo.

CHAPTER FIVE

Ezra Pound and the
Translatability of History

And the great labour, this labour of translation, of making America intelligible, of making it possible for individuals to meet across national borders.

—Pound

One never writes either in one's own language or in a foreign language.

—Derrida

Revisions of literary history, such as Harold Bloom's, often produce genealogies noted not so much for whom they include or exclude but for how they interpret the relationship between literary fathers and sons. Thus Bloom's line descending from Milton through the British Romantics and on to Emerson, Whitman, and Stevens is conspicuous more for its interpretation of what constitutes a genealogy than for the poets who make up this family. Beginning, as did Emerson, with the recognition that the poet cannot escape his belatedness, Bloom rescues poetry from writing by appealing to the psyche as that which effaces the past even as it repeats it.

Controlling Bloom's metaphoric economy is the figure of the father. This becomes crucial when he defines the American sublime as that moment in a poem when the poet becomes his own father. The mapping of tradition depends upon an exchange of tropes between texts whereby the precursor is, to use Bloom's term, transumed by the new poem. Thus, when the reader returns to the precursor, he finds him imitating the poetic son. But when Bloom writes that "Emerson therefore founds his sublime upon a refusal of history, particularly literary history,"he covers over Emerson's double sense of history that accounts for both the metaphoric exchange of texts and the entropic dispersal of writing.[1] For every one of Emerson's statements confirming the power of the central man, we have another Emer-

1. Bloom, *Poetry and Repression*, 244, 254.

son—who, we might say, fathers another family—saying the opposite: "Evolution was not from one central point, but coactive from three or more points. Life has no memory" (W.III.70). The Scene of Instruction has gone into extra sessions, and the curriculum has not been coordinated.

The economic topos of a primordial gnosis passed from father to son in chronological succession cannot control the entropic force of writing, which can never overcome the chaos of its indeterminable history. Therefore, we have Bloom's resistance to poets whose writings further entangle the much-tangled question of genealogy. The American author absent from Bloom's scheme who looms most conspicuously in any discussion of entropy and history is Henry Adams. His speculations on history, economics, and physics—all topics that profoundly interested Emerson—suggest the existence of a second Emersonian family that can never be reconciled with the first. If, as Bloom says, "the origins of the American Sublime are connected inextricably to the business collapse of 1837,"[2] we can say that another American sublime, also stemming from Emerson, originates in the depression of 1893 that resulted from a shortage of gold. Adams responded to this crisis in modern capitalism by joining his brother Brooks not only in the campaigns for bimetalism and the presidential candidacy of William Jennings Bryan but also in the intellectual exchange that led to their respective works on history and economics.

Although Adams' great distrust of bankers and the financial oligarchy that had emerged in America during the second half of the nineteenth century led to his alliance with the populist free silver movement, his theory of history, as well as his dislike of the middle and lower classes, led him to condemn liberal democracy for pushing civilization toward chaos, which he associated with socialism. The alternative would be centralization; nevertheless, his dynamic theory of history led him to believe that socialism was inevitable. A rapid increase in the random mixture of molecules leading to maximum entropy meant that civilization would eventually cease to exist.

In his dynamic theory of history, Adams proposes that the centralization of power would allow the most efficient utilization of available energy. Henry, however, left it to Brooks to formulate a theory of history that expresses the fascist impulse behind a threatened bourgeois class. In a series of books beginning with The Law of Civilization and Decay (first edition

2. Ibid., 236.

published in 1896), Brooks sets forth a theory of force in history based upon the accumulation of wealth. According to Brooks, when the surplus wealth exceeds the forces of production, capital becomes an autocratic power seeking to expand its control over other nations by either military or economic conquest. This process would lead to the inevitable collapse of a great power as wealth begins to be expended on war or on purchasing materials from outlying domains, thus draining capital away from the center of power. As a witness to the decline of Britain and France, Brooks foresaw a shift of power to America, Germany, and Russia. Applying a theory of acceleration similar to Henry's, Brooks postulates that "if Americans are to outstrip their opponents, they must do so by having a compacter and more flexible organization and shorter and cheaper communications." In a world where greatly expanding masses of people must be controlled by the most efficient means possible, the government takes on the features of a corporation: "If expansion and concentration are necessary, because the administration of the largest mass is the least costly, then America must expand and concentrate until the limit of the possible is attained; for Governments are simply huge corporations in competition, in which the most economical, in proportion to its energy, survives, and in which the wasteful and the slow are undersold and eliminated."[3]

Although he fashions his government on the model of a corporation, Adams not only despises capitalism, he also fears that the capitalist class will lead America to its doom. The centralization of power must be carried on by the government, not a financial oligarchy that taxes the majority for private interests. As power concentrates in fewer and fewer hands, there will be a simultaneous expansion of control over the masses and vast geographical domains. Ultimately, the consolidation of capital will lead to widespread disorder which can only be put down by the army. This is precisely what Brooks foresees for any government that captial might organize. In Theodore Roosevelt, whom Brooks served as an unofficial advisor, Adams finds the leader who will break up capital and act as the charismatic dictator in a state based upon what Antonio Gramsci called "Caesarism." In his *Prison Notebooks*, Gramsci writes how Caesarism "always expresses the particular solution in which a great personality is entrusted with the

3. Brooks Adams, *America's Economic Supremacy*, 232, 133.

task of 'arbitration' over a historico-political situation characterized by an equilibrium of forces heading toward catastrophe."[4] For Brooks and Henry Adams, these conflicting forces were socialism and capitalism, as they were for Wyndham Lewis, T. S. Eliot, and Ezra Pound. The Adamses' economics, not to say their historical speculations, have had a certain impact on modernist literature, none more direct or curious than in Pound's fascination with Brooks's cranky theory predicting the failure of capitalism and the rise of a fascist state.

As Marx suggests, language and money have always been bound together in an economy of translation in which the universal equivalent can never govern the rate of exchange. Money, the universal commodity, is a language that has no respect for nationality or origins (such as those which make an American sublime possible): "Commodities as such are indifferent to all religious, political, national and linguistic barriers. Their universal language is price and their common bond is money." But money itself has no intrinsic value; its value is purely imaginary. (Perhaps this is what Wallace Stevens had in mind when he wrote, "Money is a kind of poetry.")[5] Consequently, money and commodities, like words and meaning, do not exist in an indissociable relation. Translation cannot arrest the exchange between commodities, or between texts, in order to regulate an economy without reserves. An excess always remains behind in the *différance* that always escapes the machinery of language. And it is Ezra Pound, a son Emerson would be embarrassed to acknowledge, who reminds us that history lies in the untranslatable remnant which refuses to be sublimated.

Perhaps more than any other of our modern poets, even Frost, Pound has brought with him into the twentieth century the intellectual heritage of the nineteenth. Several critics, most prominently John Espey and Donald Davie, have shown how Pound's aesthetic tastes and doctrines were determined by his readings of nineteenth-century French writers and the Pre-Raphaelites.[6] Similarly, Pound's anti-Semitism and fascism can be seen as

---

4. See Brooks Adams, *The Theory of Social Revolutions*, 21–29; Gramsci, *Selections from the Prison Notebooks*, 219.

5. Marx, *A Contribution to the Critique of Political Economy*, 152; Marx, *Capital*, I, 190; Stevens, *Opus Posthumous*, 165.

6. Espey, *Ezra Pound's "Mauberley"*; Davie, *Ezra Pound*.

an anachronistic return to the anticapitalist impulse that lay behind Henry and Brooks Adams' support of William Jennings Bryan and the free silver campaign, as well as their fears of Jewish control of international finance.

Such historical formulations, however, do little to explain the relation between fascist ideology and modernism. Although the appeal to socioeconomic conditions, such as the financial crisis during the early 1890s, may explain the outpouring of anti-Semitic invectives in Henry Adams' writings, it fails to resolve the connection between the inherently nostalgic force underlying fascism and the modernists' radical revision of history. In a superb analysis of Wyndham Lewis, Fredric Jameson has pointed out that modernists, in the canonical interpretation, seek to "reappropriate an alienated universe by transforming it into personal styles and private languages: such wills to style have served in retrospect to reconfirm the very privatization and fragmentation of social life against which they meant to protest."[7] Yet if one is to claim Henry Adams for a modernist, as I have, it cannot be done on the grounds of a private language. This most reticent of writers—the *Education* and *Mont-Saint-Michel and Chartres* were privately printed and circulated among friends—writes in anything but a private language. Even in his letters, he exhibits a formal elegance and sophisticated irony that both draws the reader to him and yet keeps before his audience an impenetrable mask. As far as prose style is concerned, Adams is a child of the eighteenth century.

If we are to search for a theory of modernism, it must be in terms of a poetics of history. The problematical relationship between modernism and history has been examined anew in the wake of a rereading of Nietzsche, whose *Use and Abuse of History* provides the pre-text of Paul de Man's analysis of modernism in "Literary History and Literary Modernity." De Man argues that the term *modern* is used for a privileged moment of spontaneity free from the determinism of history. Yet in the desire to assert itself as an origin, modernism severs itself from the present as certainly as it rejects the immediate past. The contradictory basis for the relation, de Man says, "goes beyond antithesis or opposition": "If history is not to become sheer regression or paralysis, it depends on modernity for its duration and renewal; but modernity cannot assert itself without being at once

7. Jameson, *Fables of Aggression*, 2.

swallowed up and reintegrated in a regressive historical process." The modernist's ambivalent attitude toward the past distinguishes him from the historian who remains remote from the facts he collects by recording them in a language he believes to be adequate to the phenomenal world. The writer's language, however, "is to some degree the product of his own action; he is both the historian and the agent of his own language. The ambivalence of writing is such that it can be considered both an act and an interpretation process that follows after an act with which it cannot coincide."[8] The writer, therefore, inscribes an act as a moment distinct from the process of writing and nevertheless dependent on it for its being. The modernist's situation is best expressed in Tristram Shandy's plan to record every moment of his life, only to fail, not because it would require him to spend his entire life with pen in hand, but because he cannot find the point in time when his history begins. The act of writing implies the successive movement of discrete events that forever displaces the present by transforming the myth of origin into a problematic of belated interpretation whereby the past remains beyond the reach of language. Adams' position as a modernist rests on a poetics of history that marks this division between the event and its interpretation in the space of writing.

On these grounds, Ezra Pound's modernism is perhaps even more questionable than Adams'. If the sequence of cause and effect which historians traditionally take for granted is, as both Adams and Nietzsche argue, a product of language and not a series of events organized within a diachronic system, then how can the reader reconcile Pound's critical theories with his admiration of Mussolini as an unself-conscious man of action? Fascism represents a reaction to the advanced technology of a capitalist culture and to the failure of liberal democracy. In several cantos, for instance, Pound condemns the loss of craftsmanship that comes with industrialization. In Canto 22, he opposes the care in the making of handcrafted works to the waste of mass production:

> An' the inspector says: "How many rejects?"
> "What you mean, rejects?"
> And the inspector says; "How many do you get?"
> And Joe said: "We don't get any rejects, our . . ."

8. De Man, Blindness and Insight, 151, 152.

> And the inspector says: "Well then of course you
> can't do it."
> Price of life in the occident.[9]

Pound's attitude toward money and language, both of which he considers mediums of exchange, are also tangled in the same problematic that includes his politics. The question of Pound's nostalgia for an irrecoverable age is an old one. It is at least as old as readers' claims that his greatest poetry appears in his translations. This, in fact, is Wyndham Lewis' argument in a chapter of *Time and Western Man* significantly titled "A Man in Love with the Past." To accuse Pound of nostalgia, however, is to ignore his theory of language as a system of mechanical reproduction. Through this process of repetition, translation escapes the opposition of freedom versus fidelity.

Before I turn to Pound's theory of translation, I first wish to confront his political and historical formulations in his most infamous work, *Jefferson and/or Mussolini*. Early in the book he warns the reader how he is to be read: "I am not putting these sentences in monolinear syllogistic arrangement, and I have no intention of using that old form of trickery to fool the reader, any reader, into thinking I have proved anything, or that having read a paragraph of my writing he KNOWS something that he can only *know* by examining a dozen or two dozen facts and putting them all together" (*J/M*, p. 28). Pound here dismisses more than just the syllogism and the confusion of linear sequence with cause and effect. What proves so unsettling in Pound is his insistence that a relative handful of isolated facts reveals a pattern in history that normally remains obscure to anyone but the artist. Thus, he continually returns to Mussolini's draining of the swamps as proof of his administrative ability to get things done. But the relation between events in history is as tenuous as the relation between the sentences in some of Pound's writings from the thirties on.

In *Guide to Kulchur*, he suggests that his essay be read like a crossword puzzle. Following an attack on professors who "fall for the stability racket" by accepting as a necessity fixed prices and, consequently, an unchanging

---

9. Pound, *Cantos*, 22:101, hereinafter cited by canto and page number. The following abbreviations will be used for citations from Pound's works: *ABC—ABC of Reading*; *GB—Gaudier-Brzeska*; *GK—Guide to Kulchur*; *J/M—Jefferson and/or Mussolini*; *LE—Literary Essays*; *SL—Selected Letters, 1907–1941*; *SP—Selected Prose, 1909–1965*; *SR—The Spirit of Romance*.

relation between goods and money, Pound writes: "The hurried reader may say I write this in cypher and that my statement merely skips from one point to another without connection or sequence. The statement is nevertheless complete. All the elements are there, and the nastiest addict of crossword puzzles shd. be able to solve this or see this" (*GK*, p. 48). Linear sequence falsifies not only history but writing as well. Thus, we can no longer follow such critics as Daniel Pearlman and speak of the *Cantos*, or any modernist text, as "bridging the gap between Spirit and Time, self and society."[10] This formalist analysis transforms a linguistic system of exchange into a sequential narrative, only to appeal outside of language to spirit and thereby fix the relation between signifier and signified, as well as past and present, in an unchanging transcendent realm where the end marks a return to a genuine point of origin. A belief in fixed relations in economics and language lies behind the practice of explaining history by recording facts as if they were stable entities free from the process of writing.

Pound's disjointed style is an attempt to impress upon the reader the immediacy of the words on the page (thus all the typographic tricks), for language alone constitutes knowledge. As Richard Sieburth points out, in the *Cantos* language itself is "the very object of representation."[11] Consequently, history discloses itself in the guise of its record: "We do NOT know the past in chronological sequence. It may be convenient to lay it out anesthetized on the table with dates pasted on here and there, but what we know we know by ripples and spirals eddying out from us and from our own time" (*GK*, p. 60). Pound's simultaneous attack on the diachronic structure of historicism and the sentence reveals the complicity between language and the desire to transform the particulars of history into a genetic sequence. When he resorts to the metaphor of the spiral, he expresses a desire to redefine the origin in terms of the present moment.

A similar argument appears in *The Spirit of Romance*: "It is dawn at Jerusalem while midnight hovers above the Pillars of Hercules. All ages are contemporaneous. It is B.C., let us say, in Morocco. The Middle Ages are in Russia. The future stirs already in the minds of the few. This is especially true of literature, where the real time is independent of the apparent, and where many dead men are our grandchildren's contemporaries, while

10. Pearlman, *The Barb of Time*, 85.
11. Sieburth, *Instigations*, 121.

many of our contemporaries have been already gathered into Abraham's bosom, or some more fitting receptacle" (*SR*, p. 6). History exists as a synchronic entity, not as a genetic sequence. The geographical juxtaposition of various epochs redefines history in terms of the present moment. The desire we have seen in Emerson to deny the past does not appear to have been felt by Pound (unless it meant some aspects of his American past), for the past is but a point in a field existing in a synchronic relationship with the present. Therefore, Pound can say along with Fenollosa, "Relations are more real and more important than the things which they relate. The forces which produce the branch-angles of an oak lay potent in the acorn." In fact, Pound resorts to the same metaphor in order to explain the process of thought: "Man is—the sensitive physical part of him—a mechanism, for the purpose of our further discussion a mechanism rather like an electric appliance, switches, wires, etc. . . . Their thoughts are in them as the thought of the tree is in the seed, or in the grass, or the grain, or the blossom" (*SR*, p. 92). In Pound's text, Fenollosa's organic metaphor, with all its connotations of New England transcendentalism, is equated with the mechanical metaphor of the switchboard. Nature, for Pound and Fenollosa, and perhaps also for Emerson, as Joseph Riddel has argued, is a sign-producing machine governing the exchange between past and present. The author merely serves as a circuit through which this exchange takes place.[12]

De Man also speaks of the ceaseless process whereby the modern writer moves between the dream of immediacy given form in the symbolic text and "the compulsion to return to a literary mode of being, as a form of language that knows itself to be mere repetition, mere fiction, and allegory, forever unable to participate in the spontaneity of action or modernity." Pound's concept of language as machine circumvents this dilemma. De Man recognizes that his own characterization of modernism is based on the writer as subject: "It seems that there can be no end, no respite in the ceaseless pressure of this contradiction, at least as long as we consider it from the point of view of the writer as subject."[13] Language conceived of as a machine exchanging past and present, sign with sign, goods with money, functions independently from the subject, who, in fact, is merely a product

---

12. Fenollosa, *The Chinese Written Character as a Medium for Poetry*, 22; Riddel, "Pound and the Decentered Image," 584.

13. De Man, *Blindness and Insight*, 161, 162.

of the machine. I will return to this concept when I discuss Pound's politics, but here I want to emphasize that Pound's affirmation of the status of the text as repetition also affirms the absence of the subject. Thus, he freely denies being the proprietor of what he produces: "There is no ownership in most of my statements and I can not interrupt every sentence or paragraph to attribute authorships to each pair of words, especially as there is seldom an a priori claim even to the phrase or the half phrase" (GK, p. 60). Pound thus transforms the question of impersonality in Imagist poetics from epistemology into grammatology.

The juxtaposition of sources implied here by Pound disposes of the author as the creative producer of language. The power of what Pound called the ideogramic method derives from the displacement of the subject by the machine of language. He defines the ideogramic method in Guide to Kulchur: "The ideogramic method consists of presenting one facet and then another until at some point one gets off the dead and desensitized surface of the reader's mind, onto a part that will register. The 'new' angle being new to the reader who cannot always be the same reader" (GK, p. 51). The breaking up of clichés of thought, as well as phrase, can only be achieved by presenting ideas in a discontinuous fashion. The name ideogramic, however, misleads the reader into associating the method with Pound's study of Chinese, whereas it could just as well have come from his reading of Remy de Gourmont on the dissociation of ideas, and Pound calls it "interpreting detail" in an earlier essay. In his definition of ideogramic method, Pound suggests that the reader himself is translated with each new interpretation of a passage. Through the presentation of dissociated events and/or ideas, Pound impresses upon the reader, whose status as subject is as uncertain as the writer's, the task of interpretation.

This task proves particularly important when it comes to the image. In the early manifesto of 1913, "A Few Dont's," Pound calls for "direct treatment of the 'thing' whether subjective or objective" (LE, p. 3). But when it comes to defining the image, we find direct treatment is unattainable: "An 'Image' is that which presents an intellectual and emotional complex in an instant of time. . . . It is the presentation of such a 'complex' instantaneously which gives that sense of sudden liberation; that sense of freedom from time limits and space limits; that sense of sudden growth, which we experience in the presence of the greatest works of art" (LE, p. 4). The image, which is supposed to free us from the constraints of space and time, is by definition itself bound by the temporal and the spatial. Rather than present to the reader the "thing," the poet can only present the sign as a repetition of what must already be a doubled sign. In other words, the image is bound to language, hence the stress on the *gram* (Greek for "written"), or grammatical, in the ideo-gram. The apparent spatial form of the image is interpreted as a spatio-temporal complex experienced as the repetition of a previous interpretation. According to Riddel, "If the Image is a 'complex' condensed into an 'instant of time,' it is a displacement of linearity into a cycle, that is, a repetition which composes an irreducibly temporalized space."[14]

The image, then, is already marked by a radical temporality that displaces the object from the realm of direct experience. Thus when Pound comes to consider the symbol, he claims that "the proper and perfect symbol is the natural object, that if a man use 'symbols' he must so use them that their symbolic function does not obtrude; so that *a* sense, and the poetic quality of the passage, is not lost to those who do not understand the symbol as such, to whom, for instance, a hawk is a hawk" (*LE*, p. 9). Pound's statement that the natural object is the symbol should not be taken as a belief in the permanent value of nature. When he says that the symbolic object, the "hawk," is to be understood as standing for itself, he insists that it can only be taken as a linguistic sign, unlike the symbol, which he calls elsewhere a "permanent metaphor."

In an essay reprinted in his memoir *Gaudier-Brzeska*, he attacks the symbolists for dealing in " 'association,' that is, in a sort of allusion, almost of allegory. They degraded the symbol to the status of a word. They made it a form of metonymy. . . . The symbolist's *symbols* have a fixed value, like numbers in arithmetic, like 1, 2, and 7. The imagiste's images have a variable significance, like the signs *a*, *b*, and *x* in algebra" (*GB*, p. 84). The difference, we might say, between the symbol and the image is that the latter contains an untranslatable remnant. The permanent signification of the symbol implies identity between words—an identity that depends heavily upon convention. In addition, the symbolist relies upon the stability of the natural world, but the word, suggests Pound, always

14. Riddel, "Pound and the Decentered Image," 575.

exceeds that which it signifies. In fact, the object itself is but a translation. The hawk, as William Carlos Williams said of Gertrude Stein's rose, is always already a sign.[15]

In *Gaudier-Brzeska*, Pound discusses the relation between sign and truth: "In the 'search for oneself,' in the search for 'sincere self-expression,' one gropes, one finds some seeming verity. One says 'I am' this, that, or the other, and with the words scarcely uttered one ceases to be that thing" (*GB*, p. 85). Self, then, is but self-expression, with the emphasis on expression. Self can only have existence in language, but the self is always deferred from existence as language marks the difference between speaker and subject. This search, Pound explains, was important for his poetry: "I began this search for the real in a book called *Personae*, casting off, as it were, complete masks of the self in each poem. I continued in long series of translations, which were but more elaborate masks" (*GB*, p. 85). We might say that translation is the casting off of masks, for translation always involves a residue of meaning that exceeds what is supposed to name it.

Pound prefers the image to the symbol, for the former's inherent instability admits to the impossibility of the spatial form of an autotelic poem. The temporality of the image ties it to history, whereas the symbol, according to Pound's interpretation, is guilty of bad faith in positing an ahistorical language rooted in a fixed nature, or in abstract idea. Therefore, I find myself disagreeing with Michael Bernstein's argument for the ideogramic method as retaining, like the Chinese sign, "an intimate link to a natural process." Having grounded the ideogram in nature and the subject who perceives the "hitherto unperceived relations between existing phenomena," Bernstein can then argue that Pound's method aims for the same standard of truth as conventional historiography because it "allow[s] the

---

15. Williams, *The Embodiment of Knowledge*, 22–23.

The writer is to describe, to represent just as the painter must do—but what? and how?

It is the same question of words and technique in their arrangement—Stein has stressed, as Braque did paint, words. So the significance of her personal motto: A rose is a rose—which printed in a circle means two things: A rose is, to be sure, a rose. But on the other hand the words: A rose is—are words which stand for all words and are very definitely not roses—but are nevertheless subject to arrangement for effect—as are roses—and shall be, for themselves, as meaningless—or as the arrangement which is jointed upon them shall please. In this case the words are put there to represent words, the rose spoken of being left to be a rose.

conclusions to arise 'inductively' in the reader's mind from the mass of details assembled by the poem."[16] This ahistorical reading of the *Cantos* rests upon an organic theory of language wherein history and myth coalesce in a timeless harmony. This interpretation, however, is essentially an epistemological one in which language serves as the medium through which the perception of timeless relations is conveyed. In Bernstein's reading, Pound's text achieves epistemological authority—that is, it produces the understanding of truth—by reducing the tropological dimension of language to a strictly performative function. Pound's distinction between symbol and image, however, points toward a rhetorical, rather than epistemological, reading, wherein truth is exposed, in a manner reminiscent of Nietzsche's "On Truth and Lie in an Extra-Moral Sense," as a worn-down trope, a metaphor reduced to a false literal meaning, or what Pound calls a symbol. The image, we might say, "remembers" the figural, and therefore fictive, nature of language.

In Pound's texts, a gap, or what de Man calls an aporia, opens up between the ideogram considered as persuasion—it awakens the reader to "new" relations—and the image as trope—its "meaning" is determined by its relation to other signs, and thus it has no truth value. By refusing to be reduced to some opposition between the literary or fictive, on the one hand, and the historical or real, on the other, Pound's text insists on itself as being both true and false simultaneously; that is, it insists on itself as literature. Our understanding of history, therefore, arises out of the aporia between trope and persuasion, or the figurative and referential functions of language, that requires us to abandon a notion of history as either a generative process or a synchronic structure; instead, we are left with discontinuous images arranged in a diachronic sequence that, as de Man says of Nietzsche's rhetoric, "both generates and paralyzes rhetoric and thus gives it the appearance of a history."[17]

The temporality of the image is not to be confused with linear sequence, which would be a regression to symbolism. Nor is Pound suggesting that the image can be read solely as the reader chooses, for such a reader-oriented aesthetic would be just as dependent upon a traditional notion of the self as is an idealist aesthetic of poetic imagination. This aspect of Pound's

16. Bernstein, *The Tale of the Tribe*, 37, 42, 40.
17. De Man, *Allegories of Reading*, 131. For a discussion of the aporia between literature and history, see de Man, *Blindness and Insight*, 163–65.

thought comes to the fore in his distinction between the methods of "luminous detail" and "multitudinous detail." The basis for this distinction rests upon the interpretive wealth of a fact, not its significance: "Any fact is, in a sense, 'significant'. Any fact may be 'symptomatic', but certain facts give one a sudden insight into circumjacent conditions, into their causes, their effects, into sequence, and law" (SP, p. 22). Historians normally concern themselves with identification of names, dates, places, and events. These facts, Pound tells us, "are of any time and any country. By reading them with the blanks filled in, with the name written, we get no more intimate acquaintance with the temper of any period; but when in Burckhardt we come upon a passage: 'In this year the Venetians refused to make war upon the Milanese because they held that any war between buyer and seller must prove profitable to neither,' we come upon a portent, the old order changes, one conception of war and of the State begins to decline. The Middle Ages imperceptibly give ground to the Renaissance" (SP, p. 22).

Pound's example of luminous detail refers not to a verifiable historical fact, but to an interpretation of "facts." The choice of a passage from Burckhardt is revealing, and not only because Burckhardt's interpretation of the Renaissance is as controversial as it is influential. Pound's focus on the most undecidable of events, the transition from one epoch to another, tells a great deal about his theory of interpretation. His tendency to latch onto an event, or a sentence in a book, finding in it a cluster of significance, suggests the limitations a luminous detail has for universal application. What makes him so disturbing is his apparent insistence on his privileged position as interpreter. Hugh Kenner has become the foremost advocate of Pound's ability to select the key particulars of culture and enlighten the less fortunate reader. Thus, however much Kenner may write of the primacy of language in the Cantos, he consistently appeals to a transcendent meaning revealed through language but not a part of it: "The poem is not its language. It exists, just here and now, in this language, this niceness of linguistic embodiment, inspection of which will tell us all we shall ever know about it."[18]

Kenner's logocentric theory of language dissociates meaning from language in an un-Poundian way, thus transforming the indeterminable lu-

---

18. Kenner, The Pound Era, 149.

minous detail into a fixed relation of form and content. Contrary to this closing off of language to the untranslatable, there recurs in Pound's texts an excess that cannot be subsumed under this ideal of translation. When Pound insists that the reader must decode the "fact" if it is to have any interpretative significance, he pushes the luminous detail into the ungovernable border between translatability and untranslatability. The primacy of interpretation in Pound's idea of history emerges when he renames luminous detail "interpreting detail": "In the history of the development of civilization or of literature, we come upon such interpreting detail. A few dozen facts of this nature give us intelligence of a period—a kind of intelligence not to be gathered from a great array of facts of the other sort. These facts are hard to find. They are swift and easy of transmission. They govern knowledge as the switchboard governs an electric circuit" (*SP*, pp. 22–23).

I have already quoted Pound on the ideogramic method and his refusal to put into monolinear order the dozen or so facts a reader must gather and, we might add, interpret for himself. The renaming of luminous detail reinforces the status of facts as textual entities subject to varying meanings. In the introduction of the metaphor of electricity, Pound once more suggests that facts, or details, do not house meaning within, but are signs requiring interpretation. The interpreter, however, does not occupy a privileged position from which he selects and passes on the essence of culture. The artists serves as the medium of transmission: "The artist seeks out the luminous detail and presents it. He does not comment." The interpretative faculty, therefore, does not reside in the poet but in the luminous detail: "Each historian will 'have ideas'—presumably different from other historians—imperfect inductions, varying as the fashions, but the luminous details remain unaltered" (*SP*, p. 23). In contrast to Eliot, Pound's concept of persona excludes the notions of self and personality.

Eliot's theory of personality finds its most famous expression in "Tradition and the Individual Talent": "The point of view which I am struggling to attack is perhaps related to the metaphysical theory of the substantial unity of the soul: for my meaning is, that the poet has, not a 'personality' to express, but a particular medium, which is only a medium and not a personality, in which impressions and experiences combine in peculiar and unexpected ways."[19] Eliot's psychological construct of persona

19. Eliot, *Selected Essays*, 9, hereinafter cited as *SE*.

may be distinguished from Pound's linguistic one. For Eliot, personality, though excluded from poetry, remains a real entity rooted in the self. If he excludes it from poetry, he does so in fear of its power over him: "Only those who have personality and emotions know what it means to want to escape from these things" (SE, pp. 10–11).

This tendency can be made clearer if we compare Eliot's metaphor of the catalyst with Pound's metaphor of the switchboard. Eliot explains the process of depersonalization in poetry through the analogy of a catalyst entering a solution. In his example, a filament of platinum enters into a mixture of oxygen and sulfur, transforming the mixture into sulfurous acid. The acid contains no trace of the platinum, which remains unchanged. "The mind of the poet," writes Eliot, "is the shred of platinum." He soon revises his analogy: "The poet's mind is in fact a receptacle for seizing and storing up numberless feelings, phrases, images, which remain there until all the particles which can unite to form a new compound are present together" (SE, p. 8). The mind is no longer the catalyst but is now the receptacle in which change takes place. The poet is both performative agent and the container in which the materials of experience are transformed to produce the work of art. While Eliot's concept of the self requires a more detailed study than is appropriate here, I suggest that by reinstating the self as a catalyst which is at once absorbed by its environment and unchanged by it, he reveals his Puritan concept of the self; that is, the individual must be subsumed under authority not merely to preserve authority but, more important, to preserve the self.

On the other hand, Pound's metaphor of the switchboard, to which he returns several times in "I Gather the Limbs of Osiris," avoids the Eliotesque relapse into theology. Having said that luminous detail governs knowledge as the switchboard governs electric current, he adapts his simile to define the role of words in poetry. Starting from the commonplace that a word's meaning is arbitrary and defined by convention, he goes on to compare "the masterly use of words" to hollow steel cones of varying sizes and electrical charges. The aim is to place the cones/words in such an order as to radiate a high degree of energy. Whereas Eliot conceives of poetry and tradition within psychological and institutional forms, Pound's emphasis on language itself as the generator of meanings breaks down the notion of unified meaning since energy (meanings) has "sources" but "not ultimate sources." Pound warns that the placement of cones/words depends upon "the juxtaposition" in order to produce a high intensity of energy: "This peculiar energy which fills the cones is the power of tradition, of centuries of race consciousness, of agreement, of association; and the control of it is the 'Technique of Content', which nothing short of genius understands" (*SP*, p. 34). As words are bound by the conventional, they lose whatever force might have inhered in them. To break up clichés and open everyday speech to luminous detail requires the careful arrangement of words, which Pound, after Gourmont, calls the "dissociation of ideas." The power of tradition is but undifferentiated energy that can only be utilized by the method of interpretative translation.

This last term occurs in the conclusion of Pound's essay on Cavalcanti:

> In the long run the translator is in all probability impotent to do *all* of the work for the linguistically lazy reader. He can show where the treasure lies, he can guide the reader in choice of what tongue is to be studied, and he can very materially assist the hurried student who has a smattering of a language and the energy to read the original text alongside the metrical gloze.
>
> This refers to "interpretative translation". The "other sort". I mean in cases where the "translater" is definitely making a new poem, falls simply in the domain of original writing. (*LE*, p. 200)

Pound extends the method of luminous detail to include translation, the supreme, and only, form of poetry. He repeatedly warns us that it is impossible to "think with only one language." A portion of one's thought goes untouched if, for instance, the English speaker knows no French: "Different languages—I mean the actual vocabularies, the idioms—have worked out certain mechanisms of communication and registration. No one language is complete" (*LE*, p. 36). Language creates thought, thus the necessity of knowing several. But Pound also implies that all languages are ultimately one. In a letter to Iris Barry advising her what to read, he says, "I believe language *has* improved; that Latin is better than Greek and French than Latin for everything save certain melodic effects" (*SL*, p. 95). This comment suggests that the aim of translation is to uncover the universal language hidden within the original work. This concept of translation bypasses the idea of fidelity, as well as creative translation.

Walter Benjamin, in one of his more provocative and bewildering essays, "The Task of the Translator," dismisses translations that seek to render information, to convey the likeness of the original, or to capture the original's "poetic" quality (which itself is an "inessential content"). All these common criteria for translation rely on a definition of the original as a solid structure of form and content aimed at an audience. Although Benjamin uses the term *original* throughout the essay, he transforms the meaning of the word by introducing history into the formally unified edifice: "A translation issues from the original—not so much from its life as from its afterlife."[20] The only life a work has is its afterlife or, as Benjamin says, "continued life" in translation. The translation, we might say, gives the work life or, what is the same thing, history.

In a hundred-page footnote to his translator, Jacques Derrida translates Benjamin's thesis without ever referring to him: "A text lives only if it lives *on* [*sur-vit*], and it lives *on* only if it is *at once* translatable *and* untranslatable (always 'at once . . . and . . .': *hama*, at the 'same' time). Totally translatable, it disappears as a text, as writing, as a body of language [*langue*]. Totally untranslatable, even within what is believed to be one language, it dies immediately. This triumphant translation is neither the life nor the death of the text, only or already its living *on*, its life after life, its life after death." Derrida echoes Benjamin's argument that all texts are translatable but no translation is. The translation is untranslatable because it leaves out the content; the original is thereby raised to the level of pure language. Elsewhere, Benjamin defines pure language as that which communicates "the linguistic being of things." Referentiality, whether autotelic or semantic, has no place in a theory in which the thing language communicates is always language itself. Translation, to return to Derrida, always leaves out an untranslatable remnant, which is a "semantic accumulation and overloading" that "opens polysemia (and its economy) in the direction of dissemination." The classical model of translation is governed by "univocality" or "formalizable polysemia"; dissemination moves Benjamin's/Derrida's/Pound's translations toward the ungovernable. Derrida emphasizes for his readers that "if there is someting that arrests translation, this limit is not due to some essential indissociability of meaning and language, of signified and signifier, as they say. It is a matter of *economy* . . . and retains an essential relationship with time, space, counting words, signs, *marks*. . . . Economy: stricture and not *coupure*, rupture. It is always an *external* constraint that arrests a text in general, i.e., *anything*, for example life death."[21]

20. Benjamin, *Illuminations*, 71.
21. Derrida, "Living On/Border Lines," 102n., 91n., 169n.–71n.; Benjamin, *Reflections*, 316.

Think of how Pound's *Cantos* is constrained by such arbitrary events as his chance happening upon Andreas Divus' *Odyssey*. In Canto 1, Pound writes in several languages—Anglo-Saxon, Latin, Greek, English—every language but his own. The Nekuia traces the voyage of the poet into the realm of death and mourning. Odysseus discovers among the dead the unmourned Elpenor, who bids him

> "remember me, unwept, unburied,
> "Heap up mine arms, be tomb by sea-bord, and inscribed:
> "*A man of no fortune, and with a name to come.*
> "And set my oar up, that I swung mid fellows." (1:4)

Odysseus is to undertake what Freud calls the work of mourning. Through assimilation—introjection, in psychoanalytic terms—he is to sustain the memory of his shipmate and free his libido to attach itself to a new object of affection. But what can this tale be but an allegory of Pound's theft of Divus' translation of Homer's *Odyssey*, which is itself a theft? In fact, Pound carries into his text Divus' corrupted text that reads " 'A second time?' "[22] The whole canto is riddled with repetitions that mark the failure to carry over into Pound's own language the translation unmarred by the presence of death. For as Pound repeats the text in another language, he seeks to assimilate the Homeric epic into his own poem, but like Elpenor in the underworld, Divus, and with him Homer, arises from the grave. Thus, Pound tells Divus to "Lie quiet." The resurrection, though, is a partial one. A remnant always stays beyond the grasp of translation, hence the absence of the proper name on the tomb. But it is the absent name that allows the continuation of the journey and the narrative. The name Elpenor will be translated in later cantos when Pound puns on the *el* in Sordello, Elizabeth, Helen, and Eleanor. He even steals from Aeschylus' *Agamemnon* a series of puns on Helen—"helandros," "helenaus," and "heleptolis" ("man-destroying," "ship-destroying," and "city-destroying")—which he then applies to Eleanor of Aquitaine (7:24, 25). Pound also weaves the epitaph on Elpenor's tomb into this complex of puns when in the *Pisan Cantos* he too becomes "a man of no fortune and with a name to come" (74:439; 80:513, 514). Finally, the man with no name is Odysseus himself, who tells Polyphemus that he is called "No-man."

Pound's periplus takes him back to the books and places he has already visited, just as Odysseus, after his second visit to the underworld, must re-

22. Terrell, *Companion to the Cantos*, I, 2.

turn to Circe's island to bury Elpenor on the sea-bord. Indeed, the sea-bord is but the border between texts and between languages that sets Pound's text afloat upon a sea of texts. Another text embroiled in thefts and translations—so much so that it sinks beneath the burden—is Eliot's *Waste Land*, more specifically, "Death by Water." In its rather lengthy early version, it is a web of allusions to the Ulysses canto of Dante's *Inferno*, Tennyson's "Ulysses" and *In Memoriam*, the *Odyssey*, "The Love Song of J. Alfred Prufrock," and, most important, "Dans le Restaurant," a poem by Eliot written in French from which he translates the Phlebas passage that forms the final version of this section. (We might also say that "Death by Water" looks forward to the *Four Quartets*, as it contains Eliot's first mention of the Dry Salvages.) "Death by Water" consists of false starts—does it begin in "Dans le Restaurant," the manuscripts he sent Pound, or in the published version? Does it end in the *Four Quartets*? Eliot's final decision to follow Pound's advice to keep only the Phlebas section from "Dans le Restaurant" in the poem suggests his own inability to keep afloat in/on the edges of his text.[23]

If the *Cantos* lives on, it is as translation, as a poem that never begins but only "starts": "And it 'starts' only with living on (testament, iterability, remaining [*restance*], crypt, detachment that lifts the strictures of the 'living' *rectio* or direction of an 'author' not drowned at the edge of his text)." What comes before the "And" of line 1 is not, as Kenner claims, an ancient past "reclaimed by Homer as he [Pound] reclaims Homer now."[24] In his Eliotesque reading of Pound, Kenner interprets Pound's translations and quotations as a rejuvenation of the past; consequently, his dissociation of the poem from its language allows him to posit a metalanguage that would guarantee translation without remnants. When he quotes approvingly Pound's advice, "Don't bother about the WORDS, TRANSLATE the MEANING," he ignores Pound's comments about interpretative and exegetical translation. In a note to *Cantos LII–LXXI*, Pound says that the foreign words add little to the text and merely serve as underlinings. The foreign words serve neither as an expansion of the English (or is it American?) text into a universal language nor as an archaeological recovery of the past. The foreign words are the supplement that reveals the irreducible untranslatabil-

---

23. For the original version and Pound's remarks, see Eliot, *The Waste Land*, 54–69. For Pound's advice to keep the Phlebas section, see *Selected Letters*, 171.

24. Derrida, "Living On/Border Lines," 103n.; Kenner, *The Pound Era*, 349.

ity of all languages, thus marking the limits of a humanism that maintains national boundaries while insisting on internationalism as well.

Whether critics attack Pound for his politics or for his selection and handling of subject matter in the *Cantos*, they are in fact attacking Pound's transgression of language, for it is this which threatens the institutions that his critics hope to maintain against the assault of modernism. Today, this disruption of politico-humanistic institutions has been undertaken with an unparalleled rigor by Derrida, who has been attacked by both the Left and the Right as a nihilist. The common ground upon which his critics stand, and which Derrida undermines, is a theory of language that refuses to admit to a polysemia which would elude the grasp of man. For it is upon the faith in a governable multiplicity of meaning, if not strict univocality, that their claim to a privileged interpretation of man and history rests. This faith cannot tolerate the semantic overloading implied by Derrida's (and Pound's) model of translatability. As Derrida succinctly puts it:

> The line that I seek to recognize within translatability, between two translations, one governed by the classical model of transportable univocality or of formalizable polysemia, and the other, which goes over into dissemination—this line also passes between the critical and deconstructive. A politico-institutional problem of the University: it, like all teaching in its traditional form, and perhaps all teaching whatever, has as its ideal, with exhaustive translatability, the effacement of language [*la langue*]. The deconstruction of a pedagogical institution and all that it implies. What this institution cannot bear, is for anyone to tamper with [*toucher à*; also "touch," "change," "concern himself with"] language, meaning *both* the *national* language *and* paradoxically, an ideal of translatability that neutralizes this national language. Nationalism and universalism. What this institution cannot bear is a transformation that leaves intact neither of these two complementary poles. It can bear more readily the most apparently revolutionary ideological sorts of "content," if only that content does not touch the borders of language [*la langue*] and of all the juridico-political contracts that it guarantees.[25]

Pound's frequent polemics against universities and humanism as it is taught in America represent a related, if hardly as well articulated, protest against this solicitude for the "integrity" of a language. The same concern that seeks to protect language from the indeterminable finds expression in a philosophy of history that binds nature with origins. By introducing into

25. Derrida, "Living On/Border Lines," 93n.–95n.

history the untranslatable, Pound undoes the dream of the autotelic text. The residue of that which stays outside of the process of transportation points to the incapacity of nature to satisfy the wealth of signification in language. Complete translatability is possible only when meaning is supported by the solid edifice of a humanist ideology. Thus we have Eliot's claim that "totalitarianism can retain the terms 'freedom' and 'democracy' and give them its own meaning."[26]

Eliot never tires of arguing that coherence in literature depends upon tradition and social uniformity. As he sees it, this uniformity was once ensured by the church, which has since been supplanted by the state. With the decay of institutionalized religion and the rise of liberalism, man is no longer moving toward a definite end. Fearing that the absence of the telos will lead to chaos, Eliot seeks to mobilize the state behind a Christian education, which will preserve class distinctions as it protects a privileged minority culture. In opposition to the liberal policy of mass education and the subsequent disintegration of classes, Eliot proposes a Christian humanist system of education that would "help to preserve the class and to select the élite." The state, however, is not to tamper with culture, which would invariably lower it, for culture, or tradition, to use Eliot's other term for it, exists independent of history. In spite of his appeal to historical sense, Eliot's theory of tradition remains ahistorical: "The existing monuments form an ideal order among themselves, which is modified by the introduction of the new (the really new) work of art among them. The existing order is complete before the new work arrives; for order to persist after the supervention of novelty, the *whole* existing order must be, if ever so slightly, altered . . . this is conformity between the old and the new" (*SE*, p. 5). On the one hand, art forms a universal order free from time; hence, education serves as the arm of this transcendental order and ensures the maintenance of hierarchical order in society. On the other hand, the new work supplements the existing order and at once completes it and exceeds it. As Derrida points out, "The supplement supplements. It adds only to replace." Eliot would like to believe that art is a plenitude existing in a suprahistorical realm and, at the same time, present in the world in the form of the new work. The presence of the Word, in this moment, would be reappropriated by writing. Yet writing is a surplus, an uncontrollable economy, which once added to

26. Eliot, *The Idea of a Christian Society*, 17.

the plenitude of the Word reveals that plenitude as a void. Thus, when Eliot speaks of the autotelic text, he expresses his desire to grant the literary work the atemporal status of tradition; however, as the new work adds itself to the preexisting body of literature, it opens Eliot's text, in spite of Eliot, to history and repetition. In Derrida's terms, the new work is a substitute: "It intervenes or insinuates itself *in-the-place-of*; if it fills, it is as if one fills a void. If it represents and makes an image, it is by the anterior default of a presence. . . . Somewhere, something can be filled up of *itself*, can accomplish itself, only by allowing itself to be filled through sign and proxy. The sign is always the supplement of the thing itself."[27]

Pound's theory of translation accounts more fully for the excess of signification that Eliot seeks to control by appealing to the model of an institution based upon a transcendent order. Whereas Eliot's quotations appeal to the living presence of the past, Pound's quotations and foreign words point toward the irreducible anteriority of the past which his text can only repeat: "I believe that when finished, *all* foreign words in the Cantos, Gk., etc., will be underlinings, not necessary to the sense, in one way. I mean a complete sense will exist without them; it will be there in the American text, but the Greek, ideograms, etc., will indicate a *duration* from whence or since when. If you can find any *briefer* means of getting this repeat or resonance, tell papa, and I will try to employ it" (*SL*, p. 322). The foreign words will mark the spatio-temporal distance between the "original" text and Pound's own. The *Cantos* watches over the history of language in the process of producing their new repetition—a repetition that will displace the original. Elsewhere, in a letter to his father, Pound calls this "the 'repeat in history' " (*SL*, p. 210). Kenner has remarked that "the norm is now speech, which binds men, which flows through minds and cultures. . . . So writing is largely quotation energized, as a cyclotron augments the energies of common particles circulating."[28] While Pound's *Cantos*, like Eliot's *Waste Land*, is a compendium of quotations, Kenner, by emphasizing speech, thinks quotations recapture the immediacy of life, thereby revitalizing tradition. In the metaphor of the cyclotron, the particles are the living speech which the poet re-creates in his works. This better describes Eliot's theory than Pound's.

27. Eliot, *Notes Towards the Definition of Culture*, 100; Derrida, *Of Grammatology*, 145.
28. Kenner, *The Pound Era*, 126.

The fragments woven together in *The Waste Land* serve as the reminder of the absence of the Word:

> Son of man,
> You cannot say, or guess, for you know only
> A heap of broken images.[29]

Within the tradition the new poem stands as a monument to the eternal presence of the past. The disappearance of the self allows tradition to speak through the individual and thus absorb him in the Word. In contrast to Eliot, who reconfirms the logocentric history that collapses theology and aesthetics, Pound wrenches art from the theological, as well as the aesthetic, for the latter has always been bound up in theology. The orderly hierarchy of genres and of individual works rests upon the transcendental concept of the Word, of which the individual creation partakes. This common basis of humanistic studies conforms to traditional historical methodology, which Pound explicitly attacks for its undefined and surreptitious assumptions: "If the instructor would select his specimens from works that contain these discoveries [in poetic expression] and solely on the basis of discovery . . . he would aid his student far more than by presenting his authors at random, and talking about them *in toto*" (*LE*, p. 19). Humanistic instruction in the universities is founded upon a random selection of texts which are then presented as a whole and unified body. This uncritical theory was given new currency in Eliot's "Tradition and the Individual Talent."

Pound distinguishes between the recovery of fragments à la Eliot and the recovery of modernity through technique. This returns us to his method of interpreting detail and the rewriting of the past. Each age tries to rewrite, or "compound," a "new sacred book." I use *rewrite*, for the compilation of the sacred book is the (re-)creation of an anthology; thus, Pound acknowledges that some people say he dumps his "note-books on the public." Nevertheless, the poet must attempt to master the techniques of his art. Only after such a struggle will poetry "attain such a degree of development, or, if you will, modernity, that it will vitally concern people who are accustomed, in prose, to Henry James and Anatole France, in music to Debussy" (*LE*, p. 9).

The unusual significance of the anthology throughout Pound's career is explained by his pedagogic streak and his theories of language and history.

29. Eliot, *Collected Poems*, 53.

Such works as *Guide to Kulchur*, "How to Read," *ABC of Reading*, *Confucius to Cummings*, and his translation of the *Shih-ching* all attest to Pound's belief that "no single language is CAPABLE of expressing all forms and degrees of human comprehension" (*ABC*, p. 34). To this list I would like to add the *Cantos*. Although Pound frequently referred to the *Cantos* as an epic, in a letter of 1924 to William Bird, he reminds him that the title is "*A DRAFT* of 16 Cantos for a poem of some length." He then declares, "Also it ain't an epic. It's part of a long poem" (*SL*, p. 189). In addition to the obvious model of Homer's *Odyssey*, Pound also took, among many others, Dante and Ovid for precursors, neither of whom he considered as writers of epics. He thought it best to define the *Commedia* as "a cycle of mystery plays" (*SR*, p. 154). Ovid's *Metamorphoses*, like Chaucer's *Canterbury Tales*, is a "compendium" (*ABC*, p. 92), a term that best describes the *Cantos*—a collection of all the quotations Pound thought necessary for a modernist literature. He would recover Provence, Renaissance Italy, Jeffersonian America, Confucius' China, and prewar London.

Pound had what appears to have been an unflagging faith in the educability of the masses. This faith seems to have grown out of the same populist impulses that led him to support Mussolini's Italy. The importance of this for Pound's works, and the *Cantos* in particular, emerges in his idea of the writer as critic and, conversely, the critic as reader. The best criticism, Pound thought, would be an anthology consisting of the gleanings, the interpretative translations, of world literature. In a similar fashion, the poet aims to present without comment the luminous details he has translated from a life's work of reading. (As an aside, I should point out that luminous detail, interpreting detail, and interpretative translation are ultimately interchangeable terms for Pound.) One of the great paradoxes of Pound's career is that the *Cantos*, on the surface, the most forbidding of modernist poems, was written by someone who felt the importance of reaching a wide public. (It should not be forgotten, however, that Pound thought it necessary to educate the reader to the poet's level.) The *Cantos* is public property. Compiled out of the fragments of culture, it provides an anthology of literature, philosophy, history, and economics for modern man.

But Pound's encyclopedia does not partake of the nineteenth century's dream of the whole book, the universal work embodying all of history. His method acknowledges that the essence of history is its iterability. What is too often taken to be his nostalgia for earlier ages can best be explained in terms of his notion of the book. The "repeat in history" is not the same as recuperation of the past; recuperation, unlike repetition, is an unproblematical recovery of what is thought to be an authentic object. The archaeological uncovering of facts will permit a restoration of the past, however fragmentary the evidence may be. Pound's use of repetition is closer to what may be called, in the manner of his "interpretative translation," interpretative rhyme. The subject rhymes of the Cantos, which Kenner treats strictly as thematic repetitions, are the historical interpretations that simultaneously point to a past event and remind the reader of the artifice underlying history. Thus, in Canto 31 we find Pound quoting Thomas Jefferson on the transmission of errors:

> A tiel leis....en ancien scripture, and this
> they have translated Holy Scripture...
> > Mr. Jefferson
> and they continue this error. (31:156)

In Pound's version, Jefferson's remark becomes a debunking of Scripture, which derives its authority solely from its age. Jefferson's letter on how common law agrees with ecclesiastical law reads: "Here then we find ancien scripture, ancient writing, translated 'holy scripture.' . . . Thus we find this string of authorities all hanging by one another on a single hook, a mistranslation."[30] In his remark, Pound confirms the persistence of this error. The word scripture, however, is not what is normally called a mistranslation; it is a direct borrowing from the Latin, but in its transference from Latin to English, it too has a new and unsubstantiated meaning as a synonym for the Bible.

The quotation also draws attention to Pound's method of rummaging through archives and cataloguing quotations to be incorporated into the Cantos. Pound warns his readers to be wary of the text at hand. The problem of his method becomes oppressive in the Adams and the Chinese cantos. The wholesale use of quotations modified by slight verbal changes, rearrangements of sentences, and occasional commentary makes it difficult for the most sympathetic reader—and Pound does not lack his defenders— to praise these cantos as poetry. Peter Shaw, one of Pound's more vocal detractors, attacks Pound's Adams cantos as an incoherent jumble of randomly selected quotations. Pound's critics come in for a lashing because they appeal to "modernist dogmas" when praising his poetry. I have no inten-

---

30. Kenner, The Pound Era, 423; Terrell, Companion to the Cantos, I, 124.

tion of defending these cantos. Their interest lies in Pound's extension of his theories of poetry and history. Shaw's criticism is reminiscent of the attacks by Latinists on *Homage to Sextus Propertius* for its schoolboy howlers. And as these poems were defended as creative translations, so defenders of the Adams cantos repeat the argument that Pound's histories must be read as creative reimaginings of the past.

Shaw focuses on these lines from Canto 62:

> Routledge was elegant
> "said nothing not hackneyed six months before"
> wrote J.A. to his wife. (62:345)

Shaw points out that in Pound's source, Charles Francis Adams' biography of his grandfather, it is Hamilton who says that Edward *Rutledge* is an elegant speaker. The line in quotation marks does not refer to Rutledge, and Adams' comment does not come in a letter to his wife.[31] Shaw's attack rests upon the assumption that this grouping composes a grammatical order of subject/object, that is to say, of cause and effect. He further assumes that such juxtapositions of words, if they are to be read, as they must be read, as coherent, constitute a grammar which imitates historical fact, which is itself a grammar. This theory of history, which is also a theory of language, ignores the antimetaphysical thrust of Pound's method of dissociation. It is no accident that Pound's most explicit attacks on the logic of the sentence, which I have quoted above, come in two of his most historical texts, *Guide to Kulchur* and *Jefferson and/or Mussolini*. And if the *Cantos* is "a poem including history" (*LE*, p. 86), then it too must dissociate history from grammar.

Pound's waywardness with facts in the *Cantos* is well known; he himself acknowledged in a letter to John Quinn that he must ensure that his history of Malatesta is interesting. Following a description of the complexities his research has uncovered, he remarks, "I suppose one has to 'select.' If I find he was TOO bloody quiet and orderly it will ruin the canto. Which needs a certain boisterousness and disorder to contrast with his constructive work."[32] Historians are guilty of the same error Pound complained of in literary critics—they both select what must be random facts and present them as unified wholes. Pound's *Cantos* is the receptacle of modernist forces

---

31. Shaw, "Ezra Pound on American History," 118–19. I thank Kathryne Lindberg for drawing my attention to this article.
32. Quoted in Pearlman, *The Barb of Time*, 302.

in art and politics. The notebooks presented as poetry transform culture into a personal language disseminating an ungovernable surplus of meaning. As Pound's critics have remarked, the Adams cantos, as well as the Chinese cantos, are of a piece with Pound's method. The fact that they are dull is less a revelation of the extremity, even the bankruptcy, of Pound's technique, and more an unconscious critique of the vacuity of a belief in origins and the protofascist's inability to turn anticapitalist impulses into a progressive force.

I use the word *unconscious* for several reasons. First, in all of his writings on Mussolini, fascism, and America, Pound reveals an astounding ignorance of what was taking place during the thirties and forties. Like Wyndham Lewis, whose sexism, in Fredric Jameson's analysis, "is so extreme as to be virtually beyond sexism," Pound's anti-Semitism and fascism are so intense as to go beyond the level of personal opinion and operate as the unconscious field upon which fascist ideology is recorded. The obvious danger of the preceding remark lies in its appearance as an apology for Pound's, or any rabid fascist's, politics. But the question of condemnation or exculpation is out of place precisely because of Pound's rigorous attack upon the theological status of the subject. In Pound we are forced to see the relationship as one between an object and its producer. Furthermore, as Pound dissolves the concept of subjectivity, the producer is not to be confused with any traditional notion of the artistic creator; instead, the producer is, as Louis Althusser says, "the *ideology* from which it [the work of art] is born."[33] Thus, the producer is like Pound's switchboard registering the forces of the age in which it exists. That critics are drawn to either defending or condemning Pound indicates the danger of his work. The *Cantos* depicts the relations between the reader and the fascist ideology that most are so anxious to condemn or ignore.

Through the course of the *Cantos* we are offered what Pound's readers have called glimpses of paradise. But as Pound is fond of repeating,

Le Paradis n'est pas artificiel

> but spezzato apparently
> it exists only in fragments unexpected excellent sausage,
>> the smell of mint, for example,
>> Ladro the night cat.   (74:438)

33. Jameson, *Fables of Aggression*, 20; Althusser, *Lenin and Philosophy and Other Essays*, 222.

Paradise is not artificial; it is Baudelaire's (or is it Poe's?) drug-induced dreams. The *Cantos* is these fragments of literature reassembled to expose heaven as an artifice unable to cover the ill-constructed seams binding the work together:

> I don't know how humanity stands it
> with a painted paradise at the end of it
> without a painted paradise at the end of it. (74:436)

The *Cantos* is an assemblage of fragments dislocating the reader from the object, as it reveals the distance between the disjointed parts and their producer. The quotations do not conform to a source from which we can reconstruct a coherent history (this would be Eliot's method), nor do they achieve unity in their own right. They destroy the dream of totality that existed in art. Pound's politicizing of art succeeds in disrupting the historical relation existing between reader, writer, and text. The reader of Pound is no longer the secondary figure who passively responds to an object. Pound's wrenching of texts to reproduce his poem continues the violation that Emerson defined as reading and writing. Pound obsessively calls attention to himself as a reader in order to implicate his own readers in the ravaging of culture that allows poetry to live on.

It is through Pound's role as reader that the *Cantos* comes to resemble what Walter Benjamin has called "baroque allegory." In *The Origin of German Tragic Drama*, Benjamin refers to the relation between writing and history in *Trauerspiel* as an allegory for the death of nature and the gods. For the allegorist, the contemplation of history comes to signify the "unity of guilt and signifying." The place where history enacts the drama of the death of man is in/as writing: "When, as is the case in the *Trauerspiel*, history becomes part of the setting, it does so as script. The word 'history' stands written on the countenance of nature in the characters of transience." According to Benjamin, allegory reveals history in the form of "irresistible decay." Thus the most fitting form for baroque is the ruin; yet for all the allegorist's fascination with antiquity, the ruin comes to signify the present: "What prevails here is the current stylistic feeling, far more than the reminiscences of antiquity. That which lies here in ruins, the highly significant fragment, the remnant, is, in fact, the finest material in baroque creation. For it is common practice in the literature of the baroque to pile up fragments ceaselessly, without any strict idea of a goal, and, in the unremitting expectation of a miracle, to take the repetition of stereotypes for a process of intensification." Pound's *Cantos* is just such a piling up of fragments, which obsessively repeat the themes of classical literature, medieval mysticism, Renaissance Neoplatonism, social credit, and American mythology, but they do so in such an unsettling manner that the reader finds that the meaning inhering in the remnant stays beyond the reach of language. The text lives on/in/as the border between languages where history is reassembled as the edge between signs—in an untranslatable excess: "The writer must not conceal the fact that his activity is one of arranging, since it was not so much the mere whole as its obviously constructed quality that was the principal impression which was aimed at."[34] The poet is no longer the namer of nature, man, and spirit; instead, he is a reader of texts, at once the assembler and the dissembler of fragments.

34. Benjamin, *The Origin of German Tragic Drama*, 234, 177, 178, 179.

CHAPTER SIX

William Carlos Williams' Search for an "American" Place

History, history! We fools, what do we know or care? History begins for us with murder and enslavement, not with discovery.

—Williams

We are moderns—madmen at Paris—all lacking in a ground sense of cleanliness.

—Williams

I recall Williams writing somewhere, "If there is evolution, then there is no America." For if there were such a thing as evolution, or what Williams also calls "progress," then America would be the culmination of European history—an end, not a beginning. His assault on history conceived on the model of Darwinian evolution starts by acknowledging the deprivation out of which writing begins. As early as "The Wanderer," he asserts his poetic strength the very instant he recognizes the belatedness that deprives the American writer of originality:

> I know now all my time is forespent!
> For me one face is all the world!
> For I have seen her at last, this day,
> In whom age in age is united—
> Indifferent, out of sequence, marvelously!
> Saving alone that one sequence
> Which is the beauty of all the world.[1]

To achieve the full play of mind that makes all poets contemporaries, the writer must reject the teleological movement toward fixed goals. The pres-

---

1. Williams, *The Collected Earlier Poems*, 4, hereinafter cited as *CEP*. The following abbreviations will be used for citations to Williams' work: A—*The Autobiography of William Carlos Williams*; CLP—*The Collected Later Poems*; EK—*The Embodiment of Knowledge*; Imag.—*Imaginations*; IAG—*In the American Grain*; IWWP—*I Wanted to Write a Poem*; P—*Paterson*; PB—*Pictures from Brueghel and Other Poems*; SE—*Selected Essays*; SL—*Selected Letters*; VP—*A Voyage to Pagany*. All citations from Williams' manuscripts at the Beinecke Library, Yale University, will be cited as Yale MS.

ent moment in which writing begins appears only out of sequence, that is, in the imagination, or what he often calls "spring." And it is in spring that evolution ends: "It is spring. That is to say, it is approaching THE BEGIN-NING" (*Imag.*, p. 94). With the approach of spring, we draw near to the death of man: "In that colossal surge toward the finite and the capable life has now arrived for the second time at that exact moment when in the ages past the destruction of the species *Homo sapiens* occurred" (*Imag.*, p. 94).

The death of man frees the imagination from the chains of tradition:

> Having died
> one is at great advantage
> over his fellows—
> one can pretend.   (*CEP*, p. 119)

Death, then, signifies the willful forgetting of the past whereby the poet is able to begin once again. For life, like evolution, is a plagiarism each age must repeat: "Each age brings new calls upon violence/ for new rewards, variants of the old" (*CLP*, p. 8). These lines come from a poem significantly titled "Catastrophic Birth." Perhaps it requires a physician who is also a poet to recognize the indissociable link in writing between violence and beginnings. At spring, the poem, like a flower, bursts through the earth, sundering the rock that blocks its growth. Breaking through the reified structures of grammar, the poem returns language to writing once again. And if the poet is a horticulturist preserving pressed flowers in a book,[2] the physician is the diagnostician watching these flowers grow: "*Pathology literally speaking is a flower garden. Syphilis covers the body with salmonred petals. The study of medicine is an inverted sort of horticulture. Over and above all this floats the philosophy of disease which is a stern dance*" (*Imag.*, p. 77).

In his *Autobiography*, Williams writes how the physician watches over language "to witness words being born." But beneath everyday language

---

2. The metaphor of the poem as a pressed flower appears in *Asphodel, That Greeny Flower*:

> When I was boy
>   I kept a book
>   to which, from time
> to time,
>   I added pressed flowers
>   until, after a time,
> I had a good collection.   (*PB*, p. 155)

lies "a more profound language. . . . It is what they call poetry"(A, p. 361). The language of poetry is not different from everyday language; it simply requires that we listen to recover a meaning obscured by the mundane: "The poem that each is trying actually to communicate to us lies in the words. It is at least the words that make it articulate. It has always been so. Occasionally that named person is born who catches a rumor of it, a Homer, a Villon, and his race and the world perpetuate his memory" (A, p. 362). Joseph Riddel has already pointed out that the poet/physician is a belated interpreter grasping at the rumors of meaning.[3] The hidden rumor, or phantom, however, is not only a shadow of truth, it is also the ghost of Emerson. In his reduction of the poet to a mere name, Williams echoes the Emersonian theme that the poet is the least personal of all men. Even more striking is how closely Williams echoes this passage from "The Poet": "For poetry was all written before time was, and whenever we are so finely organized that we can penetrate into that region where the air is music, we hear those primal warblings and attempt to write them down, but we lose ever and anon a word or a verse and substitute something of our own, and thus miswrite the poem" (W.III.8).

Belatedness always confirms that poet's need to reinterpret, and thereby miswrite, that which has been written before he arrived. Therefore, writes Williams, "everything new must be wrong" (Imag., p. 356.) Like the physician, the poet penetrates everyday speech to catch the new word, itself a belated interpretation of an older word: "You cannot recognize it [the poem] from past appearances—in fact it is always a new face. . . . The poem springs from the half-spoken words of such patients as the physician sees from day to day. He observes it in the peculiar, actual confirmations in which its life is hid. Humbly he presents himself before it and by long practice he strives as best he can to interpret the manner of its speech. In that the secret lies" (A, p. 362). Physicians diagnose language to disclose the presence hidden in the familiar verbiage of everyday speech, and thus they "have been the words' very parents" (A, p. 361). The body under examination can be none other than language, and if the doctor, who delivers the new word, is also the parent, he can be so only by adoption. Reinterpretation, or diagnosis, will make the son into the grandfather, as Williams says in a letter to a young Indian writer, Srinivas Rayaprol: "I think you will, by understanding your father's position, come finally to accept him and understand him

3. Riddel, " 'Keep Your Pecker Up,' " 203.

and become, curiously enough HIS father" (SL, p. 289). Contrary to Harold Bloom's American sublime, the poet becomes not his own father, but his own grandfather. But even this rewriting of the genealogy, however many displacements there must be, depends upon the skill of the diagnostician, for only a correct diagnosis will displace the father from the genealogical succession that condemns the son to belatedness.

In what may be the most graphic passage in the Autobiography, Williams links the death of his father and the failure of diagnosis to the question of origins and the writing of poetry. In the introduction to the account of his father's death, Williams mentions his regret that "when he went he carried the secret of his birth with him" (A, p. 166). Dying from cancer, Williams' father submits without complaint as his son struggles to push a tube for an enema into his emaciated body. The next day, Williams' mother calls him to come right away:

> It must have been a cerebral accident, perhaps from my efforts to relieve him the day before.
> "He's gone," I said. But he shook his head slowly from side to side. It was the last thing I could ever say in my father's presence and it was disastrous.
> At that moment the telephone rang. It was a maternity case at the hospital. . . . There was no one to take my place, and I had to leave Pop forthwith. When I returned he was gone. (A, pp. 166–67)

It is curious how Williams coolly mentions the possibility that his efforts to give the enema precipitated his father's death, only to emphasize his father's correction of his diagnosis. (We might recall in Paterson when Williams quotes Norman Douglas' remark, "The best thing a man can do for his son, when he is born, is to die" [P, p. 171]). The figurative murder of his father frees him from his English ancestry (his father never gave up his British citizenship) and closes the past to him. He is now an American free to create his own history, but this same freedom condemns him to repetition. The incorrect diagnosis, in light of his later chapter "The Practice," suggests a failure of language, and the cruelty of his error points to the violence underlying language. To kill the English father is to separate himself from his European background, thereby breaking off from it a language free from the determinacy of origins.

Of course, Williams wrote more frequently of his mother than of his father. In the Autobiography he tells how Pound tried to redress this neglect: "Ezra's insistence has always been that I never laid proper stress in my life upon the part played in it by my father rather than my mother. Oh, the woman of it is important, he would acknowledge, but the form of it, if not the drive, came unacknowledged by me from the old man, the Englishman" (*A*, p. 91). It is curious to note that Dorothy Pound once remarked that "Ezra got his charm from Homer, his push from Isabel."[4]

Williams, nevertheless, looks upon his father as the keeper of the past which he wishes to recover. In the late poem *Asphodel, That Greeny Flower*, he describes seeing a man on a subway whom he suddenly recognizes as his father:

> I am looking
> > into my father's
> > > face! Some surface
> > of some advertising sign
> > > is acting
> > > > as a reflector. It is
> my own. (*PB*, p. 173)

Williams gazes into an advertising sign, the cheapened words of everyday life, which mirrors his own face, thus obscuring the father whom he has now replaced. The recovery of the father's secret demands an act of violence, a usurpation whereby the son becomes the father and thereby unblocks access to his origins, the source of poetry. Yet this origin is figurative; it is itself a poem, or "a flower/some exotic orchid/that Herman Melville had admired/in the/Hawaiian jungle" (*PB*, p. 174). Melville, whose *Pierre* demystifies the myth of a genealogical order of intertextuality, is Williams' father. But Williams' reference is to *Typee*, in which Melville describes the marriage customs of Polynesian natives. Among the Typees, where men outnumber the women, an adult tribesman marries a young girl and her lover, and thus marries a son who will eventually succeed him as husband and father.[5]

We should keep in mind that the *Autobiography* was undertaken after a heart attack, and he suffered his first stroke before completing it. In *I Wanted to Write a Poem*, he says, "It was good therapy for me. It got me back to the typewriter in high spirits" (*IWWP*, p. 86). Yet he was to write Marianne Moore that the book nearly killed him.[6] Writing was literally a matter of survival, and writing is what his father denied him. The fourth

---

4. Stock, *The Life of Ezra Pound*, 425.
5. Melville, *Typee*, 191.
6. Mariani, *William Carlos Williams*, 637.

chapter, "Pop and Mom," begins with a description of the only dream Williams claims to have had of his father after he had died:

> I saw him coming down a peculiar flight of exposed steps, steps I have since identified as those before the dais of Pontius Pilate in some well-known painting. . . . He was bare-headed and had some business letters in his hand on which he was concentrating as he descended. I noticed him and with joy cried out, "Pop! So, you're *not* dead!" But he only looked up at me over his right shoulder and commented severely, "You know all that poetry you're writing. Well, it's no good." I was left speechless and woke trembling. I have never dreamed of him since. (*A*, p. 14)

Williams is such a self-conscious writer that I hesitate to pursue the Oedipal theme of the son's murder of the father, but even he once wrote, "It took a poet to be the Oedipus too" (Yale MS). Furthermore, his father's appearance as the keeper of letters, and thus the foreign guardian of writing, reveals Williams' resentment toward him for never becoming an American citizen. And if we recall the many diatribes he wrote against the English language when we read this passage with its obvious references to writing, genealogy, the Crucifixion, and the Oedipus complex, we are overwhelmed by his deliberate overdetermination of this dream. This dream of emptiness, the absence of the father, displaces an act of murder, not necessarily of George Williams, but of the poet's literary fathers.

Perhaps the victim of this murder is Emerson. The rumor hidden in the stolen quotation appears disguised as the father who controls access to the language. Williams kills him for perpetuating English hegemony over American culture: "We care nothing at all for the complacent Concordites? We can look at that imitative phase with its erudite Holmeses, Thoreaus, and Emersons. With one word we can damn it: England" (*Imag.*, p. 211). In his condemnation of Emerson, Williams indicates how arbitrary literary parents must be. By grafting Emerson's texts onto the European canon of Romantic writers, Williams challenges literary historians who place Emerson at the source of American literature. Yet when he speaks most vehemently of his modernism, Williams recuperates the Emerson who castigated the age for living in the past. Here is Emerson: "The poet chanting was felt to be a divine man: henceforth the chant is divine also. The writer was a just and wise spirit: henceforward it is settled the book is perfect; as love of the hero corrupts into worship of his statue. Instantly the book becomes noxious: the guide is a tyrant" (*W*.I.88–89). Williams sees this as an inevitable process of history: "Each age wishes to enslave the others.

Each wishes to succeed. It is very human and completely understandable. It is not even a wish. It is an inevitability. If we read alone we are now somehow convinced that we are not quite alive, that we are less than they—who lived before us" (*EK*, p. 107). Although he rejects Emerson as an imitator of the English, his attack centers on language, not personality. To overthrow the burden of the past, Williams says, we must write, not read. Reading prolongs the tyranny of the past: "Reading shows, you say. Yes reading shows reading. What you read is what they think and what they think is twenty years old or twenty thousand" (*Imag.*, p. 61). Without writing, the book is hollow, "an inverted/ bell resounding" (*P*, p. 123). To destroy the past, one must write and thereby demystify the sacredness of the book: "I shall never be satisfied until I have destroyed the whole of poetry as it has been in the past" (Yale MS).

The question of originality, Williams says over and over again, is one of writing. Words are bound to history and what Williams variously calls the "local" or the "ground": "Words are not permanent unless the graphite be scraped up and put in a tube or the ink lifted. Words progress into the ground. One must begin with words if one is to write" (*Imag.*, p. 158). To begin with words, then, one must dig into the ground, not to seek a *point d'appui*, as did Thoreau, but to come into contact with words themselves. Williams' concept of the local is not a nostalgia for nature or place or a simple adherence to some form of positivism, but rather an extension of textuality beyond the printed page. Thus we have his Emersonian insistence on the fitness of any subject for poetry, because the subject of a poem is always the words themselves. Although there exists the temptation to say writing transforms the subject into pure poetry, writing never transforms anything because language functions independent of the phenomenal world. Nor does pure language exist, for words can never be thought of outside a notion, however figural, of inscription, itself a profanation of the idea of purity.

The problem for American writers is that "we have no words. Every word we get must be broken off from the European mass" (*Imag.*, p. 175). As words constitute everything, the poet must make us forget their old associations, hence Williams' praise of Gertrude Stein's and James Joyce's destruction of verbal and syntactical patterns in language. Williams himself was engaged in a similar effort. To open literature to the new, the poet must dissolve the calcified grammar and syntax and reestablish the primacy of writing. Any attack on language therefore constitutes an attack on thought, "the mechanism with which we make our adjustments to things and to each other" (SE, p. 165). Williams recognizes, as did Nietzsche, that the two poles of Western dialectic, I and other, are grammatical functions, not ontological truths. The modernist must therefore distance himself from both expressive and mimetic aesthetics.

In his notes for a book on education, *The Embodiment of Knowledge*, he dissociates writing from mimesis: " 'Realism' has one inevitable catch in it: it is not susceptible to writing, to being written as transcription of events or even facts. . . . To transcribe the real creates, by the same act, an unreality, something besides the real which is its transcription, since the writing is one thing, what it transcribes another, the writing a fiction, necessarily and always so" (EK, p. 13). The logical consequence of this assertion is the total breakdown of generic distinctions. Williams also undercuts philosophers' and historians' claims to truth by dismissing that which forms the basis of their discourse—referentiality. Words refer to neither nature nor thought; "words . . . represent words": "The only real in writing is writing itself" (EK, pp. 23, 13).

Williams finds himself in a double bind that parallels the same difficulty we have found in the debate between modernity and history. By breaking the bonds between words and things, he discovers his passage to an American place blocked by an abyss separating language from the local. The dependence of the American language on English threatens him with the specter of producing facsimiles of a foreign literature. As much as he would like to believe that "the American background is America," he finds himself saying, "The American background? It is Europe" (Imag., pp. 195, 196). The way out of this trap lies through repetition: "Everything that is done in Europe is a repetition of the past with a difference" (Imag., p. 210). We should not read this statement as a compromise between an established European culture and a nascent American one; to do so would ignore the many difficulties raised by Williams' polemical stance as the loyal American decrying Eliot's and Pound's flight to Europe. For all his confessions of ignorance and lack of sophistication, Williams was as international in his appreciations, if not his formal knowledge, as Eliot and Pound.

More significantly, for him, America occupies not a geographical location, but a figural one, with violence and repetition as its native ground. To break words from the European mass also means that violence must be directed at the American ground. Hence, when he hails Poe as a beginner of a local literature, he calls it "a movement, first and last to clear the GROUND" (*IAG*, p. 216). This praise is not, as some critics have said, a projection of Williams' own methods onto Poe. The local in Poe, as Riddel has said, appears only in the writing.[7] Williams will thus speak indifferently of the ground and words, for both require clearing: "It's the words, the words we need to get back to, words washed clean" (*SE*, p. 163). Yet writing does not reproduce nature as something external to language, for nature is inaccessible—the only ground man stands on is composed of graphite: "The tree as a tree does not exist literally, figuratively or any way you please—for the appraising eye of the artist—or any man—the tree does not exist. What does exist, and in heightened intensity for the artist is the impression created by the shape and color of an object before him in his sensual being—his whole body (not his eyes) his body, his mind, his memory, his place: himself—that is what he sees—And in America—escape it he cannot—it is an American tree" (*EK*, p. 24).

The impression made by the undefined object proves to be American in name only. There is no tree to be captured and translated into language; there is, instead, a nameless experience that must be disclosed in words while remaining distinct from the words themselves. The tree, we might say, becomes American in its inscription. Efforts to capture the American landscape in writing fail in their inception. Hawthorne, for example, in his rendering of New England life, is merely doing for his milieu what European writers have done for theirs; he "is no more than copying their *method* with another setting" (*IAG*, p. 229). Poe, on the other hand, tried to "invent the ORIGINAL terms" whereby Americans could recognize themselves: "Thus Poe must suffer by his originality. Invent that which is new, even if it be made of pine from your own yard, and there's none to know what you have done. It is because there's no *name*. This is the cause of Poe's lack of recognition. He was American. He was the astounding, inconceivable growth of his locality" (*IAG*, p. 226). Poe confronts the American tree and seeks to reinvent it; for if he were to give the old names, he would confine himself to European dominion. Poe looks at the tree only to turn away from the scene and "put all the weight of effort into the WRITING" (*IAG*, p. 227).

7. Riddel, *The Inverted Bell*, 22.

For Williams, Poe represents the first American writer, which is to say he is a modernist. The curious importance of Poe for Williams' poetics lies in what others have called Poe's aestheticism but what Williams calls his concern for writing. In fact, Williams looks upon Poe as a forebear of Stein and Joyce. Whitman also takes part in this revolution in writing. With the appearance of "Song of Myself," writing "had gone over to the style of the words as they appeared on the page."[8] Yet it is Poe, the first to create an American place in writing, who stands out as Williams' self-chosen precursor. But language fails Poe as he is unable to find the words adequate to his vision; thus, we have the Poe who writes macabre stories of the unreal and his French ephebes who take his failure for their model. In what the French take for the bizarre or supernatural mystery, Williams finds the nexus of Poe's genius: the search for an original language to express a new locality, "*not* 'originality' in the bastard sense, but in its legitimate sense of solidity which goes back to the ground, a conviction that he *can* judge within himself" (*IAG*, p. 216). Originality is not some sort of creation *ex nihilo*. It is, in fact, just the opposite; it is thoroughly antimetaphysical precisely because it is attached to the ground, that which always stands before man. Like Williams, Poe is an American, a beginner: "His greatness is in that he turned his back and faced inland, to originality, with the identical gesture of a Boone. And for *that* reason he is unrecognized. Americans have never recognized themselves. How can they? It is impossible until someone invent the ORIGINAL terms. As long as we are content to be called by somebody's else [*sic*] terms, we are incapable of being anything but our own dupes" (*IAG*, p. 226).

The search for a new language becomes a search for an American place. One's physical presence hardly guarantees access to the local—this is evident throughout *In the American Grain*. The Poesque turn inland, the descent to the ground, and the violence of writing form a pattern of metaphors intersecting each other on the field of action, that is, on the page. Everywhere Williams turns in nature, he finds the traces of writing. He never writes about anything but writing. In the *Autobiography*, he traces this tendency back to the play of memory. Reminiscing about girls he desired when he was a boy, he writes, "They flatter my memory. The thing, the thing, of which I am in chase. The thing I cannot quite name was there

8. Williams, "An Essay on *Leaves of Grass*," 903.

then. My writing, the necessity for a continued assertion, the need for me to go on will not let me stop" (A, p. 288). This search for "an identifiable thing" (A, p. 289) leads him into a process of perpetual beginning, a tracing of an event he has forgotten. To name the event would be the end of writing, for meaning only appears in the pursuit and disappears when writing stops. The name must therefore always elude the writer if he is to "touch the bottom of thought" (A, p. 390).

The resistance to naming leads us to the famous declaration, "No ideas but in things." Riddel argues convincingly that Williams does not grant a primacy to things over words: "The utterance does not say that ideas emerge from things, but that there are no ideas unrealized and thus no thing except in the identity and difference of things."[9] The play of difference reappears in the tropes of marriage and measure, which I will return to later in this chapter. Here I wish to add to Riddel's analysis Williams' comment upon his own process of thought: "It is seldom, arguing from the general to the particular, that any but a laborer can follow the trend of thought I espouse, which goes mostly—if it goes at all and seldom in professional minds does it go at all—from the particular, soon abandoned, to the general, its origins then forgot" (A, p. 311). The play of difference between idea and thing is situated in the relation between particular and universal, but as a play of figuration, not as sign and symbol. The measure within the utterance that sets forth the movement of the particular to the general receives its impetus from the abandonment of origins. Words are cut free from the fixities of nature and are given over to différance.

Whitman was the first to introduce a new measure to American poetry. He heard it in the waves breaking on the New Jersey coast: "There is a very moving picture of Whitman facing the breakers coming in on the New Jersey shore, when he heard the onomatopoeic waves talk to him direct in a Shakespearean language which might have been Lear himself talking to the storm. But it was not what it seemed; it was a new language, an unnamed language which Whitman could not identify or control."[10] The waves carry with them the English language Williams forswears, but this foreign language is broken upon American grounds, leaving the poet to regather the scattered fragments into a poem. In a canceled passage from Paterson, Book Four, he writes,

9. Riddel, The Inverted Bell, 9.
10. Williams, "An Essay on Leaves of Grass," 907.

> Whitman saw it: The classic is
> the past, columns regularly carved and
> arranged, the new is like the waves
> of the sea. . . .
>
> . . . .
>
>   The level of the sea is
> a field of unequal waves but all
> ranged, measured into a pattern of
> speech. No one is like another but they
> are sternly ordered by the wind.   (Yale MS)

In a curious reversal of the turn inland to Camden, Whitman, who is to be replaced by Williams, stands by the sea and hears the new measure which will eventually be copied down as Williams' variable foot. The approaching waves are, paradoxically, forever new in their perpetual sameness—although no two are alike, repetition dissolves their uniqueness into an atemporal pattern in space. In a letter written during his 1927 voyage from Europe to America, Williams tells how the sea, like writing, makes him the contemporary of his precursors: "The sea as I looked at it is exactly the same sea, given the right day and weather, that Columbus, Eric the Red, and the Puritans looked at. Thus it annihilates time and brings us right up beside these men in the imagination" (*SL*, p. 88). Williams' identity with Columbus, Eric, and the Puritans lies in the power of writing to break through uniformity to measure the difference out of which poetry is made.

In a letter to John C. Thirlwall, Williams writes: "The first thing you learn when you begin to learn anything about this earth is that you are eternally barred save for the report of your senses from knowing anything about it. Measure serves for us as the key: we can measure between objects; therefore, we know that they exist. Poetry began with measure, it began with the dance, whose divisions we have all but forgotten but are still known as measures. Measures they were and we still speak of their minuter elements as feet" (*SL*, p. 331). Measure is the spatio-temporal play between which writing begins—poetry originates in/as *différance*. Contact with the ground is always a dance— it is a marriage dance in which the separateness of man and woman generates the play of language.[11] The couple do not, cannot, achieve unity, for in unity lies the calcified grammar that kills meaning and deadens the poet to life. The dance of the poetic measure, like the dance between man and woman, prevents the synthe-

---

11. For a discussion of marriage and the play of language in Williams, see Riddel, *The Inverted Bell*, 25–26.

sizing of the elements—words and things in the poem—but releases them in the perpetual play of repetition with a difference.

In another canceled passage intended for the conclusion of *Paterson*, Book, Four, the metaphors of the sea, the woman, naming, and history all meet together:

> Europe has remained
> for us, the sea has been for us, no matter
> what it was for others, has remained for us
> the woman, Europa (we know nothing of that history)
> but a woman representing knowledge. . . .
>
> . . . .
>
> Woman has been for us unreal.
> We balk or turn away or trample them, our women
> are not the sea to us.
>
> They are not the sea, they are
> not knowledge. In a moment we bolt from them,
> we bolt from knowledge, we bolt from the names
> we give our mountains and our plain, they seem
> saltless. Who can use our names in a major work.
> We say Concord (and what does it do to our
> minds?
>
> A regression, a dissonance, an irritation,
> certainly not a fulfilment. We look to some other
> source of pleasure.
>
> We say Emerson. Oh well, we
> say. Well   .   and turn to some other source
> of inspiration, to England   to France. To
> Cervantes to Cavalcanti
>
> Whitman we say, and turn
> to Pope or Donne. We turn perhaps to chemistry
> not knowing it is the sea
>
> Thalassa, the sea. It
> is to the sea of abstract chemistry we turn. We say
> there are some bright young men in Chicago and
> Our world is a world of two women—sacred
> and profane. Our women, our own women, are the
> profane but the sea.   (Yale MS)

The woman, Europe, and the sea—all are the inaccessible, the *aletheia*, that Williams seeks to disclose. But as soon as he tries to name it, he finds the names obscure that which they were to reveal. To hear the new language is never a simple matter of paying attention to the American scenery and speech. Thus he rejects Emerson, as well as Cavalcanti, not to mention Pound and Eliot. It is to the sea that he turns, but Thalassa carries with it the weight of Greek mythology, Homer, Pound's appropriation of Homer, and the unconscious. Thalassa—the sea is a woman, both "sacred and profane": "the virgin and the whore,/ an identity" (P, p. 237).

The sea gathers together all the rivers, including the Passaic. The river bears the seeds of language:

> But lullaby, they say, the time sea is
> no more than sleep is   .   afloat
> with weeds, bearing seeds   .
>
>   Ah!
>
> float wrack, float words, snaring the
> seeds.   (P, p. 200)

The image of the sea appears a few pages earlier where Williams makes the sexual metaphor even more explicit than it is above:

> Here's to the baby,
> may it thrive!
> Here's to the labia
> that rive
>
> to give it place
> in a stubborn world.
> And here's to the peak
> from which the seed was hurled!   (P, p. 193)

The seeds bearing the fecundating power of words turn out to be mere flotsam, the wrecked particles of a language that was never unified, never one. The run to the sea is not the regathering of the assorted particulars of life into a union of signifier and signified, man and woman, Europe and America: "The sea is not our home/ —though seeds float in with the scum/ and wrack" (P, p. 201). There can never be a wedding of river and sea, of the sacred and the profane, for the woman is always two women, always double. And the sea, which is a woman, bears within it that which shatters the "dream of/ the whole poem," which has always been a dream of the Word, the One Language. The sea-bord on which Whitman and Williams stand is overrun by the excess of a heterogenenous language that cannot be controlled by the edges of the text. Much as he would like to, Williams cannot keep out the foreign language. The phallus that penetrates the sea translates the deprivation from which all writing emerges into a mythos of origins, but as Williams insists, penetration of the sea/woman signifies the desire for life/death. That is, the other, Europe, must die if America is to live on, but the womb out of which America issues serves as the crypt of the other. Thus, it is in/as America that Europe lives and dies: [12]

> Thalassa
> immaculata: our home, our nostalgic
> mother in whom the sea, enwombed again
> cry out to us to return.
> the blood dark sea! (*P*, p. 202)

Death calls the poet to return to the sea, not in expectation of renewal, but to continue the process of translation by which texts live on. In fact, Williams' "blood dark sea" translates Pound's "wine-dark sea," itself a translation from "The Seafarer," which he quotes earlier in *Paterson* (p. 115). A canceled passage makes explicit how poetry emerges from a state of privation:

> Thalassa, the sea! is another
> woman, translated—to anything, if you like,
> even to one of our fellows: the seaman has been,
> curiously, unguessed our principal translation—
> —what privation implied! a substitute for woman
> —literal and real (unguessed in point of fact). (Yale MS)

In a rather obvious pun on seaman/semen, Williams indicates that all writing is a cross-fertilization between texts and languages—in other words, a dissemination that neither issues from a center nor produces an authoritative book. The sea, or language, is a substitute for woman, or nature. The substitute is "literal and real," because the real is always an artifice and the literal is always literary, a fiction. The language that Whitman heard when facing the sea was the measure separating the poet from the mythic origin of the Word promising renewal in the womb of the sea. At the same time, measure marks the distance between man and nature that frees the poet "to dance to a measure/ contrapuntally" (*P*, p. 239), to continue in the irresolvable play of identity and difference.

12. For an analysis of the double bind of life/death, see Derrida, "Living On/Border Lines."

In *Paterson*, Book One, when Williams announces his decision to remain in America while others, obviously Pound and Eliot, run off to Europe, he rejects their nostalgia for the dream of the whole poem:

> Moveless
> he envies the men that ran
> and could run off
> toward the peripheries—
> to other centers, direct—
> for clarity (if
> they found it)
> loveliness and
> authority in the world—   (*P*, p. 36)

Although he stands motionless, he is not at the center, for centers are always plural and always peripheral. Unlike Williams, who renounces beauty
and authority as the goals of the modern writer, Pound and Eliot, in Williams' eyes, seek access to the truth. As the prologue to *Kora in Hell* makes
clear, this opposition is not between those who go to Europe and those who
choose to make a homemade world, [13] but rather between the classical and
the modern. Williams underscores his awareness that the opposition is not
a national one, not between Europe and America, but between Greece and
Rome. The choice, once again, is between remaining at home or going
abroad, but Williams here sides with those who leave: "The Greek tem-
perament lent itself to a certain symmetrical sculptural phase and to a fat
poetical balance of line that produced important work but I like better the
Greeks setting their backs to Athens. The ferment was always richer in
Rome, the dispersive explosion was always nearer, the influence carried
further and remained hot longer" (*Imag.*, p. 12). Williams' preference for
"dispersive explosion" over the symmetrical order of Greece is in accordance with his commitment to writing as that which forever dispenses with
the desire for permanence.

This passage from one of Williams' most heated arguments for an
American literature suggests that those critics who insist on Williams as a
native son are on uncertain ground. Although they certainly do not need
to search far in Williams for support for their argument, they nevertheless

---

13. I refer, of course, to the title and thesis of Kenner, *A Homemade World*.

pass over much in his works that undercuts his polemics. It is, after all, Sterne and Rabelais whom he turns to in his defense of the most radical works of Stein and Joyce, works for which Pound had neither understanding nor sympathy.[14] But his novel based on his 1924 visit to Europe, *A Voyage to Pagany*, provides a more startling example of Williams' dissolution of the borders separating homemade worlds from their foreign designs.

As in the earlier *Kora in Hell*, the question of American literature leads Williams to Rome, "the place of his birth," that is, the place of language, for the problem of modernity resolves itself in writing, not nationality: "But now he was in Rome, in Rome while passing back to the point of his departure, the place of his birth. What is the place of my birth? The place of my birth is the place where the word begins" (*VP*, p. 116). Rome is a point of passage on his return to America and, at the same time, the place where writing begins. Yet Williams does not reduce the origin of writing to some moment of creative inspiration in which a word is produced. Writing is never born for Williams; it emerges in the play of *différance*, in marriage: "It was Rome, in fact, during these days, that he most made a wife of his writing, his writing—that desire to free himself from his besetting reactions by transcribing them—thus driving off his torments and going often quietly to sleep thereafter" (*VP*, pp. 108–109). It is during his visit to Europe that Dev Evans, Williams' protagonist, determines to be a writer. When Williams declares "I am a beginner. I am an American" (*Imag.*, p. 175), he is not so much stating his nationalistic prejudices as he is declaring he is a writer, that is, a perpetual beginner. To be a beginner means always to write, never to revise: "Here's a man wants me to revise, to put in order. My God what I am doing means just the opposite from that. *There is no revision, there can be no revision—* (*Imag.*, p. 176; my emphasis). The same theme appears in *A Voyage to Pagany*: "No use to revise—for the presence is fleeting; revise and the thing escapes; only the footprints are left" (*VP*, p. 109).

---

14. In a letter to Joyce acknowledging receipt of a portion of *Finnegans Wake* in manuscript, Pound writes, "I will have another go at it, but up to present I make nothing of it whatever. Nothing so far as I make out, nothing short of divine vision or a new cure for the clapp can possibly be worth all the circumambient peripherization" (*SL*, p. 202). Williams, however, privately expressed his agreement with Pound: "I am inclined to agree with Pound—that Joyce (and Stein) are 'picking in the wrong ash can' in their recent work" (*EK*, p. 34).

And Dev finds among the traces of Rome the material for writing: "All this Roman mortar would yield up a poem." In this line from "Rome," a posthumously published fragment written during the European sabbatical that produced a *A Voyage to Pagany* and *In the American Grain*, Williams hints that Rome's fascination for the American writer lies in its ancient memorials of violence and fragmentation. Williams invokes this fertile chaos in his improvisational piece on writing, sex, and violence. Although these are also themes Pound discovered in Italian history, his interest lay largely in the Renaissance, not in ancient Rome. Williams thus follows Henry Adams, who also found in Rome the anarchy conducive to writing, if not for education. In a key passage from the chapter "Rome," which I quoted earlier, the ancient city remains a "flat contradiction" for Adams, as it previously was for Gibbon, who did not progress "an inch . . . towards explaining the Fall" (*EHA*, p. 93). Rome, the anarchistic city exempt from evolution, is synonymous with writing. In his *Autobiography*, Gibbon writes, "It was at Rome . . . that the idea of writing the decline and fall of the city first started to my mind."[15] If Rome was England, that was because its historian was English, and if it is to become America, a new historian must appear. Yet this historian does not rewrite Gibbon's history of Rome; he translates it into American history. Rome can be anything to anybody because, as Adams muses, "it meant nothing" (*EHA*, p. 93). Adams could hardly be more explicit about the figural status of Rome when he writes that the Eternal City always raises "the eternal question:—Why": "Substitute the word America for the word Rome, and the question became personal" (*EHA*, p. 92). In his emphasis on the universality of Rome—it is England and America—he hints at the familiar adage "All roads lead to Rome." This may well be true, for these roads are sentences and Rome is writing. Underlying Adams' conflation of Rome and history with England and America is a challenge to England, represented by Gibbon, as the dominant influence on American culture. Though Adams does not insist as much as Williams that Rome is the figure of a figure, he is equally adept at turning the topos of American literature into a trope of writing.

Critics have pointed out that American literature is defined by its modernism and not by its geographical location, but their heavy emphasis on America's recent origins vitiates their insight into the relation between

15. Williams, "Rome," 12; Gibbon, *Autobiography*, 160.

writing and modernism. By interpreting the relation between writing and history as a "preoccupation with the medium" or as an "antinomian, Adamic impulse," the critic either pushes language toward autonomy or turns style into the outward form of a central self.[16] Both theories remain within a dialectic of symbol and sign, with an emphasis on symbol, or poetic language and referential language. If we trace these linguistic systems back to America's Puritan tradition and to American poetry's emergence in the wake of British Romanticism, we find the question of modernity trapped within a chronological system that has for its most representative text Eliot's *Waste Land* and its reputed adaptation of classical mythology for the twentieth century. Thus, we have a poem that asserts its autonomy as a self-referential work of art (Eliot calls this the autotelic text) and nevertheless claims to recuperate the past. The paradox reappears in the title of Eliot's best-known essay, "Tradition and the Individual Talent."

Against this theory of a recuperative and autotelic poetics—with all its contradictory appeals to organicism, the self, the social community, and linear historicism—is set a practice, not a theory, of writing that rigorously excludes from its purview the theological desire for the totalizing book which would be the telos of a linear and progressive history that, at the same time, remains unaffected by temporality. Thus, when critics say that American literature has always been modern and, in fact, is inherently modern, they repeat the nineteenth-century topos wherein America is the end of history.

Therefore, when Williams and Adams turn to Rome as a trope for the beginning of American writing, they defy the nineteenth century's desire to complete history in the totalizing book. In other words, they refuse to close the book and/of history. For in the metaphor of the book, history has its most congenial representation, hence Williams' emphasis on writing as that which perpetually begins but never ends. All great literature, says Williams, is modern; if not, it is worthless. Yet he is not overawed by the past: "The master is he whom one may approach without prostituting himself. It is because in the masters' works all things go back to the ground. But the thing that continually baffles men is that this ground is a peculiarity" (*SE*, p. 36). Consequently, his focus on the local and the actual, like

16. Feidelson, *Symbolism and American Literature*, 45; Pearce, *The Continuity of American Poetry*, 5. For a discussion of symbol and sign, see Feidelson, p. 71.

the dictum "No ideas but in things," should be taken as a statement on the irreducibly linguistic grounds of knowledge. He therefore rejects the "tyranny of the symbolic" without forgoing his search "to find a basis (in poetry, in my case) for the actual" (*SL*, p. 257). The symbol draws the reader away from the word, from writing, and thus from the actual.

It should not, therefore, come as a surprise that Williams praises the importance of words: "Surrealism does not lie. It is the single truth. It is an epidemic. It is. It is just words" (*Imag.*, p. 281). The dadaists come in for similar praise for having recognized the universality of writing. "So that when we say, Long live dada! we are praising that which has already, in some one of its phases, long since outlived the pyramids." Dada, which Williams credits with having insisted on the ephemeral conditions of art, is also the most permanent of art movements. All art is dada, for no other theory embraces the radical temporality of art. Therefore, Williams can say that all art is ephemeral and, nevertheless, contemporary: "I say that Chaucer, Villon and Whitman were contemporaries of mind with whom I am constantly in touch—through the art of writing" (*SE*, p. vii).

This constant renewal, whereby writing breaks up the calcified structures of grammar and thought, submits art to an irreducible temporality, and so writing bursts through to the actual, making all poetry one. Consequently, readings such as Cary Nelson's, which turn Williams' poetry into a realization in space of the poet's consciousness, grant a corporeality to the image that seems to resemble Pound's Imagism reinterpreted through Fenollosa (that is Hugh Kenner's reading) more closely than it does Williams' poetics of writing as perpetual dance. Nelson writes, "We approach the page committed to the established boundaries of the self, boundaries which do not yet include the poem. Yet the reading process creates a unique verbal space in which consciousness is identified with the formal properties of the poem. Interaction with poetry gives our consciousness the shape and texture of inhabited space." Kenner advances a similar position when discussing Williams' theory of the imagination: "It is the place where mental clarities occur, for you no more experience clarities in your head than you experience vision in your eye. Where is the seen world? It is behind the eye, in a space you have learned to create."[17] By interpreting Williams as some sort of phenomenalist, the critic takes the actual as the immediate en-

17. Nelson, *The Incarnate Word*, 194; Kenner, *A Homemade World*, 60.

vironment that the poet represents in his works. The actual, however, appears nowhere outside of the words on the page. The poem is neither an autotelic structure nor an expression of the poet's consciousness, hence Williams' frequent declarations "that writing deals with words and words only and that all discussions of it deal with single words and their associations in groups" (*Imag.*, p. 145).

The job of the writer, then, is "to knock off every accretion from the stones of composition. . . . [I]t is a way to realize the classical excellences of language, so that it becomes writing again, and not an adjunct to science, philosophy and religion—is to make the words into sentences that will have a fantastic reality which is false" (*Imag.*, p. 280). Destruction of grammar and logic restores language to writing: "Language is the key to the mind's escape from bondage to the past. There are no 'truths' that can be fixed in language. It is by the breakup of the language that the truth can be seen to exist and that it becomes operative again" (*EK*, p. 19). Truth can only be made operative through the violence of writing; in other words, writing must violate language in order to allow truth to emerge. The place of violation is where writing begins: "for from place, a place, begins everything—is in fact a place" (*EK*, p. 130). And this place, Williams repeatedly tells us, is America.

After reading Williams' attack on him in the prologue to *Kora in Hell*, Pound fired back and reminded Williams that as a son of immigrants he really was not a genuine American, unlike the Idaho-born Pound:

> There is a blood poison in America; you can idealize the place . . . all you like, but you haven't a drop of the cursed blood in you, and you don't need to fight the disease day and night; you never had to. Eliot has it perhaps worse than I have—poor devil.
>
> You have the advantage of arriving in the milieu with a fresh flood of Europe in your veins, Spanish, French, English, Danish. You had not the thin milk of New York and New England from the pap; and you can therefore keep the environment outside you, and decently objective. (*SL*, p. 158)

Although Pound suggests that Williams' foreign blood isolates him from America and thereby allows him to deal with it, Williams did write much of *In the American Grain* during his 1924 visit to Europe, a visit he made at Pound's insistence. It may well be, as James Breslin writes, that "Williams strongly felt the need . . . to distance himself from his native environment." His "native environment," however, is the scene of writing. The importance of his decision to live in America cannot be gainsaid; it is, however, easy to confuse his sense of the local with either nationalism, something D. H. Lawrence astutely avoided and warned against, or a version of phenomenalism. The latter seems to be the more common error since the American landscape, usually thought of as a vast wilderness, becomes one-half of a dialectic between European man and the new continent. Lawrence describes Williams' history as "a sensuous record of the Americanization of the white man in America, as contrasted with ordinary history, which is a complacent record of the civilization and Europizing (if you can allow the word) of the American continent."[18] In distinguishing Europeanization from Americanization, Lawrence not only dismisses a simplistic belief that America is but a distant outpost of Europe, he also reveals that the white man is always a foreigner in America.

In Williams' rather anthropocentric figure for the process of Americanization, the continent is forever being violated but never settled. I wish to emphasize that the motif of violence running throughout In the American Grain cannot be separated from Williams' reading and writing of American history. To a certain degree, his extensive use of quotation (some chapters consist entirely of quotations) suggests the piecemeal nature of both writing and history. He describes his method of composition in the Autobiography:

> The plan was to try to get inside the heads of some of the American founders or "heroes," if you will, by examining their original records. I wanted nothing to get between me and what they themselves had recorded: a translation of a Norse saga, The Long Island Book, the case of Eric the Red, would be the beginning; Columbus' Journal; the letters of Hernando Cortez to Philip of Spain; Daniel Boone's autobiography; and so forth, to a letter, entire, written by John Paul Jones on board the Bonhomme Richard, after his battle with the Serapis. So it would go. (A, p. 178)

But we should not reduce Williams' historical method to a rummaging through documents out of which he can reconstruct America's past. The intertextual relation between Williams' work and his sources is not a pro-

18. Breslin, William Carlos Williams, 90; Lawrence, Review of In the American Grain, 334.

cess of reduplication or reconstruction, but a writing that repeats history in/as a destruction of preexisting interpretations. In other words, Williams' writing re-marks the violence of naming that is American.

His emphasis on violence serves as a reminder that America has been contaminated at its very source. Red Eric brings to Greenland a legacy of murders, yet this violence cannot be separated from writing—as if history were a documentation of an original event marking the birth of a new world. Williams' treatment of *The Long Island Book* shows his text is a failed reappropriation of an unattainable source: "Obviously I couldn't imitate the Norse but I chose a style that was barbaric and primitive, as I knew Eric the Red to be" (*IWWP*, p. 42). In his misappropriation of his "source," Williams identifies history as the violence of an "original" renaming. He says: "In these studies I have sought to re-name the things seen, now lost in chaos of borrowed titles, many of them inappropriate, under which the true character lies hid. In letters, in journals, reports of happenings I have recognized new contours suggested by old words so that new names were constituted" (*IAG*, p. v). His renaming does not re-create a hidden America; he has constructed his book out of the fragments of diverse texts. His renaming, therefore, is a rereading of history whereby the copied texts destroy the edifice of old interpretations and uncover that which lies without names: "It has been my wish to draw from every source one thing, the strange phosphorus of the life, nameless under an old misappellation" (*IAG*, p. v). Life, however, removes itself from language even as the writer breaks through the reified interpretations that insist on being regarded as authentic. The destructive force of writing discloses the original violation in history obscured by language. Thus the violence surrounding the colonizing of the New World is the figure for the writing of history—to enter into history is to be violated.

"Red Eric" introduces this double inscription of history as murder and naming. Having killed a man, Eric is forced to flee Norway and thus comes to discover what he calls Greenland. America thus begins as a figural substitution for the lost home: "Eric was Greenland: I call it Greenland, that men will go there to colonize it" (*IAG*, p. 1). Eric's misnomer is a trope of a trope—"Greenland" signifies the belatedness of the discoverer, for he has been anticipated by the myth of a fertile and virgin land which he invokes in the name. "Greenland" also designates the New World as a trope of desire, of the privation from which poetry begins. To name something is, by most accounts, the primordial act of originality, but "Greenland" signifies what Eric has lost and futilely desires to recover. The New World begins in what can only be a repetition of an original misappellation.

Beginning with Eric, Williams reflects on the peculiar urge of the poet—if Eric is a name-giver, he is a poet—for contact with the uniqueness of the American place. Success demands a descent to the ground, an opening of the place to memory:

> The descent beckons
> as the ascent beckoned
> Memory is a kind
> of accomplishment
> a sort of renewal
> even
> an initiation, since the spaces it opens are new
> places
> inhabited by hordes
> heretofore unrealized,
> of new kinds—   (P, pp. 77–78)

Memory, contra Eliot, can never recuperate a lost plenitude; it opens the place to writing, a perpetual play wherein the place is reconstituted as a lost presence:

> A
> world lost,
> a world unsuspected
> beckons to new places
> and no whiteness (lost) is so white as the memory
> of whiteness.   (P, p. 78)

Only in memory does the world attain being. Thus when Eric names his new land, he measures the distance separating him from a lost home. The New World is not an Eden contaminated by the presence of a European; it is a memorial figure for a lost purity, but a purity that has no existence outside of language. The New World does not exist outside its inscription—the orderly movement from Old World to New repeats an original reappropriation of configuration, the double inscription whereby words are set free from the chains of referentiality to constitute themselves as a pattern, a "representation of knowledge from an illegible script" (EK, p. 75).

Therefore, Columbus' discovery does not open America to the Old World; the new land forever eludes the grasp of knowledge that would make it into a continuation, and possible end, of Europe's history. Yet America is not impregnable; in fact, it bears fruit before it is ravished: "A predestined and bitter fruit existing, perversely, before the white flower of its birth, it was laid bare by the miraculous first voyage. For it is as the achievement of a flower, pure, white, waxlike and fragrant, that Columbus' infatuated course must be depicted, especially when compared with the acrid and poisonous apple which was later by him to be proved" (*IAG*, p. 7). The fruit precedes the flower, which is ravished the moment Columbus lands. The virgin land has always been deflowered. As the chapter itself begins belatedly with Columbus' return and ends with the discovery of America, we are reminded that discovery is never original. Williams manages to tell of all three voyages and still end with the first; in violating the logic of the narrative, he designs Columbus' voyages as an initial repetition, a reproduction of previous discoveries.

When the sailors land and shout, "*Nuevo Mundo*," they say in their own language what the Asian discoverers and Eric said before them. Yet Williams insists, "it was indeed a new world," new not because they are the first Europeans, but because the land had no language: "They [Columbus' men] the product of an age-long civilization beginning in India, it is said, and growing through conquest and struggle of all imaginable sorts through periods of success and decline . . . through the changes of speech: Sanscrit, Greek, Latin growing crooked in the mouths of peasants who would rise and impose their speech on their masters . . . words accurate to the country, Italian, French and Spanish itself not to speak of Portuguese. Words! Yes this party of sailors . . . ambassadors of all the ages that have gone before them, had indeed found a new world, a world, that is, that knew nothing about them" (*Imag.*, pp. 181–82). Just as Latin and Greek were to be replaced by modern languages, "accurate to the country," so America will need a new language. In the absence of such a language, the old words are loosened from the ground that gave them authority, initiating the new in history. The words have become outmoded "because meanings have been lost through laziness or changes in the form of existence which have let words empty. Bare handed the man contends with the sky, without experience of existence seeking to invent and design" (*Imag.*, p. 100). America casts out the old words and, with them, the past. Yet the poet does not turn to nature, for it too is an imitation of the past: "Every step once taken in the first advance of the human race, from the amoeba to the highest type of intelligence, has been duplicated, every step exactly paralleling the one that preceded it in the dead ages gone by. A perfect plagiarism results. Everything is and is new. Only the imagination is undeceived" (*Imag.*, p. 93).

Nature is a plagiarist; it produces an endless series of copies. And if nature itself is a copy, there can be no basis for a mimetic theory of art, which demands that the work faithfully reproduce the original. To be engaged with nature, therefore, the writer must construct a work equally detached and apposed to it. Thus, the writers who copy the American scenery only reproduce European literature in a foreign setting, the American being a reproduction of the European. But the imagination does not create the new; it re-creates it: "Yes, the imagination, drunk with prohibitions, has destroyed and recreated everything afresh in the likeness of that which it was. Now indeed men look about in amazement at each other with a full realization of the meaning of 'art'" (*Imag.*, p. 93). Destruction must precede reconstruction, for words must break loose from the debris of nature if they are to become new once more. Therefore, Williams' attacks on nature are also directed against books:

> And there rises
> a counterpart, of reading, slowly, overwhelming
> the mind; anchors him in his chair. So be
> it. He turns   .   O Paradiso! The stream
> grows leaden within him, his lilies drag. So
> be it. Texts mount and complicate them-
> selves, lead to further texts and those
> to synopses, digests and emendations. So be it.
> Until the words break loose or—sadly
> hold unshaken. Unshaken! So be it.   (*P*. p. 130)

Williams seizes upon nature and the book as symmetrical figures supporting a logocentric theory of history. In *Paterson*, he appropriates the classical form of four books corresponding to the four seasons. But the poem mocks this structural design modeled on nature's cyclical renewal:

> —you cannot believe
> that it can begin again, again here
> again   .   here
> Waken from a dream, this dream of
> the whole poem.   (*P*, p. 200)

Williams calls upon the writer to destroy nature and burn the library, not that he may create anew, but that he may repeat the past in a play of

difference. Repetition is the new; it is the falls, the "common language . . .
combed into straight lines/ from that rafter of a rock's/ lip" (P, p. 7). The
crashing water of the falls echoes with the rumor of meaning which the
poet strains to catch:

> falling
> and refalling with a roar, a reverberation
> not of the falls but of its rumor
> > unabated. (P, p. 96)

In the iterability of the falls, the poet hears the repetition of a rumored beginning; he hears the approach of spring: "It is spring: life again begins to
assume its normal appearance as of 'today.' Only the imagination is undeceived" (Imag., p. 94). Spring is repetition, not renewal.

In Paterson, Williams accuses Eliot of a belief in the recuperation of the
past:

> Who is it spoke of April? Some
> insane engineer. There is no recurrence.
> The past is dead. (P, p. 142)

Unlike the recuperative dream of The Waste Land, Paterson abjures the
desire to recapture a lost plenitude and, instead, commits poetry to a perpetual beginning:

> How to begin to find a shape—to begin to begin again,
> turning the inside out :   to find one phrase that will
> lie married beside another for delight . ?
> —seems beyond attainment. (P, p. 140)

Williams' violent response to Eliot's Waste Land stems not only from Eliot's
desire to resuscitate tradition but also from Eliot's turning his back on the
privation out of which the American poet struggles to emerge. In the prologue to Kora in Hell, Williams dismisses Pound and Eliot as "men content
with the connotations of their masters." They would employ their admit-
tedly sophisticated techniques to measure themselves against the past: "It
is convenient to have fixed standards of comparison: All antiquity!" (Imag.,
p. 24). Williams' ridicule is directed not at their craftsmanship but at their
belief in a hierarchical order which the present may resurrect and even sur-
pass. Against this, Williams sets the imagination, which is not a recuperative power, but a force that draws upon the loss of presence: "Rich as are
the gifts of the imagination bitterness of world's loss is not replaced thereby.

On the contrary it is intensified, resembling thus possession itself" (*Imag.*, p. 18). Imagination intensifies and does not replace what has been lost, and thus absence comes to resemble possession. The power of imagination allows the poet to break through the emptiness and establish contact with the ground, but that power does not recover a lost presence. Contact exists in what Williams variously calls marriage, the dance, and the measure—the new ground out of which language emerges:

> Let the snake wait under
> his weed
> and the writing
> be of words, slow and quick, sharp
> to strike, quiet to wait,
> sleepless.
> —through metaphor to reconcile
> the people and the stones.
> Compose. (No ideas
> but in things) Invent!
> Saxifrage is my flower that splits
> the rocks. (*CLP*, p. 7)

Williams' snake is a trope for tropes, a turning of the words that leads to other words. Metaphor joins man to the ground without their ever becoming one, for writing can only be realized in the identity and difference of things. The flower of imagination blooms in the difference that is measured by words. Only in figures can there be a meeting between idea and thing, man and woman:

> I speak in figures,
>   well enough, the dresses
> you wear are figures also,
>   we could not meet
>   otherwise. (*PB*, p. 159)

Man and woman do not join together and dissolve all differences between them; they remain two in the figure. In the dance, "there are always two,/ yourself and the other" (*PB*, p. 32), and self and other exist only in the difference measured by the dance:

> But only the dance is sure!
> make it your own.
> Who can tell
> what is to come of it? (*PB*, p. 33)

In *Poets of Reality*, J. Hillis Miller speaks of "the state of deprivation which was [Williams'] starting point." Miller insists, however, that "it appears only once because it was so soon transcended. The poet does not become himself, nor is his writing possible, until he has gone beyond it."[19] I would modify this to say that every poem begins out of a deprivation that is not so much transcended as it is made fecund by the imagination. By accepting the loss of unity which the imagination intensifies, the poet draws together the words of a shattered language: "Thus a poem is tough by no quality it borrows from a logical recital of events nor from the events themselves but solely from that attenuated power which draws perhaps many broken things into a dance giving them thus a full being" (*Imag.*, pp. 16–17). In the "logical recital of events" and "the events themselves," Williams takes aim against the division, and reification, of idea and thing into the two poles of existence. Out of this dualism comes the emptiness that can never be overcome.

The vehemence with which Williams rejects the slightest taint of dualism explains the repulsion the Puritans aroused in him. In their rigid division of nature and spirit is a denial of the ground in the name of God. For Williams, the Puritans' moral vacuity is measured by their devotion to God. Finally, their religion embodied all that Williams detested in the New World. In Cotton Mather's books, Williams finds "the flower of that religion": "Its virtue is to make each man stand alone, surrounded by a density as of the Lord: a seed in its shell. The Kingdom of God; the Devil at fault fighting for souls; Christ the Divine sacrifice; the Bible the guide; the Church its apostle. There it is, concise, bare, PURE: blind to every contingency, mashing Indian, child and matron into one *safe* mold" (*IAG*, pp. 11–12). Puritan dogma represents the absolute limits of a tradition that closes the world to the possibility of contact and thus the reinvention of the new.

Yet Williams recognizes that it is precisely their emptiness that gave them their strength: "By their very emptiness they were the fiercest element in the battle to establish a European life on the New World" (*IAG*, p. 63). Having nothing, they imagine they are full, thereby protecting themselves from the encroachments of the land. Their "spirit *is* an earthly pride which

19. J. H. Miller, *Poets of Reality*, 285.

they, prideless, referred to heaven and the next world (*IAG*, p. 65). In his attack on Puritan dogma, Williams also assaults a theory of reading. As Perry Miller and Sacvan Bercovitch have argued, the Puritans introduced into America a hermeneutics which transformed their experience into the fulfillment of biblical typology.[20] Williams thus directs his argument at the Puritans' belief in the correspondence between language and the world, a belief which has had a tyrannical hold on American history: "The Puritan, finding one thing like another in a world destined for blossom only in 'Eternity,' all soul, all 'emptiness' then here, was precluded from SEEING the Indian. They never realized the Indian in the least save as an unformed PURITAN" (*IAG*, p. 113).

Although Williams' condemnation surely shares a great deal with the popular conception of the Puritan as the stern denier of all that is generous in man, it is also aimed at a theory of reading that finds in every text, including nature, a fixed relation with a personal concept of God raised into a transcendent principle. As the universal signifier, God guarantees the stability of the text, and thus ensures that the end of art is the ends of man. Consequently, Williams writes, "All that will be new in America will be anti-Puritan. It will be of another root" (*IAG*, p. 120). The new in America will only emerge when the reader comes into contact with the ground, that is, when he recognizes the necessity of interpretation: "That unless everything that is, proclaim a ground on which it stand, it has no worth; and that what has been morally, aesthetically worth while in America has rested upon peculiar and discoverable ground. But they think they get it out of the air or the rivers, or from the Grand Banks or wherever it may be, instead of by word of mouth or from records contained for us in books—and that, *aesthetically, morally we are deformed unless we read*" (*IAG*, p. 109; my emphasis). The descent to the ground leads to writing, not nature, and it is there, in the text, that America will be discovered. Puritanism stands for a refusal to read, in spite of any appeal to the book of nature, which merely rehashes what they find in the Bible. To read demands a recognition of the indeterminable ground upon which America rests, for interpretation only begins when reading is stripped of the institutional supports embodied

---

20. See Perry Miller, *The New England Mind*; Bercovitch, *The Puritan Origins of the American Self*.

in tradition. Consequently, God must be destroyed: " 'God' it destroys everything that interferes with simple clarity and apprehension" (*Imag.*, p. 259).

Opposed to Puritan hermeneutics is a French method of reading which is free from the dogmas that block access to the ground. Thus in Champlain, Williams finds a man who can live in the New World and, it seems, in a book: "Here *is* a man after my own heart. Is it merely in a book? So am I then, merely in a book" (*IAG*, p. 69). Although the book Williams refers to is obviously his source for the chapter, it is also the reader and his subject, that is to say, a figure for the intertextuality of the historical subject and its interpreter. Unlike the Puritans, Champlain is free to invent: "He . . . sets out with two vessels for New France, a country almost invented, one might say, out of his single brain" (*IAG*, p. 70). While much of Williams' praise for Champlain, particularly his "energy for detail," reflects his own views on writing, Champlain's strength proves to be his undoing: "It is why France never succeeded here. It is the Latin, or Gaelic or Celtic sense of historic continuity" (*IAG*, p. 74). In the belief that physical presence will make the land French, Champlain shuts himself off from the freedom of interpretation—"the absolute new without a law but the basic blood where the savage become brother. That is generous. Open. A break through" (*IAG*, p. 74). The white man, says Williams, interposes Europe—that is, the past—between himself and America and thus fails to break through to the new.

It is Champlain's compatriot, Sebastian Rasles, who opposes the Puritan dogma erected between the white man and the Indian. In Père Rasles' *Lettres Edifiantes*, Williams discovers how much Americans are like Indians: "I do believe the average American to be an Indian, but an Indian robbed of his world" (*IAG*, p. 128). In the conflict between Père Rasles and the English, Williams offers his models for two readings of the New World—the open and the closed. This distinction, however, is figural, not geographical, for Boone embraces the savage, as did Père Rasles, in what will be a "new wedding" between the white man and the Indian. On the other hand, "Franklin is the full development of the timidity, the strength that denies itself" (*IAG*, p. 155). In "Jacataqua," this curse of self-denial which interposes God between man and the actual becomes translated into a subservience to America's European past: "It is our need that is crying out, that and our immense wealth, the product of fear,—a torment to the spirit; we sell—but carefully—to seek blessings abroad. And this wealth, all that is not pure accident—is the growth of fear" (*IAG*, p. 174). This fear, writes Williams, is "a mechanism to increase the gap between touch and thing, *not* to have a contact" (*IAG*, p. 177).

American history is the repeated story of a failure, with few exceptions, to attain contact with the local, and those who do succeed are hounded by the rest of society. The inability to dwell in the particularity of the American scene drives the country to seek approval abroad. Instead of turning to Europe, Williams seeks to uncover the significance of history at home. Thus he denies Valéry Larbaud's accusation that he wishes "to uproot history, like those young men of the Sorbonne. No, I seek the support of history but I wish to understand it aright, to make it SHOW itself" (*IAG*, p. 116). Just as Williams poetry is a destruction of the classical forms, so his history is a destruction and, thereby, an opening of history to the new: "History must stay open, it is all humanity" (*IAG*, p. 189). History, however, is a method of reading, not a linear development: "It portrays us in generic patterns, like effigies or the carving of sarcophagi; which say nothing save, of such and such a man, that he is dead. That's history. It is concerned only with one thing: to say everything is dead" (*IAG*, p. 188). Conceived as the record of the past rather than an opening of the local to man, history becomes merely a funerary monument. History that fixes man into a single unchanging image is false: "It's lies, such history, and dangerous. Just there may lie our one hope for the future, beneath that stone of prejudice" (*IAG*, p. 190). In his egregious pun on *lies*, Williams suggests that in recognizing the fictive grounds of history, the reader frees himself to reinterpret the past and uncover whatever is usable for man. Writing history, then, is reinterpreting the texts and interpretations that have solidified into accepted truths.

Williams characterizes the destruction of these reified interpretations of America as a descent to the ground, and in this, history is inseparable from writing: "He [the poet] wants to have the feet of his understanding on the ground, his ground, *the* ground, the only ground that he knows, that which *is* under his feet. I speak of aesthetic satisfaction. This want, in America, can only be filled by knowledge, a poetic knowledge, of that ground" (*IAG*, p. 213). This return to authenticity, however, is an original repetition: "However hopeless it may seem, we have no other choice: we must go back to the beginning; it must all be done over; everything that is must be destroyed" (*IAG*, p. 215). And every time Williams begins to write, he destroys everything once again.

CHAPTER SEVEN

Quotation, Originality
and the Poetry of Hart Crane

Language has built towers and bridges,
but itself is inevitably as fluid as
always.
                                —Hart Crane

The difficulty of Crane's verse has attained a notoriety in literary history
that, we might say, has only been rivaled by his scandalous biography. A
reputation for obscurity plagued him from the beginning of his career, as
he acknowledges in an often quoted letter to Yvor Winters: "It's all an accident so far as my style goes. It happens that the first poem I ever wrote
was too dense to be understood."[1] To defend his poetry against charges of
willful obscurity, Crane could have turned to the example of T. S. Eliot,
whose poetry he read throughout his career. In fact, Crane may well be the
greatest poet, perhaps the only great poet, upon whom Eliot exerted a lasting influence. Despite this debt, Crane's style seems as far removed from
Eliot's as that of Eliot's most vocal denigrator, William Carlos Williams.

In a letter to Allen Tate, Crane tells of having to face Eliot for *"four* years"
in order to go *"through* him toward a *different goal.* . . . You will profit
by reading him again and again. I must have read 'Prufrock' twenty-five
times and things like the 'Preludes' more often. His work will lead you back
to some of the Elizabethans and point out the best in them. And there is
Henry James, Laforgue, Blake and a dozen others in his work" (*L*, p. 90).
Before the appearance of *The Waste Land*, Crane recognized how Eliot used
quotation to assert his place within the tradition. In his letter to Tate, Crane
describes Eliot's poetry as a critical anthology containing, in Poundian

---

1. Weber (ed.), *The Letters of Hart Crane*, 301, hereinafter cited as *L*. All references to
Crane's poetry and critical prose are from Weber (ed.), *The Complete Poems and Selected
Letters and Prose*, hereinafter cited by page number.

fashion, the necessary fragments of the tradition. Eliot's method not only served as a model for Crane, it also formed the very material of his poetic education. But as John Irwin has pointed out, "In writing *The Bridge*, Crane planned to use the poetic artistry of *The Waste Land* against the content of *The Waste Land*." In other words, Crane hoped to counteract Eliot's pessimism, only to find that in adapting the technique, he "got the pessimistic content along with it."[2] What is in doubt for both Crane and Eliot is the possibility of recovering the Word.

For Eliot, and this is where he and Crane part company, the tradition, like God's Word, belongs to an ideal order exempt from time and recognized by what he calls the "historical sense": "The historical sense involves a perception, not only of the pastness of the past, but of its presence" (*SE*, p. 4). To recognize the presence of the past, the poet must absorb all of the European tradition since Homer; only then will he perceive the ideal order that remains free from time and gives significance to the contemporary poem. The tradition is, for Eliot, the Word that descends to lend meaning to language. Hence Eliot professes to be comfortable with the past: "This historical sense, which is a sense of the timeless as well as of the temporal and of the timeless and of the temporal together, is what makes a writer traditional. And it is at the same time what makes a writer most acutely conscious of his place in time, of his own contemporaneity" (*SE*, p. 4). In "Little Gidding," he arrives at the theological consequences of this theory—history is the infinite recurrence of "timeless moments" repeating an ideal order:

> A people without history
> Is not redeemed from time, for history is a pattern
> Of timeless moments.

Eliot's insistence upon a fixed order of tradition inevitably meant that the poem would be theologized as an autotelic structure (meaning inheres in the internal self-references, thus freeing the poem from history) and that the logos would be aestheticized. The logos is the Word sustaining the tradition; it is "The point of intersection of the timeless/ With time."[3] In the earlier poem "Gerontion," history is a nightmare of unrequited desire to be redeemed from time, that is, to escape an empty present unsustained by

2. Irwin, "Figurations of the Writer's Death," 252.
3. Eliot, *Collected Poems*, 144, 136, hereinafter cited as *CP*.

the Word. For the faithful in the later poems, the Word will harmonize language around a silence, an absence that will be filled by a music that reverberates within the hollow center to remind man of the eternal Word outside history, that is to say, outside language.

Although Crane was disturbed by Eliot's pessimism, and wrote "Faustus and Helen" as a response to it, a more important distinction for modernist poetics lies in their different attitudes toward tradition, a difference that is accentuated by their similarities. In one of the several letters acknowledging his debt to Eliot, Crane condemns those artists who strive for novelty: "GOD DAMN this constant nostalgia for something always 'new.' This disdain for anything with a trace of the past in it!!! This kind of criticism is like a newspaper, always with its dernier cri. It breeds its own swift decay because its whole theory is built on an hysterical sort of evolution theory" (L, p. 114). Crane's disdain for those who reject the past is at once a confession to conservative tastes and a fairly radical critique of originality that separates his notion of tradition from Eliot's. Although Eliot thought that a novel work was possible, he ultimately granted true originality to the work in which the tradition is fully felt. Crane, on the other hand, dismisses a belief in originality along with a genetic view of history that considers the present an evolutionary product of the past. And as the phrase "nostalgia for the new" suggests, originality has meaning only in terms of a linear historicism, according to which the present is the accretion of past moments in a chain of cause and effect. To be original, one must step over the immediate past and reach back to a lost or primitive origin. According to this linear sense of history, originality is reduced to empty repetition—a continual re-production of the new. The poem, therefore, stands outside history and, hence, language, a notion that Eliot never entertained even in his most logocentric pronouncements.

Crane's theory of metaphor separates him both from the dadaists, who in his eyes sought to deny the past, and from Eliot's aesthetic theory of history. In "General Aims and Theories," Crane states that the task he posed for himself in writing "Faustus and Helen" consisted "in a reconstruction in these modern terms of the basic emotional attitude toward beauty that the Greeks had." The favorable reception of "Faustus and Helen" encouraged Crane to begin work on The Bridge, which he apparently had in mind when he wrote of reconstructing ancient Greek myth: "And in doing so I

found that I was really building a bridge between so-called classic experience and many divergent realities of our seething, confused cosmos of today, which has no formulated mythology yet for classic poetic reference or
for religious exploitation" (p. 217). Crane's method involved a search for
correspondences "between two widely separated worlds." Amid the fragments of modern life, he hopes to find signs of the permanence of tradition.
His method, as he acknowledged, owes a great deal to Eliot's *Waste Land*,
but whereas Eliot's compilation of fragments was a means of asserting history's hold over the ruins of modern culture, Crane held that the poet's job
was to transfigure history in the making of the poem.

Comparison with Eliot's thematic reflection in "*Ulysses*, Order, and
Myth" is fruitful here. Both Eliot and Crane characterize twentieth-century civilization as an age of radical uncertainty and purposelessness—a
formulation, one must suspect, that was already hackneyed by the close of
the century's second decade (Crane's phrase "seething, confused cosmos of
today" must have sounded like a cliché the day it was written). But Eliot
sought in myth a preformed set of images that would organize the literary
work and place it within the tradition. Crane, on the other hand, looked
upon myth not as a totalizing system but as a purely linguistic structure
without a transcendent referent; it is what he calls a "bridge." Mythology,
for Crane, is a language, not a set of beliefs, as it is for Eliot. Crane's bridge,
therefore, is a figure for figurality, that which allows the substitution of
tropes for one another. Mythology, in other words, serves as a vehicle for
"reference" or "exploitation." It bypasses the logic of onto-theology for
what Crane calls the "logic of metaphor" and Emerson simply calls poetry.
In fact, Crane's speculations on the bridge and metaphor echo Emerson's
call for a poet who will supersede the philosopher: "I think metaphysics a
grammar to which, once read, we seldom return. . . . I want not the logic,
but the power, if any, which it brings into science and literature; the man
who can humanize this logic, these syllogisms, and give me the results. The
adepts value only the pure geometry, the aërial bridge ascending from earth
to heaven with arches and abutments of pure reason. I am fully contented
if you tell me where are the two termini" (W.XII.13). Crane's bridge is a
trope for the power of language over history.

To reconstruct the Greek attitude toward beauty, Crane is to design a
bridge that, unlike classical allusion, will permit access to ancient myth. In
his theory, Crane eschews allusion, or direct reference, in favor of analogy,

or metaphor, which will lead language back to the idea of the "beautiful" he always associates with the logos. The return to the logos, however, is neither the recovery of a lost unity nor the teleological unfolding of destiny; instead, it is an interiorizing of the cipher in which history is written. The past returns via quotation of the texts that form the substance of his poetry. Furthermore, we might add that his bridge is without termini— neither a modern nor an ancient myth that will serve in a referential system. Figuration, therefore, must create the illusion of meaning by a process of substitution. Thus, Crane finds " 'Helen' sitting in a street car," Helen being the Greek experience of beauty, that is, another trope and not an ideal referent to beauty.

For Crane, recovering the past is inimical to appropriating its cultural signposts and mythological denominators, which he dismisses as "useless archeology." To revive the past, he writes, the poet must be attentive to present experience and relate "his experience to a postulated 'eternity' " (p. 218). In Whitmanesque fashion, his attempt to recover a living past forces him to look toward America's future, where he hopes to discover "a new hierarchy of faith" (p. 219). His recovery of the past, therefore, will take place in the future, and his bridge will extend between experience and a "postulated 'eternity.' "

To span this distance, Crane replaces the logic of referential language with the associational power of metaphor: "The entire construction of the poem is raised on the organic principle of a 'logic of metaphor,' which antedates our so-called pure logic, and which is the genetic basis of all speech, hence consciousness and thought-extension" (p. 221). Crane's notion of an ur-logic grounded in metaphor shifts the genetic basis of a literary language from an organic model to a rhetorical one. The poem does not recount a movement from origin to end wherein the end conforms to its source. *The Bridge* has been read as the poet's search for a myth that would give meaning to modern America, which thus turns the poem itself into the object of the search and the psyche of the poet into the fecundating source of an American mythology. What Crane's logic of metaphor calls into question is the status of the psyche as an originating source. In its place stands language, a "source" without a center.

Like Nietzsche, Crane finds that the first metaphor was itself a metaphor. The "genetic basis" of speech and consciousness, which, Crane suggests, is itself a language, can only be an origin without a fixed point or, in other words, a bridge without termini, a nonorigin. The genetic pattern of metaphor joins together what Paul de Man, in an essay on *The Birth of Tragedy*, identifies as the "distinction between essence and appearance."[4] Metaphor, which always insists that it means something other than what it says, posits a link between the literal and/or representational function of language and the figurative and/or rhetorical function. Hence, the genetic pattern that begins with Columbus' voyage and closes with a vision of Atlantis depends upon the *archē*-tectural metaphor of the bridge to "link/ What cipher-script of time no traveller reads" (p. 115). Crane's bridge is constituted of texts, not prophecy, and it is the crossing of texts that undoes the myth of the visionary who gazes at the bridge to catch a glimpse of infinity. I therefore disagree with Harold Bloom's analysis of Crane's poetry in *Agon*, which I will discuss later in this chapter.

In one of his earlier poems, "Possessions," Crane characterizes the urge for sublime vision as a desire for his lover. Typically read in terms of the sexual imagery of the bolts of lightning, the poem is said to move toward the purification of lust. "Possessions" becomes the archetypical statement of Crane's dependence upon suffering for the subsequent release of the imagination. Consummation of the self means propagation of the Word. According to these readings, the identity of tenor and vehicle in metaphor indicates the recuperative power of language. The sacrificial motif of the final stanza makes this a powerful interpretative approach to Crane's exceedingly difficult poetry. Thus, his poetry is almost universally read as a nonironic assimilation of the past in the name of the present and the imagination.[5]

The Shelleyan pathos of the final stanza seems to confirm the triumph of imagination over lust:

> Tossed on these horns, who bleeding dies,
> Lacks all but piteous admissions to be spilt
> Upon the page whose blind sum finally burns
> Record of rage and partial appetites.
> The pure possession, the inclusive cloud
> Whose heart is fire shall come,—the white wind rase
> All but bright stones wherein our smiling plays.   (p. 18)

---

4. De Man, *Allegories of Reading*, 102.
5. For readings of Crane's poem as purification through art, see Uroff, *Hart Crane*, 28–30; Dembo, *Hart Crane's Sanskrit Charge*, 5–8; R. W. B. Lewis, *The Poetry of Hart Crane*, 132–35.

The poet offers himself as a sacrifice to history, the "smoked forking spires,/ The city's stubborn lives, desires." The poet's failure to consummate his desire brings the poem into existence; consequently, he leaves it for the future to transform the "stones of lust" into the "bright stones" of a purified love. "Possessions," therefore, recounts the making of the poem. As Joseph Riddel has argued, Crane writes "poems in which the poet rehearses the act of creating the poem, poems in which life is explored and virtually lived by holding it within the intense focus of the moment of its creation— poems, that is, which create a world rather than discover one."[6] The search for love purified of lust is an allegory of the poet's search for the Word free from a referent, a quest that can only end in failure, hence the deferral of the vision at the poem's conclusion. Yet the echoes of Shelley's "Ode to the West Wind" and "The Cloud" suggest that the poet laments not just the failure of a "pure possession" but also the failure to purify language of history, which haunts the poem in the form of quotation.

Read as a poetry that creates the world in the act of writing the poem, Crane's lyrics enact a genetic narrative confirming the correspondence of inside to outside, or inner desire to its expression in metaphor. Yet in aligning metaphor with prophetic vision and, therefore, with truth, Crane denies the temporal pattern on which his poem is built. When he turns to Shelley for his pathos-laden image of sacrifice upon the "thorns of life" and the redemptive images of wind and cloud, he transforms the visionary impetus of the poem from an imagistic identity between appearance and essence, or metaphor as a closed system of resemblance, to the open temporality of what Paul de Man calls allegory.[7] In other words, allusion in Crane breaks the symmetrical relation between appearance and essence by introducing into symbol as prophecy the disruptive figure of narrative as allegory. Crane switches from the representational property of metaphor to the nonreferential linguistic process of transumptive allusion, which is quite distinct from the recuperative nostalgia of classical allusion. The wind that promises the coming of spring in Shelley transforms the "stones of lust" into "bright stones," or figures. In a text that presumably narrates the purification of the self, the figures that first represent the self become

6. Riddel, "Hart Crane's Poetics of Failure," 475.
7. De Man, *Allegories of Readings*, 74–78.

figures of figures, thereby transforming the teleological promise of purification into a process of repetition.

"Possessions" dramatizes what Riddel has recognized as the paradigmatic theme of Crane's poetry—it expresses his "desire to transmute the
temporal self into pure space—to purify himself virtually into the form of
a poem." But although Riddel characterizes Crane as doomed to acknowledge the irreducible temporality of writing as process, Crane's transformation of the self into poetry is less the phenomenalization of the creative
consciousness in the product and more accurately an allegory of the uncertain relationship between self and language. The gesture toward the redemptive power of imagination to purify the emotions remains simply a
gesture, a figure for the self as figuration or, in Crane's trope, the transformation of passion into writing, the "piteous admissions to be split/ Upon
the page." Yet Crane's trope operates not within the framework of an expressive theory of poetry but within a Nietzschean process of metamorphosis wherein passion itself is metaphor, or what Nietzsche, in *The Birth
of Tragedy*, calls the "vicarious image": "The images of the *lyrist* are
nothing but *his very* self and, as it were, only different projections of himself, so he, as the moving center of this world, may say 'I': of course, this
self is not the same as that of the waking, empirically real man, but the
only truly existent and eternal self resting at the basis of things, through
whose images the lyric genius sees this very basis." Consciousness of the
world of symbols requires the surrender of "subjectivity in the Dionysian
process." The "I" of the lyrist, therefore, is a fiction, the trope that allows
the continual metamorphosis of the world that begins with the metamorphosis of the self. Yet the lyrist's image in which he sees himself is not the
mirror image that, in autotelic fashion, closes history, as Eliot would have
it, "About the centre of the silent Word" (*CP*, p. 65). When the lyrist beholds himself in the medium of music, "his own image appears to him as
unsatisfied feeling: his own willing, longing, meaning, rejoicing, are to him
symbols by which he interprets music." The lyrist ultimately cannot interpret music because language always remains an appendage to music.
Language itself is the belated, the translation of primordial phenomena
symbolized by music. The desire for language to attain the status of music
and, thereby, "To purify the dialect of the tribe" (*CP*, p. 204), not only
ends in failure but dooms the poet to a false aesthetic, one that distin-

guishes between metaphorical and referential language. Because music itself, as well as phenomena, is already a symbol, then all language is metaphorical and without appeal to essence or truth.[8]

Crane's desire to translate his vision into poetry embroils him in the failed
quest for love and the embodiment of the Word in an image of song. This
search takes him to Brooklyn Bridge, where he found for one brief time in
his life the sublime experience wherein he beheld the Logos:

> I have seen the Word made Flesh. I mean nothing less, and I know now
> that there is such a thing as indestructibility. In the deepest sense, where
> flesh became transformed through intensity of response to counter-
> response, where sex was beaten out, where a purity of joy was reached that
> included tears. . . . And I have been able to give freedom and life which
> was acknowledged in the ecstasy of walking hand in hand across the most
> beautiful bridge of the world, the cables enclosing us and pulling us up-
> ward in such a dance as I have never walked and never can walk with an-
> other. (L, p. 181)

One is almost tempted to say that what Crane describes in this letter es-
caped him in all his poetry: the merger of self, the Word, and music. Riddel
has already remarked that "in the poet, as Crane idealizes him, resides the
power to recognize the Word become flesh; his role is to transform that
flesh back into the Word." Crane finds in the body of man the "imaged
Word," but he must translate this Word with words; therefore, he denies
history as that which would erode his sublime vision. Yet he must continually seek to reconcile the temporality of language with his faith in the Logos. Ultimately, it is Crane's insistence on the poet as seer that makes him
so averse to history, which, as Riddel argues, the poet must transform into
myth.[9]

Commentators have frequently pointed out that Crane's poetry typically gives us the search for vision rather than the visionary moment itself.[10] Fulfillment of the visionary quest requires a loss of self—a loss to

---

8. Riddel, "Hart Crane's Poetics of Failure," 474; Nietzsche, *The Birth of Tragedy*, 50, 79,
55. For a discussion of the relation between metaphor and concept in Nietzsche, see Kofman,
Nietzsche et la métaphore, a chapter of which is translated in *The New Nietzsche*, 201–214.
Also see de Man's chapters on Nietzsche in *Allegories of Reading* for a thorough analysis of
Nietzsche's demystification of the term *symbol*. Joseph Riddel discusses Nietzsche's theory
of metaphor and its place in the poetics of Pound, Crane, and Stevens in " 'Neo-Nietzschean
Clatter,' " 209–239.

9. Riddel, "Hart Crane's Poetics of Failure," 478–80.

10. For example, see Vogler, *Preludes to Vision*, 142–96.

which Crane cannot willingly submit himself. Yet the merger of self with the Word—for the Logos and vision are one and the same for Crane—promises to sustain the self. In the essay "Modern Poetry," he describes poetic prophecy as "a peculiar type of perception, capable of apprehending some absolute and timeless concept of the imagination with astounding clarity and conviction" (p. 263). Although Crane, like Eliot, speaks of the poet's need to recognize the permanence of the tradition, he does not share Eliot's sense of historical time as a linear descent. The living presence of great art lies, for Eliot, in the poet's submission of himself to the existing order, thereby surrendering his personality and allowing himself to be the vehicle of *"significant* emotion" (*SE*, p. 11). Crane, on the other hand, demands a new expression, a new Word, to body forth an eternal truth that history obscures: "It is as though a poem gave the reader as he left it a single, new *word*, never before spoken and impossible to actually enunciate, but self-evident as an active principle in the reader's consciousness henceforward" (p. 221).

Crane's aesthetic requires that the reader experience in the poem the "original" experience that led to the poem's creation. Allen Grossman argues that Crane "situates the reader internal to the poem, and assigns him the task of completing rather than deriving significances."[11] In Crane's affective theory, the temporal experience is transformed through language into an eternal truth, a new Word. The reader closes the hermeneutic circle by experiencing a repetition of the poet's originary imaginative act. The lyric, in Poesque fashion, overcomes history as its spatial form captures a moment of time in a self-mirroring free from the representational function of language. Both Poe and Crane seek to overcome the dispersal of the Word in time, only to reveal that the Word refers to nothing. As long as history is thought of in terms of a sequential narrative, then it measures the distance that separates the poet from a unitary origin. In order to overcome this abyss, the poet must build some structure, either a bridge or a tower, that will carry him back to the origin.

In a letter written around the time he was beginning to formulate his conception of *The Bridge*, Crane describes the poem as "a synthesis of America and its structural identity" (*L*, p. 127). In another letter, he writes that "it

---

11. Grossman, "Hart Crane and Poetry," 226.

concerns a mystical synthesis of 'America.' History and fact, location, etc., all have to be transfigured into abstract form that would almost function independently of its subject matter. The initial impulses of 'our people' will have to be gathered up toward the climax of the bridge, symbol of our con- structive future, our unique identity, in which is included also our scientific hopes and achievements of the future" (L, p. 124). Despite the appearances of Columbus, Pocahontas, and the pioneer, Crane really has little interest in the historical figures of America's past. He wishes to move beyond them to some vision of eternity. The bridge gathers into the presence of the vi- sionary poet both past and future, but the past merely serves as the abstract signs, the symbols of the future he foresees.[12]

As Crane progressed on *The Bridge* he came to doubt that he possessed the prophetic vision necessary for his poem. In an important letter to Waldo Frank, Crane writes of "the idea of a bridge":

> Emotionally I should like to write *The Bridge*; intellectually judged the whole theme and project seems more and more absurd. A fear of personal impotence in this matter wouldn't affect me half so much as the convic- tions that arise from other sources. . . . I had what I thought were authen- tic materials that would have been a pleasurable-agony of wrestling, even- tuating or not in perfection. . . . These "materials" were valid to me to the extent that I presumed them to be (articulate or not) at least organic and active factors in the experience and perceptions of our common race, time and belief. The very idea of a bridge, of course, is a form peculiarly de- pendent on such spiritual convictions. It is an act of faith besides being a communication. The symbols of reality necessary to articulate the span— may not exist where you expected them, however. By which I mean that however great their subjective significance to me is concerned—these forms, materials, dynamics are simply non-existent in the world.
> (L, p. 261)

Crane's idea of a bridge is inseparable from his poetic project—a mystical synthesis of America. This synthesis, however, is the figure of the bridge itself as that which spans the literal and figural dimensions of metaphor. The bridge brings into play the two poles of metaphor and insists upon a genetic link between them.

The language of a bridge is a second metaphor, a derivative of the "first" trope, nature. Beginning with the faith that his bridge will span the ocean

---

12. Donald Pease offers one of the more compelling readings of Crane's epic as prophecy in "Blake, Crane, Whitman, and Modernism," 64–85.

separating America's past from the fulfillment of its spiritual destiny, Crane discovers that the future is but a shadow cast by the past and is, thus, a type and not the fulfillment: "The form of my poem rises out of a past that so overwhelms the present with its worth and vision that I'm at a loss to explain my delusion that there exist any real links between that past and a future destiny worthy of it. The 'destiny' is long since completed, perhaps the little last section of my poem is a hangover echo of it—but it hangs suspended somewhere in ether like an Absalom by his hair" (L, p. 261). "Atlantis," the first section of the poem to be completed, is but a repeat of a finished destiny. Crane took obvious pleasure in noting that bridges, like his long poem, are "begun from two ends at once" (L, p. 270), although he cannot say with Eliot, "In my end is my beginning" (CP, p. 190). For Eliot, the coincidence of end and beginning is a sign of the teleological order governing existence, but for Crane, ends fail to meet; they hang suspended between myth and history, or the figural and the literal.

The bridge does not, as Bloom, among others, claims, lead "to Atlantis, in fulfillment of the Platonic quest of Crane's Columbus." The bridge remains suspended, a trope, between tropes. Caught between the figural and the literal, the bridge hangs in what de Man calls the aporia: between language considered as a system of tropes or as constative, that is, as the grounds of knowledge.[13] Considered as a figure for language itself, the bridge at once posits an identity between past and future, sensible and nonsensible, and it also functions as a system of metaphorical substitutions. In other words, the bridge, as language, generates the impression of a history moving from visionary promise to fulfillment in the transcendental. This impression, however, is based on the substitution of the tropes of word as graphic mark for word as song.

R. W. B. Lewis, however, writes that Crane's equation of the bridge with music opens the poem to the sacred. According to Lewis' reading of "Atlantis," the final aim of the poem is "the musical creation of a godhead." And Bloom takes Crane as an Orpheus whose "night-illuminated bridge becomes a transparent musical score" carrying the past upward beyond time.[14] I will return to the Orphic figure of the poet in The Bridge, but here I wish to suggest that the typology of the bridge is linked to another of

13. Bloom, Agon, 264; de Man, Allegories of Reading, 131, 122.
14. R. W. B. Lewis, The Poetry of Hart Crane, 371; Bloom, Agon, 265.

Crane's favorite tropes, the sea. In "Ava Maria," Columbus floats "between two worlds," Old World and New, upon another: "This third, of water, tests the word" (p. 50). The ocean is a bridge carrying Columbus' word, which is literally a message in a "casque." The sea is the abyss of history that the bridge must overcome:

> And through that cordage, threading with its call
> One arc synoptic of all tides below—
> Their labyrinthine mouths of history. (p. 114)

Along with the cables and towers of the bridge, the ship's cordage and mast are the graphic marks in a synoptic text. Further in the poem, Crane addresses the bridge as the "Vision-of-the-Voyage," a choir

> translating time
> Into what multitudinous Verb the suns
> And synergy of waters ever fuse, recast
> In myriad syllables,—Psalm of Cathay! (p. 115)

The bridge is simultaneously image and voice translating time into a "multitudinous Verb"; it is, finally, a symbol of language unable to purify itself of history.

In the "Voyages" sequence, Crane addressed the sea as "this great wink of eternity." Anticipating the poet's death in "Atlantis," Crane recounts a failed search for a bridge that will span the sea and reunite him with his lover, who is transfigured as the Logos, "The imaged Word" (p. 41). The sea, "whose diapason knells/ On scrolls of silver snowy sentences," foretells death, as it did for Whitman:

> Mark how her turning shoulders wind the hours,
> And hasten while her penniless rich palms
> Pass superscription of bent foam and wave,—
> Hasten, while they are true,—sleep, death, desire,
> Close round one instant in one floating flower. (p. 36)

The sea is Crane's scene of writing, the place where death is textualized as the superscription—as writing, a seal or address, and as a prescription—consigning man to be set adrift in history. The transformation into the imaged Word is the sacrifice of self into poetry and is, hence, a sea change, that is, death:

> and where death, if shed,
> Presumes no carnage, but this single change,—

> Upon the steep floor flung from dawn to dawn
> The silken skilled transmemberment of song. (p. 37)

The single change wrought by death will be the transmemberment of song, a crossing of texts to produce a single Word.

Crane echoes Eliot's *Waste Land*:

> Here, said she,
> Is your card, the drowned Phoenician Sailor,
> (Those are pearls that were his eyes. Look!) (*CP*, p. 54)

The link between the two texts is, of course, these lines from *The Tempest*:

> Full fathom five thy father lies;
>   Of his bones are coral made;
> Those are pearls that were his eyes;
>   Nothing of him that doth fade
> But doth suffer a sea-change
> Into something rich and strange. (I.ii.397–402)

Transmemberment is translation, the metamorphosis of texts into a Word beyond time, Belle Isle, which Eliot mentions in "Gerontion." Here is Crane's "Voyages" (VI):

> The imaged Word, it is, that holds
> Hushed willows anchored in its glow.
> It is the unbetrayable reply
> Whose accent no farewell can know. (p. 41)

Crane's antipathy to time surfaces in this acceptance of the lover's death. Crane seeks to translate the dismembered body of his text back into the Word, but he produces a transmemberment, a patchwork of texts. Ultimately, he is left not with the Word made flesh but with the Word as image or metaphor.

This belief that death promises translation into the eternal hardly makes Crane unique. If his obsession with death has any significance beyond some version of literary biography on the one hand, or Christian eschatology on the other, it lies in his peculiar linking of death with the Word. (In this he resembles Hegel.) This coupling has its parallel in the sculptural basis of Appollonian art and the musical basis of Dionysian art. For all of Crane's references to the "imaged Word" or "unfractioned idiom," his complex metaphors often result in visual confusion, not spatial imagery. In fact, the words seem chosen for their sound or musical effect, not for the image they might evoke.[15] This particular distinction between the Apollonian and the Dionysian belongs to Nietzsche, who in *The Birth of Tragedy* describes the emotional power of music: "In the Dionysian dithyramb man is incited to the greatest exaltation of all his symbolic faculties; something never before experienced struggles for utterance—the annihilation of the veil of *māyā*, oneness as the soul of the race and of nature itself. The essence of nature is now to be expressed symbolically; we need a new world of symbols; and the entire symbolism of the body is called into play, not the mere symbolism of the lips, face, and speech but the whole pantomime of dancing, forcing every member into rhythmic movement." Opposed to the loss of self in the Dionysian dance is the Apollonian illusion and the principle of individuation. Paul de Man has characterized this opposition between appearance and the thing itself as a genetic relation between meaning and metaphor: "The genetic version of the polarity Appearance/Thing is that of an entity that can be said to be identical with itself and that would engender, through a process of mediation, an appearance of which it is the origin and the foundation. Such a model can be understood in linguistic terms as the relationship between figural and proper meaning in a metaphor. . . . The meaning engenders and determines the metaphor as the appearance or sign of this meaning."[16] De Man goes on to show how Nietzsche undercuts the genetic grounds of his argument, and thus the privileged place given to Dionysian music at the expense of Apollonian symbol, by undermining the authority that could guarantee the conformity of end to origin.

Although Crane could repeatedly refer to *The Bridge* as a mystical synthesis of America and thus attest to a unity beneath the fragmentary appearances of everyday American life, his concept of metaphor as the origin of consciousness shifts the ground of being from self to language. As the figure of figurality, the bridge is less a conceptual key to the poem's meaning and more a rhetorical device to structure the poem. Critics have judged from Crane's youthful essay on Nietzsche that he was not a sophisticated reader of philosophy, yet his poetry represents a Nietzschean undermining of the very terms he so depends upon—the self and the primal being of the Word. Thus critics, like Joseph Riddel, who argue from Nietzsche's text that

15. John Irwin makes a strong case for a "special kind of nominalization in which Crane links things through a similarity in their names rather than in the things themselves." See his "Hart Crane's 'Logic of Metaphor,'" 294.
16. Nietzsche, *The Birth of Tragedy*, 40; de Man, *Allegories of Reading*, 90.

the villain is Apollonian individuation, the division of the One into the many, portray Crane as if he were perpetually seeking to reintegrate the self in a moment of ecstacy, only to fail as that rapturous moment is predicated upon a fragmentation of self, which is the price the poet must pay for his vision.[17]

Crane's visionary poetry asserts itself as the verbal equivalent of the Dionysian dance in which the dancer loses consciousness and attains vision in his moment of rapture: "Lie to us,—dance us back the tribal morn!" (p. 73). In a letter to Yvor Winters, Crane defends this passage against charges that it is a reversion to nostalgia and claims it is merely a request for the medicine man to "mimic" a scene from the past.[18] The return to origins is a fiction, the lie of representational language. Crane's "poetics of failure," to borrow Riddel's term, depends upon the genetic descent of the Word to words. If the poet fails to cross the threshold to become one with the Word, he yet maintains, and in fact confirms in his very failure, the sustaining power of the Word as the ground of being to perpetually renew the language that the poet inevitably contaminates. Crane's adaptation of an epic design to a series of lyrics heightens the characteristic tension between the timeless and the temporal in his poetry. By taking on the machinery of the epic, Crane assumes the convention of transforming American history into myth, but the lyric conventions undermine the narrative continuity, despite the fact that the lyric seems to be suited to the declared intention of writing a mystical synthesis of America—that is, transforming American history into myth.

In terms of his "General Aims and Theories," *The Bridge* offers Crane's most sustained effort to substitute for the degraded language of spent emotions one that would recapture the immediacy of a transcendental essence that he calls " 'absolute' experience" (p. 219), an experience, in other words, that has its origins beyond the epistemological boundaries of the sensuous apprehension of the natural world. It is, therefore, a recovery of an originary consciousness that predates the sensuous and psychological apprehension of nature.

In a remarkable essay written relatively early in his career, Paul de Man comments on the incompatibility of a transcendental principle, or epi-

---

17. Riddel, "Hart Crane's Poetics of Failure," 485.
18. Pemberton, "Hart Crane and Yvor Winters," 280.

phany, and the desire to recover an origin through language: "Strictly speaking, an epiphany cannot be a beginning, since it reveals and unveils what, by definition, could never have ceased to be there. Rather, it is the rediscovery of a permanent presence which has chosen to hide itself from us."[19] We find in Crane's poetics this Romantic dialectic relatively unchanged—the poetry of "'absolute' experience" unveils the permanent presence of an ideal of human experience that man has forgotten how to name. Crane's poetry re-presents what may best be called his redundant efforts to disclose experience through metaphor. Poetry as trope, consequently, seeks to substitute itself in place of nature. Hence, Crane's bridges and towers exist independent of natural origin—trope is a *return* to "'absolute' experience." Yet Crane must speak of his "logic of metaphor" in tropes borrowed from the secondary source of nature.

We fool ourselves, he writes, if we think our poetry is modern when we refer to skyscrapers and machines. To refer to the "surface phenomena of our time is merely to paint a photograph" (p. 219). The adaptation of referential language to modern poetry will result in a hybrid of an archaic technique applied to a modern subject. In place of referential language, Crane turns to organicism: "I think that what is interesting and significant will emerge only under the conditions of our submission to, and examination and assimilation of the organic effects on us of these and other fundamental factors of our experience. It can certainly not be an organic expression otherwise" (p. 219). In what seems a crossing of Eliot with Emerson, Crane argues that the poet is a medium through which flows, not the tradition as Eliot would have it, but the facts of modern existence. The poem, then, would be dependent upon the ontological priority of nature, yet Crane entertains the hope of going "*through* the combined materials of the poem, using our 'real' world somewhat as a spring-board, and to give the poem *as a whole* an orbit or predetermined direction of its own. I would like to establish it as free from my own personality as from any chance evaluation on the reader's part" (p. 220). Crane's poetry aims at the recovery of a lost state of consciousness that exists before the natural world, just as the "logic of metaphor" antedates "pure logic." Yet his poetry is inherently belated, as it borrows from the fallen world of natural existence the metaphors that will propel the poem in an orbit that returns it to its

19. De Man, "Intentional Structure of the Romantic Image," 68.

origin. This circle, however, does not close, for the origin does not coincide with a beginning in nature but exists permanently beyond nature.

Crane's organic principle posits a syntagmatic relation between words and experience whereby lived experience is metonymically displaced by an experience attained in language, a language, as I have said, that is borrowed from nature. Thus, consciousness converges with nature through the mediary properties of language. But Crane's poetry can be characterized by anything but the syntagmatic pattern of metonymy. His mode tends toward substitution, hence the desire that the poem leave the reader with "a single, new *word*, never before spoken and impossible to actually enunciate, but self-evident as an active principle in the reader's consciousness henceforward" (p. 221). The poem should, as it were, substitute a new word for the old ones out of which the poem is made. This "self-evident" word, the product of the "logic of metaphor" and, hence, the "genetic basis of all speech," proves older than the words it displaces. Crane's reestablishment of the "true" descent of language restores a syntagmatic dimension to his poetry. Nevertheless, these two poles disrupt one another even as they make each other possible. We might call this, after de Man, the grammatization of rhetoric.[20] The "logic of metaphor" comes into being through the hidden dependence of metaphor, or substitution, on the opposing figure of metonymy, or contiguity.

This pattern itself can be reversed when Crane argues that the basis of poetry is rhetoric as persuasion, not trope: "It may not be possible to say that there is, strictly speaking, any 'absolute' experience. But it seems evident that certain aesthetic experience . . . can be called absolute, *inasmuch as it approximates a formally convincing statement of a conception or apprehension of life that gains our unquestioning assent,* and under the conditions of which our imagination is unable to suggest a further detail consistent with the design of the aesthetic whole" (p. 219; my emphasis). In order to maintain continuity between lived experience and the experience of reading, Crane must switch his argument from rhetoric as trope to rhetoric as persuasion. If the new word is to enter our consciousness, it must be translated into a language with which we are familiar, a conceptual language of logical persuasion. Consequently, there must be a continual forgetting of the transcendental source hidden within lived experience in or-

20. De Man, *Allegories of Reading*, 15.

der that it be recovered anew in the poem. To translate this into Crane's terms, we might say that the poet must choose between the bridge and the tower, that is, between the temporality of the verb and the transcendent Word.

The impulse to link the poet's song with the Logos runs as strongly through Crane as it does through Eliot. Since both poets borrow their themes from the Word as the sustaining creator, their poetry measures the distance separating the Logos from language. Words are part of the Word, and all poetry, as Emerson claims, is quotation—unless one says with Wallace Stevens, " 'Words are not forms of a single word. / In the sum of the parts, there are only the parts' " ("On the Road Home"). In Stevens' centerless world, words are the making of the world, but in Eliot's Christian theology, the Word is the making of the world—it is the sustaining creator, the ever-present origin. In accordance with the logocentric logic of epiphany, the Word is hidden from us; it is drowned out by the chatter of what Heidegger calls idle talk. The Word, therefore, is present as an absence: "the Word within/ The world" shall not be found here, for "there is not enough silence." Nevertheless, "the unstilled world still whirled/ About the centre of the silent Word" (CP, p. 92). Eliot seeks the "stillpoint," without which "There would be no dance" (CP, p. 177). When every word is in its proper place, "The complete consort dancing together," the poet will have arrived at his beginning "And know the place for the first time" (CP, p. 208). And in so doing, he will repeat, in finite form, God's "I Am"—he will have achieved the sublime.

I allude, of course, to Coleridge's famous definition of the primary imagination "as a repetition in the finite mind of the eternal act of creation in the infinite I AM."[21] For the modernist poet, however, the repetition of the logos must take the form of quotation—as the Word is known only in its absence, the poet is compelled to disclose the Word in the signs that are semblances of an absent presence. The disclosure of the Word must take place in the body of the past, the tradition, which records that presence as an absence. This process has no end, says Eliot, "Because one has only learnt to get the better of words/ For the thing one no longer has to say, or the way in which/ One is no longer disposed to say it" (CP, p. 188–89). Po-

21. Coleridge, *Biographia Literaria*, I, 202.

etry, therefore, records the failed search for an original presence that forever exceeds language.

Harold Bloom has been the most prominent defender of the Romantic sublime, which he calls "the reader's Sublime," the will to power that dismisses all history and, therefore, all precursors. "The Sublime," Bloom writes, "is always a quotation, a *measuring* (etymological meaning of 'quoting') that becomes a quota, and so destroys the context of a text." Faced with the anterior voice of a strong precursor, the poet must free himself from what has already been said by quoting or recollecting the texts of the other and presenting them as his own. Thus, the "Sublime, of strong poetry, is a chiasmus, a diagonal *lying against time.*" Bloom, as we should expect, finds in Emerson his representative poet of the sublime: "He tended to fragment all anterior texts into 'quotations,' so as to keep the continuity of his own literary discourse going."[22] Bloom's model for the relation between the poet and the tradition is a rather conventional Hegelianism. Even the tripartite structure of text/reader/precursor conforms to a familiar Hegelian dialectic of the master/slave relationship. Moreover, with the obvious religious symbolism of this triadic structure, Bloom's description of Emerson's use of quotation owes more to Eliot's *Waste Land* than it does to "Quotation and Originality."

Finally, Bloom locates the sublime in the Orphic poet of *Nature*'s conclusion where Emerson prophesies the kingdom of man over nature and the past. If we turn to the Orphic chants of "Prospects," we find they are quotations telling us of the Fall of Man:

> Man is the dwarf of himself. Once he was permeated and dissolved by spirit. He filled nature with his overflowing currents. Out from him sprang the sun and the moon; from man the sun, from woman the moon. The laws of his mind, the periods of his actions externalized themselves into day and night, into the year and the seasons. But, having made for himself this huge shell, his waters retired; he no longer fills the veins and veinlets; he is shrunk to a drop. He sees that the structure still fits him, but fits him colossally. Say, rather, once it fitted him, now it corresponds to him from fear and on high. (W.I.71)

The Orphic poet sings a lament for the distance separating man from his origins. The colossal shell housing man is a crypt, a monument housing a

22. Bloom, *Agon*, 170, 241, 244, 229.

foreign body, a quotation. For as the excess of spirit, the universe is the thought of man and comes back to us in the alienated majesty of quotation, the creation of another, the logos.

As a quotation, the Orphic song is a doubled inscription marking the song as an image of writing, a crypt, not an image of voice. Man, according to this fable, created the universe out of himself, but the Emersonian self, as I have argued earlier, is none other than language. The self, then, is a "first" metaphor and phenomena a second metaphor, the ill-fitting correspondences between man and nature, or between trope and trope. When Emerson's Orpheus advises, " 'Build therefore your own world,' " he calls upon man to repeat in finite form the first metaphor. Hence, the Orphic poet sings of man's belatedness.

Emerson's trope of the colossus follows the logic of incorporation and introjection that I have outlined in the first chapter. To build one's own world is to introject the lost creation, the natural and spiritual universe from which man has unwittingly cut himself off, but the enlargement of the self required by introjection cannot be achieved because the universe remains excluded and maintained as a foreign body or unincorporated corpus, a tradition that can be neither successfully repressed nor transcended. Bloom's theory of quotation, we may conclude, is an idealization of the Freudian process of introjection—the past is reappropriated and kept alive in the body of the tradition. This process is facilitated by Bloom's surprisingly Eliotesque belief in the continued presence of the past—the tradition lives in/ as the truly new work.

Crane's use of quotation may be that aspect of his poetics which owes most to Eliot, although Crane does not employ the fragments of the tradition as a defense against his ruin. Whereas the early Eliot's appropriation of the past insists upon both his place within tradition and the historical distance that transfigures the past, Crane stresses the repetitive patterns that exist across time. In this, he is closer to the Eliot of *Four Quartets* than to the Eliot of *The Waste Land*. Eliot desires that language attain the status of music, and, thus, freedom from the impurities of mediacy: "every word is at home,/ Taking its place to support the others" (*CP*, p. 207). A language that attains the immediacy of music translates a "history" that can only be perceived as "timeless moments." According to Eliot's poetics, history is the return to the origin, a rediscovery of the beginning that is our end. This "origin" is the fold wherein the timeless intersects with time; it is, in other words, history constituted as the Logos:

> When the tongues of flame are in-folded
> Into the crowned knot of fire
> And the fire and the rose are one.   (*CPP*, p. 209)

Earlier in this concluding passage from "Little Gidding," Eliot hears the voice of the origin, the Logos, "in the stillness/ Between two waves of the sea." For Eliot, history is not a process but those moments of being wherein end and beginning meet in the silence of the Word that redeems.

In the paradoxical, and therefore totalizing, logic of Eliot's theology, the timeless and time meet, as do the Word and words. Yet the Word, for Eliot, is approached only through history, that is to say, through language:

> Every phrase and every sentence is an end and a beginning,
> Every poem an epitaph. And any action
> Is a step to the block, to the fire, down the sea's throat
> Or to an illegible stone: and that is where we start.   (*CP*, p. 208)

We start in death, the descent to the sea that is a dying into life. Moreover, to start in the end is to begin with writing, the "illegible stone." Eliot desires to escape history by means of history, to hear the Word in the spaces between the waves, which in the *Four Quartets* means between the lines. This is Eliot's version of the Kabbalistic fantasy of divining God's secret wisdom in the white spaces surrounding the letters of the Hebrew alphabet. The word out of the sea, however, bears with it an irredeemable past, a language that can be neither repressed nor sublimated; it is the word "death," the graphic mark inhabiting voice:

> A word then, (for I will conquer it,)
> The word final, superior to all,
> Subtle, sent up—what is it?—I listen;
> Are you whispering it, and have been all the time,
>   you sea-waves?
> Is that it from your liquid rims and wet sands?
>
> Whereto answering, the sea,
> Delaying not, hurrying not,
> Whisper'd me through the night, and very plainly before
>   daybreak,
> Lisp'd to me the low and delicious word death,
> And again death, death, death, death.   (*LG*, p. 252)

The similarities between Eliot's and Crane's association of the sea with death and writing can be explained, of course, by Whitman's influence. Yet neither poet can accept, as did Whitman, the openness of history because neither could renounce his nostalgia for the Logos. Consequently, where Whitman discovers in the sea a scene of writing that perpetuates poetry, Eliot and Crane listen for a voice and, thus, fail to read the "cipher-script of time" (p. 115). Yet to satisfy the desire for presence makes the poem unnecessary. In "Ava Maria," God's presence must be deferred for fear that the Word will consume the poet and his poem:

> O Thou who sleepest on Thyself, apart
> Like ocean athwart lanes of death and birth,
> And all the eddying breath between dost search
> Cruelly with love thy parable of man,—
> Inquisitor! incognizable Word
> Of Eden and the enchained Sepulchre,
> Into thy steep savannahs, burning blue,
> Utter to loneliness the sail is true.   (p. 51)

God fails to materialize; "Elohim" can only be heard in the wake of his "sounding heel," that is, in the traces left by his absence. Apostrophe is the paradigm for poetry, for writing begins in the absence of the receiver. Caught between death and birth, end and beginning, God is a bridge re-counting the parable of man's entrance into history when the "incogniz-able Word" expelled him from Eden. Man now seeks to return, but only to find that the sealed sepulcher contains no body.

In his poetry, Crane seeks a myth beyond language, an "unfractioned idiom" that would "condense eternity." Yet he catches "sight" of the Word—for the bridge is the "imaged Word"—in the dark: "Only in dark-ness is thy shadow clear" (p. 46). The bridge is the shadowy double of ab-sence, a figure of the absent Logos. Thus, when he asks, "And of the curve-ship lend a myth to God," he calls upon the bridge as trope to create belatedly the "source" of his myth—the trope, or "curveship," is the turn of lan-guage that is always a return, a belated repetition that masquerades as an origin. It is what Williams called beginning again. Crane uses the very same trope in "Cape Hatteras" in his tale of the poet as pilot who wears a "San-skrit charge/ To conjugate infinity's dim marge—Anew" (p. 92). Joseph Riddel offers a most convincing reading of these lines: "To conjugate 'Anew' is to conjugate belatedly, and to derive one's myth not from the *logos* but from the sign of its absence, the 'dim marge' or shadow figuration. But Crane's poet far from piercing or transcending this margin is revolved within it. His plane (language) tropes and returns."[23]

23. Riddel, " 'Neo-Nietzschean Clatter,' " 230.

In the concluding section, "Atlantis," Crane desires to remove the myth from under the shadow of language: "Swift peal of secular light, intrinsic Myth/ Whose fell unshadow is death's utter wound" (p. 116). The bridge's "unshadow" does not negate language, for the poem can never erase the marks of writing that tie it to history:

> Of thy white seizure springs the prophecy:
> Always through spiring cordage, pyramids
> Of silver sequel, Deity's young name
> Kinetic of white choiring wings . . . ascends.　　　　　　(p. 116)

The bridge, as Riddel remarks, prophesies "an ideal poem for which the poem is only a sign."[24] The cordage, graphic marks of ascent, is also the funerary monument to the "Deity's young name," for the cordage echoes Crane's warning in "Voyages" (I) to the children never to cross the line of the seaboard. And it also refers to the "cordage tree" of Columbus' ship, around which the sailors sing the Angelus, a prayer for their savior to protect them from the threatening sea.

As the epigraph from Plato indicates, Crane desires that his poem achieve the status of music: "—One Song, one Bridge of Fire! Is it Cathay?" (p. 117). The poem is an uncertain promise that leaves America still in search of what Columbus thought he discovered. Crane's poem repeats in "Whispers antiphonal in azure swing" the failure to escape history; the double voice of the bridge is the "Inquisitor! incognizable Word," and the daughter of the wind, Anemone, "Answer of all." The answer is the petals blown by the wind, "a scattered chapter" that fails to keep the Orphic singer afloat. The "casque" containing the message of Columbus' visionary dream now sinks. (According to the myth of Orpheus, his head was cut off and set afloat. Thus, Crane's so-called misspelling of *cask* proves appropriate, as the casque, or helmet, in which the message is sealed may, by metonymy, stand for mind or head.) The severed head of Orpheus was transported to Lesbos and his lyre was transformed into a constellation. But this transfiguration of the bridge, the harp and altar of the proem, plays an antiphonal tune; it is at once a voice and a place, a tautology for the poem as myth that repeats the ur-myth, that of Orpheus, who first sang of loss and lamented the poet's descent from and, hence, removal from the presence of the gods. The antiphonal song repeats a myth about myths and is, as such, the history of visionary poetry which tells of the failed efforts to escape

24. *Ibid.*, 233.

death by water. Henceforth, the myth is but a shadowy figure for figurality, a trope that tells of the return to language and history, the shadow cast by time, and "This fabulous shadow only the sea keeps" (p. 34).

Crane's Orpheus does not, in the end, signify the fusion of "Platonic myth to a higher world of forms." Bloom's version of Orpheus is that of a "religion of 'freedom and mastery'" leading to the triumph over time, which brings us back to the figure of central man. The severed head of Orpheus singing its prophecies is Bloom's ultimate image of voice, the voice that breaks free from time. In "*The Native Strain*: American Orphism," Bloom remarks that Emerson, without having read Vico, arrived at the Viconian connection tracing "the lyre of Orpheus to the original possession of Hermes." This connection, however, discloses that Orpheus' lyre is a stylus, for Hermes is a Greek derivation of the Egyptian Thoth, the god of laws and letters. Vico tells us that "the lyre was invented by the Greek Mercury, just as law was invented by the Egyptian Mercury." Orpheus' songs are a scene of writing, the transmission of legal codes to Greece: "So that the lyre was the union of the cords or forces of the fathers."[25] Even the serpent and eagle may be traced to Thoth and Hermes and through Hermes to Orpheus. Whether Crane actually knew Vico's work is doubtful, but his readings in mystic writers, such as Ouspensky, may have introduced him to this lore. Orpheus, the ur-poet, is already belated, as Crane realizes when he writes, "Atlantis,—hold thy floating singer late!"

I now turn to "The Broken Tower" for a final look at Crane's use of quotation and his sense that "the poem arises out of a past that . . . overwhelms the present" (L, p. 261). John Irwin has shown how Eliot's poetry and his technique of "fragmented cultural allusion" threatened Crane's faith in the originality of his own verse, but it is instructive to examine a poem firmly placed in a tradition that Eliot publicly denounced, Romanticism.[26] Nevertheless, "The Broken Tower" may stand in relation to Crane's poems as "Ash-Wednesday" does to Eliot's. Just as Eliot asks, "Where shall the word be found?" so Crane declares himself creator of the word only to retreat before the Word: "My word I poured. But was it cognate?" (p. 193). In his question Eliot declares what he holds to be the true descent of lan-

25. Bloom, *Agon*, 269, 163; Bloom, *Figures of Capable Imagination*, 71; Vico, *The New Science*, 227, 228.
26. Irwin, "Figurations of the Writer's Death," 253.

guage, but Crane, having been cast into the world, traces the "visionary company" to rechart the genesis of poetry.

The poet is sentenced to wander in the fallen world:

> The bell-rope that gathers God at dawn
> Dispatches me as though I dropped the knell
> Of a spent day—to wander the cathedral lawn
> From pit to crucifix, feet chill on steps from hell. (p. 193)

God's presence banishes the poet, who, unlike Keats's visionary of *The Fall of Hyperion*, fails to "gain the lowest step" that leads to heaven. Crane condemns himself with "All else who find a haven in the world" (Canto I, 128, 150). The search for "A scattered chapter, livid hieroglyph" ("At Melville's Tomb") leads him to the tower, for in the silence intervening between the strokes of the bells, he hears the absence that marks the iterability of the Word and allows the poet to break his repetition from this putative origin:

> The bells, I say, the bells break down their tower;
> And swing I know not where. Their tongues engrave
> Membrane through marrow, my long-scattered score
> Of broken intervals . . . And I, their sexton slave! (p. 193)

The rupture that wrenches the Word from one context to set it in another implies that with every repetition a new poem is written. As Derrida has pointed out in various contexts, it is this iterability, the dissociation of the sign from the presence of a sender or receiver, that links writing with death.[27] The writer, to borrow Crane's metaphor, is the "sexton slave" consigned to burying the dead and to ringing the church bell as a reminder to man of his separation from the divine author. Like Donne before him, Crane hears in the tolling of the bell the death of man. Crane's association of bells with death could well come from Poe's "The Bells," but "The City in the Sea" is also a likely source for the association of death with towers. Crane had already alluded to the following couplet in "The Tunnel," the poem where Poe, one of the "visionary company," appears: "While from a proud tower in the town/ Death looks gigantically down." Death inscribes the mark, the "Oval encyclicals," in which poetry lives on:

> And so it was I entered the broken world
> To trace the visionary company of love, its voice

27. See Derrida, *Margins of Philosophy*, 307–330.

An instant in the wind (I know not whither hurled)
But not for long to hold each desperate choice.

My word I poured. But was it cognate, scored
Of that tribunal monarch of the air
Whose thigh embronzes earth, strikes crystal Word
In wounds pledged once to hope—cleft to despair?   (p. 193)

Cut off from the Father, the poet cannot answer for what he has written, but it is in the cleft Word, a Word divided from itself, that the poet seeks to insinuate himself. This median, the between, is the "sweet mortality [that] stirs latent power":

And through whose pulse I hear, counting the strokes
My veins recall and add, revived and sure
The angelus of wars my chest evokes:
What I hold healed, original now, and pure . . .

And builds, within, a tower that is not stone
(No stone can jacket heaven)—but slip
Of pebbles,—visible wings of silence sown
In azure circles, widening as they dip

The matrix of the heart, lift down the eye
That shrines the quiet lake and swells a tower . . .
The commodious tall decorum of that sky
Unseals her earth, and lifts love in its shower.   (p. 194)

The tolling bell echoes in the pulsation of blood announcing a new incarnation of the Word building within the heart of man a new temple, a new tower. The poet's eyes that once lifted altars to heaven now cast their gaze downward to find love lifted in a shower from the earth. The "slip/ Of pebbles" with which the poet reconstructs the world within consists of stolen tropes. The bands extending from the sides of Crane's book (this is one of the many meanings of *slip*) hold sewn together Crane's precursors. It is also the mooring place where his poetic ancestors rest. In the "visible wings of silence" can be heard Wallace Stevens' "casual flocks of pigeons" from "Sunday Morning"; George Herbert's "broken Altar" and groans "full of Wings" make up the tower's stones ("The Altar" and "Sion"); Blake's "Universe within" which is measured in the interval between a pulsation of the artery strikes the angelus within the poet's chest (*Milton*); Shelley's "caverns of rain" which arise "Like a child from the womb, like a ghost from the tomb" rise from the unsealed earth ("The Cloud"); and so much of Wordsworth goes to construct the "matrix of the heart" as to be beyond citation. These echoes, marks of the poet's belatedness, break down Crane's tower to unseal the body and reveal the dismembered texts that every poem resurrects.

CHAPTER EIGHT

Wallace Stevens and the Question of the Book

It was a rabbi's question, let the rabbis reply.

           —Stevens

Onto an answer Elohim grafted a question. Thus the innumerable supplanted the Unique.

           —Reb Redel

Before Stevens had ever eaten the fruit which "might be a cure of the ground,"[1] he first had to read what he was about to consume:

> An apple serves as well as any skull
> To be the book in which to read a round,
> And is as excellent, in that it is composed
> Of what, like skulls, comes rotting back to ground.   (CP, p. 14)

The fruit that would be "a cure of the ground/ Or a cure of ourselves" (CP, p. 526) itself rises from the ground; hence the disease produces its own antidote. The devourer of this homeopathic cure, therefore, seeks to restore the ground on which he stands and from which he can begin to write, for the fruit also cures leaves, that is, books. The site where writing begins lies elsewhere; it is not empirical, but calls to us from beyond memory.[2] It is the father before speech and, thus, a call to the future. Yet these leaves are rotted pages driven to the ground by Shelley's (ode to the) west wind. To read the sibylline leaves one must regather them into a book and thus come to repossess the poem. But our voracious reader devours much more than

---

1. Stevens, *The Collected Poems*, 526, hereinafter cited as *CP*. The following abbreviations will be used for Stevens' texts: *L—Letters of Wallace Stevens*; *NA—The Necessary Angel*; *OP—Opus Posthumous*; *SP—*Holly Stevens, *Souvenirs and Prophecies*. All ellipses in poetry quotations are in the original except where placed in brackets.

2. For an analysis of the homeopathic cure in Plato, see Derrida, *Dissemination*, 61–171. My discussion of the site of writing is indebted to Derrida, *Writing and Difference*, 64–78. Derrida says, "The site is not the empirical and national Here of a territory. It is immemorial, and thus also a future. Better: it is tradition as adventure" (p. 66).

an apple, or a mango's rind, or even a pineapple pieced together—"the irreducible X" (*NA*, p. 83)—he must eat the rotted remains of literature. Both apples and skulls have an attraction to the ground from which they have risen because compost proves the richest of soils for literature. The apple served Milton as well as the skull served Shakespeare in their respective meditations on death; now Stevens meditates on the book, which must be a regathering of his precursors' remains and thus a meditation on death.

J. Hillis Miller provides the most thorough examination of Stevens' metaphors of the cure in "Stevens' Rock and Criticism as Cure." In an earlier work, *Poets of Reality*, Miller had pointed out the importance of the ground as a figure for reality, but he argued convincingly that reality and imagination are never reconciled in Stevens' poetry, for "at the moment they touch . . . the poet finds himself face to face with a universal nothing." Although he has changed his critical perspective since writing this, Miller has not significantly revised his reading of Stevens. What was formerly an existential nothingness is now an abyss of endless interpretations leading him from Stevens through Whitman, Emerson, and Milton to the *OED* and *The American Heritage Dictionary*. Despite his appeals to the openness of the modern poem to interpretation, Miller's metaphors, particularly that of the *mise en abyme*, return literature to a genealogical sequence and thus set the text on solid ground. The *mise en abyme* is, shall we say, the mirror image of genealogy; it is a series of reproductions stretching back to a promised but indiscernible origin. Miller's two key examples of this effect are the heraldic shield, which implies "some break in the genetic line of filiation," and what he calls "the Quaker Oats box effect." Although metaphors drawn from feudalism and corporate America are rich in their suggestiveness (both systems depend upon an unquestioned acceptance of hierarchical order), I here wish to emphasize the symmetry of this schema, even if, as Miller astutely points out, "without the production of some schema, some 'icon,' there can be no glimpse of the abyss, no vertigo of the underlying nothingness." The abyss, says Miller, is created even as it is covered over. By turning Stevens into the demystified heir of Emerson and Whitman, Miller sets him in a tradition in which the deviation from his literary parents, or what Miller calls Stevens' "deconstruction" of Emerson and Whitman, keeps him within the genealogical line and at the same time reaffirms that this line progresses to a clearer vision of the illusion of onto-theological beliefs.[3] However, before we start "deconstructing the deconstructors," that is, Emerson and Stevens, we would do well to keep in mind Stevens' warning against the "Inescapable romance . . . disillusion as the last illusion" (CP, p. 468).

As the above suggests, the *mise en abyme* is but a metaphor for inter-textuality, a gathering of allusions to forebears that grounds a text in an ascertainable order whereby the descent of tropes is mapped out in genea-logical reconstructions. Stevens appeared to be excruciatingly self-con-scious of the nature of influence, and thus of genealogy, and he stubbornly disavowed any suggestion that he was indebted to other poets. In a letter to José Rodríguez Feo, he denies that he reads "a lot of poetry." What makes this claim more interesting than similar remarks is the way Stevens turns the question into one of reading, not creativity:

> My state of mind about poetry makes me very susceptible and that is a
> danger in the sense that it would be so easy for me to pick up something
> unconsciously. In order not to run that danger I don't read other peoples'
> poetry at all. There seem to be very few people who read poetry at the fin-
> ger tips, so to speak. . . . Most people read it listening for echoes because
> the echoes are familiar to them. They wade through it the way a boy
> wades through water, feeling with his toes for the bottom: the echoes are
> the bottom. This is something that I have learned to do from Yeats who
> was extremely persnickety about being himself. It is not so much that it is
> a way of being oneself as it is a way of defeating people who look only for
> echoes and influences. (L, p. 575)

With his nearly Emersonian capacity for contradiction, Stevens credits Yeats for having taught him how to avoid being indebted to others. Usually, he reserves his rare acknowledgments of debts for letters in which he is not denying them, such as one to Bernard Heringman in which he reverses his normal position and says, "I never plan to do a lot of writing without also planning at the same time to do a lot of reading" (L, p. 798). The strength that allows him to reject those who hunt for influences does not, Stevens suggests in his letter to Rodríguez Feo, lie in the self, for it is those who listen for echoes who believe in psyches and selves. Reading, like writing, must be guided by the hand, not by eyes and ears, the portals of the psyche. Reading at one's fingertips requires an openness to the text, thereby allow-

---

3. J. H. Miller, *Poets of Reality*, 279; J. H. Miller, "Stevens' Rock and Criticism as Cure," 12, 23.

ing the reader to break through the familiar and, without touching some
solid though earthy foundation, to tread water in an unfathomable sea, "a
sea of ex" (*CP*, p. 175).[4]

To hear the echoes of, say, Whitman, Emerson, and Shelley is to touch
bottom or, to borrow another of Thoreau's metaphors, to find a *point d'appui*. We might say, in fact, that the water upon which the reader floats is
Walden, whose depth Thoreau measured to see how much room it left for
writing: "The greatest depth was exactly one hundred and two feet. . . .
This is a remarkable depth for so small an area; yet not an inch of it can be
spared by the imagination. What if all ponds were shallow? Would it not
react on the minds of men? I am thankful that this pond was made deep
and pure for a symbol" (*W*, p. 196). The pond, we can easily surmise, is a
book containing the tradition, and Thoreau is not the first to fathom it:
"Successive nations perchance have drank at, admired, and fathomed it, and
passed away, and still its water is green and pellucid as ever. . . . Who knows
in how many unremembered nations' literatures this has been the Castal-
ian Fountain? or what nymphs presided over it in the Golden Age?" (*W*,
p. 124). Unlike Stevens, who chooses to float, however uncomfortably, over
measureless depths, Thoreau finds "a solid bottom everywhere" (*W*, p.
225). What Miller finds in an advertisement and calls the *mise en abyme*,
Thoreau finds in nature, albeit a literary one, and calls kittlybenders, a child's
game in which the aim is to skate quickly over thin ice and risk breaking
through. The most adept player of this game among Thoreau's readers is
Walter Michaels, who writes, "To read *Walden*, then, is precisely to play
at kittlybenders, to run the simultaneous risks of touching and not touching bottom."[5]

Thoreau, as I have argued earlier, would like to touch solid bottom, but
the echoes of the past reverberate with an unending series of puns and allusions that mark him as a belated writer. Thoreau, who so wanted to be
the father of an American literature, seems to be the perpetual son unable

---

4. Concerning the "sea of ex," Stevens wrote in 1940 to Hi Simons, "The imagination takes
us out of (Ex) reality into a pure irreality. One has this sense of irreality often in the presence
of morning light on cliffs which then rise from a sea that has ceased to be real and is therefore
a sea of Ex. So long as this sort of thing clearly expresses an idea or impression, it is intelligible
language" (*L*, p. 360). And in a 1953 letter to Renato Poggioli, Stevens said, "A sea of ex
means a purely negative sea. The realm of has-been without interest or provocativeness" (*L*,
p. 783). Two more divergent interpretations can hardly be imagined.

5. Michaels, "*Walden*'s False Bottoms," 148.

to assume his independence. Although Joseph Riddel has suggested that Stevens' rock may have its origin in Thoreau's *point d'appui*, Thoreau usually appears as an appendage to Emerson, if he appears at all, in critical evaluations of Stevens' literary genealogy. As Stevens suggests, the hunt for allusions is the reader's way of taming a poet by uncovering the roots that extend from his poems into the ground or, in other words, into the past and into pre-texts. Now that we have Stevens' genealogy charted, we can erase the negative of *unheimlich* (unhomely and what Freud called uncanny) and make his poetry *heimlich* (homely and canny). Having caught an echo of Emerson or Whitman, we now know, or think we know, where Stevens lives and who he is; we have touched "the visible rock, the audible" (*CP*, p. 375). We have given ourselves over to an empirical Here that confuses the visible with the audible. The rock, however, is a site that opens history to the adventure of reading. It is from this rock that we gaze down to the sea:

> The exact rock where his inexactnesses
> Would discover, at last, the view toward which they had edged,
>
> Where he could lie and, gazing down at the sea,
> Recognize his unique and solitary home.   (*CP*, p. 512)

The poet spies the unique home, not because he rests upon the rock of certainty, but because he himself is the uncertain, the inexact child who must re-create the home. To be at home in Stevens is to hear the echoes of "An ancestral theme" (*CP*, p. 412) of fathers, mothers, and children. It is to dwell in the "mythology of modern death": "an alphabet/ By which to spell out holy doom and end,/ A bee for the remembering of happiness" (*CP*, p. 434). There is a lapse between parents and child, a gap that cannot be bridged by discourse. It is not, however, a rupture within a genealogical line; it is writing, a fragment that is "neither a determined style nor a failure, but the form of that which is written."[6] And between the letters that recall a lost happiness walks death. The images of sleep, peace, and memory, "the mother of us all," protect us from the encroachments of nothingness. They are the grammar and syntax of being in which we read life as the memorial to death; for in man's faith in the continuity between life and death, there lies a debilitating servitude to the past as the origin of the present. The

---

6. Riddel, *The Clairvoyant Eye*, 244; Derrida, *Writing and Difference*, 71.

modern myth of death is the myth of genealogy: "These are death's own supremest images,/ The pure perfections of parental space" (*CP*, p. 436).

In "The Rock," the desire to return to that most unhomely of places, the "parental space," is dismissed as the myth of origins (a myth of endings requires a myth of beginnings): "It is an illusion that we were ever alive,/ Lived in the houses of mothers" (*CP*, p. 525). This is the illusion of genealogy, of a genetic line that takes us back before language to the father:

> Who is my father in this world, in this house,
> At the spirit's base?
>
> My father's father, his father's father, his
> Shadows like winds
>
> Go back to a parent before thought, before speech,
> At the head of the past. (*CP*, p. 501)

The father is but a shadow, a ghost at the threshold who has no need to write; he is the God who does not question the distance between himself and language, for his son is the Word made flesh. And it is to God the father that another son, who is a writer, turns as he seeks to restore the home. But in his turning, he measures the distance between himself and his desire.

In a poem about his grandfather, "The Bed of Old John Zeller," Stevens uncovers the "ghostly sequences" hidden within a belief in the structure of ideas:

> This structure of ideas, these ghostly sequences
> Of the mind, result only in disaster. It follows,
> Casual poet, that to add your own disorder to disaster
>
> Makes more of it. It is easy to wish for another structure
> Of ideas and to say as usual that there must be
> Other ghostly sequences and, it would be, luminous
>
> Sequences, thought of among spheres in the old peak of night:
> This is the habit of wishing, as if one's grandfather lay
> In one's heart and wished as he had always wished, unable
>
> To sleep in that bed for its disorder, talking of ghostly
> Sequences that would be sleep and ting-tang tossing, so that
> He might slowly forget. It is more difficult to evade
>
> That habit of wishing and to accept the structure
> Of things as the structure of ideas. It was the structure
> Of things at least that was thought of in the old peak of night.
> (*CP*, pp. 326–27)

Logical thought—that is, thought as it is determined by grammar—harbors an implicit genealogy, a sequence that binds the chaos of things to the order of the sentence. Yet the incompatibility of "the structure of ideas" with "the structure of things" disturbs the grandfather, who is unable to sleep in a disorderly bed, that is, in an open book. The ghostly presence of the grandfather sleeps within the book and dreams the dream of the total book, or the dream of the family—these two are one—and expresses the desire to break through language to a "Pure rhetoric of a language without words" (CP, p. 374) and "step barefoot into reality" (CP, p. 423).

This desire to recover the "parent before thought" not only appears as a motivating force in many of Stevens' greatest poems, it also occupied his personal affairs from 1942 until his death. There exist several hundred letters devoted entirely to his efforts to trace his genealogy. The reasons for this interest are somewhat obscure. Holly Stevens suggests it may have been prompted by her decision to leave school and not pursue the academic career her father had hoped for her. Around this time his sister Elizabeth died, leaving Stevens as the last member of his generation, and perhaps he saw himself as the guardian of the family's history. Finally, he very much desired to be admitted to the Holland Society, which meant he had to show an unbroken line of Dutch ancestry on the male side back to 1674 or earlier. These reasons are hardly satisfactory. And Stevens' infrequent personal remarks in his correspondence concerning this matter are of only limited value. In a letter to Emma Stevens Jobbins, a first cousin he discovered thanks to the research of his genealogists, he says that when the genealogy is complete, "we shall really know who we are, without any fiction." To Charles Baker he says he wishes "to ascertain as a matter of fact who I am," and he speaks of this interest at greater length in a letter to Hi Simons: "This was a subject that I scorned when I was a boy. However, there has become a part of it something that was beyond me then and that is the desire to realize the past as it was. . . . It is extraordinary how little seems to have survived when you first begin to study this sort of thing and then later on, when you have learned how to go about it, what an immense amount has survived and how much you can make of it" (L, p. 457).[7]

7. Wallace Stevens to Emma Stevens Jobbins, December 27, 1944, and Stevens to Charles R. Baker, March 17, 1944, both in Stevens Collection, Huntington Library, San Marino.

It is startling to read Stevens expressing the desire to know "the past as it was." Is this the poet who refuses to play "A tune beyond us, yet ourselves" (*CP*, p. 165)? "The Irish Cliffs of Moher" suggests that to uncover things as they are, we must "Go back to the parent before thought." To play a tune—that is, to reduce the world to language—is to open the world to metaphor. Yet Stevens' obsession with genealogy seems to belie his insistence that "It is a world of words to the end of it,/ In which nothing solid is its solid self" (*CP*, p. 345). The world for Stevens, as it is for Edmond Jabès, is in a book, but "the book is not in the world."[8] To trace the genealogy is to bind the world in a book: "I don't suppose anyone is in a hurry about genealogy because piecing the past together is very much like binding a book" (*L*, p. 406). The reluctance to conclude the genealogy is a reluctance to close the book, which must remain open to writing, and thus to the son's questionings. And it is through his questions that the reader feels for the earth, but solid ground is a first metaphor, a filling of nothingness with the words of the world.

To inhabit a world of words, we must read, thus the desire to trace the genealogical line back before language, to the fecund minimum out of which writing begins. Reading, for Stevens, as it was for Emerson, is another name for writing:

> It is difficult to read. The page is dark.
> Yet he knows what it is that he expects.
>
> The page is blank or a frame without a glass
> Or a glass that is empty when he looks.
>
> The greenness of night lies on the page and goes
> Down deeply in the empty glass . . .
>
> Look, realist, not knowing what you expect.
> The green falls on you as you look,
>
> Falls on and makes and gives, even a speech.
> And you think that is what you expect,
>
> That elemental parent, the green night,
> Teaching a fusky alphabet. (*CP*, p. 267)

The page is the dark receptacle of the reader's expectations, a frame without a mirror in which to see the self. Stevens' tone indicates his impatience with the reader who is unable to put aside his expectations, which is to rec-

8. Derrida, *Writing and Difference*, 76.

ognize his self, when he confronts the book. The green to which Stevens refers is a trope for nature, the "elemental parent" of a "natural" language. Unable to illuminate the writings of "a fusky alphabet," Phosphor listens for echoes, the voice of an author in the poem; he clings to the myths of speech and origin, of a parent who oversees the descent of meaning and language.

In order to rethink the meaning of descent, Stevens had to turn to the family, his reality, as the metaphoric substitution for the idea of textuality. Thus he comes to look upon the family as he would a book: "My father came from Bucks County. He was a farmer's son although he himself was a lawyer and lived and practiced in Berks County. My brother came to own the farm and eventually sold it to one of the Cornells who still lives there. I look back to that farm and the people who live in it the way American literature used to look back to English literature" (*L*, p. 732). The home of one's parents serves as the trope of desire for a metaphysical origin. Yet Stevens' comparison suggests that he has declared his independence from the ancestral home just as Emerson and, after him, the modern American writer successively made such declarations of freedom from the past. Nevertheless, the home remains indissociable from the self, even though Stevens recognizes that to possess the home would be to close the book. In a letter of 1951 to Thomas McGreevy, he writes, "I should like to do as you do: go back to the original chez moi. When I was boy and used to go home from college, I used to feel as if it was going back to mother earth" (*L*, p. 728). The return to mother earth would be a return to the mother tongue, the words growing from the ground, and thus a return to the home and nature (a mother language).

From his scattered comments on genealogy and his vast correspondence devoted entirely to tracing his family line, we get a strong sense of his ambivalence toward the past. Although he once told someone that "the way to read American history . . . is to interest yourself in your family" (*L*, p. 479), he also knew that family histories are subject to as many interpretations as they have readers: in his "Adagia," he writes, "Genealogy is the science of correcting other genealogists' mistakes" (*OP*, p. 170). But it is in such late poems as "The Auroras of Autumn" that Stevens' massive strength emerges, breaking through the pessimism of a poem such as "The Comedian as the Letter C" and its nostalgia for "Loquacious columns" (*CP*,

p. 41) to an uncompromising awareness of the illusion of the parental home that has nothing to do with either pessimism or optimism:

> Farewell to an idea . . . A cabin stands,
> Deserted, on a beach. It is white,
> As by a custom or according to
>
> An ancestral theme or as a consequence
> Of an infinite course. The flowers against the wall
> Are white, a little dried, a kind of mark
>
> Reminding, trying to remind, of a white
> That was different, something else, last year
> Or before, not the white of an aging afternoon,
>
> Whether fresher or duller, whether of winter cloud
> Or of winter sky, from horizon to horizon.   (CP, p. 412)

In this, the second canto of the "Auroras," along with the third and fourth cantos, Stevens proceeds to negate the ideas of the home, the mother, and the father. As Joseph Riddel has remarked, "Each beginning again is a turning of an image that repeatedly dismantles the 'ancestral theme' of continuity, of the passage of truth from origin to end or from father to son."[9] The whiteness of the cabin suggests "The dominant blank, the unapproachable" (CP, p. 477), a past vacated by the tenants of memory leaving the poet free to imagine the present.

In a rarely discussed late poem, "The Role of the Idea in Poetry," Stevens reexamines the descent of the idea from father to son:

> Ask of the philosopher why he philosophizes,
> Determined thereto, perhaps by his father's ghost,
> Permitting nothing to the evening's edge.
>
> The father does not come to adorn the chant.
> One father proclaims another, the patriarchs
> Of truth.   (OP, p. 93)

Meaning inhabits the philosopher's chant, or the poem, as a ghost announcing the presence of other ghosts and other fathers. The idea in poetry is the bloodless abstraction of the patriarchal descent of truth from parent to son, for truth inheres in linear descent. Stevens, however, transforms the diachronic descent of parentage into a synchronic pattern of relation—fathers do not breed sons; they bear the dream of patriarchal order:

9. Riddel, "Metaphoric Staging," 334.

> They strike across and are masters of
> The chant and discourse there, more than wild weather
> Or clouds that hang lateness on the sea. They become
> A time existing after much time has passed.   (*OP*, p. 93)

Fathers are the masters of language and nature at "the evening's edge," the threshold of the imagination. And their temporal priority is the daily re-creation of a myth that places a father at the head of the past and, therefore, at the border of night:

> Therein, day settles and thickens round a form—
> Blue-bold on its pedestal—that seems to say,
> "I am the greatness of the new-found night."   (*OP*, p. 93)

The father is the giant guarding truth and, consequently, blocking access to the book:

> Here, then, is an abstraction given head,
> A giant on the horizon, given arms,
> A massive body and long legs, stretched out,
> A definition with an illustration, not
> Too exactly labelled, a large among the smalls
> Of it, a close, parental magnitude,
> At the centre on the horizon, concentrum, grave
> And prodigious person, patron of origins.   (*CP*, p. 443)

The giant designates the poet as a secondary man condemned to chant the "ancestral theme" of a lost home. But in the final stanza of "A Primitive like an Orb," Stevens discloses that the giant is a figure of language's eccentricity:

> That's it. The lover writes, the believer hears,
> The poet mumbles and the painter sees,
> Each one, his fated eccentricity,
> As a part, but part, but tenacious particle,
> Of the skeleton of the ether, the total
> Of letters, prophecies, perceptions, clods
> And the giant ever changing, living in change.   (*CP*, p. 443)

The "centre on the horizon" proves to be eccentric, that is, remote from the center. We know of the poem of the whole only through the lesser poems, the fragments that make of every particle an ever-changing giant on an eccentric center. To remove the giant, who is the father, from his privileged position is to free language from the regulations of a central control. No longer the "centre on the horizon," the father now stands, like Emerson on the "horizon" in "Experience," at the threshold of the book, but not in it. Like the son, he too will be a reader seeking to recapture words that he can never possess.

Stevens gives his most programatic statement on the poet's genealogy in "Recitation after Dinner," a poem published by the Saint Nicholas Society, a group composed of men descended from early Dutch settlers of America:

> A poem about tradition could easily be
> A windy thing . . . However, since we are here,
> Cousins of the calender if not of kin,
> To be a part of tradition, to identify
> Its actual appearance, suppose we begin
> By giving it a form. But the character
> Of tradition does not easily take form. (OP, p. 86)

Ostensibly addressed to his fellow members, the poem of tradition also speaks to other poets, for this family is bound, not by filiation, but by affiliation. The tradition upheld by this society is subjected to numerous questions as Stevens explores the difficulties of giving form to the book of family history. The poem of tradition is written on leaves that the wind drives to the ground. Thus, to give it form one must gather them and bind them together in a book. But tradition is not a book of laws:

> There is
> No book of the past in which time's senators
> Have inscribed life's do and don't. The commanding codes
> Are not tradition. (OP, p. 86)

Stevens dissolves the bonds between tradition and institutionalized codes, a link that must be artificial, for it is predicated on a belief in the immutability of writing. Nor is tradition memory:

> Is it the memory
> That hears a pin fall in New Amsterdam
> Or sees the new North River heaping up
> Dutch ice on English boats? The memory
> Is part of the classic imagination, posed
> Too often to be more than secondhand.
> Tradition is much more than the memory. (OP, pp. 86–87)

Stevens bows to the nostalgic desires of his Dutch cousins as he gives priority to the Dutch explorers, who preceded the English, in the navigation of the North River, a portion of the Hudson. But memory belongs to the classical imagination, a stale tradition that perpetuates such beliefs in the priority of Dutch settlers. For Stevens, the ancestral land is situated beyond memory. Tradition is a cry from beyond memory to a site that is always elsewhere, that is, in a book that remains to be written. Home lies in a memory of the cry of fallen leaves:

> It is the cry of leaves that do not transcend themselves,
>
> In the absence of fantasia, without meaning more
> Than they are in the final finding of the ear, in the thing
> Itself, until, at least, the cry concerns no one at all.　　　(*OP*, pp. 96–97)

These are the leaves that speak to the living of death. They cry for "life as it is," a life abandoned to the uncertainity of being.[10]

The questioning continues as Stevens asks, "Is it experience?" and "is tradition an unfamiliar sum,/ A legend scrawled in script we cannot read?" (*OP*, p. 87). With this final question, tradition is inscribed in an indecipherable hand as the question of the book, and as Stevens begins to define the past we confront the "original" illegibility, the indeterminable that inhabits every book. This is not a primal and irrational mystery of origins indeciperable by man. Once again, it is Derrida on the illegible in Jabès who offers the best gloss on Stevens' truly indecipherable hand: "Prior to the book (in the non-chronological sense), original illegibility is therefore the very possibility of the book and, within it, of the ulterior and eventual opposition of 'rationalism' and 'irrationalism.' The Being that is announced within the illegible is beyond these categories, beyond, as it writes itself, its own name."[11] For Stevens, this Being is the son's promised inheritance as the successor to the father as the gatherer of leaves; yet this will's illegibility, which makes it impossible to probate, allows the perpetual contestation whereby being is never named, but always waits a step beyond the threshold of the book. And at this threshold stands tradition, a son who bears the father on his back:

10. Derrida discusses the site of tradition in *Writing and Difference*, 66. For Helen Vendler, the cry of the leaves signifies Stevens' gathering together "in a single speaking voice the whole psychology, the self" (*On Extended Wings*, 277). Also see Riddel's review of Vendler; "Interpreting Stevens," 79–97.
11. Derrida, *Writing and Difference*, 77.

It has a clear, a single, a solid form,
That of the son who bears upon his back
The father that he loves, and bears him from
The ruins of the past, out of nothing left
Made noble by the honor he receives,
As if in a golden cloud. The son restores
The father. He hides his ancient blue beneath

His own bright red. But he bears him out of love,
His life made double by his father's life,
Ascending the humane. This is the form
Tradition wears, the clear, the single form
The solid shape, Aeneas seen, perhaps,
By Nicholas Poussin, yet nevertheless
A tall figure upright in a giant's air.   (*OP*, p. 87)

Perhaps the ceremonial occasion of the poem explains why this is Stevens' most generous acceptance of the father's priority. The son serves as an undertaker in a duet with dead fathers. Stevens rests only momentarily in the dream of recuperation as he inscribes the past in a double inscription that folds in upon itself and thus is the reflection of its own beginning as a figure of a figure. The past is Nicholas Poussin's reimagining of Vergil's allegory of genealogical order, and thus the legitimacy of the Caesars, in the tale of Aeneas' bearing his father on his shoulders after the destruction of Troy. This "solid shape" inhabits "a giant's air" which, we know from other Stevens poems, is a trope of origins.

The final stanza leaves little room to doubt the thoroughly fictive grounds of genealogy:

The father keeps on living in the son, the world
Of the father keeps on living in the world
Of the son. These survivals out of time and space
Come to us every day. And yet they are
Merely parts of the general fiction of the mind:
Survival of a good that we have loved
Made eminent in a reflected seeming-so.   (*OP*, pp. 87–88)

The continuity of the past lies within the fiction of the mind, the desire to give reality to what remains of faith in orderly descent. The father, however, is but a reflection of a fiction, a double of trope itself.

One of Stevens' favorite figures of the parent is the giant, for it is he who stands like the sun "on the horizon": "a close, parental magnitude,/ At the centre on the horizon, concentrum, grave/ And prodigious person, patron of origins" (*CP*, p. 443). The central being of the central poem—in other words, the parent—is the supreme fiction. (Harold Bloom identifies the "you" to whom Stevens addresses the introductory verse of "Notes Toward a Supreme Fiction" as the family.[12]) For to believe in the family is to believe in origins and ends, and, thus, in divinity: "We knew one parent must have been divine" (*CP*, p. 331). And like parents, the poem shares in "the first idea":

<blockquote>

It satisfies

Belief in an immaculate beginning

And sends us, winged by an unconscious will,

To an immaculate end. We move between these points:

From that ever-early candor to its late plural.   (*CP*, p. 382)

</blockquote>

The poem situates man between beginnings and ends, between the pure origin and the innumerable. The "ever-early candor" opens the poem to the "late plural" out of which the first idea is reimagined; the first idea, then, is never original, or derived, and like Nietzsche's "first metaphor" is always already (in) language.

In the fourth canto of "It Must Be Abstract," Stevens undoes the myth of the first idea:

<blockquote>

The first idea was not our own. Adam

In Eden was the father of Descartes

And Eve made air the mirror of herself,

Of her sons and of her daughters. They found
   themselves

In heaven as in a glass; a second earth;

And in the earth itself they found a green—

The inhabitants of a very varnished green.   (*CP*, p. 383)

</blockquote>

The Fall is Cartesian dualism; thus Adam is neither the author nor the issue of the first idea but is the father of self-consciousness, a son who is a father, a doubled father. In a complementary manner, Eve, like Narcissus, finds her image wherever she looks. The "original" parents are writers, makers of metaphors. Heaven is but a "glass," or a mirror of earth, a "varnished green," that is, an artifice or an artificial nature. In "The Pure Good of Theory," these same metaphors are reshaped to form the myth of metaphor:

12. Bloom, *Wallace Stevens*, 167.

> Man, that is not born of woman but of air,
> That comes here in the solar chariot,
> Like rhetoric in a narration of the eye—   (*CP*, p. 331)

The son is an ephebe, a diminutive Phoebus, who is himself a rhetorical figure dragging his father on his back like a double inscription. The eye's, or I's, narration tells the story of perception, which Stevens says is always an aftering: "The idea that because perception is sensory we never see reality immediately but always the moment after is a poetic idea. We live in mental representations of the past" (*L*, p. 722). The past, however, is not recuperated by the eye, for when "Man" (the son as Adam) woke, "He woke in a metaphor: this was/ A metamorphosis of paradise,/ Malformed, the world was paradise malformed . . ." (*CP*, pp. 331–32). Contrary to Keats, "Man" does not wake to find his dream is reality; he wakes to a dream of a dream, a "mal" form, a metaphor—an aesthetic of "mal." Thus Stevens declines to rest in a metaphor because it is too comfortable a place for so severe a reader:

> Yet to speak of the whole world as metaphor
> Is still to stick to the contents of the mind
>
> And the desire to believe in a metaphor.
> It is to stick to the nicer knowledge of
> Belief, that what it believes in is not true.   (*CP*, p. 332)

If we speak of the world as metaphor, and thus turn our backs on what Stevens calls "reality," we have merely given ontological priority to mind over nature.

Stevens evades settling for either imagination or reality out of a distrust of metaphor as a bridge between man and nature, or idea and thing. In his "Adagia," he writes, "There is no such thing as a metaphor of a metaphor. One does not progress through metaphors. Thus reality is the indispensable element of each metaphor. When I say that man is a god it is very easy to see that if I also say that a god is something else, god has become reality" (*OP*, p. 179). Stevens implies that reality emerges only in naming; to say man is a god displaces previous notions of god, who must be named anew. Reality is therefore indistinguishable from unreality: "Metaphor creates a new reality from which the original appears to be unreal" (*OP*, p. 169). Reality is neither some prior absolute, a rock upon which man and language rest, nor a supreme fiction. Once we appeal to reality and metaphor we enter into a search for the present, the governing idea that will root metaphor in a solid edifice. Stevens dramatizes the search as the descent from the first idea:

> But the first was not to shape the clouds
> In imitation. The clouds preceded us
>
> There was a muddy centre before we breathed.
> There was a myth before the myth began,
> Venerable and articulate and complete. (CP, p. 383)

Stevens exposes mimesis as a genealogical descent from the first idea to nature. The copy exists as the variation of an original untouched by time; this is as true for nature as it is for poetry. Nor will he rest in some belief in the priority of nature; the muddy center is that ground which is neither solid nor water, neither an earthy foundation nor an abyss. It is myth, for, as Stevens writes in another poem, "The origin could have its origin" (OP, p. 85). While myths preceding myths and origins before origins appear to throw Stevens into an infinite regress whereby illusion succeeds illusion, the "venerable and articulate" myth shatters the specular descent into infinity and displaces the central poem of being. The frame bordering the *mise en abyme* is broken open to the uncertainty of writing, a process that refuses to settle either on solid ground or in a specular descent that controls the indeterminable by framing it within a recognizable image. For in the muddy center, the irreducible myth, the poem has its beginning:

> From this the poem springs: that we live in a place
> That is not our own and, much more, not ourselves
> And hard it is in spite of blazoned days. (CP, p. 383)

Homelessness, or "the celestial ennui of apartments," is what "sends us back to the first idea" (CP, p. 381). The world consists of rooms for rent and the manager is nowhere to be found. And to be without a home is to be without what Stevens variously calls the "first idea," the "myth before myth began," or the muddy center—all of which tropes of generation or, more particularly, of the single parent who determines the descent of language. Yet, for Stevens, the first idea functions not as a source but as an elemental blank situated in language. Therefore, when he speaks of the disappearance of the gods in "Two or Three Ideas," he interprets it as a displacement of beliefs embodied in language, since the gods are a matter of style. The starting point of his discussion is Baudelaire's "La Vie Antérieure" and the line "J'ai longtemps habité sous de vastes portiques." When we read this, Stevens says, "It is as if we had stepped into a ruin and were startled by a flight of birds that rose as we entered. The familiar experience is made unfamiliar. . . . We stand looking at a remembered habitation. All old dwelling-places are subject to these transmogrifications and the experience of all of us includes a succession of old dwelling-places: abodes of the imagination, ancestral or memories of places that never existed" (*OP*, p. 204). The ancestral home exists only as a belated fiction of the familiar or what Freud calls *das heimlich*. But the repressed in Freud is never a lost presence; it is known only in its double, that is, as a belated reimagining of a first desire. Similarly, for Stevens, the home is the most unhomely (*unheimlich*) of places because it is the reminder of the gods' and the parents' absence.[13]

In the same essay, Stevens refers to the disappearance of the gods not only as their own annihilation but also as man's: "It was their annihilation, not ours, and yet it left us feeling that in a measure, we, too, had been annihilated. It left us feeling dispossessed and alone in a solitude, *like children without parents, in a home that seemed deserted*, in which the amical rooms and halls had taken on a look of hardness and emptiness. *What was most extraordinary is that they left no momentoes behind, no thrones, no mystic rings, no texts either of the soil or of the soul*. It was as if they had never inhabited the earth" (*OP*, p. 207; my emphasis). Stevens' poetry will serve as the mementoes, the archival remains, of these absent gods. The reimagining of the first idea discloses metaphor as a perpetual naming that at once points to the gods and annihilates them, along with man, by the same stroke of the pen.

Stevens' most dramatic treatment of the reimagining of the gods, which is also their annihilation, comes in the first canto of "It Must Be Abstract":

> Begin, ephebe, by perceiving the idea
> Of this invention, this invented world,
> The inconceivable idea of the sun.
>
> You must become an ignorant man again
> And see the sun again with an ignorant eye
> And see it clearly in the idea of it.
>
> Never suppose an inventing mind as source
> Of this idea nor for that mind compose
> A voluminous master folded in his fire.　　　　　(*CP*, pp. 380–81)

---

13. Freud, *On Creativity and the Unconscious*, 122–61. For an analysis of the doubled nature of repression in Freud's texts, see Derrida, *Writing and Difference*, 196–231.

Asked to perceive the idea of the sun, the ephebe, a youth just entering manhood, must strip away all the metaphors that this metaphor, the sun, has accrued. Yet the sun is present to neither the mind nor the senses; man only perceives the world in and as a metaphor, thus the need to be ignorant again, for it is only the ignorant man, one free from the accretions of language, who has access to the first idea: "The poem reveals itself only to the ignorant man" (OP, p. 160). The first idea, however, is a fiction, a belated reimagining of origins in which the lateness of the son is inscribed in the father's instructions for him to forget the old names. As Riddel has argued, the ephebe "can only recapitulate the fiction of Adamic naming by using an old memory system (language) to forget or overwrite that system, so as to overcome, if only in a fiction, the belatedness signified by all naming."[14] And as the third stanza instructs us, the first idea is also a fiction; there is no "inventing mind as source," no "voluminous master"—that is, no transcendent author situated within either nature or the book.

When the ephebe has proceeded by an act of willful forgetting to pass through memory to a "first idea," he can then see the sun:

> How clean the sun when seen in its idea,
> Washed in the remotest cleanliness of a heaven
> That has expelled us and our images . . .
>
> The death of one god is the death of all.   (CP, p. 381)

Heaven is the other of man; it can only be seen when it is stripped of human trappings. But to do so would be to hide it. This other is not the dialectical opposite, and thus partner, of man; it is a metaphor for what cannot be named:

> Phoebus is dead, ephebe. But Phoebus was
> A name for something that never could be named.
> There was a project for the sun and is.
>
> There is a project for the sun. The sun
> Must bear no name, gold flourisher, but be
> In the difficulty of what it is to be.   (CP, p. 381)

In the absence of the gods, man must face the simultaneous project of naming and being, for naming is being, even if the sun is to "bear no name." Escape from language is impossible, as Stevens lapses into words to speak

14. Riddel, "Metaphoric Staging," 317. The definitive examination of the metaphoricity of the sun is Derrida, *Margins of Philosophy*, 207–271.

of the sun's project, which bears the father (Phoebus) inscribed within itself. The sun is already language, and "gold flourisher" is a rather hackneyed metaphor.

Stevens will return again and again to the myth of proper naming, and thus to tales of absent gods, deserted homes, and nascent poets. These metaphors, along with the terms *reality* and *imagination*, are part of Stevens' inheritance from Romantic poetry. He seemed to require the polar concepts of reality and imagination as the instruments of thought. In a letter to Richard Wilbur, Stevens explains the polar and the antipolar: "The greater part of the imaginative life of people is both created and enjoyed in polar circumstances. However, I suppose that without being contrary, one can say that the right spot is the middle spot between the polar and the antipolar. It is the true center always that is unapproachable or, rather, extremely difficult to approach" (*L*, p. 740). In adopting these terms from Romantic philosophy and aesthetics, he declares his literary genealogy. Yet to do so was to confess to a secondary stature that he simply could not accept. Thus, his letter can be taken as a rejection of dialectics (the polar) and both monism and anarchy (the antipolar), hence the impossibility of locating a center and origin from which a genealogy can be mapped. Furthermore, we find him undercutting these tropes in his early works as well as in the late poems of his greatest phase when age begins to impress upon him the essential poverty from which poetry emerges. In "Extracts from Addresses to the Academy of Fine Ideas," he writes of the poet's need to live "naked of any illusion, in poverty,/ In the exactest poverty" (*CP*, p. 258).

Stevens is at his most eloquent in his elegy for the dying Santayana when the poem is transformed into a meditation on his own impending death and the "grandeur" that is found

> Only in misery, the afflatus of ruin,
> Profound poetry of the poor and of the dead,
> As in the last drop of the deepest blood,
> As it falls from the heart and lies there to be seen,
>
> Even as the blood of an empire, it might be,
> For a citizen of heaven though still of Rome.
> It is poverty's speech that seeks us out the most.
> It is older than the oldest speech of Rome.
> This is the tragic accent of the scene. (*CP*, pp. 509–10)

"Poverty's speech" has existed before the tradition, before Rome. It is "the irreducible X" (*NA*, p. 83) that Santayana discloses "On the threshold of heaven" (*CP*, p. 508):

> It is a kind of total grandeur at the end,
> With every visible thing enlarged and yet
> No more than a bed, a chair and moving nuns,
> The immensest theatre, the pillared porch,
> The book and candle in your ambered room,
>
> Total grandeur of a total edifice,
> Chosen by an inquisitor of structures
> For himself. He stops upon this threshold,
> As if the design of all his words takes form
> And frame from thinking and is realized. (*CP*, pp. 510–11)

The "total edifice" is realized in what is, for Stevens, an uncharacteristic affirmation of closure of the total book. Perhaps, as Harold Bloom suggests, "Freed by an identification with Santayana as a liminal figure, Stevens for once allowed himself to repress his strong awareness that the mind could never be satisfied lest it fall into the error of ceasing to remember that ceaselessly it was an activity."[15] While Stevens' elegy is free from irony, its celebration of Santayana's devotion to thought gently acknowledges that the vision of heaven is the last illusion afforded by a belief in the "total book"; it is a lapse into the evasions of metaphor. Santayana is like the "harassing master" of another poem who, dissatisfied with "the theory of poetry,/ As the life of poetry," extemporizes:

> Subtler, more urgent proof that the theory
> Of poetry is the theory of life,
>
> As it is, in the intricate evasions of as,
> In things seen and unseen, created from nothingness,
> The heavens, the hells, the worlds, the longed-for
>   lands.   (*CP*, p. 486)

Stevens refuses to console himself in the "evasions of as," that is, in tropes. For Santayana's vision is realized in a trope, in the "As if" of the final stanza. The threshold Santayana stands on leads from the pure good of theory to a final belief that Stevens could never allow himself.

In an earlier poem, "Crude Foyer," Stevens bitterly denies that thresholds lead to vision upon death:

15. Bloom, *Wallace Stevens*, 363.

Thought is false happiness: the idea
That merely by thinking one can,
Or may, penetrate, not may,
But can, that one is sure to be able—

That there lies at the end of thought
A foyer of the spirit in a landscape
Of the mind, in which we sit
And wear humanity's bleak crown;

In which we read the critique of paradise
And say it is the work
Of a comedian, this critique;
In which we sit and breathe

An innocence of an absolute,
False happiness, since we know that we use
Only the eye as faculty, that the mind
Is the eye, and that this landscape of the mind

Is a landscape only of the eye; and that
We are ignorant men incapable
Of the least, minor, vital metaphor, content,
At last, there, when it turns out to be here.   (CP, p. 305)

This is perhaps as vehement a rejection of a belief in thought free from reality as one may find in Stevens. The foyer points to the threshold of "To an Old Philosopher in Rome"—it is the vestibule situated between life and death. But a vestibule is, according to the *OED*, "the principal seat (in the body)" of a disease. For Stevens, this is a dis-ease of false beliefs in mind and in endings. But the foyer lying at the "end of thought" is, after all, only a waiting room, a threshold opening onto an end that does not exist. We are incapable of the "vital metaphor" that will transform the landscape of the mind into paradise. Stevens relentlessly disabuses his readers of whatever faith they may have in transcendence as he reduces man's yearnings for the divine to a satisfaction with the illusion that "there," or heaven, may be found here on earth. In this poem ignorance means a belief in paradise, unlike the use of the word in "Notes Toward a Supreme Fiction," where it means precisely the opposite, a stripping away of all false beliefs reified in language.

As is well known, Stevens knew Santayana at Harvard, where the young teacher invited the future poet to his rooms occasionally. Holly Stevens has said, "It is obvious that Santayana had a lifelong influence on my father"

(*SP*, p. 69). Frank Doggett has made a rather thorough study of Santayana's influence on Stevens' poetry.[16] Santayana provided Stevens with a necessary model for his belief in the unity of poetry and philosophy. But it was as a man of reason, a scholar, that Santayana seems to have impressed Stevens the most. The frequent appearance of the word *scholar* in Stevens' poetry indicates its importance to him, for the scholar occupies a unique position as a reader in Stevens' canon. "An Ordinary Evening in New Haven" contains one of the most striking passages on the scholar:

> A scholar, in his Segmenta, left a note,
> As follows, "The Ruler of Reality,
> If more unreal than New Haven, is not
>
> A real ruler, but rules what is unreal."
> In addition, there were draftings of him, thus:
> "He is the consort of the Queen of Fact.
>
> Sunrise is his garment's hem, sunset is hers.
> He is the theorist of life, not death,
> The total excellence of its total book." (*CP*, p. 485)

The scholar, Professor Eucalyptus, conceives this god, the ruler of reality, as a scholar or a seeker of "the extremest book" (*CP*, p. 380). Married to Fact, the ruler of reality is thus wedded to a belief that life is a unity reducible to the book; hence, he seeks reality "In the metaphysical streets of the physical town" (*CP*, p. 472). Belief in reality requires the same leap of faith as does belief in God:

> Professor Eucalyptus said, "The search
> For reality is as momentous as
> The search for god." It is the philosopher's search
>
> For an interior made exterior
> And the poet's search for the same exterior made
> Interior: breathless things broodingly abreath
>
> With the inhalations of original cold
> And of original earliness. Yet the sense
> Of cold and earliness is a daily sense,
>
> Not the predicate of bright origin.
> Creation is not renewed by images
> Of lone wanderers. To re-create, to use
>
> The cold and earliness and bright origin
> Is to search. (*CP*, p. 481)

16. Doggett, *Stevens' Poetry of Thought*.

Harold Bloom has called these lines "Stevens' conscious palinode in the matter of the First Idea. . . . The First Idea is no longer seen as a reduction, 'the predicate of bright origin,' but simply as the eye's plain version, the daily sense of cold and earliness."[17] The search for an "original cold," which, as Bloom says, is a search to make the Not Me of nature into the Me, does not, however, lead to contact with the world through the immediacy of perception. To use origins is to dissociate the "bright origin" from its generative capacity and to displace it from the head of the past. The origin is to be used, not found, in the daily search in which "The point of vision and desire are the same" (CP, p. 466). This search, then, is an evening's gathering of "days' separate several selves . . . together as one." In this identity of day and night, self and other, the scholar uncovers the absence that perpetuates the search:

> In this identity, disembodiments
>
> Still keep occurring. What is, uncertainly,
> Desire prolongs its adventure to create
> Forms of farewell, furtive among green ferns.   (CP, p. 482)

The scholar creates by night the fragments, the "Segmenta," that remind him by day of the "total book." Between the issue and the absence of these writings lies the perpetual, and thus unfulfilled, devotion to reality, a reality known only in and as the book.

The scholar's search for the total book is a substitute for faith in God. And perhaps it was Stevens' professed agnosticism that restrained him from endorsing Santayana for Henry Church's projected Poetry Chair: "The holder of the Chair would necessarily have to be a man of a dynamic mind and, in this field, something of a scholar and very much of an original force. A man like Dr. Santayana illustrates the character, although in him the religious and the philosophic are too dominant" (L, p. 378). The scholar's religious fetish of the book is, nevertheless, attractive to Stevens, for he recognized the close ties between reading and faith: "I believe in pure explication de texte. This may in fact be my principal form of piety" (L, p. 793).

Despite his atraction to the book, Stevens withheld his endorsement of the scholar as priest. The poet must himself be free from the pieties of his readers. And to be a strong poet, one must deny himself the scholar's hunger

17. Bloom, Wallace Stevens, 328.

> for that book,
> The very book, or, less, a page
>
> Or, at the least, a phrase, that phrase,
> A hawk of life, that latined phrase:
>
> To know; a missal for brooding-sight. (CP, p. 178)

The scholar seeks the poem that would be a New Testament "like a missal found/ In the mud" (CP, p. 177). This is the dream of the total book. In the final canto of "The Man with the Blue Guitar," Stevens refers to this desire as "That generation's dream, aviled/ In the mud, in Monday's dirty light" (CP, p. 183). The book, or its dream, has been lost in the mud; it has been degraded by life in the world, "Monday's dirty light."

The scholar's dream recuperates God in what Stevens calls "the extremest book of the wisest man"(CP, p. 380). By turning the poem into Scripture, the scholar is tempted to substitute the illusion of God for the abyss opening up between the poet and his subject, or, as Stevens puts it, "Theology after breakfast sticks to the eye" (CP, p. 245). The scholar would be content with a poetry that affirms the One in face of the chaos of experience. This is what Stevens cannot accept:

> After all the pretty contrast of life and death
> Proves that these opposite things partake of one,
> At least that was the theory, when bishops' books
> Resolved the world. We cannot go back to that. (CP, p. 215)

Yet Stevens will not turn around and accept disorder, for it is only "a violent order." Unwilling to resurrect theology through its negation, Stevens entertains the possibility of order in disorder:

> But suppose the disorder of truths should ever come
> To an order, most Plantagenet, most fixed . . .
> A great disorder is an order. Now, A
> And B are not like statuary, posed
> For a vista in the Louvre. They are things chalked
> On the sidewalk so that the pensive man may see. (CP, p. 216)

The model for order comes from royal succession; order is guaranteed by genealogy (though we might think of it as an imposed order, rather than natural, because the Plantagenets were Normans living in and ruling a foreign land). Stevens, however, reimagines this order so that it resembles no other. In his world, writing, or a scrawl upon a sidewalk, is the poem waiting for the pensive man; there is no "missal" to be found in "the mud" (*CP*, p. 177).

Stevens' world is not a world for scholars, who are, after all, only students, too old to be ephebes and too young to be poets. The priestly robes of these youth must be cast off for the somber garb of the rabbi, who is not a student but a teacher. And in Stevens' world "the poet would be the Metropolitan Rabbi, so to speak" (*L*, pp. 292–93). Late in life, Stevens wrote of the significance of rabbis in a letter to Bernard Heringman: "In the view of Mr. Wagner's very philosophic papers on my things, I am beginning to feel like a rabbi myself. I have never referred to rabbis as religious figures but always as scholars. When I was a boy I was brought up to think that rabbis were men who spent their time getting wisdom. And I rather think that that is true. One doesn't feel the same way, for instance, about priests or about a Protestant pastor, who are almost exclusively religious figures" (*L*, p. 751). Here Stevens uses the word *scholar* in what the *OED* calls the "vulgar" sense as a man of learning, rather than simply as a disciple or a university student. Nevertheless, this letter is much more helpful than his gloss of "The Sun This March" in a letter to Renato Poggioli: "The rabbi is a rhetorical rabbi. Frankly, the figure of the rabbi has always been an exceedingly attractive one to me because it is the figure of a man devoted in the extreme to scholarship and at the same time to making some use of it for human purposes" (*L*, p. 786). Stevens' prose commentaries are reassuring—no one can offer a weaker reading of his poems than he does. What, I ask, is a "rhetorical rabbi"?

"The Sun This March" is a particularly important poem because it broke six years of silence. The poem concerns the loss of poetic spirit:

> The exceeding brightness of this early sun
> Makes me conceive how dark I have become,
>
> And re-illumines things that used to turn
> To gold in broadest blue, and be a part
>
> Of a turning spirit in an earlier self.   (*CP*, pp. 133–34)

Although the poem begins as a reawakening of the self, it quickly turns into an acknowledgment of a loss of self that has fundamentally altered the poet. Hence, the solemnity and the pathos of these lines bespeak a reimagining of the poet rather than an awakening of a lost self. Instead of the opulent poetry of *Harmonium*, the poems of "gold in broadest blue," he will need to write poems of "winter's air." Yet there seems to be a hesitancy before the cold, and Stevens cries, "Oh! Rabbi, rabbi, fend my soul for me/ And true savant of this dark nature be" (CP, p. 134). Bloom has commented that "the rabbi, like the poet, is always in the sun, and his function is both to defend and to shift Stevens, to reilluminate the poet's dark nature so that he can write poems again."[18] Although it wasn't till twelve years later that Stevens denied the existence of "A voluminous master folded" in the sun's fire, the sun has always been foreign to the poet. If the rabbi is the reader of Stevens' soul, and thus his defender, it is because he lives with him in the darkness of a winter's night.

The "dark rabbi" himself had previously appeared in the final canto of "Le Monocle de Mon Oncle":

> Like a dark rabbi, I
> Observed, when young, the nature of mankind,
> In lordly study. Every day, I found
> Man proved a gobbet in my mincing world.
> Like a rose rabbi, later, I pursued,
> And still pursue, the origin and course
> Of love, but until now I never knew
> That fluttering things have so distinct a shade.   (CP, pp. 17–18)

The rabbi, like the scholar, is a figure for the reader. In this rejection of "The honey of heaven," the rabbi passes from a devourer of man to a reader of the fluctuations and shades of difference in human love. Stevens' rabbi strikes a more optimistic note than does his "dull scholar," who beholds in love the new mind, perhaps an ephebe, that "bears its fruit and dies," and thus he laments, "Our bloom is gone. We are the fruit thereof" (CP, p. 16).

Unlike the priest, or the priestly scholar, the rabbi is the secular reader of man and his texts; thus, in "Notes Toward a Supreme Fiction," he is told to observe the poet as tramp, as "The man/ In that old coat, those sagging pantaloons," and "to confect/ The final elegance, not to console/ Nor sanctify, but plainly to propound" (CP, p. 389). But it is in the final canto of "The Auroras of Autumn" that the rabbi appears most forcefully:

> An unhappy people in a happy world—
> Read, rabbi, the phases of this difference.
> An unhappy people in an unhappy world—

18. *Ibid.*, 89.

Here are too many mirrors for misery.
A happy people in an unhappy world—
It cannot be. There's nothing there to roll

On the expressive tongue, the finding fang.
A happy people in a happy world—
Buffo! A ball, an opera, a bar.

Turn back to where we were when we began:
An unhappy people in a happy world.
Now, solemnize the secretive syllables.

Read to the congregation, for today
And for tomorrow, this extremity,
This contrivance of the spectre of the spheres,

Contriving balance to contrive a whole,
The vital, the never-failing genius,
Fulfilling his meditations, great and small.

In these unhappy he meditates a whole,
The full of fortune and the full of fate,
As if he lived all lives, that he might know,

In hall harridan, not hushful paradise,
To a haggling of wind and weather, by these lights
Like a blaze of summer straw, in winter's nick.   (*CP*, pp. 420–21)

The rabbi is the reader situated not only between man and world but also between language—in a play of prefixes, negatives, and adjectives that multiply reproductions, and thus interpretations, of the text. The rabbi must therefore be a reader of difference, which is the linguistic play in which man and nature are situated without ever coming into contact. To keep with the initial text, "unhappy people in a happy world," the rabbi must seek to balance the difference and thereby "contrive a whole." It is the rabbi's "never-failing genius" to meditate a whole in the unhappy people as if he had lived their lives, had lived in the harridan halls, in the haggling and shrewish weather of winter, and still be able to "know [. . .] by these lights/ Like a blaze of summer straw, in winter's nick." To know is to lighten the dark soul; it is a contrivance of the whole, but a moment's interpretation, a lighting of a text "at the finger tips" and not a resting in a final object, as the absence of an object for the verb "to know" suggests.

There is a far-reaching significance in Stevens' desire that the rabbi interpret the differences in the words "An unhappy people in a happy world." Hegel defined the unhappy consciousness as the "dualizing of self-consciousness within itself," whereupon self-consciousness is perceived as divided and double. Thus we have "the *Unhappy Consciousness*, the Alienated Soul which is the consciousness of self as a divided nature, a doubled and merely contradictory being. This unhappy consciousness, divided and at variance within itself, must, because this contradiction of its essential nature is felt to be a single consciousness, always have in the one consciousness the other also; and thus must be straightaway driven out of each in turn, when it thinks it has therein attained to the victory and rest of unity."[19] In the dialectic of master and slave, dualism was embodied in two individuals; now it is concentrated into one, which subsequently perceives the consciousness that exists for itself and the consciousness that exists for others as the divided consciousness of a single, but contradictory, being. It gazes at itself as a double consciousness and thus its unity is not a true unity of both.

In Stevens, the unhappy people perceive the other, the world, as happy: the world is a reality foreign to the individual's consciousness. Aware of this difference, it seeks to overcome the contradiction of the self, but for an unhappy consciousness to rest in an unhappy world is to remain in the duality of a contradictory being. But when Stevens turns to "A happy people in an unhappy world," he rejects it as an impoverished language. The contradiction of being and the world inheres in language, in the words of the world. Thus, the reconciliation of "A happy people in a happy world" is a comedy, a joke, while the belief that man can be happy in a foreign world is a tragedy. Consequently, in the return to the original proposition, he dismisses the possibility of sublation for the unchangeable existence of the unhappy consciousness.

The unhappy consciousness is what Alexandre Kojève called the "Judaic attitude,"[20] which Hegel, without actually using this term, describes as the process whereby consciousness assumes the simple as the essential and the manifold as unessential, or as two foreign realities, whereupon it identifies its own contradictory consciousness with the unessential and is thus unable to free itself from the unessential that inhabits it as the definition, the essence, of its own consciousness.

Derrida, following Kojève and Hegel, has remarked on Jabès' convergence with Hegel: "The Jewish consciousness is indeed the unhappy consciousness." For Stevens, as for Jabès, the unhappy consciousness finds it-

19. Hegel, *The Phenomenology of Mind*, 251.
20. Kojève, *Introduction à la lecture de Hegel*, 68.

self "inscribed just beyond the phenomenology of the mind" in a book in which the absence of nature and God is announced "and is lost in being pronounced." Absence "knows itself as disappearing and lost, and to this extent it remains inaccessible and impenetrable. To gain access to it is to lose it; to show it is to hide it; to acknowledge it is to lie." Derrida here follows both Hegel and Heidegger in describing God, nature, and consciousness as an other that "cannot be found where it is sought; for it is meant to be just a 'beyond,' that which cannot be found." "This is where the serpent lives, the bodiless" (*CP*, p. 411), on a horizon where the flash of an unnatural light, a light without origins, illuminates an empty home: "Upstairs/ The windows will be lighted, not the rooms" (*CP*, p. 413). The auroras are a figure for the impossibility of language's tracing back to an origin a governing power that can control the force of writing. In Riddel's words, "The auroras, like a 'serpent body flashing without the skin' (*CP*, p. 411), are 'light' without a proper origin, a natural aberration, flashings not of the sun but of the clashing play of unequal forces, a light of morning as cold as the end of an autumn's day. The 'auroras' have no origin, and even their northern place is inconceivable outside of some eschatological fiction." We know the home, the "original chez moi," only by a foreign light, not by an eternal source, and thus we know it only as the impenetrable, as the grave of the unhappy consciousness. And as Hegel writes, "Consciousness . . . can only come upon the *grave* of its life. But since this is itself an actuality to afford a lasting possession, the presence even of that tomb is merely the source of trouble, toil, and struggle, a fight which must be lost."[21] For Hegel, the unhappy consciousness will eventually abandon the concrete and seek particularity in a force that is universal, but for Stevens' rabbi, as for Jabès, the unhappy consciousness finds the tomb in a book, a book that can never be possesed but only traced in the path of writing:

> Thus the theory of description matters most.
> It is the theory of the word for those
>
> For whom the word is the making of the world,
> The buzzing world and lisping firmament.   (*CP*, p. 345)

God's "I Am" is a splintered speech, a "latent double" that separates God from his creation and thus usurps speech from man, who must always write

---

21. Derrida, *Writing and Difference*, 68, 69; Hegel, *The Phenomenology of Mind*, 258 and 259; Riddel, "Metaphoric Staging," 332–33.

and can never speak. The original voice has been shattered with the Tables of the Law and now only rabbis can read the broken words which are our freedom. To be secondary, displaced from God's original speech, is to be free, for freedom exists only in the indeterminability of writing, a negation of the "patron of origins," of God the Father, and a relocation of the site of Being in the book:

> The house was quiet and the world was calm.
> The reader became the book; and summer night
> Was like the conscious being of the book. (CP, p. 358)

The rabbi is the only reader free from the bondage of genealogy. He alone stands outside the linear descent of father to son, teacher to student, or priest to congregation.

Bibliography

Adams, Brooks. *America's Economic Supremacy*. 1900; rpr. with a new evaluation by Marquis W. Childs. New York: Harper & Brothers, 1947.
———. *The Law of Civilization and Decay: An Essay on History*. 1896; rpr. New York: Knopf, 1943.
———. *The Theory of Social Revolutions*. New York: Macmillan, 1913.
Adams, Henry. *The Degradation of the Democratic Dogma*. Introduction by Brooks Adams. New York: Macmillan, 1919.
———. *The Education of Henry Adams*. Edited by Ernest Samuels. 1918; rpr. Boston: Houghton Mifflin, 1973.
———. [Francis Snow Compton, pseud.]. *Esther: A Novel*. 1884; rpr. New York: Scholars' Facsimiles & Reprints, 1938.
———. *History of the United States of America During the Administrations of Jefferson and Madison*. Abridged and edited by Ernest Samuels. Chicago: University of Chicago Press, 1967.
———. *Letters to a Niece and Prayer to the Virgin of Chartres, with "A Niece's Memories" by Mabel La Farge*. Boston: Houghton Mifflin, 1920.
———. *Mont-Saint-Michel and Chartres*. 1905; rpr. Boston: Houghton Mifflin, 1933.
Adams, Richard P. "Emerson and the Organic Metaphor." *PMLA*, LXIX (1954), 117–30.
Allen Gay Wilson. "Mutations in Whitman's Art." In *Walt Whitman: A Collection of Criticism*, edited by Arthur Golden. New York: McGraw-Hill, 1974.
Althusser, Louis. *Lenin and Philosophy and Other Essays*. Translated by Ben Brewster. New York: Monthly Review Press, 1971.
Anderson, Quentin. *The Imperial Self: An Essay in American Literary and Cultural History*. New York: Knopf, 1971.
Benjamin, Walter. *Illuminations*. Translated by Harry Zohn. Edited by Hannah Arendt. New York: Schocken Books, 1969.
———. *The Origin of German Tragic Drama*. Translated by John Osborne. London: New Left Books, 1977.
———. *Reflections: Essays, Aphorisms, Autobiographical Writings*. Translated by Edmund Jephcott. Edited by Peter Demetz. New York: Harcourt Brace Jovanovich, 1978.
Bercovitch, Sacvan. *The Puritan Origins of the American Self*. New Haven: Yale University Press, 1975.
Beringause, Arthur F. *Brooks Adams: A Biography*. New York: Knopf, 1955.
Bernstein, Michael André. *The Tale of the Tribe: Ezra Pound and the Modern Verse Epic*. Princeton: Princeton University Press, 1980.
Blackmore, John T. *Ernst Mach: His Work, Life, and Influence*. Berkeley: University of California Press, 1972.

Bloom, Harold. *Agon: Towards a Theory of Revisionism*. New York: Oxford University Press, 1982.
———. *Figures of Capable Imagination*. New York: Seabury Press, 1976.
———. *Poetry and Repression: Revisionism from Blake to Stevens*. New Haven: Yale University Press, 1976.
———. *Wallace Stevens: The Poems of Our Climate*. Ithaca: Cornell University Press, 1977.
Boltzmann, Ludwig. *Theoretical Physics and Philosophical Problems: Selected Writings*. Translated by Paul Foulkes. Edited by Brian McGuinness. Dordrecht and Boston: D. Reidel, 1974.
Borges, Jorge Luis. *Ficciones*. Translated by Anthony Bonner. New York: Grove Press, 1962.
Bové, Paul A. *Destructive Poetics: Heidegger and Modern American Poetry*. New York: Columbia University Press, 1980.
Breslin, James E. *William Carlos Williams: An American Artist*. New York: Oxford University Press, 1970.
Brush, Stephen G. *The Kind of Motion We Call Heat: A History of the Kinetic Theory of Gases in the Nineteenth Century*. 2 vols. Amsterdam: North-Holland Publishing Co., 1976.
Bucke, Richard Maurice, Thomas B. Harned, and Horace Traubel, eds. *The Complete Writings of Walt Whitman*. 10 vols. New York: G. P. Putnam's Sons, 1902.
Buell, Lawrence. *Literary Transcendentalism: Style and Vision in the American Renaissance*. Ithaca: Cornell University Press, 1973.
Carlyle, Thomas. "On History." In *Critical and Miscellaneous Essays*. Vol. II of 4 vols. 1839; rpr. Boston: Dana Estes, n.d.
Carnot, Sadi. *Reflections on the Motive Power of Fire and Other Papers on the Second Law of Thermodynamics by E. Clapeyron and R. Clausius*. Edited by E. Mendoza. New York: Dover Publications, 1960.
Cater, Harold Dean, ed. *Henry Adams and His Friends: A Collection of His Unpublished Letters*. Boston: Houghton Mifflin, 1947.
Cavell, Stanley. *The Senses of Walden*. New York: Viking Press, 1972.
Chambers, Robert. *Vestiges of the Natural History of Creation*. 3rd ed. London: John Churchill, 1845.
Coffman, Stanley K., Jr. "'Crossing Brooklyn Ferry': A Note on the Catalogue Technique in Whitman's Poetry." In *Walt Whitman: A Collection of Criticism*, edited by Arthur Golden. New York: McGraw-Hill, 1974.
Colacurcio, Michael. "The Dynamo and the Angelic Doctor: The Bias of Henry Adams' Medievalism." *American Quarterly*, XVII (Winter, 1965), 696–712.
Coleridge, Samuel Taylor. *Aids to Reflection*. Edited by Henry Nelson Coleridge. Vol. I of *Complete Works*, edited by W. G. T. Shedd. 7 vols. New York: Harper & Brothers, 1854.
———. *Biographia Literaria*. Edited by J. Shawcross. 2 vols. Oxford: Oxford University Press, 1907.
———. *Confessions of an Inquiring Spirit*. Edited by H. StJ. Hart. 3rd ed. 1853; rpr. Stanford: Stanford University Press, 1967.
———. *The Friend*. Edited by Barbara E. Rooke. Princeton: Princeton University Press, 1969. Vol. IV of *Collected Works*, edited by Kathleen Coburn. 16 vols. projected.

————. *Lay Sermons.* Edited by R. J. White. Princeton: Princeton University Press, 1972. Vol. VI of *Collected Works,* edited by Kathleen Coburn. 16 vols. projected.

Comte, Auguste. *Philosophie première: Cours de philosophie positive, Leçons 1 à 45.* Edited by Michel Serres, François Dagognet, and Allal Sinaceur. Paris: Hermann, 1975.

Curtius, Ernst Robert. *European Literature and the Latin Middle Ages.* Translated by Willard R. Trask. 1953; rpr. Princeton: Princeton University Press, 1973.

Cuvier, Georges. *The Animal Kingdom Arranged in Conformity with Its Organization.* Translated by Edward Griffith *et al.* 15 vols. London: G. B. Whittaker, 1827–32.

————. *A Discourse on the Revolutions of the Surface of the Globe, and Changes Thereby Produced in the Animal Kingdom.* Philadelphia: Carey & Lea, 1831.

Darwin, Charles. *The Origin of Species by Means of Natural Selection, or the Preservation of Favoured Races in the Struggle for Life.* Edited by J. W. Burrow. 1859; rpr. New York: Penguin Books, 1968.

Davie, Donald. *Ezra Pound.* New York: Viking Press, 1975.

Davis, Merrell R., and William H. Gilman, eds. *The Letters of Herman Melville.* New Haven: Yale University Press, 1960.

De Man, Paul. *Allegories of Reading: Figural Language in Rousseau, Nietzsche, Rilke, and Proust.* New Haven: Yale University Press, 1979.

————. *Blindness and Insight: Essays in the Rhetoric of Contemporary Criticism.* New York: Oxford University Press, 1971.

————. "Hypogram and Inscription: Michael Riffaterre's Poetics of Reading." *Diacritics,* XI (Winter, 1981), 17–35.

————. "Intentional Structure of the Romantic Image." In *Romanticism and Consciousness,* edited by Harold Bloom. New York: Norton, 1970.

————. "The Rhetoric of Temporality." In *Interpretation: Theory and Practice,* edited by Charles S. Singleton. Baltimore: Johns Hopkins University Press, 1969.

————. "Shelley Disfigured." In *Deconstruction and Criticism.* New York: Seabury Press, 1979.

Dembo, L. S. *Hart Crane's Sanskrit Charge: A Study of "The Bridge."* Ithaca: Cornell University Press, 1960.

Derrida, Jacques. "Coming into One's Own." In *Psychoanalysis and the Question of the Text,* edited by Geoffrey H. Hartman. Baltimore: Johns Hopkins University Press, 1978.

————. *Dissemination.* Translated by Barbara Johnson. Chicago: University of Chicago Press, 1981.

————. "Fors." Translated by Barbara Johnson. *Georgia Review,* XXXI (Spring, 1977), 64–116.

————. "Living On/Border Lines." Translated by James Hulbert. In *Deconstruction and Criticism.* New York: Seabury Press, 1979.

————. *Margins of Philosophy.* Translated by Alan Bass. Chicago: University of Chicago Press, 1982.

————. *Of Grammatology.* Translated by Gayatri Chakravorty Spivak. Baltimore: Johns Hopkins Press, 1976.

————. *Writing and Difference.* Translated by Alan Bass. Chicago: University of Chicago Press, 1978.

Doggett, Frank. *Stevens' Poetry of Thought*. Baltimore: Johns Hopkins University Press, 1966.

Donato, Eugenio. "Divine Agonies: Of Representation and Narrative in Romantic Poetics." *Glyph*, VI (1979), 90–122.

———. "'A Mere Labyrinth of Letters'/Flaubert and the Quest for Fiction/A Montage." *Modern Language Notes*, LXXXIX (December, 1974), 885–910.

———. "The Museum's Furnace: Notes Toward a Contextual Reading of *Bouvard and Pécuchet*." In *Textual Strategies: Perspectives in Post-Structuralist Criticism*, edited by Josué V. Harari. Ithaca: Cornell University Press, 1979.

———. "The Ruins of Memory: Archeological Fragments and Textual Artifacts." *Modern Language Notes*, XCIII (May, 1978), 575–96.

Dryden, Edgar A. "The Entangled Text: Melville's *Pierre* and the Problem of Reading." *Boundary 2*, VII (Spring, 1979), 145–73.

Eco, Umberto. *A Theory of Semiotics*. Bloomington: Indiana University Press, 1976.

Eliot, Thomas Stearns. *Collected Poems, 1909–1962*. New York: Harcourt, Brace, Jovanovich, 1963.

———. *The Idea of a Christian Society*. New York: Harcourt, Brace, 1940.

———. *Notes Towards the Definition of Culture*. London: Faber and Faber, 1948.

———. *Selected Essays*. Expanded edition. New York: Harcourt, Brace & World, 1960.

———. *The Waste Land: A Facsimile and Transcript of the Original Drafts Including the Annotations of Ezra Pound*. Edited by Valerie Eliot. Preface by Ezra Pound. New York: Harcourt Brace Jovanovich, 1971.

Emerson, Edward Waldo, ed. *The Complete Works of Ralph Waldo Emerson*. 12 vols. Boston: Houghton Mifflin, 1903–1904.

Espey, John. *Ezra Pound's "Mauberley."* 1955; rpr. Berkeley: University of California Press, 1974.

Feidelson, Charles, Jr. *Symbolism and American Literature*. Chicago: University of Chicago Press, 1953.

Fenollosa, Ernest. *The Chinese Written Character as a Medium for Poetry*. Edited by Ezra Pound. San Francisco: City Lights Books, 1936.

Ferguson, Frances. *Wordsworth: Language as Counter-Spirit*. New Haven: Yale University Press, 1977.

Findlay, Alexander. *The Phase Rule and Its Applications*. Revised with the assistance of A. N. Campbell. 8th ed. New York: Dover Publications, 1945.

Ford, Worthington Chauncey, ed. *Letters of Henry Adams (1858–1891)*. Boston: Houghton Mifflin, 1930.

———, ed. *Letters of Henry Adams (1892–1918)*. Boston: Houghton Mifflin, 1938.

Foucault, Michel. *The Order of Things: An Archaeology of the Human Sciences*. A translation of *Les Mots et les choses*. New York: Vintage Books, 1973.

Freud, Sigmund. *General Psychological Theory*. Edited by Philip Rieff. New York: Collier Books, 1963.

———. *On Creativity and the Unconscious: Papers on the Psychology of Art, Literature, Love, Religion*. Edited by Benjamin Nelson. 1925; rpr. New York: Harper & Row, 1958.

Gibbon, Edward. *Autobiography of Edward Gibbon*. Edited by Lord Sheffield. 1907; rpr. London: Oxford University Press, 1967.

Gilman, William H., *et al.*, eds. *The Journals and Miscellaneous Notebooks of Ralph Waldo Emerson.* 16 vols. Cambridge: Harvard University Press, 1960–82.

Glacken, Clarence J. *Traces on the Rhodian Shore: Nature and Culture in Western Thought from Ancient Times to the End of the Eighteenth Century.* Berkeley: University of California Press, 1967.

Gramsci, Antonio. *Selections from the Prison Notebooks.* Edited and translated by Quintin Hoare and Geoffrey Nowell Smith. New York: International Publishers, 1971.

Grossman, Allen. "Hart Crane and Poetry: A Consideration of Crane's Intense Poetics with Reference to 'The Return.'" In *Critical Essays on Hart Crane,* edited by David R. Clark. Boston: G. K. Hall, 1982.

Hartshorne, Charles, and Paul Weiss, eds. *Collected Papers of Charles Sanders Peirce.* 8 vols. Cambridge: Harvard University Press, 1931–58.

Hegel, G. W. F. *Aesthetics: Lectures on Fine Art.* Translated by T. M. Knox. 2 vols. Oxford: Oxford University Press, 1975.

———. *The Phenomenology of Mind.* Translated by James Ballie. 2nd rev. ed. 1931; rpr. New York: Harper & Row, 1967.

———. *Philosophy of Mind.* Translated by William Wallace. *Zusätze.* Translated by A. V. Miller. Part 3 of *Encyclopedia of the Philosophical Sciences.* Oxford: Oxford University Press, 1971.

———. *Reason in History: A General Introduction to the Philosophy of History.* Translated by Robert S. Hartman. Indianapolis: Bobbs-Merrill, 1953.

Heidegger, Martin. *Being and Time.* Translated by John Macquarrie and Edward Robinson. New York: Harper & Row, 1962.

———. *On the Way to Language.* Translated by Peter D. Hertz. New York: Harper & Row, 1971.

———. *Poetry, Language, Thought.* Translated by Albert Hofstadter. New York: Harper & Row, 1971.

Irwin, John T. *American Hieroglyphics: The Symbol of the Egyptian Hieroglyphic in the American Renaissance.* New Haven: Yale University Press, 1980.

———. "Figurations of the Writer's Death: Freud and Hart Crane." In *The Literary Freud: Mechanisms of Defense and the Poetic Will,* edited by Joseph H. Smith, M.D. New Haven: Yale University Press, 1980. Vol. IV of *Psychiatry and the Humanities.* 5 vols.

———. "Hart Crane's 'Logic of Metaphor.'" *Southern Review,* New Ser., XI (April, 1975), 284–99.

Jabès, Edmond. *The Book of Questions.* Translated by Rosmarie Waldrop. Middletown, Conn.: Wesleyan University Press, 1976.

———. *The Book of Questions: II & III. The Book of Yukel. Return to the Book.* Translated by Rosmarie Waldrop. Middletown, Conn.: Wesleyan University Press, 1976.

Jacob, François. *The Logic of Life: A History of Heredity.* Translated by Betty E. Spillman. 1973; rpr. New York: Pantheon Books, 1982.

Jameson, Fredric. *Fables of Aggression: Wyndham Lewis, the Modernist as Fascist.* Berkeley: University of California Press, 1979.

———. *The Prison-House of Language: A Critical Account of Structuralism and Russian Formalism.* Princeton: Princeton University Press, 1972.

Jordy, William H. *Henry Adams: Scientific Historian.* New Haven: Yale University Press, 1952.
Kenner, Hugh. *A Homemade World: The American Modernist Writers.* New York: William Morrow, 1975.
————. *The Pound Era.* Berkeley: University of California Press, 1971.
Kierkegaard, Søren. *The Concept of Dread.* Translated by Walter Lowrie. 2nd ed. Princeton: Princeton University Press, 1967.
Kippur, Stephen A. *Jules Michelet: A Study of Mind and Sensibility.* Albany: State University of New York Press, 1981.
Kofman, Sarah. "Metaphor, Symbol, Metamorphosis." Translated by David B. Allison. In *The New Nietzsche: Contemporary Styles of Interpretation,* edited by David B. Allison. New York: Delta, 1977.
————. *Nietzsche et la métaphore.* Paris: Payot, 1972.
Kojève, Alexandre. *Introduction à la lecture de Hegel.* Edited by Raymond Queneau. 1947; rpr. Paris: Gallimard, 1968.
————. *Introduction to the Reading of Hegel.* Assembled by Raymond Queneau. Edited by Allan Bloom. Translated by James H. Nichols, Jr. 1969; rpr. Ithaca: Cornell University Press, 1980.
Lawrence, David Herbert. Review of *In the American Grain,* by William Carlos Williams. In *Phoenix: The Posthumous Papers of D. H. Lawrence, 1936,* edited by Edward D. McDonald. 1936; rpr. New York: Penguin Books, 1978.
Layzer, David. "The Arrow of Time." *Scientific American* (December, 1975), 56–69.
Lewis, R. W. B. *The American Adam: Innocence, Tragedy, and Tradition in the Nineteenth Century.* Chicago: University of Chicago Press, 1955.
————. *The Poetry of Hart Crane: A Critical Study.* Princeton: Princeton University Press, 1967.
Lewis, Wyndham. *Time and Western Man.* 1927; rpr. Boston: Beacon Press, 1957.
Lindsay, Robert Bruce, and Henry Margenau. *Foundations of Physics.* New York: John Wiley & Sons, 1936.
Lyell, Charles. *Principles of Geology: Being an Inquiry How Far the Former Changes of the Earth's Surface are Referable to Causes Now in Operation.* 2 vols. From 5th London edition. 1st American edition. Philadelphia: James Kay, Jr., & Brother, 1837.
Mane, Robert. *Henry Adams on the Road to Chartres.* Cambridge: Harvard University Press, 1971.
Mariani, Paul. *William Carlos Williams: A New World Naked.* New York: McGraw-Hill, 1981.
Marx, Karl. *Capital: A Critique of Political Economy.* Vol. I of 3 vols. Translated by Ben Fowkes. New York: Vintage Books, 1977.
————. *A Contribution to the Critique of Political Economy.* Translated by S. W. Ryazanskaya. Edited by Maurice Dobb. New York: International Publishers, 1970.
Matthiessen, F. O. *American Renaissance: Art and Expression in the Age of Emerson and Whitman.* New York: Oxford University Press, 1941.
McIntyre, John P., S.J. "Henry Adams and the Unity of Chartres." *Twentieth Century Literature,* VII (1962), 159–71.

Melville, Herman. *The Confidence-Man: His Masquerade*. Edited by Hershel Parker. New York: Norton, 1971.
———. *Moby-Dick*. Edited by Harrison Hayford and Hershel Parker. New York: Norton, 1967.
———. *Pierre, or The Ambiguities*. Edited by Harrison Hayford, Hershel Parker, and G. Thomas Tanselle. Evanston: Northwestern University Press, 1971.
———. *Typee: A Peep at Polynesian Life*. Edited by Harrison Hayford, Hershel Parker, and G. Thomas Tanselle. Evanston: Northwestern University Press, 1968.
Michaels, Walter Benn. "*Walden*'s False Bottoms." *Glyph*, I (1977), 132–49.
Michelet, Jules. *Introduction à l'histoire universelle*. In *Oeuvres complètes*. Paris: Ernest Flammarion, n.d.
Middlebrook, Diane Wood. *Walt Whitman and Wallace Stevens*. Ithaca: Cornell University Press, 1974.
Miller, Edwin Haviland. *Walt Whitman's Poetry: A Psychological Journey*. New York: New York University Press, 1968.
Miller, J. Hillis. "The Critic as Host." *Critical Inquiry*, III (Spring, 1977), 439–47.
———. *Poets of Reality: Six Twentieth-Century Writers*. Cambridge: Harvard University Press, 1966.
———. "Stevens' Rock and Criticism as Cure." *Georgia Review*, XXX (Spring, 1976), 5–31.
Miller, Perry. *Errand into the Wilderness*. Cambridge: Harvard University Press, 1956.
———. *The New England Mind: The Seventeenth Century*. 1939; rpr. Boston: Beacon Press, 1961.
Milton, John. *Complete Poems and Major Prose*. Edited by Merritt Y. Hughes. Indianapolis: Odyssey Press, 1957.
Nelson, Cary. *The Incarnate Word: Literature as Verbal Space*. Urbana: University of Illinois Press, 1973.
Nietzsche, Friedrich. *The Birth of Tragedy*. In *Basic Writings of Nietzsche*, translated and edited by Walter Kaufman. New York: Modern Library, 1968.
———. *The Will to Power*. Translated by Walter Kaufman and R. J. Hollingdale. Edited by Walter Kaufman. New York: Vintage Books, 1968.
Novalis [Friedrich von Hardenberg]. *Henry von Ofterdingen*. Translated by Palmer Hilty. New York: Frederick Ungar, 1964.
Orr, Linda. *Jules Michelet: Nature, History, and Language*. Ithaca: Cornell University Press, 1976.
Packer, Barbara. *Emerson's Fall: A New Interpretation of the Major Essays*. New York: Continuum, 1982.
———. "The Instructed Eye: Emerson's Cosmogony in 'Prospects.'" In *Emerson's "Nature": Origin, Growth, Meaning*, edited by Merton M. Sealts, Jr., and Alfred R. Ferguson. 2nd ed., enlarged. Carbondale: Southern Illinois University Press, 1979.
Paul, Sherman. *Hart's Bridge*. Urbana: University of Illinois Press, 1972.
Pearce, Roy Harvey. *The Continuity of American Poetry*. Princeton: Princeton University Press, 1961.
———. *Historicism Once More: Problems and Occasions for the American Scholar*. Princeton: Princeton University Press, 1969.

Pearlman, Daniel S. *The Barb of Time*. New York: Oxford University Press, 1969.
Pease, Donald. "Blake, Crane, Whitman, and Modernism: A Poetics of Pure Possibility." *PMLA*, XCVI (1981), 64–85.
Pemberton, Vivian H. "Hart Crane and Yvor Winters, Rebuttal and Review: A New Crane Letter." *American Literature*, L (May, 1978), 276–81.
Poirier, Richard. *A World Elsewhere: The Place of Style in American Literature*. London: Chatto & Windus, 1967.
———. "Writing Off the Self." *Raritan*, I (Summer, 1981), 106–133.
Porte, Joel. *Representative Man: Ralph Waldo Emerson in His Time*. New York: Oxford University Press, 1979.
Pound, Ezra. *ABC of Reading*. 1934; rpr. New York: New Directions, 1960.
———. *The Cantos of Ezra Pound*. New York: New Directions, 1972.
———. *Gaudier-Brzeska: A Memoir*. 2nd ed. New York: New Directions, 1970.
———. *Guide to Kulchur*. 1938; rpr. New York: New Directions, 1970.
———. *Jefferson and/or Mussolini: L'Idea Statale, Fascism as I Have Seen It*. 1935; rpr. New York: Liveright, 1970.
———. *Literary Essays of Ezra Pound*. Edited by T. S. Eliot. 1954; rpr. New York: New Directions, 1968.
———. *Selected Letters, 1907–1941*. Edited by D. D. Paige. 1950; rpr. New York: New Directions, 1971.
———. *Selected Prose, 1909–1965*. Edited by William Cookson. New York: New Directions, 1973.
———. *Spirit of Romance*. 1910; rpr. New York: New Directions, 1952.
Riddel, Joseph N. *The Clairvoyant Eye: The Poetry and Poetics of Wallace Stevens*. Baton Rouge: Louisiana State University Press, 1965.
———. "The 'Crypt' of Edgar Poe." *Boundary 2*, VII (Spring, 1979), 117–44.
———. "Decentering the Image: The 'Project' of 'American' Poetics?" In *Textual Strategies: Perspectives in Post-Structuralist Criticism*, edited by Josué V. Harari. Ithaca: Cornell University Press, 1979.
———. "Hart Crane's Poetics of Failure." *English Literary History*, XXXIII (1966), 473–96.
———. "Interpreting Stevens: An Essay on Poetry and Thinking." *Boundary 2*, I (Fall, 1972), 79–97.
———. *The Inverted Bell: Modernism and the Counterpoetics of William Carlos Williams*. Baton Rouge: Louisiana State University Press, 1974.
———. " 'Keep Your Pecker Up'—*Paterson Five* and the Question of Metapoetry." *Glyph*, VIII (1981), 203–231.
———. "Metaphoric Staging: Stevens' Beginning Again of the 'End of the Book.' " In *Wallace Stevens: A Celebration*, edited by Frank Doggett and Robert Buttel. Princeton: Princeton University Press, 1980.
———. " 'Neo-Nietzschean Clatter'—Speculation and the Modernist Poetic Image." *Boundary 2*, IX/X (Spring/Fall, 1981), 209–239.
———. "Pound and the Decentered Image." *Georgia Review*, XXIX (Fall, 1975), 565–91.
Rowe, John Carlos. *Henry Adams and Henry James: The Emergence of a Modern Consciousness*. Ithaca: Cornell University Press, 1976.
Royce, Josiah. *The Problem of Christianity*. 2 vols. New York: Macmillan, 1913.

Rusk, Ralph L. *The Life of Ralph Waldo Emerson*. New York: Charles Scribner's Sons, 1949.

Said, Edward, "On Repetition." In *The Literature of Fact*, edited by Angus Fletcher. New York: Columbia University Press, 1976.

Schlegel, Friedrich. *The Philosophy of Life, and Philosophy of Language, in a Course of Lectures*. Translated by A. J. W. Morrison. London: Henry G. Bohn, 1847.

Schwab, Raymond. *La Renaissance orientale*. Paris: Payot, 1950.

Serres, Michel. *Hermes III: La Traduction*. Paris: Minuit, 1974.

Shaw, Peter. "Ezra Pound on American History." *Partisan Review*, XLIV (1977), 112–24.

Sieburth, Richard. *Instigations: Ezra Pound and Remy de Gourmont*. Cambridge: Harvard University Press, 1978.

Stallo, John Bernhard. *The Concepts and Theories of Modern Physics*. 1881; rpr. New York: D. Appleton, 1897.

Stapleton, Laurence, ed. *H. D. Thoreau: A Writer's Journal*. New York: Dover Publications, 1960.

Stevens, Holly. *Souvenirs and Prophecies: The Young Wallace Stevens*. New York: Knopf, 1977.

Stevens, Wallace. *The Collected Poems of Wallace Stevens*. New York: Knopf, 1954.

———. Correspondence. Stevens Collection, Henry E. Huntington Library, San Marino, California.

———. *Letters of Wallace Stevens*. Edited by Holly Stevens. New York: Knopf, 1966.

———. *The Necessary Angel: Essays on Reality and the Imagination*. New York: Knopf, 1951.

———. *Opus Posthumous*. Edited by Samuel French Morse. New York: Knopf, 1957.

Stock, Noel. *The Life of Ezra Pound*. New York: Random House, 1970.

Terrell, Carroll F. *A Companion to the Cantos of Ezra Pound*. Vol. I of 2 vols. projected. Berkeley: University of California Press, 1980.

Thomson, William (Lord Kelvin). "On a Universal Tendency in Nature to the Dissipation of Mechanical Energy." *Philosophical Magazine and Journal of Science*, 4th ser., IV (July-December, 1852), 304–306.

———. *Popular Lectures and Addresses*. 3 vols. 2nd ed. London: Macmillan, 1891.

Thoreau, Henry David. *"Walden" and "Civil Disobedience."* Edited by Sherman Paul. Boston: Houghton Mifflin, 1957.

———. *A Week on the Concord and Merrimack Rivers*. Edited by Carl F. Hovde et al. Princeton: Princeton University Press, 1980. *The Writings of Henry D. Thoreau*, edited by William L. Howarth. 10 vols. projected.

Truesdale, Clifford. *The Tragicomedy of Classical Thermodynamics*. Vienna: Springer Verlag, 1971.

Uroff, M. D. *Hart Crane: The Patterns of His Poetry*. Urbana: University of Illinois Press, 1974.

Valéry, Paul. *Leonardo, Poe, Mallarmé*. Translated by Malcolm Cowley and James R. Lawler. Princeton: Princeton University Press, 1972. Vol. VIII of *Collected Works of Paul Valéry*, edited by Jackson Mathews. 15 vols.

Vendler, Helen Hennessy. *On Extended Wings: Wallace Stevens' Longer Poems*. Cambridge: Harvard University Press, 1969.

Vico, Giambattista. *The New Science*. Translated by Thomas Goddard Bergin and Max Harold Fisch. Ithaca: Cornell University Press, 1968.

Vogler, Thomas A. *Preludes to Vision: The Epic Venture in Blake, Wordsworth, Keats, and Hart Crane*. Berkeley: University of California Press, 1971.

Wasser, Henry. *The Scientific Thought of Henry Adams*. Thessalonica: N.p., 1956.

Weber, Brom, ed. *The Complete Poems and Selected Letters and Prose of Hart Crane*. New York: Liveright, 1966.

—————, ed. *The Letters of Hart Crane, 1916–1932*. 1952; rpr. Berkeley: University of California Press, 1965.

West, Michael. "*Walden's* Dirty Language: Thoreau and Walter Whiter's Geocentric Etymological Theories." *Harvard Library Bulletin*, XXII (April, 1974), 117–28.

Wheeler, Lynde Phelps. *Josiah Willard Gibbs: The History of a Great Mind*. Rev. ed. New Haven: Yale University Press, 1952.

Whicher, Stephen E., Robert E. Spiller, and Wallace E. Williams, eds. *The Early Lectures of Ralph Waldo Emerson*. 3 vols. Cambridge: Harvard University Press, 1959–72.

White, Hayden. *Metahistory: The Historical Imagination in Nineteenth-Century Europe*. Baltimore: Johns Hopkins University Press, 1973.

Whitman, Walt. *Leaves of Grass*. Edited by Sculley Bradley and Harold W. Blodgett. 1965; rpr. New York: Norton, 1973.

—————. *Leaves of Grass: Facsimile Edition of 1860 Text*. Edited by Roy Harvey Pearce. Ithaca: Cornell University Press, 1961.

—————. *Leaves of Grass: The First (1855) Edition*. Edited by Malcolm Cowley. New York: Viking Press, 1959.

—————. *New York Dissected*. Edited by Emory Holloway and Ralph Adimari. New York: R. R. Wilson, 1936.

—————. *Prose Works 1892*. Edited by Floyd Stovall. 2 vols. New York: New York University Press, 1963. *The Collected Writings of Walt Whitman*, edited by Gay Wilson Allen and Sculley Bradley. 17 vols. projected.

Williams, William Carlos. *The Autobiography of William Carlos Williams*. 1951; rpr. New York: New Directions, 1967.

—————. *The Collected Earlier Poems*. New York: New Directions, 1951.

—————. *The Collected Later Poems*. Rev. ed. New York: New Directions, 1967.

—————. *The Embodiment of Knowledge*. Edited by Ron Loewinsohn. New York: New Directions, 1974.

—————. "An Essay on *Leaves of Grass*." First published in *Leaves of Grass: One Hundred Years After*, edited by Milton Hindus. Stanford: Stanford University Press, 1955. Rpr. Walt Whitman, *Leaves of Grass*, edited by Sculley Bradley and Harold W. Blodgett. New York: Norton, 1973.

—————. *Imaginations* [contains *Kora in Hell*, *Spring, and All*, *The Great American Novel*, *The Descent of Winter*, and *A Novelette and Other Prose*]. Edited by Webster Schott. New York: New Directions, 1970.

—————. *In the American Grain*. 1925; rpr. New York: New Directions, 1956.

—————. *I Wanted to Write a Poem: The Autobiography of the Works of a Poet*. Reported and edited by Edith Heal. 1958; rpr. New York: New Directions, 1978.

—————. *Paterson*. New York: New Directions, 1963.

————. *Paterson* MS. Collection of American Literature, Beinecke Library, Yale University, New Haven.

————. *Pictures from Brueghel and Other Poems*. New York: New Directions, 1962.

————. "Rome." *Iowa Review*, IX (Summer, 1978), 12–65.

————. *Selected Essays*. 1954; rpr. New York: New Directions, 1969.

————. *The Selected Letters of William Carlos Williams*. Edited by John C. Thirlwall. New York: McDowell, Obolensky, 1957.

————. *A Voyage to Pagany*. 1928; rpr. New York: New Directions, 1970.

Winters, Yvor. *In Defense of Reason*. Chicago: Swallow Press, 1947.

Yoder, R. A. *Emerson and the Orphic Poet in America*. Berkeley: University of California Press, 1978.

Zall, Paul M., ed. *Literary Criticism of William Wordsworth*. Lincoln: University of Nebraska Press, 1966.

Ziff, Larzer. *Literary Democracy: The Declaration of Cultural Independence in America*. New York: Viking Press, 1981.

Index

Abelard, Peter, 162
Abraham, Nicolas, 15
Adamic myth, 4, 5, 44, 90, 98
Adams, Brooks, 128–29, 134n, 135, 138,
    164, 167–69, 170
Adams, Charles Francis, 129, 192
Adams, Henry: anti-semitism of, 170; and
    literary history, 167, 213; as modernist,
    171; politics of, 167, 169, 170; men-
    tioned, 6, 50
Adams, John, 192
Adams, John Quincy, 128–29
Adams, Richard P., 1
Aeschylus, 187
Allegory, 63–66, 107, 109, 114, 120, 184,
    194–95, 234. See also Benjamin, Wal-
    ter; Coleridge, Samuel Taylor
Althusser, Louis, 193
Aquinas, Saint Thomas, 159, 162–63, 164
Archaeology: and history, 42, 44–45, 51,
    56, 57, 62, 146, 185, 191; and language,
    61, 63; and evolutionary theory, 150.
    See also Darwin, Charles (and Darwin-
    ism); Geography; Geology; Philology;
    Thermodynamics
Augustine, Saint, 130, 132, 155

Baudelaire, Charles, 146, 194, 272
Benjamin, Walter, 182–83, 194–95
Bercovitch, Sacvan, 225
Bernstein, Michael André, 177–78
Bhagavad-Gita, 48
Biology, 77–78
Blake, William, 254
Bloom, Harold, 1, 3, 4, 17–18, 49, 62, 103,
    118–20, 166, 167, 199, 233, 239, 247,
    248, 252, 270, 279, 282
Boltzmann, Ludwig, 139–48 passim, 153,
    154, 159, 162
Boone, Daniel, 226
Borges, Jorge Luis, 38
Bové, Paul, 95–98, 101
Breslin, James, 216
Browning, Robert, 18

Brush, Stephen, 141, 142
Bryan, William Jennings, 167, 170
Burckhardt, Jacob, 179

Carlyle, Thomas, 49, 52, 81, 89, 127, 128
Carnot, Sadi, 48, 73, 136, 137
Cavalcanti, Guido, 209
Cavell, Stanley, 33
Chambers, Robert, 72
Champeaux, William of, 162
Champlain, Samuel de, 226
Champollion, Jean François, 61
Chaucer, Geoffrey, 190
Clausius, Rudolf, 136, 137, 138, 140, 141,
    147, 149, 159
Colacurcio, Michael, 161
Coleridge, Samuel Taylor: The States-
    man's Manual, 63–64; Essays on the
    Principles of Method, 64–65; Aids to
    Reflection, 66–67; Biographia Literaria,
    246; on symbol and allegory, 63–69
    passim, 120; on biblical exegesis, 70;
    mentioned, 48, 49, 60, 74, 89
Columbus, Christopher, 219–20, 233, 251
Comte, Auguste, 37–38, 74, 75, 78, 79, 80,
    88, 152, 157
Crane, Hart, 7
Cuvier, Georges, 42–45, 47–48, 50, 58, 59,
    63, 72, 79, 149

Dadaism, 215, 230
Dante (Alighieri), 184, 190
Darwin, Charles (and Darwinism), 58, 125,
    131–32, 133, 134, 137, 149–50. See also
    Evolutionary theory
Davie, Donald, 169
De Man, Paul, 5, 22, 64, 102, 107, 109–12
    passim, 119, 120, 170–71, 174, 178, 233,
    234, 239, 242, 243
Derrida, Jacques, 5, 15, 16, 23, 26–27, 29,
    57n, 80, 83, 119, 129, 183, 186, 187,
    188, 253, 284–85
De Saussure, Ferdinand, 48
Doggett, Frank, 278